# On Power

BERTRAND DE JOUVENEL

# On Power

*The Natural History of Its Growth*

BERTRAND DE JOUVENEL

*Foreword by D. W. Brogan*

*Translation by J. F. Huntington*

*Liberty Fund*

*Du Pouvoir: Histoire Naturelle de sa Croissance* © 1945 by Les Éditions du Cheval Ailé, Geneva. *On Power: Its Nature and the History of Its Growth* © 1948 by Hutchinson & Co., London, and © 1948 by Viking Press, Inc. Copyright renewed by Viking Penguin, 1976. Reprinted by arrangement with Random House/Hutchinson and by arrangement with Viking Penguin, a division of Penguin Books USA, Inc. All rights reserved. All inquiries should be addressed to Liberty Fund, Inc., 11301 North Meridian Street, Carmel, IN 46032-4564. This book was manufactured in the United States of America.

Frontispiece photo: Ulf Anderson/Gamma Liaison. Used by permission. Jacket and cover illustration: Louis XIII at the promotion of Chevaliers of the Order of St. Esprit at Fontainebleau, 1633. *Le Roi Donnant l'Accolade . . .*, etching and engraving by Abraham Bosse. Published in Paris by Melchior Tavernier, c. 1635. Library of Congress.

*Library of Congress Cataloging-in-Publication Data*
Jouvenel, Bertrand de, 1903–1987
[Du pouvoir. English]
On Power : the natural history of its growth / Bertrand de Jouvenel ; foreword by D. W. Brogan ; translation by J. F. Huntington.
p.    cm.
Includes bibliographical references and index.
ISBN 0-86597-112-9.—ISBN 0-86597-113-7 (pbk.)
1. Power (Social sciences)   2. State, The.   I. Title.
JC330.J613   1993   93-1656
303.3′3—dc20

06   22   23   24   25   C   6   5   4   3   2
22   23   24   25   26   P   13   12   11   10   9

libertyfund.org

QUAERITUR:
*Pone seram, cohibe. Sed quis custodiet ipsos Custodes?*
                                                    —Juvenal, VI, 347

RESPONDENDUM:
*Nisi Dominus custodierit civitatem, frustra vigilat qui custodit eam.*
                                                    —Solomon


THE QUESTION:
"Keep your wife under guard." Yes, but who
will guard the guardians?

THE ANSWER:
Unless the Lord watches over the city, the watchman stays
awake in vain.

Laborem extulisti Helena ut confovente dilectione hoc evigilaretur opus dum evertuntur funditus gentes.

[Helen, you produced this work, in that this endeavor was awakened because your love was nurturing while the world was being completely destroyed.]

# Contents

# *Foreword*

IN THESE OMINOUS TIMES, when the pressure of events makes calm thought difficult and when the apparent need of drastic measures makes hesitation, scepticism, criticism seem a form of petty treason, a book like M. de Jouvenel's may seem to need some justification. For it is a plea for hesitation and scepticism; it is an argument for not letting necessity, "the tyrant's plea," have all its own way. Or, rather, it is an argument for a repeated stocktaking, for the scrutiny of every new proposal for extending the power of the state or of *any other power-monopolizing body*. And so it can be made to seem an argument that will weaken the will to action of the government and the will to obedience of the governed.

It is not that: M. de Jouvenel has too acute a sense of the world and age in which we live to ignore the necessities of that age. But his book is an argument—and a powerful argument—against leaps in the dark when they can be avoided, and an argument against the popular pretence that the darkness is in fact well lighted and the cliff merely a slight declivity.

In this book our attention is called, first of all, to what is, at any rate a striking coincidence: the power of the state has steadily increased and the power of the human race for deadly mischief has increased at the same time. Written as the book was before Hiroshima, the most striking example of this parallel progress was not to the author's hand. But it is worth noting that when we regard with legitimate fear the potentialities of mischief inherent in modern science, we should continually remind ourselves that potentialities have only been actualized by the will of the state. It was not a spontaneously acting group of "scientists" who made the atomic bomb. It was a group of employees of the government of the United States who made the bomb, and the most important of them were scientists. But the decision to make it was the decision of President Roosevelt, as the decision to use it was the decision of President Truman. To state this is not to impute wickedness to either statesman; it is merely to call attention to the fact that only the state is powerful enough to do damage on this scale—and that the state always means politicians, whether they be politicians in the White House or in the Kremlin. It is a dangerous and idle dream to think that the state can become rule by philosophers turned kings or scientists turned commissars. For if philosophers become kings or scientists commissars, they become politicians, and the powers given to the state are powers given to men who are rulers of states, men subject to all the limitations and temptations of their dangerous craft. Unless this is borne in mind, there will be a dangerous optimistic tendency to sweep aside doubts and fears as irrelevant, since, in the state that the projectors have in mind, power will be exercised by men of a wisdom and degree of moral virtue that we have not yet seen. It won't. It will be exercised by men who will be men first and rulers next and scientists or saints a long way after. It was an illusion of the framers of the early American constitutions that they could set up "a government of laws and not of men." All governments are governments of men, though the better of them have a high admixture of law too—that is, of effective limitations on the free action of the rulers.

It is possible, of course, to believe that a new system or a new doctrine will alter these empirically established laws of politics. It is possible to believe that only some easily identifiable and eradicable flaw in the older systems makes the doubts and fears of M. de Jouvenel plausible. In a world without private property,* or without race prejudice, or without religion, or without rain on holidays, these depressing considerations will no longer apply. If you can believe that, as the Duke of Wellington said, you can believe anything. But it may be worth while recalling the disillusionment of Lenin (whom no one has ever accused of romantic optimism). Yet in *State and Revolution* Lenin, on the eve of the seizure of power, saw in the apparatus of the state a mere transitory and soon to

---

* Cf. Aristotle, *Politics,* 1263b: "None of these evils is due to the absence of property in common. They all arise from the wickedness of human nature."

be evanescent phenomenon. He learned better, and could he return to Leningrad, thirty years later, he would see installed there a state power more formidable than any known to the Czars, not because the "Revolution has been betrayed" but because, as M. de Jouvenel puts it, "Power changes its appearance but not its reality." Politics are about power; we cannot evade that truth or its consequences. We dream of a better world but it is in Utopia—that is, nowhere.

It is in the popularity of the pursuit of Utopia that the aggrandizers of state power find their most effective ally. Only an immensely powerful apparatus can do all that the preachers of panaceas promise, so we accept the apparatus but find that we have not got the beneficial effects of the panacea, or have got them at a very high, perhaps ruinous, price. It is one of the many merits of this book that it insists on the price paid even for historical triumphs like the French Revolution. Perhaps the Revolution was the only way out of the dilemma in which the French state under the *ancien régime* had involved itself. M. de Jouvenel's highly critical account of the behaviour of the French *élites* on the eve of the Revolution at any rate suggests that this was the case. But the price paid was terribly high. The Republic demanded sacrifices that no king had dared ask for, and these sacrifices were offered up. Perhaps the only way that the decadent Czardom could be replaced as the centre of Russian state authority was by the Bolshevik Revolution, but think of the price paid and still being paid for that achievement! If a religion or a general cause not identified with the nation-state asked for these sacrifices, we should be far more critical than we are. And even if we put at its highest the success of the modern state in doing what it promises to do, we have to notice that nothing is done free and that the price can be ruinous.

Another lesson is the necessity for scrutinizing all claims to political infallibility and impeccability.

"The right divine of kings to govern wrong" is a doctrine we can all laugh at today. But its defender did not deny that kings could govern wrong; that was their fault and their sin. But some modern deifiers of the state, democratic as well as totalitarian, preach and practise a doctrine of Divine Right far more uncritical than Filmer's. For their rulers, the Führer or the Duce, the Party or the Sovereign People cannot do wrong, morally or intellectually. We are, most of us in the West, immunized against the doctrine of political infallibility and impeccability when it comes to us in the discredited forms it took in Berlin and Rome or even in the more sophisticated form it takes in Moscow. But we are not immune from "democratic" arguments which state or imply that a majority can do no wrong, if it is *our* majority; that, if we are part of it, it cannot do anything disastrously silly. It can and does. And M. de Jouvenel has rightly stressed the dangerous results of this illusion (whether Rousseau was its legitimate begetter or no matters little), for, of course, if the people is always right and the people is the state, then there can be no danger in surrendering into the hands of its mandatories complete, uncontrolled, and irrecoverable power.

But, since the people is not always right, is capable of going wrong morally and prudentially, it would be dangerous to relax the vigilance that is the price of liberty simply because power is in the hands of "the people." And in any case, power will not be in the hands of the people, but in the hands of rulers. For they are rulers, however chosen. "There is more in common between two deputies of whom one is a revolutionary and the other isn't, than between two revolutionaries of whom one is a deputy and the other isn't." And what Robert de Jouvenel wrote of the Third Republic is true of all commonwealths. Being a ruler is a trade. So we can apply to all types of ruler the judgment of Swift. "Arbitrary power is the natural object of temptation to a prince, as wine or women to a young fellow, or a bribe to a judge, or vanity to a woman." For the best of motives, rulers will, like courts, try to add to their jurisdiction.

How is this never-ending audacity to be, at any rate, limited? By making sure that effective power is not monopolized. Writing from a French point of view, M. de Jouvenel is conscious of the harm done to France by the withering away, in face of the power of the French state, of all intermediate organizations of power. We have been less tolerant of state greed, of state jealousy, and France serves rather as an example to teach us caution than as an exact parallel to our own situation. But it would be foolish to pretend that the power of the British state is not growing and growing at the expense of the independent bodies, which, in the past, have been such a source of varied strength. The Minotaur, as M. de Jouvenel calls the engrossing state, is permanently greedy.

But it would also be foolish not to notice that the greed of the state finds justification in the failure of the intermediate bodies either to do well what they used to do well, or to find functions in the modern world to replace those which were once their justification. The brilliant analysis here of the decline in public utility of such French corporations as the *parlements,* the descent of the French legal leaders into being a merely selfish and largely parasitic body, ensures that M. de Jouvenel's readers will not be misled into thinking that the decline in independent sources of authority is due merely to state aggression. It may be due to the failure in adjustment of once useful bodies. Of course, we can all see, in 1949, the faults of the *Parlement de Paris*. It is a little harder to examine the possibility that Oxford and Cambridge, the Federation of British Industries, and the Trade Union Congress are the equivalent bodies in modern Britain and that they may be dying of their own faults as well as of the more or less deliberate aggression of the state!

And lastly, M. de Jouvenel is too wise not to notice and to state that the acceptance of omnicompetent state authority is largely due to the fatigue and despair bred by endemic disorder. The French people accepted, even welcomed, Louis XIV, to put an end to civil war; it was internal peace at almost any price. We may be provoked into doing the same to put an end to the threat of another and more terrible war. It was after a nine years' war that it was possible to create the "Brave New World" of Mr. Huxley's fable. "The world will never be safe for democracy," wrote Chesterton after the First World War; "it is a dangerous trade." One of the reasons why it is dangerous is brilliantly set out here, and one of the duties of the good citizen who treasures liberty is to reflect on the problems so set out and developed in this book.

D. W. BROGAN

*Dr. Denis William Brogan (1900–1974) was Professor of Political Science at Cambridge University.*

# *Translator's Note*

THROUGHOUT THIS BOOK, its title included, the word "Power," whenever it begins with the capital letter, denotes the central governmental authority in states or communities— *l'ensemble des éléments gouvernementaux,* as the author himself defines it.

The notes which appear without brackets are the author's. Those few which appear in brackets are my own. These latter are in the main directed to informing the reader on matters with which Englishmen and Americans would tend naturally to be less well acquainted than Frenchmen. I have repressed the temptation to add greatly to their number.

The introductory epigraph does not appear in the original but is inserted here with the author's warm approval.

In an article entitled "Concerning Translation," which appeared in the *Edinburgh Review* for January 1927, Mr. Lewis May tells this story: "I remember saying to Anatole France that translation was an impossible thing. . . . He replied: 'Precisely, my friend; the recognition of that truth is a necessary preliminary to success in the art.' " My "impossible" labours have been much cheered by this consideration. It has in any case been a privilege to have translated this great book.

The absence of any reference to the important books of Ferrero and Russell on the same subject is due to the fact that they were not, unfortunately, available to the author when he was writing.

J. F. HUNTINGTON

# On Power

# The Minotaur Presented

THE WAR THROUGH WHICH WE HAVE LIVED has surpassed in savagery and destructive force any yet seen by the Western World.

This force has been generated by the unparalleled scale on which men and materials have been thrown in. Not only have armies been raised to the number of ten, of fifteen, of twenty millions of men, but also, behind the lines, whole populations have been conscripted that these armies might not lack the latest and deadliest weapons. Every inhabitant of a country with breath in him has served war's turn, and the non-essential tasks which sweeten life have come to be tolerated at all only so far as they have been thought necessary to sustain the spirit of the one vast instrument of war into which whole peoples have been forged.[1]

In this war everyone—workmen, peasants, and women alike—is in the fight, and in consequence everything, the factory, the harvest, even the dwelling-house, has turned target. As a result the enemy to be fought has been all flesh that is and all soil, and the bombing plane has striven to consummate the utter destruction of them all.

---

1. "The needs of the civilian population must receive sufficient satisfaction *to ensure that its work on war production will not suffer,*" wrote the *Frankfurter Zeitung* of December 29, 1942. The paper was inspired by a "liberal" motive! It was concerned to justify the survival of a remnant of life's ordinary activities. That could be done only by demonstrating that the activities of death could not be carried on without them. In England, too, the release of miners from the Forces was urged in numerous debates in Parliament, the argument advanced being the capital importance of coal-mining *for the war*.

3

The war would have counted fewer participants, it would have wrought a less frightful havoc, had not certain passions, fiercely and unanimously felt, so transformed men's natures that a total distortion of their normal modes of doing became possible. The task of stirring and sustaining these passions has been that of a munition of war without which the others must have proved ineffectual—propaganda. Savagery in act is sustained by savagery of feelings; this has been the work of propaganda.

The most surprising feature of the spectacle which we now present to ourselves is that we feel so little surprise at it.

## 1. The Proximate Cause

That the entire populations of Great Britain and the United States, countries where there was no military conscription and the rights of the individual were held sacred, should have become merely so much "human potential," distributed and applied by Power as might best maximize the war effort,[2] is easily explained. Germany was employing in her design of world conquest all her national resources, and there was no restraining her by other countries with only a part of theirs. That had been the mistake of France,[3] whose subsequent fate taught Great Britain and the United States their lesson. The former, indeed, went to the length of the conscription of women.

In like manner, the enemy who, to render its bodies more docile, mobilizes the thoughts and feelings of men, must be copied by the other side, who will otherwise fight at a disadvantage. Thus it comes about that, just as duellists follow each other's thrusts and feints, nations at war copy each other's "total" methods.

The total militarization of whole societies is, then, the work—in Germany the direct work, in other countries the indirect—of Adolf Hitler. And the reason for this achievement of his was, in his own country, this— that nothing less than the whole of her resources was adequate to his will to power.

2. The formula is President Roosevelt's.

3. In my book *Après la défaite,* published in November 1940, I have demonstrated how the pressing of all its resources, economic and intellectual, into the service of one idea gives a country which is subjected to such a discipline an immense advantage over one which has not been concentrated to the same extent. This sort of monolithism, the product of our monolithic age, is now, alas, the one condition on which a society can survive in war.

There is no disputing this explanation, but it does not explain enough. Hitler was not the first of Europe's would-be conquerors. How comes it that neither Napoleon, nor Frederick II, nor Charles XII, ever achieved the total mobilization of his entire people for war? Simply because they were unable to. And there have been other occasions in history when, with some formidable aggressor to repel, rulers would dearly have liked to dip deeply into the national resources; it will be enough to instance the emperors of the sixteenth century, who, even when the Turk was ravaging their lands, were never able, for all their wide domains, to raise armies which were more than moderate in size.

Therefore, neither the aggressor's will nor the needs of his victims suffice of themselves to explain the vastness of the resources deployed in today's war. Rather the explanation must be sought in the controls, both spiritual and material, which modern governments have at their disposal. It is the power of these controls which has made possible, whether for purposes of attack or of defence, the total mobilization which we see.

## 2. The Growth of War

War is not necessarily, has not always been, what we see it today.

In the time of Napoleon only the men of military age were taken—and not all of them, for as a general rule the Emperor would call up only half a class. All the rest of the population were left, apart from having to pay war taxes of moderate size, to lead their normal lives.

In the time of Louis XIV less still was taken: conscription was unknown, and the private person lived outside the battle.

We may say, then, that it is not an unavoidable result of an outbreak of war that every member and every resource of society must be involved in it: may we also say that the circumstances of the outbreak of which we are at once the spectators and the victims are due to chance?

Assuredly not. And the proof is that if we arrange in chronological order the various wars which have for nearly a thousand years ravaged our Western World, one thing must strike us forcibly: that with each one there has been a steady rise in the coefficient of society's participation in it, and that the total war of today is only the logical end of an uninterrupted advance towards it, of the increasing growth of war.

For an explanation, then, of the evil which besets us we must look not to the actual events which we see, but to history.

What is the continuously operative reason which has made ever wider the area of warfare? (By "area of warfare" I mean, and shall mean throughout, the extent, whether more or less complete, to which the forces of society are sucked into it.)

The answer is given by the known facts.


### 3. Kings in Search of Armies

When we go back to the time—it was in fact the eleventh and twelfth centuries—in which the first modern states began to take shape, what at once strikes us is that, in times which have always been depicted as much given to war, the armies were very small and the campaigns very short.

The king could count on the troops mustered for him by his vassals, but their obligation to serve him was for no more than forty days. He had on the spot some local militia, but these were troops of poor quality[4] and could hardly be relied on for more than two or three days' campaigning.

How could he hope, with such an army, to undertake large-scale operations? For them he needed more disciplined, long-term troops, but troops of that kind had to be paid for.

But how could the king pay for them when the only resources immediately available to him were the revenues of his private domains? No one would let him impose taxes on any account,[5] and his main source of additional revenue was the Church, which, assuming that it approved his projected campaign, might let him have a tenth of its revenues over several years. Even with this support, and even as late as the end of the thirteenth century, the hundred and fifty-three days which the "Crusade of Aragon"[6] lasted made it seem to contemporaries a tremendous undertaking and caused considerable financial embarrassment to the monarchy.

War in those days was always a small-scale affair—for the simple reason

4. Great emphasis is laid on the part which they played at Bouvines, but what happened at Crécy illustrates their more usual role. There, says Froissart, after drawing their swords while the enemy was still two miles off and shouting, "To the death, to the death," they took to their heels precipitately as soon as the English army came in sight.

5. Cf. A. Caullery, *Histoire du pouvoir royal d'imposer depuis la féodalité jusqu' à Charles V* (Brussels: 1879).

6. [The disastrous crusade against the King of Aragon was undertaken, at the prompting of the then Pope, by Philip III, "the Bold," who ruled France from 1270 to 1285.]

that Power was a small-scale affair and entirely lacked those two essential controls, the conscription of men and the imposition of taxes.

But the struggle to magnify itself is of Power's essence, and the kings of other days were forever striving, at intervals which became ever shorter, to extract grants in aid, not only from the clergy, but from the nobility and commonalty as well. The period covered in England by the reigns of the first three Edwards, and in France from the reign of Philip the Fair to that of Philip of Valois,[7] saw a steady development of this tendency. The calculations made by Charles IV's[8] advisers for a campaign in Gascony have come down to us: they were for 5,000 horsemen and 20,000 foot-soldiers, all hired and all under a five months' contract. Twelve years later we find yet another calculation for a four months' campaign in Flanders, this time for 10,000 horsemen and 40,000 foot-soldiers.

To collect the necessary ways and means the king had to visit in succession all the principal centres of population in his realm and, having gathered the inhabitants together from highest to lowest, expound his requirements and request their help.[9]

We find that the course of the Hundred Years' War—in reality a succession of short campaigns each of which had to be financed in turn—was continually marked by begging approaches of this kind. And in the English camp the same process went on;[10] here the king had relatively more authority, and was able to extract larger and more regular grants even though his country was much the poorer and less populous of the two.[11]

The various levies, like those needed for the ransoming of King John of France, had to continue over many years. Their permanence, even so, was never admitted, and before long the French and English peoples rose in almost simultaneous rebellion against them.

7. [I.e., approximately, the last quarter of the thirteenth century and the first half to three-quarters of the fourteenth.]

8. [Charles IV, who ruled France from 1322 to 1328, was the last of the Capetian kings. The House of Valois succeeded.]

9. According to the documents published by M. Maurice Jusselin in *Bibliothèque de l'école des Chartes,* 1912, p. 209.

10. Baldwin Schuyler Terry, *The Financing of the Hundred Years' War, 1337–1360* (Chicago and London: 1914).

11. Of the wealth of France at the start of the war, Froissart writes: *"Adonc était le royaume de France gras, plains et drus, et les gens riches et possessans de grand avoir, et on' i savait parler de nulle guerre."*

Only at the war's end, when sacrifice had become second nature, was it possible to establish a levy permanently—the *taille* (poll-tax), as it was called—for the purpose of maintaining an army on a permanent footing in the shape of the orderly companies.

And now indeed Power had taken a big step forward. It need no longer go a-begging from popular assemblies in times of crisis: it was henceforward permanently endowed. Its next task, into which it would throw all its energies, would be to increase the endowment fund.

### 4. Power Extended, War Extended

How to do it? How increase the share of the national wealth which Power takes and converts into strength?

So long as it lasted, the monarchy never dared attempt the conscription of men. It always hired its soldiers for cash.

Now, its civil duties, which, by the way, it came to perform quite well, justified it in acquiring a legislative capacity—a thing unknown to the Middle Ages, but with possibilities of growth. This legislative capacity carried in its womb the right to impose taxes, though the period of gestation was to be a long one.

The great crisis of the seventeenth century which saw the revolutions in England and in Naples—the latter a hardly remembered but highly instructive one!—and the rise of the Fronde as well, marked the clash between the three great Western monarchies trying to increase their taxes[12] and their peoples violently resisting their efforts.[13]

When Power had once safely rounded that cape, the results were clear to see: 200,000 men engaged in killing each other at Malplaquet against 50,000 at Marignan.[14]

---

12. An increase was to some extent necessitated by the general rise in prices following the influx of precious metals from America.

13. [The revolt against Spanish rule in Naples occurred in 1647. Its immediate occasion was a tax on fruit and it started as a riot between the fruit venders and the customs officers.

The Fronde was the name given (meaning toy catapult and derived from the pelting of Mazarin's windows by the Paris mob) to certain French factions during the minority of Louis XIV which were hostile to the Court and the Minister, Mazarin, and gave rise to a series of disturbances between 1648 and 1654. The trouble started with a tax levied in the former year on the judicial officers of the Parlement of Paris.]

14. [The Battle of Marignan was fought in 1515 between the French army under Francis I and the Swiss troops of Maximilian Sforza, Duke of Milan.]

Louis XVI had 180,000 men-at-arms against Charles VII's (King of France, 1403–1461) 12,000. The King of Prussia of the time of Louis XVI had 195,000 and the Emperor 240,000.

This growth frightened Montesquieu.[15] "And soon," he wrote prophetically, "having soldiers will result in having nothing but soldiers, and we shall become like the Tartars." And he went on with remarkable prescience: "All that is necessary for that to come about is that the new invention of militias set up in nearly the whole of Europe should become the normal rule and that their effectives should be pushed to as high a level as that which those of the regular forces have already attained."[16]

But to do that was quite beyond the power of the monarchy. Louvois[17] had created some territorial regiments to be drawn from their own districts and to give service—or that was the idea—nowhere else; when he tried to convert them into reserves for general service units he met with strong opposition. In Prussia, on the other hand, the same project, embodied in the rescript of 1733, fared better. But all the same, and to a much greater extent than the resulting increase of taxation, the peoples hated these first attempts at conscription, which constituted a major grievance against Power.

To say that the monarchy did no more than increase the size of armies would be ridiculous. That it established internal order, that it protected the weak against the strong, that it raised the community's standard of life, that it conferred great benefits on industry, commerce, and agriculture—all that is well enough known.

But, for the very reason that it had to make itself competent in the role of benefactor, it had to set up in concrete form a governmental machine— an executive, laws, a legislature—which may fairly be compared to a power house setting the governed in motion by means of ever more powerful controls.

15. "A new disease has broken out in Europe: it has infected our rulers and caused them to maintain armies which are out of all proportion. It has its recurrences and soon becomes contagious; inevitably, because as soon as one State increases the number of its troops, as they are called, the others at once increase theirs, so that the general ruin is all that comes out of it. Every monarch keeps permanently on foot armies which are as large as would be needed if his people were in imminent danger of extermination; and this struggle of all against all is called peace." *Esprit des Lois*, Livre XIII, chap. xvii.

16. *Loc. cit.*

17. [Louvois (1641–1691) was war minister of Louis XIV. As a war minister he ranks with Carnot, but has little else to commend him.]

And it is by means of these controls, operated from this power house, that Power has become able, whenever war is actual or impending, to make such exactions from its people as were never conceived by a feudal monarch in his dreams.

Therefore the extension of Power, which means its ability to control ever more completely a nation's activities, is responsible for the extension of war.

## 5. The Men Whom War Takes

We have learned, and fairly enough, to link up the ideas of absolute monarchies, dynastic wars, and sacrifices laid on peoples. For, while it is not the case that all kings have been ambitious, yet, if one such there was, the extent of his authority enabled him to lay heavy burdens.

When the people upset the Power of kings, it was, so they thought, of just these burdens that they were ridding themselves. It was the burdens of taxation and, above all, military conscription which they hated. That being so, it is not a little surprising to see these burdens grow heavier under an up-to-date regime, and most surprising of all to see conscription instituted, not by absolute monarchy, but as the result of its fall.

Taine remarks that it was the present threat and past experience of invasion and its sufferings which won the people's consent to conscription.

The people conceived of conscription as an accidental and temporary necessity. But it became permanent and established when, after victory and peace had been achieved, the people's Government kept it on. Thus, Napoleon kept it on in France after the Treaties of Lunéville and Amiens, and the Prussian Government kept it on in Prussia after the Treaties of Paris and Vienna.

As war has followed war, the burden of conscription has grown heavier. Like a slow contagion it has spread from State to State until now the whole of continental Europe is in its grip. There it holds court along with the friend of its youth, its twin brother, that comes always just before or after it—with universal suffrage; both of them brought to birth at about the same time, the one bringing in its train, more or less openly and completely, the other, both of them the blind and terrible guides or masters of the future, the one placing in the hands of every adult person a voting paper, the other putting on his back a soldier's knapsack. The promise which they hold for the twentieth century of slaughter and bankruptcy, the exacerbation of hatred and suspicion between nations, the wastage of the work of men's hands, the perversion to base uses of the beneficent discoveries of science, the return to the low and debased shapes of primitive societies on the warpath, the retrograde movement towards a barbarous and instinctual egotism, towards the feelings, manners and morals of ancient cities and savage tribes—all this we know too well.[18]

The event, however, surpassed even the imagination of Taine. At the end of the Napoleonic Wars there were 3,000,000 men in Europe under arms. The 1914–1918 war killed or mutilated five times as many. And in the 1939–1945 war there is no counting the men, and the women and children, engaged in the struggle—as long ago those on Ariovistus's chariots were counted.

We are ending where the savages began. We have found again the lost arts of starving non-combatants, burning hovels, and leading away the vanquished into slavery. Barbarian invasions would be superfluous: we are our own Huns.

### 6. Absolute Power Is Not Dead

How very strange! When their masters were kings, the peoples never stopped complaining at having to pay war taxes. Then, when they have overthrown these masters and taken to taxing themselves, the currency in which they pay is not merely a part of their incomes but their very lives!

How do we explain this amazing somersault? Has the rivalry of nations taken the place of that of dynasties? Is the popular will so warlike and expansionist that the ordinary citizen likes paying for wars and joining armed forces? So that we now bear with enthusiasm self-imposed sacrifices which are far heavier than those at which in other times we kicked?

Nonsense!

When he gets a warning from the tax collector or a summons to barracks from the policeman, the recipient is far from seeing in the warning or in the travel voucher an exercise of his own will, however much extolled and transfigured for him that will may be. Rather they are to him the dictates of a foreign power, of an impersonal master, now popularly called "they" but in other days known as "the evil spirits." " 'They' increase our taxes, 'they' mobilize us"—that is the language of the man in the street. So far as the ordinary man is concerned it is as if a

18. H. Taine, *Les Origines de la France contemporaine*, Vol. X, pp. 120–23.

successor to the vanished monarchy had brought to fruition the interrupted tasks of absolutism.

In the past armies and taxes have been seen to grow with the growth of the royal Power, so that there was a correspondence between the peak of taxation and military effectives, and the peak of absolutism: must we not say, then, when we see the curve of these two irrefutable indices, taxes and soldiers, still moving onwards and upwards and the same effects still monstrously expanding, that the same cause is at work, and that, though in another shape, Power has increased and is increasing?

Viollet was conscious of this: "The modern State is just the king of other days bringing to a triumphal end his unremitting work."[19]

All that has happened is that the royal power house has been improved on: its controls, moral and material, have been made progressively more efficient so as to drive ever deeper into society and to take from it in an ever tighter clutch its goods and men.

All that has changed is that Power in its present swollen form has become a stake in a political contest.

> This Power [said Marx] with its vast bureaucratic and military organization and its complicated and artificial mechanism, this frightful parasite which enmeshes as in a net the body of French society and obstructs all its pores, started at the time of absolute monarchy, when the feudal system, in whose overthrow it helped, was in decline. . . . The effect of overthrows of Power has been merely to improve the government machine, not to smash it. The political parties which in turn fought for Power conceived of the seizure of this vast edifice as the spoils of victory.[20]

## 7. The Minotaur Masked

From the twelfth to the eighteenth century governmental authority grew continuously. The process was understood by all who saw it happening; it stirred them to incessant protest and to violent reaction.

In later times its growth has continued at an accelerated pace, and its extension has brought a corresponding extension of war. And now we no longer understand the process, we no longer protest, we no longer react. This quiescence of ours is a new thing, for which Power has to

19. Paul Viollet, *Le Roi et ses ministres pendant les trois derniers siècles de la monarchie* (Paris: 1912) p. 8.

20. Karl Marx, *Le dix-huit brumaire de Louis Bonaparte.*

thank the smoke-screen in which it has wrapped itself. Formerly it could be seen, manifest in the person of the king, who did not disclaim being the master he was, and in whom human passions were discernible. Now, masked in anonymity, it claims to have no existence of its own, and to be but the impersonal and passionless instrument of the general will.

But that is clearly a fiction.

> By a fiction, or, as some would say, by an abstraction, it is claimed that the General Will, which in reality emanates from the persons invested with political power, emanates from a collective being, the Nation, of which the rulers are nothing more than the instruments; and the rulers are always anxious to drive this idea into the heads of their peoples. They well understand its usefulness to them in making their power or their tyranny acceptable.[21]

Today as always Power is in the hands of a group of men who control the power house. The so-called Power is this group, whose relationship with their fellow-men is that of the ruler with the ruled. All that has changed is that it has now been made easy for the ruled to change the personnel of the leading wielders of Power. Viewed from one angle, this weakens Power, because the wills which control a society's life can, at the society's pleasure, be replaced by other wills, in which it feels more confidence.

But, by opening the prospect of Power to all the ambitious talents, this arrangement makes the extension of Power much easier. Under the *ancien régime*, society's moving spirits, who had, as they knew, no chance of a share of Power, were quick to denounce its smallest encroachment. Now, on the other hand, when everyone is potentially a minister, no one is concerned to cut down an office to which he aspires one day himself, or to put sand in a machine which he means to use himself when his turn comes.[22] Hence it is that there is in the political circles of a modern society a wide complicity in the extension of Power.

The most striking example of this is offered by the socialists. Here is what their doctrine teaches them:

21. L. Duguit, *L'État, le droit objectif et la loi positive* (Paris: 1901) Vol. I, p. 320.

22. Cf. Benjamin Constant: "Your party man, however excellent his intentions may be, is always opposed to any limitation of sovereignty. He regards himself as the next in succession, and handles gently the property that is to come to him, even while his opponents are its tenants." *Cours de politique constitutionelle*, ed. Laboulaye (Paris: 1872) Vol. I, p. 10.

The State is nothing but an instrument of oppression of one class by another—no less so in a democratic republic than in a monarchy.[23]

Through all the innumerable revolutions which have taken place in Europe since the end of the feudal system, this bureaucratic and military machine has developed, improved and strengthened. . . . Every revolution of the past has done no more than improve the government machine, when its real task was to smite and smash it.[24]

But this does not prevent the socialists from viewing the growth of this "instrument of oppression" with much favour; their plan is not to "smash" it but to get hold of it.[25] Rightly denouncing war, as they do, they do not realize that there is a link between its monstrous extension and the extension of Power.

To no purpose was Proudhon's lifelong denunciation of the perversion of democracy into a mere competition for the *imperium*.[26]

This competition brought forth in time its inevitable fruits—a Power which was at once widespread and weak. But it is of Power's essence not to be weak. Circumstances arise which make the people themselves want to be led by a powerful will. Then comes the time when whoever has taken hold of Power, whether it be a man or a gang, can make fearless use of its controls. These users quickly demonstrate the crushing enormity of Power. They are thought to have built it, but they did not. They are only its bad tenants.

## 8. The Minotaur Unmasked

The power house was there before them: they do no more than make use of it. The giant was already up and about: they do no more than furnish him with a terrible spirit. The claws and talons which he then makes felt grew in the season of democracy. It is he that mobilizes the

23. Engels, in his 1891 preface to Marx's *Guerre civile*.

24. Lenin, *L'État et la Révolution*, ed. *Humanité* (1925) p. 44.

25. "What they distrust," Constant went on to say, "is this or that form of government and this or that class of governors; but once allow them to organize government in their own way, once let them entrust it to mandatories chosen by themselves, and there are no limits to what they will think its desirable extension." *Loc. cit.*

26. [*Imperium* denotes here, as elsewhere, the sovereign authority, as distinct from the *potestas* of a subordinate office. Proudhon (1809–1865), French socialist writer, was called by Morley "the trenchant genius of French Socialism in 1840 and onwards." To the modern socialist the libertarian cast of his thought must seem odd.]

population, but the principle of conscription was founded in a democratic time. He is the despoiler of wealth, but democracy provided him with the inquisitorial mechanism of taxation which he uses. The tyrant would not derive legitimacy from the plebiscite if the general will had not already been proclaimed the sufficient source of authority. The weapon of party with which he consolidates himself is the offspring of the competition for Power. The way has been made straight for the conditioning of minds in childhood by the monopoly, whether more or less complete, of education. Opinion has been prepared for the seizure by the state of the means of production. Even the police regime, that most insupportable attribute of tyranny, has grown in the shadow of democracy.[27] The *ancien régime* hardly knew of such a thing.[28]

Democracy, then, in the centralizing, pattern-making, absolutist shape which we have given to it is, it is clear, the time of tyranny's incubation.

By means of the air of apparent innocence which Power derives from it, Power has attained a vastness of which a war and a despotism such as Europe never saw before give us the measure. Had Hitler succeeded Maria Theresa on the throne, does anyone suppose that it would have been possible for him to forge so many up-to-date weapons of tyranny? Is it not clear that he must have found them ready prepared? The more we think on these lines, the better we can appreciate the problem which faces our Western World.

It is, alas, no longer possible for us to believe that by smashing Hitler and his regime we are striking at the root of the evil. Even while we do it, we are already making plans for after the war, which will make the state the arbiter of every individual destiny and will place, inevitably, in Power's hands means adequate to the vastness of its task.

Can anyone doubt that a state which binds men to itself by every tie of need and feeling will be that much the better placed for devoting them all one day to the dooms of war? The more departments of life that Power takes over, the greater will be its material resources for making war; the more clearly seen the services which it renders, the readier will be the answer to its summons. And will anyone be so bold as to guarantee that

27. Cf. A. Ullmann, *La Police, quatrième pouvoir* (Paris: 1935).

28. The reason is that in a stratified society the police agent is afraid to attack anyone of importance. He is never free of the fear that he will come off second best in such a conflict, and that fear keeps him down and renders him inactive. It is only in an egalitarian society that the nature of his activities elevates him above everyone else, and this inflation of the man contributes to the inflation of the office.

this vast mechanism of state will never fall into the hands of a glutton of empire? Is not the will to Power rooted deep in human nature, and have not the outstanding qualities of leadership needed for the handling of a machine which goes ever from strength to strength often had for companion the lust of conquest?

### 9. Ubiquity of the Minotaur

Now it suffices, as we have just seen and as the whole of history teaches us, for only one of the great powers of the future to produce a leader who will convert into sinews of war the powers taken for social advancement, and then all the others must follow suit. For the more complete the hold which the state gets on the resources of a nation, the higher, the more sudden, the more irresistible will be the wave in which an armed community can break on a pacific one.

It follows that, in the very act of handing over more of ourselves to the state, no matter how benevolent a face it wears today, we may be fostering tomorrow's war and ensuring that it will be to the last one as the last one was to the wars of the Revolution.

In saying this I am not setting up as an enemy of the growth of Power and of the distension of the state. I know well the hopes that men have of it, and how their trust in the Power which shall be warms itself at the fire of the sufferings which the Power that was inflicted on them. The desire of their hearts is social security. Their rulers, or those who hope to become their rulers, feel no doubt that science now enables them to condition the minds and the bodies of men, to fit each single person into his proper niche in society, and to ensure the happiness of all by the interlocking functions of each. This undertaking, which is not lacking in a certain grandeur, marks the culmination of the history of the West.

If it seems to some of us that there is in this design rather too much confidence here and rather too much presumption there; that premature attempts to apply an inexact science may inflict a more than barbarian cruelty—witness the experimentation in breeding—that mistakes in the switching of vast trainloads of human beings cannot but bring catastrophe; that, to conclude, the pliability of the masses on the one hand and the authority of their leaders on the other forebode wars of which the last one was but a foretaste—what is the good of being Jeremiahs?

In my view, none; and the purpose of my book is merely to examine the reasons why, and the way in which, Power grows in society.

# BOOK I

~

# Metaphysics of Power

# I.

~

# *Of Civil Obedience*

AFTER DESCRIBING IN HIS LOST TREATISES on Constitutions the various governmental structures of a large number of different societies, Aristotle, in the *Politics,* reduced them all to three basic types: monarchy, aristocracy, and democracy. The characteristics of these three types, in the various mixtures in which they were found in practice, accounted for all the forms of Power which had come under his observation.

Ever since then political science, or what passes for such, has followed obediently in the footsteps of the master. The discussion of the different forms of Power is always with us because, there being in every society a centre of control, everyone is naturally interested in the questions of its powers, its organization, and its conduct.

There is, however, another phenomenon that also deserves some consideration: the fact that over every human community there reigns a government at all. The differences between forms of government in different societies and the changes of form within the same society are but the accidents, to borrow the terminology of philosophy, of the same essence. The essence is Power. And we may well break off from inquiring into *what is the best form* of Power—from political ethics—to ask *what is the essence* of Power—to construct a political metaphysic.

The problem may also be looked at from another angle, which permits of a simpler statement of it. At all times and in all places we are confronted with the phenomenon of civil obedience. An order issued by Power gets obeyed by the community at large. When Power addresses itself to a

19

foreign state, the weight behind its words is in proportion to its own ability to make itself obeyed and win from that obedience the means of action. It all turns on that obedience. Who knows the reasons for that obedience knows the inner nature of Power.

Another point is that, as history shows, obedience has certain limits within which Power must keep, just as there is a limit to the amount of a society's resources which it can take for its own. These limits, as observation shows us, do not remain static throughout the history of a society. For example, the Capetian[1] Kings could not impose direct taxation, and the Bourbons could not exact military service.

The fraction or quantum of a society's resources which Power can take for its own is theoretically measurable. Clearly it is strictly proportioned to the quantum of obedience. And these variations in the resources available to Power are the measure of its own extent. We are safe in saying that the more completely Power can control the actions of the members of society and turn their resources to its uses, the greater is Power's extent.[2]

The study of the successive variations in its resources is to consider the history of Power by reference to its extent—a very different thing from the history usually written of it, by reference to its forms.

These variations in the extent of Power, considered as a function of the age of a society, could be represented in the form of a graph. Will the curve run in capricious indentations, or will its general direction be sufficiently defined to enable us to speak of Power being subject to a law of development in the society in question? Taking the latter hypothesis to be true, and also taking the view that human history, in so far as it has come down to us, is but the arrangement in their order of the successive histories of big societies or civilizations (into the formation of which smaller ones have gone), all carried forward on the same impulse,

---

1. [The Capetian dynasty ruled in France from 987 to 1328.]
2. [What the author has here in mind can be pictured as a mathematical relationship:

$$\frac{\text{the resources at Power's disposal}}{\text{the resources inherent in society}} = \text{Extent of Power,}$$

the numerator and the denominator both being variables by reference to time and circumstance. The study of this relationship is the main purpose of the book. This mathematical view of the matter may help to clarify the author's meaning, but it must not be supposed that the fraction can at any given moment be accurately quantified, though the proportion of the national income taken in taxation and the proportion of the nation's manpower taken in conscription would always be serviceable indications.]

then we may easily conceive that the curves of Power in all these big societies wil probably show a certain similarity to each other and that to examine them may throw some light on the course taken by civilizations.

The start of our inquiry will be an attempt to penetrate to the essence of Power. It may be that we shall not succeed in it, nor is success absolutely necessary to our purpose, for what we are really after is the relation, to put it broadly, of Power to society, the former being considered as a function of the latter. And these two we can regard, if we have to, as unknown variables of which nothing can be grasped but the relationship between them. But history, when all is said, cannot be reduced in this way to an affair of mathematics. And we must not neglect whatever aids our vision.

## 1. The Mystery of Civil Obedience

The High School of our species, curiosity, requires the unusual for its awakening. Just as it took prodigies, eclipses, or comets, to start our distant ancestors inquiring into the structure of the universe, so in our time crises have been needed for the birth of an economic science, and thirty millions of unemployed for it to become widespread. If they happen every day, then the most surprising events do not act on our intelligences. Hence it is, no doubt, that so little thought has been given to the amazing faculty for obedience of groupings of men, whether numbering thousands or millions, which causes them to obey the rules and orders of a few.

It needs only an order for the tumultuous flood of vehicles which throughout a vast country kept to the left to change sides and keep to the right. It needs only an order for an entire people to quit their fields, their workshops, and their offices, and flock to barracks.

> Discipline on such a scale as this [said Necker] must astound any man who is capable of reflection. This obedience on the part of a very large number to a very small one is a thing singular to observe and mysterious to think on.[3]

To Rousseau the spectacle of Power recalls "Archimedes sitting calmly on the shore and effortlessly launching a large ship."[4]

3. Necker, *Du Pouvoir exécutif dans les Grands États* (1792) pp. **20–22**.
4. Rousseau, *Du Contrat social,* Book III, chap. vi.

Anyone who has ever started a small society for some special object knows well the propensity of its members, even though they have entered of their own accord into a voluntary engagement for a purpose to which they attach importance, to leave the society in the lurch. We may, then, well feel surprise at the docility of men in their dealings with a large society.

Someone says, "Come," and come we do. Someone says, "Go," and go we do. We give obedience to the tax-gatherer, to the policeman, and to the sergeant-major. As it is certain that it is not before them that we bow down, it must be before the men above them, even though, as often happens, we despise their characters and suspect their designs.

What, then, is the nature of their authority over us? Is it because they have at their disposal the means of physical coercion and are stronger than ourselves that we yield to them? It is true that we go in fear of the compulsion which they can apply to us. But to apply it they must have the help of a veritable army of underlings. We have still to explain where they get this army and what secures them their fidelity: in that aspect Power appears to us in the guise of a small society commanding a larger.

It is, however, far from being the case that Power has always had at its disposal a vast apparatus of coercion. Rome, for instance, as it was for many centuries, had no permanent officials; no standing army set foot inside its walls, and its magistrates had but a few lictors to do their will. The only force of which Power then disposed to restrain an individual member of the community was what it drew from the community as a whole.

Would it, then, be true to say that Power owes its efficaciousness to feelings, not of fear, but of partnership? That a group of human beings has a collective mind, a national genius, and a general will? And that its government is the personification of the group, the public expression of its mind, the embodiment of its genius, and the promulgation of its will? So that the mystery of obedience dissolves beneath the fact that we are in reality only obeying ourselves? That has been the explanation favoured by our men of law; its vogue has been assisted both by the double meaning of the word "state" and by its conformity with certain usages of our day. The expression "state" comprises two very different meanings. First, it denotes any organized society with an autonomous government: in that sense we are all members of a state and we are the state. But the word also means the governmental machine in that society. In that sense the members of a state are those with a share of Power and they are the state. The proposition that the state, meaning thereby the governmental machine, rules a society is nothing more than a truism; but once inject surreptitiously its other meaning into the word "state," and the proposition becomes the quite unproven one that the society is ruling itself.

What we have here is, clearly, a piece of unconscious self-deception. The reason why it is not too flagrant for concealment is that in the society of our day the governmental machine is, or should be in principle, the expression of society, a mere conduit, in other words, by means of which society rules itself. Even if we choose to assume what in fact remains to be seen—that that is now the true position, it is clear that it has not been, always and everywhere, the true position in the past, but that authority has at times been exercised by Powers which were quite distinct entities from society—and yet received obedience.

Therefore the rule of Power over society is not the work of force alone, because it is met with even where the force available is very small, nor is it the work of partnership alone, because it is met with even where society has absolutely no part in Power.

It may be urged that there are really two Powers which are different in kind; that one is the Power of a small number of men over the mass, as in a monarchy or aristocracy, and that Power of this kind maintains itself by force alone; and that the other is the Power of the mass over itself, and that Power of this kind maintains itself by partnership alone.

If that were so, we should expect to find that in monarchical and aristocratic regimes the apparatus of coercion was at its zenith, because there was no other driving power, and that in modern democracies it was at its nadir, because the demands made by them on their citizens are all the decisions of the citizens themselves. Whereas what we in fact find is the very opposite, and that there goes with the movement away from monarchy to democracy an amazing development of the apparatus of coercion. No absolute monarch ever had at his disposal a police force comparable to those of modern democracies. It is, therefore, a gross mistake to speak of two Powers differing in kind, each of which receives obedience through the play of one feeling only. Logical analyses of this kind misconceive the complexity of the problem.

## 2. The Historical Character of Obedience

Obedience is, in truth, the outcome of various and very different feelings which have, as it were, the effect of seating Power on a multiple throne:

Power exists, it has been said, only through the concurrence of all the properties which go to form its essence; it draws its inner strength and the material succour which it receives, both from the continuously helping hand of habit and also from the imagination; it must possess both a reasonable authority and a magical influence; it must operate like nature herself, both by visible means and by hidden influence.[5]

This is a useful formula, so long as it is not regarded as a systematic and exhaustive catalogue. It stresses the ascendancy of the irrational factors—and it is far from being the case that obedience is mainly due either to a weighing of the risks of disobedience or to a conscious identification by the subject of his will with that of his governors. The essential reason for obedience is that it has become a habit of the species.

We find Power at the birth of social life, just as we find a father at the birth of physical life. This simile has constantly given rise in the past to comparisons between them, and will no doubt, even in the teeth of the most conclusive objections, continue to give rise to them.

Power is for us a fact of nature. From the earliest days of recorded history it has always presided over human destinies. And so its authority in our own time finds support in us from feelings drawn from very ancient times, feelings which it has with each successive change of form successively inspired.

The continuity of human development has been such that most, if not all, of the great institutions which still form the framework of civilized Society have their roots in savagery, and have been handed down to us in these later days through countless generations, assuming new outward forms in the process of transmission, but remaining in their inmost core substantially unchanged.[6]

All societies, even those which seem to us the least developed, go back into a past of several thousand years, and the authorities which ruled them in former times did not disappear without bequeathing to their successors their prestige, nor without leaving in men's minds imprints which are cumulative in their effect. The succession of governments which, in the course of centuries, rule the same society may be looked on as one underlying government which takes on continuous accretions. And

5. Necker, *op. cit.*
6. J. G. Frazer, *Lectures on the Early History of Kingship* (London: 1905) pp. 3–23.

for that reason Power is something which the historian, rather than the logician, comprehends. So that we may unhesitatingly disregard the various systematic approaches which claim to gather all its diverse attributes into a single principle, and to make of that principle both the foundation of all the rights exercised by Power's titularies and the explanation of all the obligations which they impose on others.

Sometimes this single principle is the "Divine Will" of which the titularies are the vicars on earth; sometimes it is the "general will" of which they are the mandatories; sometimes again it is the national genius of which they are the incarnation, or the collective conscience which they interpret, or the finalization of society of which they are the agents.

Clearly we cannot make of any one of the aforesaid principles the only begetter of Power, if there ever was a Power in being which lacked the backing of the particular principle. But we know that Powers have existed in periods in which it would have been nonsense to talk of "national genius"; other Powers there were which there was no general will to sustain—far from it. The one systematic approach which can be made to fulfil the fundamental condition of explaining every Power whatsoever is that by way of "the Divine Will" when St. Paul said, "There is no Power but of God: the Powers that be are ordained of God," even Nero's, he provided theologians with the explanation of Power which includes its every instance.

All other metaphysical explanations of Power are useless for the purpose, if indeed they can be called metaphysics at all. For we leave the region of true metaphysics when analysis is more or less completely submerged by ethics—when the question asked is, not "What must Power be to exist?" but "What must Power be to be good?"

### 3. Statics and Dynamics of Obedience

Should we, then, ignore these theories? Certainly not, for these ideal representations of Power have given currency in society to beliefs which play a vital part in actual Power's development.

We may study the movements of celestial bodies without concerning ourselves with astronomers' concepts which, though they were once believed, do not correspond to the reality; this is so because the movements themselves are unaffected by our beliefs about them. But the position is quite different when it comes to the ideas conceived at different times of Power; for government, being a human, and not a natural, phenomenon, is deeply influenced by the ideas men have of it. And it is true to say that Power expands under cover of the beliefs entertained about it.

With this in mind, let us take up again our musings on obedience. The proximate cause of obedience is, as we have seen, habit. But let command once step outside its usual limits and habit ceases to be a full explanation of obedience. When it is command's will to impose on men obligations in excess of those to which they have been broken in, it no longer gets the benefit of the automatic reactions which time has implanted in the commanded. To bring into being the enlarged effect, which is in this case an accretion of obedience, there must be an enlarged cause. At this point habit is not enough: there must be recourse to reason. Both logic and history lead to this conclusion, that it is in times when Power is stretching its limbs that discussion takes place of its inner nature and of the elements inherent in it which bring it obedience; and this is so whether its growth is in the end helped or hindered by the process of discussion. The opportunism which is thus seen to characterize the various theories of Power is but one more proof of the inability of such theories to provide a complete explanation of the phenomenon.

Whenever a period of discussion arrives, reason has never failed to follow the same two paths, which correspond to the theoretical and the practical sides of the human intellect. On the side of theory it has sought to justify obedience as such: on the side of practice it has opened the door to beliefs, whether in efficient or final causes matters not, which make an increase of obedience possible. Power, in other words, must be obeyed, whether in virtue of its nature or of its aims.

The arguments from its nature are based on the rise of theories of sovereignty. The efficient cause of obedience, run these theories, is to be found in a *prerogative* exercised by Power in virtue of a certain *Majestas*, of which it is either the possessor or the incarnation or the representative. This prerogative belongs to it on the one necessary and sufficient condition that it is *legitimate*—in virtue, in other words, of its origin.

The arguments from its aims are based on the rise of theories as to the purpose of government. The final cause of obedience, run these theories, lies in the *end* of Power, and that end is the *Common Good*, however the term is interpreted. Power has earned the subject's submissiveness when it seeks and gets the Common Good: no other justification for it is required.

This simple classification includes all the standard theories of Power. In general, no doubt, Powers lay claim to both the efficient cause and the final cause at one and the same time, but it will tend to much greater clarity to consider successively the attributes first of the one and then of the other.

But, before going into any detail, let us stop to see whether we cannot, in the light of this general survey, form even now some approximate idea of Power. We have found in it, through all its outward manifestations, the mysterious quality of its continuing essence, and this quality confers on it an irrational influence which cannot be brought to the bar of logical reason. Reason discerns in it three settled qualities: force, legitimacy, beneficence. But try to isolate these qualities, and, as with some chemical bodies, they steal away into thin air. And this they do because they exist, not absolutely, but only in the minds of men. What for practical purposes exists is human belief in the legitimacy of Power, hope of its beneficence, consciousness of its strength. But, quite clearly, it wins its title to be legitimate only by conforming to what is in the general view the legitimate form of Power; it wins its title to be beneficent only by making its ends conform to those which men in general esteem; lastly, its only strength is, at any rate in most cases, the strength which men think it their duty to lend to it.

### 4. Obedience Linked to Credit

It thus appears that obedience is largely compounded of creed, credence, and credit.

Force alone can establish Power, habit alone can keep it in being, but to expand it must have credit—a thing which, even in its earlier life, it finds useful and has generally received in practice. As a description of Power, rather than as a definition, we may now call it a standing corporation, which is obeyed from habit, has the means of physical compulsion, and is kept in being partly by the view taken of its strength, partly by the faith that it rules as of right (in other words, its legitimacy), and partly by the hope of its beneficence.

The role played by credit in the advancement of Power's strength needed underlining, so as to explain why the theories which stir the imagination concerning it are so valuable to it. Whether they induce greater respect for an abstract sovereignty, or whether they arouse more devotion to an abstract Common Good, they greatly aid Power and open up to it new pastures.

A remarkable feature of this process is that these abstract systems of thought can still be of use to Power even when they do not grant it this sovereignty and do not admit its role of agent for this Common Good: they have done what is needed when they have implanted in the mind these two conceptions. Rousseau, for instance, though a great believer in sovereignty, was for refusing it to Power and setting it up against it. Or again, socialism, having conjured up an exceedingly attractive vision of a Common Good, was for giving Power no share in the task of realizing it: so far from that, it was for putting the state to death. But these negations make no difference to Power; such is its position in society that it, and it only, can make itself master of this hallowed sovereignty— that there is no other agency which can materialize the fascinations of this Common Good.

We now know what is the right angle from which to examine the theories of Power. The one feature of them which is of vital importance to our inquiry is their practical assistance to Power.

# II.

# *Theories of Sovereignty*

THE THEORIES WHICH HAVE, in the course of time, had the most vogue in Western society and exercised there the most influence are those which explain and justify political authority by its efficient cause. These theories are those of sovereignty.

Obedience, it is said, becomes a duty because of the undeniable existence "of an ultimate right of command in Society," called sovereignty, a right which extends "to controlling the actions of Society's members with, in the background, power to coerce them, a right to which all private individuals have to submit without possibility of resistance."[1]

Power makes use of this right even though in the general view it does not belong to it. It is denied that this absolute and unbounded right, transcending all private rights, can possibly belong to one man or to one group of men. Only to the most august incumbent, to God, or to society as a whole, will we commit, with no thought of bargaining reserve, the entire conduct of our lives.

As we shall see, theories like those of Divine Right and Popular Sovereignty, which pass for opposites, stem in reality from the same trunk, the idea of sovereignty—the idea, that is, that somewhere there is a right to which all other rights must yield. It is not hard to discover behind this juridical concept a metaphysical one. A supreme Will, it runs, rules and disposes human societies, a Will which, being naturally good, it would

1. Burlamaqui, *Principes de droit politique* (Amsterdam: 1751) Vol. I, p. 43.

be wrong to resist: this Will is either the "Divine Will" or the "general will."

Power in being must be the emanation of this supreme sovereign, be it God or society; it must be the incarnation of this will. And its legitimacy is proportionate to its satisfaction of these conditions. Whether as delegate or mandatory, it can then exercise the right to rule. It is at this point that the two theories, in addition to their divergent conceptions as to the nature of the sovereign, become much differentiated. As to how, for instance, and to whom, and, above all, to what extent the right to rule is given. Who will watch over its exercise and in what manner, so that the mandatory does not fail the purpose of the sovereign? When can it be said, and by what signs can it be known, that Power, by betraying its trust, has lost its legitimacy, and, having now become no more than an observable fact, can no longer claim a right transcendent?

We must for the time leave these important details aside. Our present concern is with the psychological influence of these doctrines, and the way in which they have affected human beliefs in regard to Power and, through them, man's attitude of mind towards it; that in its turn has determined Power's extent. Have they acted on Power as a discipline, by forcing it to own allegiance to a beneficent being? Or have they canalized its stream, by creating checks which can bind it to keep faith? Or have they limited it, by restricting the share of sovereign right allowed it?

Many writers on theories of sovereignty have worked out one or the other of these restrictive devices. But in the end every single such theory has, sooner or later, lost its original purpose, and come to act merely as a springboard to Power, by providing it with the powerful aid of an invisible sovereign with whom it could in time successfully identify itself. The theory of a divine sovereignty led to absolute monarchy; the theory of a popular sovereignty led at first to parliamentary supremacy, and finally to plebiscitary absolutism.

## 1. Divine Sovereignty

The idea that Power is of God buttressed, so it is said, a monarchy that was both arbitrary and unlimited right through the Dark Ages. This grossly inaccurate conception of the Middle Ages is deeply embedded in the unlettered, whom it serves as a convenient starting-point from which to unroll the history of a political evolution to the winning-post, which is liberty.

There is not a word of truth in all this. Let us remember, without at the moment stressing it, that Power in medieval times was shared (with the *Curia Regis*[2]), limited (by other authorities which were, in their own sphere, autonomous), and that, above all, it was not sovereign.[3] The distinguishing characteristics of a Power which is sovereign are: its possession of a legislative authority; its capacity to alter as it pleases its subjects' rules of behaviour, while recasting at its own convenience the rules which determine its own; and, while it legislates for others, to be itself above the laws, *legibus solutus*, absolute. Now Power in medieval times was very different: it was tied down, not only in theory but in practice, by the *Lex Terrae* (the customs of the country), which was thought of as a thing immutable. And when the English Barons uttered their *Nolumus leges Angliae mutari*[4] they were only giving vent to the general feeling of the time.[5]

In fact, so far from having been a cause of greatness in Power, the conception of divine sovereignty was for many centuries the companion of its weakness. No doubt some fine phrases can be brought up. James I of England said to the heir to his throne: "God has made of you a little god, to sit on your throne and rule men."[6] Louis XIV's instructions to the Dauphin were in very similar terms: "He who gave the world kings

2. [The *Curia Regis* was in the early years of Norman England the feudal assembly of the tenants-in-chief. It is the germ from which the higher Courts, the Privy Council, and the Cabinet have sprung.]

3. By this is meant that it was not sovereign in the modern meaning of the word. Sovereignty of the medieval type is merely "superiority." It is the quality which belongs to the authority set above all the others, and which has no superior in the temporal hierarchy. But because it is the highest, it does not follow that the right of the sovereign is different in kind from the other rights which are below it: it does not offend these, of which it is not regarded as the source and author. The modern conception of sovereignty unfolded in the seventeenth century.

4. ["We object to changes in the laws of England."]

5. We find, in the great work devoted by the brothers R. W. and A. J. Carlyle to the political ideas of the Middle Ages (*A History of Political Medieval Theory in the West*, London: 6 vols., 1903–1936), this idea—conclusively proved by the whole of their researchers—constantly repeated, that the monarch was regarded by both medieval thinkers and people in general *as being below the law*, which obligated him and which he could not use his authority to change. For him law was *a premise*: it was really the sovereign.

6. Quoted by Marc Bloch, *Les Rois thaumaturges*, p. 351.

wished that they should be honoured as His representatives, by reserving to Himself alone the right to judge their actions. He who is born a subject must obey without complaining: that is God's will."[7] Even Bossuet, when preaching at the Louvre, apostrophized his royal house as follows: "You are gods even though you are mortal, and your authority is immortal."[8]

It is beyond question that if God, the Father and protector of human society, has Himself designated certain men to govern it, has called them His anointed, has made them His regents, and has armed them with a sword for the administration of justice—Bossuet again—then the king, strong in such a majesty, can be for his subjects nothing less than their absolute master. But phrases of this sort, in this acceptation of them, are only met with in the seventeenth century; in relation to the medieval theory of divine sovereignty they are the greatest heterodoxy. And here we come across a striking instance of the perversion of a theory of Power to the advantage of Power in being—a perversion which is, as we have already said and as will appear later, a very general phenomenon.

The same idea, that Power is of God, has, in the course of more than fifteen centuries, been used by its prophets for a great variety of purposes. St. Paul,[9] it is clear, was anxious to combat in the Christian community at Rome its tendencies to civil disobedience, which would, he feared, not only precipitate persecutions but also divert the community's activities from their true purpose, which was the winning of souls. Gregory the Great,[10] writing at a time when the West was a military anarchy, the East a prey to political instability, and the Roman way of life in imminent danger of destruction, felt under the necessity of shoring up Power. The canonists of the ninth century[11] strove to prop up the toppling imperial authority after the Church had, in the general interest, re-established it. As many periods and as many requirements, so many meanings. But it is not the case that the doctrine of Divine Law was dominant at any time before the Middle Ages: it was ideas derived from Roman law which formed the intellectual climate of those days. And if we take up the theory of divine sovereignty in the time of its blossoming, that is to say from

7. Louis XIV, Œuvres, Vol. II, p. 317.

8. Palm Sunday, 1662.

9. Cf. Epistle to the Romans, xiii, 1. Commentaries in Carlyle, op. cit., Vol. I, pp. 89–98.

10. St. Gregory, Regulae Pastorales, III, 4. [Gregory the Great, Pope from 590 to 604. The first monk to become a Pope.]

11. Cf. in particular Hincmar de Reims, De fide Carolo Regi servanda, XXIII.

the eleventh to the fourteenth centuries, what do we find? That people are repeating St. Paul's formula, "all Power is of God," but less with a view to inducing subjects to obey Power than to inducing Power to obey—God. So far from the Church wishing to confer on princes a divine supremacy by calling them the representatives or the ministers of God, her concern was the very opposite: to make them conscious that, since they held their authority only as a trust, it was their duty to make use of it in accordance with the intention and will of the Master from whom they had received it. It was not a question of her authorizing the prince to make whatever law he pleased, but rather of bending Power's will to a divine law which was its overriding master.

The consecrated king of the Middle Ages was a Power as tied down and as little arbitrary as we can conceive. He was simultaneously constrained by standing human law, i.e., custom, and by the Divine Law, and could hardly trust his own reading of his duty about anything. The court of peers was there to compel his respect for custom, and the Church took care that he continued as the assiduous vicerègent of the heavenly king, whose instructions in their every point he must obey.

In the act of crowning him the Church warned him: "Through this crown, you become a sharer in our ministry," as Archbishops said to French kings of the thirteenth century at the time of their consecration; "as in the spiritual sphere we are the shepherds of souls, so in the temporal you must show yourself the true servant of God. . . ." This solemn charge she incessantly reiterated to kings. Yves de Chartres, for instance, wrote in these terms to Henry I of England after his accession: "Never forget it, Prince: you are the servant of the servants of God and not their master; you are the protector and not the owner of your people."[12] Lastly we may observe that, if he proved himself an unprofitable servant, she had it in her power to lay sanctions on him which were found so formidable that they brought the Emperor Henry IV to fall on his knees before Gregory VII in the snow of Canossa.

Such, in the very heyday of its strength, was the theory of divine sovereignty; so little favourable was it to the exercise of a boundless authority that emperors and kings, seeking Power's enlargement, could not but clash with it. Sometimes, to escape the Church's yoke, we see them advance the plea that, since their authority is immediately held from God, it is not for man to supervise their use of it (this argument rests

12. *Epist.*, CVI P. L., Vol. CLXII, col. 121.

mainly on the Bible and St. Paul's Epistle to the Romans); but more often, and to more purpose, they have recourse to the tradition of the Roman jurists which ascribes sovereignty not to God, but—to the people!

It is for this reason that Marsilius of Padua—an adventurer who was pushing the claims of the then uncrowned Emperor, Louis of Bavaria—and many other champions of Power besides, supplanted the postulate of divine sovereignty with that of popular sovereignty: "The supreme legislator of the human race," he asserts, "is none other than the Totality of mankind, to whom the sanctions of Law fall to be applied. . . ."[13] The reliance of Power on this idea to render itself absolute is very significant.[14]

The idea would in time emancipate Power from the control of the Church. But there had first to be a revolution in religious ideas before Power, after arguing from the people's brief against God, could take up that of God against the people—a piece of tergiversation which was a necessary step in the build-up of absolutism.

The revolution needed was the crisis caused in European society by the Reformation, and the violent pleadings of Luther and his successors for a temporal Power which should be freed from papal tutelage and so enabled to adopt and legalize the reformers' doctrines. Such was the gift brought by the doctors of the Reformation to the reformed princes. The Hohenzollern who, in his capacity of Grand Master of the Order of Teutonic Knights, was then ruling Prussia, acting on Luther's advice, declared himself the owner of the estates which he held as administrator; the princes, breaking with the Church of Rome, took the opportunity of converting into a freehold the right of sovereignty, which had, until then, only been accorded to them as a limited mandate. Divine right, which had in the past been on the debit side of Power's account, was becoming an asset. Nor did that happen in those countries only which had adopted the Reformation, but in the others as well, for the Church, being now reduced to soliciting the support of the princes, was in no position to lay on them its time-honoured ban.[15] There lies the explanation of the "divine right of kings," as we see it in the seventeenth century; it is a fragment taken from the context of a doctrine which had made of kings the

13. Cf. the fine study by Noël Valois on John of Jandun and Marsilius of Padua in *L'Histoire littéraire de la France*, Vol. XXIV, pp. 575 *et seq.*

14. "The democratic theory of Marsilius of Padua led to the proclamation of Imperial omnipotence," says Noël Valois, *op. cit.*, p. 614.

15. "No Luther, no Louis XIV," as Figgis truly says. J. N. Figgis, *Studies of Political Thought from Gerson to Grotius* (2nd ed., Cambridge: 1923) p. 62.

representatives of God as regards their subjects, only to subject them at the same time to the law of God and to the control of the Church.

## 2. Popular Sovereignty

So far from its being the case that theology gives absolutism any justification for itself, we find the Stuart and Bourbon kings, at the time that they were raising their claims, having the political treatises of Jesuit doctors burnt by the common hangman.[16] These doctors not only prayed in aid the supremacy of the Pontiff: "The Pope can depose kings and put others in their place, as he has done already,"[17] but also constructed a theory of authority which shelved completely the idea of a direct mandate entrusted to kings by the heavenly Sovereign.

In their view, while it is true that Power is of God, it was not true that God had selected the beneficiary. Power is an emanation of His will because He has given man a social nature,[18] and has, therefore, caused him to live in a community: of this community civil government is a necessary feature.[19] But He has not Himself organized this government. That is the business of the people of this community, who must, for reasons of practical necessity, bestow it on some person or persons. These holders of Power manage something which is of God, and are therefore subjected to His law. But, in addition, it is the community which has entrusted them with this something, and on conditions laid down by itself. That makes them accountable to the community.

> It is for the will of the people [says Bellarmin] to set up a king, consuls or other magistrates. And if good cause comes, the people may exchange monarchy for aristocracy or democracy, and vice versa; history tells us that it happened so at Rome.[20]

It is easy to imagine with what fury a man of James I's arrogance read statements like these: it was then that he wrote his "Apology for the oath

---

16. For instance, the *De rege et regis institutione* of Mariana and the *Tractatus de potestate summi pontificis in temporalibus* of Bellarmin were burnt at Paris in 1610, followed by the *Defensio fidei* of Suarez in 1614. The same thing happened in London.

17. Vittoria, *De indis*, I, 7.

18. "The nature of man is such that he has to be a political and social animal and live among his fellows," as St. Thomas has said. *De regimine principum*, I, 1.

19. Cf. Suarez, *De legibus ac Deo Legislatore*, Book III, chaps. i, ii, iii, iv. In the two-volume summary at pp. 634–35.

20. Bellarmin, *De Laicis*, Book III.

of allegiance." Suarez's refutation[21] of it, written to the order of Pope Paul V, was publicly burnt in front of St. Paul's in London.

James I had claimed that, confronted by an unjust royal command, "the people may do no other than flee unresistingly from the anger of its king; its tears and sighs are the only anwer to him allowed it, and it may summon none but God to its aid." To this Bellarmin replied, "No people ever delegated its authority without reservation, by which it may in appropriate cases resume it in act.[22]

According to this Jesuit doctrine, it is the community which, by the act of forming itself, establishes Power. The city-state or republic is formed of

> a species of political union, which could not have taken shape without a sort of convention, expressed or implied, by which families and individuals subject themselves to a superior authority or social administrator, the aforesaid convention being the condition on which the community exists.[23]

In this formula of his, Suarez has anticipated the theory of the social contract. Society is formed and Power established by the will and consent of the multitude. To the extent that the people invests its rulers with the right to rule them, there is a *pactum subjectionis*.[24] The object of this reconstruction was, it is clear, to bar Power's road to absolutism. But it was soon distorted, as we shall see, in such a way that it served to justify absolutism. How was it possible to do that? Merely by taking away from the three following expressions the first one—God the author of Power, the people who confer Power, the rulers who receive it and exercise it. It is affirmed, after this abstraction, that Power belongs to society in full fee simple and is then conferred by it alone on its rulers. That is the theory of popular sovereignty.

It may be objected that, more surely than any other, this theory bars the road to absolutism. That, as we shall see, is the great illusion.

---

21. [The title of this treatise (1613) was *Defensio catholicae fidei contra anglicanae sectae errores.*]

22. Bellarmin, "Reply to James I of England." *Works*, Vol. XII, pp. 184 *et seq.*

23. Suarez, *De Opere*, LV, chap. vii, No. 3, Vol. III, p. 414.

24. Rousseau's new idea was merely to divide this original proceeding into two successive parts. In the first the city is formed and in the second it designates its government. In theory the subordination of Power is increased by this process. But his was only an enlargement of the Jesuit idea.

The medieval champions of Power conducted their case clumsily enough. Marsilius of Padua,[25] for instance, after postulating that the "supreme legislator" was the "totality of mankind," goes on to the proposition that this authority has been conferred on the Roman people; and he reaches this triumphant conclusion: "Finally, if the Roman people has conferred legislative power on its prince, then there is no escaping the conclusion that this power belongs to the prince of the Romans"— to, in other words, Marsilius's client, Louis of Bavaria. The argument makes no attempt to conceal its lack of disinterestedness. The point of it is, as any child could see, that the multitude has been endowed with this majestic authority merely that it may pass it on, stage by stage, to a despot. In course of time, however, the selfsame dialectic will find more plausible guise in which to present itself.

Here, for instance, is Hobbes, who, right in the middle of the seventeenth century, which was the heyday of the divine right of kings, wanted to undertake the defence of absolute monarchy. Notice how he avoids using the Biblical arguments which will be the stock-in-trade of Bishop Filmer a generation later—only to go down before the arrows of Locke.

Hobbes does not infer the unlimited right of Power from the sovereignty of God: he infers it from the sovereignty of the People. He assumes that men were, in the natural state, free, but he defines this primitive freedom, in terms more appropriate to a doctor than to a jurist, as the absence of every external compulsion. This freedom of action continues to the point at which it comes up against someone else's freedom, when the conflict is resolved according to the forces at the disposal of each. "Each individual," as Spinoza put it, "has a sovereign right over whatever is in his power; in other words, the right of each extends to the precise limit of the power which each has."[26] There is, therefore, no other effective right than that of tigers to eat men.

Some way out of this "state of nature," where each takes what he can and holds as best he can what he has taken, had to be found.[27] For this

---

25. [Marsilius of Padua (1270–1342), Italian medieval scholar, publisher in 1324 in conjunction with Jean de Jandun of a famous controversial work, the *Defensor Pacis*. The purpose of this work was to sustain Louis of Bavaria, King of the Romans, in his struggle with Pope John XXII, and its purport to prove the supremacy of the Empire, its independence of the Holy See, and the emptiness of the prerogatives "usurped" by the sovereign pontiffs.]

26. Spinoza, *Traité théologico-politique*, XVI: *Des fondements de l'état*.

27. T. Huxley, *Natural and Political Rights, in Method and Results* (London: 1893).

wild sort of liberty made both security and civilization equally impossible. Had not men, therefore, to come to the point of making a mutual surrender of their rights for the sake of peace and order? Hobbes goes to the length of giving the formula on which the social pact was concluded:

> I surrender my right to rule myself to this man or to this assembly on condition that you make a like surrender of yours. In this way the multitude has become a single person which goes by the name of a city or a republic. Such is the origin of this Leviathan or terrestrial deity, to whom we owe all peace and all safety.[28]

The man or assembly on whom the hitherto unlimited individual rights have now been unreservedly conferred is the possessor of an unlimited collective right. Thenceforward, the English philosopher asserts:

> Each subject having been made, by the establishment of the Republic, the author of all the actions and judgments of the sovereign established, the sovereign, whatever he does, does no wrong to any of his subjects, and can never be accused of injustice by any of them. For, acting as he does only on a mandate, what right could those who have given him this mandate have to complain of him?
> By this establishment of the Republic, each individual is the author of whatever the sovereign does: consequently, anyone who claims that the sovereign is wronging him is objecting to acts of which he is himself the author, and has only himself to accuse.[29]

Surely this is all very extravagant. But Spinoza, though in less striking language, affirms no less the unlimited right of Power:

> Whether the supreme Power belongs to one man, or is shared among several, or is common to all, it is certain that to whoever has it belongs also

---

28. Hobbes, *Leviathan*, chap. xxvii, "De cause, generatione et definitione civitatis."

29. Hobbes, *Leviathan*, 2nd part, chap. xviii. This proposition is fundamental to Hobbes' entire position. Thus, in the case of an executive act affecting an individual, done by the sovereign-representative of the people: "Whatever the sovereign-representative does to a subject, and for whatever reason, it cannot be called an injustice or a hurt; for each subject is the author of each of the sovereign's acts." *Ibid.*, chap. xxi. In the case of a law: ". . . no law can be unjust. Laws have been made by the sovereign authority and all that it does is agreed (in advance) by each subject; and what each has willed can be called unjust by none." *Ibid.*, chap. xxx.

the sovereign right of giving any order he pleases—the subject is bound to an absolute obedience as long as the king, or the nobles, or the people, retain the sovereign power which the conveyance of rights has conferred on them.

He too asserts: "The sovereign, to whom all is of right allowed, cannot violate the rights of the subjects."[30]

Here then we have two illustrious philosophers inferring the most complete despotism from the principle of popular sovereignty. Whoever has the sovereign power can do whatever he likes, and the subject who is wronged must regard himself as the actual author of the unjust act. "We are bound to execute to the limit whatever orders the sovereign gives us, even though they should be the silliest imaginable," pontificates Spinoza.[31]

How different is the language held by St. Augustine: ". . . but, inasmuch as we believe in God and have been summoned to His kingdom, we have been subjected to no man who should seek to destroy the gift of eternal life which God has given us."[32]

What a contrast is here between a Power which is held to the execution of the divine law and one which, after subsuming every individual right, has become a law to itself!

### 3. Democratic Popular Sovereignty

Given that there was at first a state of nature in which men were bound by no laws, and rights (so called) were no more than the measure of each man's strength, and on the hypothesis that they formed a society by commissioning a sovereign to establish order among them, then it follows that this sovereign received from them all their own rights, and that in consequence the individual has none in reserve wherewith to oppose him.

Spinoza has put the point very clearly:

Everyone has had, whether by an express or an implied agreement, to confer on the sovereign their entire stock of means of self-preservation—in other words, all their natural right. Had they wished to keep back for themselves any part of this right, they must at the same time have taken defensive measures for their own safety; as they have not done that and must,

30. Spinoza, *op. cit.*, xvi.
31. *Ibid.*
32. St. Augustine, *Commentary on the Epistle to the Romans.*

had they done it, have divided and in the end destroyed all rule, they have in fact subjected themselves to the will, *however it operates*, of the sovereign power.

To this it was no answer to suppose, as Locke did, that *all* individual rights were not put in the common stock and that some were kept back by the contracting parties. This hypothesis, though destined to bear fruit politically, holds no water logically. Rousseau will be found at a later date pouring scorn on Locke's reasoning: the alienation of individual rights is made unreservedly

> and none of the partners can henceforward claim back anything; for, if there were still any rights in private hands, then, as there would be no superior in common to pronounce between them and the public right, the result would be that each man, finding himself his own judge in something, would soon claim to be it in everything.[33]

"Will it perhaps seem to someone," asks a troubled Spinoza, "that by this principle we are making men slaves?" His answer is that what makes a man a slave is not obedience but obedience in the interest of a master. If the orders given are in the interests of the man who obeys, then he is not a slave but a subject.

But this raises the problem of how to ensure that the sovereign never considers the interest of the ruler but only the interest of the ruled. The solution of confronting him with an overseer, a "defender of the people," is ruled out in advance, because he is himself the people, and the individual has no rights left to him wherewith to arm against the whole any check or counter-weight. Hobbes admits that "the state of subjects who are exposed to all the irregular passions of the man or men who own such an unlimited authority, may be one of great misery.[34]

The people's only hope is in the personal excellence of the man or men whom they obey. Who is it to be?

In Hobbes' view, men had bound themselves by their original contract to obey either a monarch or an assembly—his own marked preference was for a monarch. In Spinoza's view, they had bound themselves to obey either a king, or a nobility, or a people, and he stressed the advantages of the last of these solutions. In Rousseau's view, no choice was conceivable: men could bind themselves to obey nothing but their totality. Whereas Hobbes made his man concluding the social pact say, "I surrender

33. *Du Contrat social*, Book I, chap. vi.
34. Hobbes, *Leviathan*, 2nd part, chap. xviii.

my right to rule myself to this man or to these men," Rousseau, when drafting a constitution for the Corsicans, made each contracting party say, ". . . with my body, my goods, my will and my entire strength I join myself to the Corsican nation, to whom I now belong in fee simple, I and my dependents."

Once there is postulated a right of command which has no limits and against which the private person has no rights—and that is the logical result of the hypothesis of the social pact—then it is much less terrible to conceive of this right as belonging collectively to all than as belonging to one man only or to a few.

Rousseau, like his predecessors, held that what constitutes sovereignty is the surrender without reservation of individual rights; these then go to form a collective right, the sovereign's, which is absolute. On this point all the theories of popular sovereignty are in agreement. In Hobbes' view, however, a surrender of rights presupposed someone, whether a man or an assembly, to whom to surrender them: the will of this someone, in whom is vested the collective right, would thereafter pass for, and stand legally as, the will of all. Spinoza, and others too, conceded that the collective right might be vested in the will either of one man, or of several men, or of a majority. Hence the three traditional forms of government: monarchy, aristocracy, and democracy. According to this line of thought the originating act by which a society and a sovereignty were created set up *ipso facto* the government which is the sovereign. And to many thinkers of note it seemed unthinkable that, once the fundamental hypothesis was accepted, any other course of events was possible.[35]

In Rousseau's view, however, the process has two stages: first, individuals turn themselves into a people; next, they give themselves a government. The result is that, whereas in previous systems the people gave the collective right (the sovereignty) in the act of creating it, in his they create it without giving it—in fact they never part with it. Rousseau allowed in principle all the three forms of government and considered democracy appropriate to small states, aristocracy appropriate to those of moderate size, and monarchy appropriate to large ones.[36]

### 4. A Dynamic of Power

In any case, the government is not the sovereign. Rousseau calls the government the prince or the magistrate, names which may signify a

35. Cf. Bossuet, *Cinquième avertissement aux protestants*.
36. *Du Contrat social*, Book III, chap. iii.

collection of men: thus a senate may be the prince, and in a perfect democracy the people itself is the magistrate. It is true that this prince or magistrate is the ruler. But his title to rule is not sovereign, does not derive from that limitless *imperium* which is the essence of sovereignty— all he does is to exercise such powers as have been conferred on him.

Only, when once the idea of an absolute sovereignty has even been conceived and its existence asserted to rest in the body of society, great is the temptation, and great also are the opportunities, for the ruling body to seize it. Although Rousseau was, in our opinion, quite wrong in supposing that so overpowering a right existed at all, his theory has the merit of accounting for the growth of Power, and brings into play a political dynamic. Rousseau saw very clearly that the agents of Power form a corps,[37] that this corps houses a corps mind,[38] and that its aim is to usurp sovereignty:

> The more they redouble their efforts, the more the constitution changes; and, in the absence of any other corps mind to resist the prince's [Power's] and thus bring it into equilibrium, the time must come sooner or later when the prince [Power] ends by oppressing the sovereign [the people] and thereby breaks the Social Contract. This is the inherent and inevitable weakness which, from the day that the body politic is born, tends ceaselessly to destroy it, even as old age and death destroy at last the physical body.[39]

This theory of Power marks a great advance on those so far examined by us. The others explained Power by the possession of an unlimited right of command, whether that right emanated from God or from the social totality. But none of them gave any clue to the reason why, as one Power succeeded another or one period in the life of the same Power succeeded another, the area over which command and obedience operated should show such variations.

37. "That the 'Government corps' may have a being and a life of its own distinguishing it from the nation as a whole, that all its members may act in unison and serve its specific purpose, it must have its personal ego, an *esprit de corps* in which all its members share, a strength of its own and a will to its own survival. This personal life presupposes assemblies, councils, the capacity to deliberate and decide, rights, titles and privileges, all of which are the exclusive property of the prince." (Rousseau meant by "prince" the totality of the components of government; it is what in this book I have called Power.) *Du Contrat social,* Book III, chap. ii.
38. Book III, chap. x.
39. *Ibid.*

In Rousseau's powerful reconstruction, on the other hand, we do find an attempt at explanation. If Power's extent varies from one society to another, the reason is that the body social, in which alone sovereignty resides, has made larger or smaller grants of its exercise. Above all, if the same Power's extent varies in the course of that Power's life, the reason is that it tends unceasingly to usurp sovereignty and can, in the measure of its success, dispose of the people and their resources more completely and more uninhibitedly. The result is that, the greater the element of usurpation in a government, so much the wider is the range of its authority.

What, however, is not explained is the source from which Power draws the strength necessary to effect this usurpation. For, if it owes its strength to the mass of the people and to the fact that it is the incarnation of the general will, then it must, with its every deviation from that general will, lose strength, and its authority must tend to disappear to the extent to which it separates itself from the popular desire. Rousseau's view was that government, by a natural slant, tends to move from many men to few or from democracy to aristocracy—he instances the case of Venice—and in the end to monarchy, regarded by him as the final form of society; and monarchy, by becoming despotic, causes in the end the death of the body social. But there is nothing in history to show that such a serial movement is inevitable. Nor is any light thrown on the question from what source one man gets strength enough to have executed a will which is cut off ever more completely from the general will.

The weakness of the theory lies in its heterogeneity. It has the merit of treating Power as a separate entity—a body which houses strength—but it still thinks of sovereignty, in the medieval manner, as a right. In this mix-up Power's strength remains quite unexplained, and there is no clue to the social forces which are able to moderate or check it.

All the same, what an advance this is on the earlier theories! And, on the essential points, what foresight!

## 5. How Sovereignty Can Control Power

The theory of popular sovereignty, as Rousseau left it, offers a rather striking parallel to the medieval theory of divine sovereignty. Both allow a right of command which, though it is unlimited, is not inherent in the governors. The right belongs to a superior power—whether it be God or the people—which cannot by its nature exercise the right itself. Therefore

they have to confer a mandate on a Power which can exercise it. Both
state more or less explicitly that the mandatories will be tied by rules: in
other words, Power's behaviour is subject to either the Divine Will or
the general will.

But will these mandatories necessarily be faithful to their trust? Or will
they tend to usurp the command which they at present exercise only by
delegation? Will they remember at all points the end for which they have
been established, which is the common good, and the condition to which
they have been subjected, which is the execution of the law, whether
God's or the people's?[40] Will they, in short, keep their hands off the
sovereignty? They will not; and they will in the end give themselves out
as resuming in their own persons the Divine Will or the general will, as
the case may be; Louis XIV, for instance, claimed the rights of God, and
Napoleon those of the people.[41]

Is there any way of stopping this, except by the exercise of control by
the sovereign over the Power? The sovereign's nature, unfortunately,
makes it as impossible for him to control as to govern. Hence came the
idea of having a body which would keep watch in the name of the
sovereign over the actual Power, prescribe as occasion demanded the rules
by which it must act, and, in case of need, pronounce the forfeiture of
its functions and make provision for a successor.

Under the system of divine sovereignty this body could only be the
Church.[42] Under the system of popular sovereignty it will be Parliament.
As a result of this, however, sovereignty becomes a house divided, and
the Powers in human exercise show two faces. These are either a temporal

40. We must always remember that, when Rousseau talks of the people being the only
law-making authority, he is thinking only of quite general directives, and not of all the
particular and detailed provisions which modern constitutional practice comprises under
the name of legislation.

41. He always took care to found his authority on the sovereignty of the people. As for
instance in this declaration: "The Revolution is over; its principles have come to rest in my
person. *The present government is the representative of the sovereign people;* there can be no
revolution against the sovereign."

Molé observes: "Everything spoken or written by him bore the same character, was
bound up with the same system and was directed to the same end, that of propagating the
principle of the sovereignty of the people—a principle which he thought completely
erroneous and certain to have disastrous consequences. . . ." Mathieu Molé, *Souvenirs d'un
Témoin* (Geneva: 1943) p. 222.

42. I must not be supposed to be saying that in medieval society the Church was the
only organism actually engaged in the control and check of Power. I am not now recording
events but analysing theories.

Power and a spiritual Power exercising a temporal jurisdiction, or, in the other case, an executive and a legislature. The whole metaphysic of sovereignty leads to this division—and yet abominates it. Empiricists may find in it a safeguard for liberty, but it must surely be an offence to all who believe in a sovereignty which is in essence one and indivisible. As though sovereignty could be shared between two sets of agents! If two wills clash, both cannot be the divine or popular, as the case may be. It follows that of the two bodies one only can be the true reflex of the sovereign; the will opposing is, in that case, a rebel will to be subdued. These results follow logically if the basis of Power is one will which must be obeyed. One of the bodies, therefore, had to win. At the close of the Middle Ages the winner was the monarchy.

In modern times it is either the executive or the legislature, according to which stands closer to the sovereign people.[43] The chief executive does so when, as in the case of Louis Napoleon or Roosevelt, there is direct election of him by the people; the parliament does so when, as in the France of the Third Republic, the chief executive is at a distance from the source of authority.

So far as the controllers of Power are concerned, one of two things results: either they are finally eliminated, or else, acting in the name of the sovereign, they subdue his agents and usurp the sovereignty. In this connection it is worth noting that Rousseau, while cutting down as far as was possible the authority of the rulers, had a deep distrust for "representatives," who were, in his time, greatly relied on for keeping Power within the bounds of its office. He saw no other "method of preventing usurpations of government" than that of holding periodic popular assemblies, to pronounce on the use which had been made of Power and to decide whether it would not be a good thing to change the form and the personnel of the government. As he fully admitted that his method was quite impracticable, the obstinacy with which he urged it can only be ascribed to the invincible repugnance which the method of control at that time operating in England inspired in him—the method of parliamentary control, which Montesquieu had praised to the skies. So distasteful to him is the very idea that he inveighs against it with a sort of passion:

43. "Whenever," remarks Sismondi, "the view is taken that all authority proceeds from the people by process of election, then those who derive their power from the people most immediately and have the largest number of constituents come to regard their authority as the most legitimate." Sismondi, *Études sur les Constitutions des Peuples modernes* (Paris: 1836) p. 305.

> Sovereignty cannot be represented. . . . Therefore the deputies of the people are not and cannot be its representatives. . . . This new-fangled idea of representatives comes down to us from feudal government, from that iniquitous and ridiculous form of government which made degenerates of the human species and caused the name of man to stink in the nostrils.[44]

His attack is against the representative system as it was operating in the very country of which Montesquieu had made a model of excellence:

> The English think they are free but they are quite wrong; they are only free when Parliamentary elections come round; once the members have been elected, they are slaves and things of naught. They deserve to lose Liberty by reason of the use which they make of their brief intervals of Liberty.[45]

Why all this spleen? With a sovereignty on this great scale, Rousseau felt that, once the possibility of the sovereign being represented was admitted, it would be impossible to stop the representative laying claim to the sovereignty.[46] And indeed every tyranny which has since appeared has justified its aggressions on individual rights by its usurped claim to represent the people. More especially, he foresaw what seems to have escaped Montesquieu, that the authority of Parliament, though for the time being it would grow at the expense of the executive and so act as a brake on Power, would come in the end first to dominate the executive and then to fuse it with itself, thus reconstituting a Power which could lay claim to sovereignty.

## 6. The Theories of Sovereignty Considered in Their Effects

If we now take a bird's-eye view of the theories whose natures we have just examined, we note that all of them tend to render subjects obedient by revealing to them a transcendent principle behind the Power they see; this principle, whether God or the people, is armed with an absolute

44. *Du Contrat social,* Book III, chap. xv.
45. *Ibid.*
46. We find in Kant the same distrust of "representatives." "The people," he writes, "that is represented in Parliament by its deputies, finds these guardians of its rights and liberty to be men deeply interested in the position of themselves and of the members of their family in the army, the navy and the civil administration—all of them things which are in the disposal of ministers; they do not offer resistance to the government's pretensions but are, on the contrary, always ready and prepared to divert the government into their own hands." Kant, *Métaphysique des Mœurs.* Trans. Barni (Paris: 1853) p. 179.

authority. At the same time they all tend also to subordinate Power in effect to this principle, whichever it is. Therefore their disciplinary effect is twofold: they discipline the subject, they also discipline Power.

By disciplining the subject they reinforce the Power in being. But by straitly tying this Power down, they compensate for this reinforcement—always provided that they can find some practical method of keeping the Power down. That is the difficulty. The more unlimited the conception of the sovereign authority which there is danger of Power's usurping, and the greater consequent danger to society if Power usurps it, the more important become the practical methods employed to keep Power in leading-strings.

But the sovereign cannot make the whole of his presence felt to keep his regents to their duty. Therefore he needs a controlling body; this body, whether its place is above the government or at its side, will in time try to seize it, thus joining in one the two capacities of regent and overseer and thereby securing for itself unlimited authority of command.

This danger leads to a multiplication of precautions; the Power and its controller are, by a division of functions or a rapid succession of office-holders, crumbled up into small pieces—a cause of weakness and disorder in the administration of society's business. Then, inevitably, the disorder and weakness, becoming at length intolerable, bring together again the crumbled pieces of sovereignty—and there is Power, armed now with a despotic authority.

The wider the conception held, in the time when monopoly of it seemed a vain imagining, of the right of sovereignty, the harsher will be the despotism. If the view is that a community's laws admit of no modification whatever, the laws will contain the despot. Or if the view is that something of these laws, corresponding to the ordinances of God, is immutable, that part at least will remain fast.

And now we begin to see that popular sovereignty may give birth to a more formidable despotism than divine sovereignty. For a tyrant, whether he be one or many, who has, by hypothesis, successfully usurped one or the other sovereignty, cannot avail himself of the Divine Will, which shows itself to men under the forms of a Law Eternal, to command whatever he pleases. Whereas the popular will has no natural stability but is changeable; so far from being tied to a law, its voice may be heard in laws which change and succeed each other. So that a usurping Power has, in such a case, more elbow-room; it enjoys more liberty, and its liberty is the name of arbitrary power.

# III.

# *The Organic Theories of Power*

THE EXPLANATION OF AND JUSTIFICATION FOR civil obedience is, according to the theories of sovereignty, the right of command which Power derives from its origin, whether divine or popular.

But has not Power an end as well? Must it not tend to the common good—vague and variable of content as the phrase is, its uncertain meaning corresponding to the indefinite nature of human aspiration? And can it happen that a Power, though legitimate enough in origin, governs in a way which is so flatly opposed to the common good that obedience to it may be called in question? Theologians have often debated this problem and have evolved from their debates the idea of the end. Some have argued that even an unjust Power must be obeyed; but most of them, and all the highest authorities among them, have held the contrary view that a government with an unjust end could not be legitimated by its origin. And particularly St. Thomas seems to attach more importance to the end of Power than to its origin: revolt against an authority which is not aiming at the common good ceases to be seditious.[1]

The idea of the end, after having played in medieval Catholic thought the part of a corrective to the idea of sovereignty (the obedience due to a Power by reason of its legitimacy could, that is to say, be disclaimed if

---

1. *Summa Theologica,* II, 42, 2. "Ad tertiam dicendum, quod regimen tyrannicum non est justum; *quia non ordinatur ad bonum commune,* sed ad bonum privatum regentis; et ideo perturbatio hujus regiminis non habet rationem seditionis."

the Power stopped aiming at the common good),[2] suffered eclipse in the theories of popular sovereignty. Not, to be sure, that people stopped saying that the function of Power was to achieve the general advantage: no one ever went as far as that. But the hypothesis was made that a Power which was the legitimate emanation of society would for that very reason never cease to seek the social good, because "the General Will is always righteous and always aims at the public advantage."[3]

In the nineteenth century, but not before, the idea of the end reappears, but its influence then is quite different from that which it exercised in the Middle Ages. In those days it had, in effect, served as an obstacle to the development of Power. But in the nineteenth century it will be seen furthering its development. This reversal is related to an entirely new way of picturing society, which is now regarded not as an aggregate of individuals with common legal principles, but as a developing organism. We must pause to examine this intellectual revolution, because it is from it that the new theories of the final cause derive their importance and their character.

## 1. The Nominalist Conception of Society

The explanation of, and to a large extent the corrective for, the theories of sovereignty are to be found in the conception of society which was in vogue at the time of their foundation.

Before the nineteenth century it never occurred to any Western thinker to suppose that there was, in any collection of men subject to a common political direction, anything with a real existence except individuals. That had been the point of view of the Romans. They looked on the Roman people as an assemblage of human beings: not, it is true, just any assemblage, but one which was held together by ties of law to the end of a common advantage.[4]

They never imagined that this assemblage could be the parent of a "person" who was distinct from the persons making it up. Where we now say "France," with the sensation of talking about a real person, they used

---

2. If, in medieval speech, it administers *in destructionem* instead of, as it should, *in aedificationem*.

3. *Du Contrat social*, Book II, chap. iii.

4. Cf. Cicero, *De Republica*, I, 25, 39: "Res publica, res populi, populus autem non omnis hominum coetus quoquo modo congregatus, sed coetus multitudinis juris consensu et utilitatis communione sociatus."

to say, according to the date of the speaker, either "the people and commons of Rome," or "the Senate and people of Rome," signifying, by this essentially descriptive appellation, that what they saw in their mind's eye was not a person, Rome, but rather the physical reality of a collection of individuals belonging to a group. What the word "people," in its wider acceptation, evoked for them was something entirely concrete, namely the Roman citizens gathered in conclave; they had no need of a word equivalent to our "nation" because the adding up of individuals resulted, as they saw it, only in an arithmetical total, and not in a quite different sort of creature. They had just as little need of the word "state," because they were not conscious of a thing transcendent, living above and beyond themselves, but only of certain interests which they had in common and which made up the *res publica*.

In this conception, which Rome bequeathed to the Middle Ages, the only reality is men. The medieval theologians and the philosophers of the seventeenth and eighteenth centuries were at one in proclaiming that men preceded any and every society. They established society only when, either because of the corruption of their nature (the theologians) or by reason of the savagery of their instincts (Hobbes), they found it necessary to do so. But this society of theirs is still an artificial body—Rousseau says so expressly,[5] and even Hobbes, though he had put as a frontispiece to one of his works a picture of a giant outlined in a composite of human shapes, seems never to have supposed that Leviathan lived a life of his own. He has no will, but the will of a man or of an assembly passes for his will.

This purely nominalist conception of society renders intelligible the notion of sovereignty. Society consists only of associated men, whose disassociation is always possible. An authoritarian, like Hobbes, and a libertarian, like Rousseau, are at one in this. The former sees in disassociation a disaster which must be prevented with the utmost rigour,[6] the latter a last resource for oppressed citizens.

5. For instance: ". . . although the artificial body of the government is the work of another artificial body (the body politic or Society) . . ." (*Du Contrat social*, Book III, chap. i).

6. Hobbes, whom civil commotions troubled so much that he fled the country on their appearance, wished to confer on Power this degree of absolutism only because he hated above everything the idea of humanity falling back into what he regarded, rightly or wrongly, as the primitive condition of all against all. After developing his theory of an unlimited right of command, he answered objections to it in this way: "Perhaps at this point objection will be taken that the condition of the subjects is wretched, in that they are exposed to the cupidity and other irregular passions of those who possess so unlimited a Power. And in general those who live under a monarch attack monarchy; and those who

But, given that society is but an artificial assemblage of naturally independent men, think of the effort needed to bring their separate behaviours into line and force them to admit a common authority! The mystery of the foundation of society requires a divine intervention for its explanation or, at the very least, a first solemn convention of the entire people. Think too of the prestige needed to maintain day by day the cohesion of the whole! There must have been some title to compel respect and one which could not for its purpose be too exalted—in short, sovereignty, whether or not it is agreed to confer it at once on Power.

Certain it is that, when independent persons agree to regulate their intercourse and appoint commissioners to the task of regulation, the perpetuity of the tie and the strict execution of the obligations entered into can be assured only by the ascription of the utmost majesty possible to those whose continuous duty it will be to bring back straying wills to the common path. In our own time we have seen a social contract concluded between persons in the state of nature—*bellum omnium contra omnes*. Those persons were the powerful nations of the world, and that contract was the League of Nations. And this artificial body became disassociated for the absence in it of any Power which a right transcendent had so buttressed that the rights of the component nations could not oppose it.

In just the same way a Rugby team, if I may take a more familiar illustration, must have an arbitral authority for thirty embattled giants to obey the solitary referee's whistle.

Given the abstract problem of making and maintaining an association between independent elements; given the conception that the nature of these elements underwent no substantial change by their adherence to the social pact; given the belief that nonconformity and secession were always possible courses—it will be seen that a majestic sort of sovereignty, which could cloak its weak and naked magistrates with its own dignity, was indispensable. Seen in the picture of its own postulates, the idea is not only logical but has a certain grandeur.

---

live in a democracy or are governed by any other sort of sovereign authority, ascribe their discomforts to whatever the form of government is; whereas in truth Power, under whatever form, is, if it is *sufficiently complete* to protect them, always the same.

"They do not reflect that the condition of man is never without some inconvenience, and that the worst which a government of whatever kind can inflict is nothing at all to the miseries and frightful calamities which go with civil war, or to the anarchic condition of men who, lacking masters, are exempt from all laws and from every coercive force capable of opposing their rapines and vendettas." (*Leviathan*, 1st edition of 1651, p. 94.)

Given, however, that society is a natural and necessary fact, that it is materially and morally impossible for a man to withdraw from it, and that factors quite other than the measure of force in laws and state compel his social conformity, then the support for Power which the theory of sovereignty gives becomes excessive and dangerous.

The dangers adduced by it remain partly concealed so long as minds retain the imprint of the basic hypothesis which brought sovereignty to birth, namely *that men are the reality and society a convention*. This opinion does carry with it the idea that human personality is an absolute value to which society stands only in the relation of a means. This is the source of Declarations of the Rights of Man, rights against which the right of sovereignty itself breaks in vain; this defeat of sovereignty must seem logically absurd if it is remembered that its right is, by definition, absolute, but it will seem the most natural thing in the world if it is remembered that the body politic is an artificial thing, sovereignty just a prestige with which it is armed with a view to a certain end, and that all these shadows are as dust against the reality of the human being. We may say then that, so long as social philosophy continued individualist and nominalist, the notion of sovereignty could do little harm; its ravages began as soon as this philosophy started to decay.

From this point, we may note in passing, the double acceptation of the word "democracy" begins; in the sense of individualist social philosophy it is the rule of the Rights of Man; in a political philosophy divorced from social individualism it is the absolutism of a government which draws its title from the masses.

## 2. The Realist Conception of Society

Thought is less independent than is supposed, and philosophers more indebted than they admit to fashionable idols and popular parlance. Before metaphysics could affirm the reality of society, the latter had first to take the shape of a being which bore the name of Nation.

This was an outcome, perhaps its most important, of the French Revolution. When the Legislative Assembly had plunged France into a military escapade which the monarchy would never have risked, it soon appeared that her Power's resources were insufficient for opposing the rest of Europe, and it became necessary to require the almost total participation of her people in the war; this was an unprecedented demand. In whose name to make it? In that of a discredited king? Emphatically no. It must be in the name of the nation: the patriotism which had for a thousand years taken the form of attachment to a person naturally inclined men's minds to attach to the nation the character and aspect of a person whose lineaments were promptly fixed by a thousand pencils.

Not to recognize the psychological disturbance and metamorphosis set in train by the Revolution is to linger in misconception of the whole of subsequent European history, including the history of thought. In former times, as after Malplaquet, Frenchmen ranged themselves *about* the king; it was a case of individuals bringing succour to a loved and respected chief. But now it is the nation *in* which, as members of a whole, they range themselves. This conception of a whole, leading a life of its own which is superior to that of its parts, was in all probability always below the surface. But the process of its crystallization was to be sudden.

It was not that the throne was overthrown, but that the whole, the nation-person, mounted it. Its life was as that of the king it succeeded, but it had one great advantage over him: for subjects are, in regard to a king—who is seen to be *a person different* from themselves—naturally careful to secure their rights. Whereas the nation is not *a person different*: it is the subject himself, and yet it is more than he—it is a hypostatized *We*. Nor does it make any difference to this revolution in ideas that in sober fact Power remains much more like its old self than is generally thought, and, in any case, quite distinct from the actual people it rules.

For what matters are beliefs. And the belief which then gained credit in France and later spread over Europe was that the nation-person has an existence and is the natural repository of Power. The French armies sowed the seed of this faith all over Europe, as much and more by the dis-illusionments which they occasioned as by the effect of the gospel which they brought in their train. Those who, like Fichte, had been at first the most enthusiastic in their welcome, turned in the end the most impassioned preachers of opponent nationalisms.

At the time that German national feeling had taken wing Hegel formulated the first coherent doctrine of the new phenomenon and awarded the nation a certificate of philosophical being. His doctrine, if contrasted with Rousseau's, emphasizes the extent of the change which has come over the concept of society. What Rousseau calls "civil society" corresponds to society as thought of up to the Revolution. In it the individual members are what matter, and the greatest care is due to their particular ends and interests. But, to safeguard these individuals against both danger from without and the potential injury which they may do each other, institutions are necessary. Order and Power to guarantee it are demanded by the interest of the individual himself. Yet with whatever efficaciousness it is thought needful to endow this order and with whatever range this Power, theirs is a morally subordinate position, for they have been established only with a view to enabling individuals to pursue their individual ends. Hegel's idea of "State," on the other hand, corresponds to the new conception of society. Just as a man does not regard the family as a mere convenience, but joins to it his own ego and accepts life on terms of being a member of this unit, so do there come to him the conception of being a member of the nation, the recognition that he is bound to share in a collective life, the conscious integration of his activity with the general activity, the sensation of pleasure in the society's accomplishments—in short, he makes the society an end.

### 3. Logical Consequences of the Realist Conception

Such, in as simple language as possible, is Hegel's conception.[7] The closeness of its correspondence to an evolution of political feelings is clear to see; in the nineteenth and twentieth centuries people will be found thinking of society as Hegel did without ever having heard of him, for the reason that, in this field, his work was merely to endow with form a belief which had always lurked more or less consciously in many minds.

This novel conception of society had momentous consequences. The idea of the common good now gets a completely different content from its former one. It is no longer a question simply of helping each individual to realize his own private good—which is clear-cut enough—but of achieving a social good of a much less definite character. The idea of an end in Power takes on an importance quite different from that given it in the Middle Ages. The end was then justice, "*jus suum cuique tribuere*," to ensure that each obtained his due. But what was the due? That which an immovable law-custom acknowledged to be his. Hence it resulted that the idea of an end or final cause could not be used to extend the area of Power. But all is changed when the rights that belong to individuals, their subjective rights, give place to an ever more exalted morality which must needs be realized in society. By reason of this end, there is no

---

7. I have refrained from exact quotations by reason of the peculiarity of Hegelian jargon. The important passages will be found in Vol. VII of Lasson's edition of the complete works: *Schriften zur Politik und Rechtsphilosophie*.

extension of itself which Power, as the agent of this realization, cannot justify. From that time on, then, as we can easily see, place is made for theories of the final cause of Power which Power finds exceedingly advantageous to itself. It has only, for example, to make the vague concept of social justice its end.

And Power itself—how does this new idea affect it? There is now a collective being, which is of far greater importance than individuals: clearly, then, the right transcendent of sovereignty belongs to none other. It is the sovereignty of the nation which is, as has often been stressed,[8] a very different thing from the sovereignty of the people. In the latter—Rousseau said it—"the Sovereign is only the individuals who go to the making of him."[9] But in the former, society fulfils itself as a whole only to the extent that partakers of it know themselves for members and see in it their end; from which it follows logically that those *only* who have attained to this knowledge are steering society towards its fulfilment. In them is all guidance and leadership; the general will coincides with their will only; theirs is the general will.

It is Hegel's claim to have clarified in this way an idea which, as found in Rousseau is, it must be admitted, somewhat confused. For the Genevan philosopher, after telling us that "the General Will is righteous and tends always to the public advantage,"[10] remembered too well the many unjust or disastrous decisions taken by the Athenian people not to add: "It does not follow that the people's deliberations are always on the same level of rectitude," and even further: "There is often a big difference between the Will of All and the General Will; it is the latter which looks only to the public interest." All this is meaningless unless the prescriptions, "is righteous and tends always to the public advantage" and "looks only to the public interest," are taken as the attributes of an ideal will. That is Hegel's point: general will is that which tends to the end in view (conceived no longer as that which private interests have in common but as the realization of the higher collective life). The motive force of society is the general will, which does all that needs to be done, whether or not the individuals who lack consciousness of the end are assenting parties.

It is now, in short, a question of inducing in the body social a new

8. Cf. particularly Carré de Malberg, *Contribution à la théorie générale de l'état* (2 vols., Paris: 1920) and Paul Bastid, in a work of importance: *Sieyès et sa Pensée* (Paris: 1939).
9. *Du Contrat social*, Book I, chap. vii.
10. *Du Contrat social*, Book II, chap. iii.

efflorescence, the vision of which is possessed by its conscious members only. These latter form "the universal class" in distinction to all the rest, who remain the prisoners of their own particularisms.

It is, then, the business of the *conscious part* to do for the whole the necessary willing. That, for Hegel, does not mean that the part is free to choose for the whole whatever future it pleases. So far from that, it would be truer to say that its recognition of what the whole should be both now and in the future is what makes it the conscious part. In using hothouse methods to force the whole to be what it should be it acts merely as an *accoucheur* and, even if it uses force, does the whole no violence.

It is easy to see how valuable this theory may prove to a group of men who, claiming to be the *conscious* part, claim also to know the end in view, in the assured conviction that it is their will alone which marches with "the rational Will for its sake and for its fruits" of which Hegel speaks. The Prussian administration, for instance, then in the full tide of development, found in Hegelianism the justification both for what it was doing and for its authoritarian methods of doing it. The *Beamtenstaat* (bureaucracy), the Power of expert officialdom, is sure that its will represents no arbitrary caprice but a knowledge of what should be. In the result it both can and must shove the people into such ways of acting and thinking as will best realize the end which reason has permitted these experts to envisage.

The vision of what should be, thus envisaged in a group, casts this group for a leading part. In Marx's scientific socialism there is no doubt as to what the proletariat should be. Therefore the proletariat, being the conscious part, may speak and will in the name of the whole; its duty is to give the inert mass consciousness of the building of a proletarian whole. At a later stage the proletariat, when it has come to know itself, disappears as a class and becomes the social whole.

Again, and in the same way, the Fascist party, being the conscious part of the nation, does the nation's willing and wills it to be what it should be.

All these doctrines, which sanction in practice the right of a minority, calling itself conscious, to direct a majority, spring directly from Hegelianism. It is, moreover, far from being the case that the systems with an obviously Hegelian pedigree are the only children of the conception of a social whole. This conception, as was said earlier, was widespread in the thought of the post-revolutionary period: it is not, therefore, surprising to find modern politics impregnated with it. Whereas in earlier centuries the actual people could be represented only in its multiple aspects (by the States-General) or not at all (according to Rousseau), the whole can now find expression in those who know, or claim to know, what must be its becoming, and who are for that reason, or claim to be, in a position to express the objective will. It will be either an oligarchy of elected persons or popular groupings speaking in the name of the Nation with an absolute assurance. It will be, whatever its group or party, the sole repository of truth. And opposition parties, with a different conception of the end, will also aspire to direct the whole without hindrance.

To sum up: the sensation of a common national emotion has caused society to be looked on as a whole. Not as yet a realized whole, because many of the individuals in a society do not yet behave as the members of a whole, from not knowing that they are *members* rather than *individuals*. This whole, however, fulfils itself as such to the extent that its conscious members lead the rest on to behave and think in the way that is required to enable the whole to fulfil itself as such. And for that reason the conscious members both can and must push and pull the unconscious. Hegel does not seem to have wanted to construct an authoritarian theory. But his theory is known by its fruits.

### 4. The Division of Labour and Organicism

Meanwhile, the middle of the nineteenth century found attention as much riveted on industrial progress and the social changes resulting therefrom as, in the beginning of the century, it was riveted on the phenomenon of nationalism.

This stupendous change, which had proceeded at a breakneck speed almost since the time of *The Social Contract*, had, almost in the act of taking wing, received its interpretation from Adam Smith. The author of *The Wealth of Nations*—a work whose fame has not been dimmed by time—explained the influence of the division of labour on a society's productivity. Soon the idea was widespread that the further the lengths to which the individuals in a community push the specialization of their particular activities, the greater will be the production of that community— or, as Bentham put it, the more means of happiness will they create.

The idea has won all hearts by reason of the twofold movement which it brings to light, though, to be sure, the two paths join in the end. Hegel turned it to good account: recalling that Plato in his *Republic* had rigorously stressed the importance of the citizens remaining undifferentiated and had seen in that the essential condition of social unity, Hegel asserted that the characteristic of the modern state was, contrariwise, to allow a process of differentiation, by which an ever growing diversity could be ranged within an ever richer unity.[11]

This anticipated what Durkheim says in our time; he sets off the "mechanical" solidarity of a primitive society, in which the individuals are held together by their similarity, against the "organic" solidarity of a mature society, the members of which have, just by reason of their being differentiated, become necessary to each other.[12]

Auguste Comte, who distinguished very clearly the material and the moral effects of the phenomenon, gave this concept of the division of labour its first introduction to political thought. In the material order, as he admitted, human activities, by becoming differentiated, tend to their more effective interplay between themselves.[13] And he is not convinced that the process of adjusting all these differences is as automatic as it was made out to be by the liberal economists, whose *laissez faire* he condemns, and conceives it to be the duty of the public authority to take a hand in facilitating this adjustment. But, and this above all, the process, as he notices, induces a moral differentiation which calls for remedy. It is the business of Power

> to restrain in adequate measure and to forestall as far as possible this fatal tendency towards that fundamental cleavage of sentiments and interests which results inevitably from the very principle of human development, and which, if it were allowed to follow its natural course unchecked, would end inevitably by blocking social advance.[14]

But the astounding career of the concept of the division of labour did not end here. It is now to overrun biology, and thereafter to return, by

11. "The principle of modern States has the deep-seated ability of allowing the principle of subjectivity to work itself out to the extreme limit of independent individual particularity, and of bringing it back simultaneously to the main unity; and so of maintaining this unity in the midst of this principle of license." (Hegel, *Principes de la Philosophie de Droit*. French ed. N.R. F. 1940, para. 260).

12. Cf. Durkheim, *De la Division du travail social* (1st ed. Paris: 1893).

13. Auguste Comte, *Cours de philosophie positive* (Paris: 1839), especially Vol. IV, pp. 470–80.

14. Auguste Comte, *Cours de philosophie positive* (Paris: 1839) p. 220.

way of Spencer, to the field of political thought, its content enriched and its impetus heightened.

Biology made a decisive advance when it came to see every living organism as a structure of cells; these cells show, it is true, an almost infinite diversity as between one organism and another, and even within the same organism; and the higher the form of life, the greater is the variety of cells which make it up. The loan from political economy of the concept of division of labour then brought forth the idea that all these cells had, by a process of functional differentiation, evolved from a primitive cell which was relatively simple. And the successive stages in the perfection of organisms corresponded to stages in the progress of the "natural" division of labour. So that in the end organisms came to be regarded as higher and higher forms of one and the same process—that of cellular cooperation by way of division of labour—or else as "societies of cells" of an ever growing complexity.

Here we have one of the most fruitful ideas which the history of thought has to show us. And, though modern science no longer accepts it in its original form, its appearance, as we know, shook existing ideas, over which it established an absolute predominance, and brought new ones to birth, notably in the field of political science.

If biology saw organisms as societies, how in its turn could political thought have failed to see societies as organisms?

Almost simultaneously with the publication of the *Origin of Species* (November 1859), Herbert Spencer published in the *Westminster Review* (January 1860) a reverberating article entitled "The Social Organism." There he sets out[15] the resemblances between human societies and cellular organisms. Both of them, commencing as small aggregations, insensibly augment in mass: some of them eventually reaching ten thousand times what they originally were. While at first so simple in structure as to be considered structureless, both assume, in the course of their growth, a continually increasing complexity of structure. Though in their early, undeveloped states there exists in them scarcely any mutual dependence of parts, their parts gradually acquire a mutual dependence which becomes at last so great that the activity and life of each part is made possible only by the activity and life of the rest. The life of a society, as of an organism,

---

15. Cf. H. Spencer, *Essays, Scientific, Political and Speculative* (3 vols. London). The article referred to fills pp. 384–428 of the first volume: the passage in the text summarizes pp. 391–92.

is independent of the lives of any of its component units, who are severally born, grow, work, reproduce, and die, while the whole body survives, increasing in mass, in completeness of structure, and in functional activity.

This view had at once an enormous vogue. It provided the latter-day conviction of belonging to the whole with a more intelligible explanation than that of Hegelian idealism. And after all, how often in the course of centuries has the body politic been compared to a physical body! No scientific truth finds readier admission than one which serves to justify a metaphor to which we are used.

### 5. Society, A Living Organism

The truth is that there has never been a time—the case of Menenius Agrippa[16] shows it—when in discussions on society analogies have not been drawn from man's physical body.

St. Thomas wrote:

> Any group would break up of which there was none to take good care. And in the same way the body of man, like that of any other animal, would fall to pieces were there not within it a directing force seeking the common good of all its members.[17] . . . As between the members, it is, whether it be the heart or the head, a ruling chief. In every mass of men there must in the same way be a principle of direction.[18]

The analogy had on occasion been pushed to great lengths. Forset, the Englishman, writing in 1606,[19] compared natural and political bodies organ by organ, and Hobbes, it is said, picked up from him many of his ideas. This I doubt, for Hobbes seems to me to have given Leviathan only a shadowy existence, which was but the reflex of the only real life—that of the men composing him. What is certain, however, is that metaphor is always a dangerous servant; on its first appearance it aims but to give a modest illustration to an argument, but in the end it is the master and dominates it.

16. [Menenius Agrippa, Roman patrician and statesman, Consul 503 B.C. On the occasion of the first secession of the people to the Sacred Mount he was one of the commissioners empowered to treat with the seceders, and recited to them the fable of the belly and the members.]

17. *De Regimine Principium*, I. 1.

18. *Ibid.*, I, 2.

19. E. Forset, *A Comparative Discourse of Bodies Natural and Political* (London: 1606).

Rouvray[20] and even Rousseau[21] both reason from the structure of the natural body to explain that—which they know to be artificial—of the community. In Rousseau's case, moreover, the power of metaphor over the mind employing it is very apparent.

The progress of the natural sciences has since invalidated all analogies, supported as they were by physiological examples, drawn from the human body; the examples were in any case quite irrelevant, firstly because they were based on a wholly erroneous picture of the organism and the organs taken for the purposes of comparison; and secondly, and above all, because any comparison of a society in being with an organism must be with an organism which is much lower in the scale of evolution than man and far less advanced in the twofold process of differentiation and integration.

In other words, if societies are living beings—if they form, as Durkheim unhesitatingly suggests, a "social series" on top of the animal series—then the beings of this new series can only be at a stage of their own development which places them far behind even the lowest mammifers.

As set out by Spencer, the hypothesis seemed to reconcile an intellectual propensity of long standing with recent discoveries in the field of science: from this it received a great encouragement. Moreover, by giving an impulsion and a meaning to ethnological researches, it proved itself a fertilizing stream: do not primitive societies, in their various stages of evolution, give testimony as to the successive stages through which we ourselves must have passed? We shall return to this point of view and see what should be thought of it.

20. Du Rouvray, *Le Triomphe des républiques*, 1673.

21. In the *Encyclopédie*, in the article "Économie politique," he writes: "The body politic, taken in itself, may be likened to a living body with organs, like that of a man. The sovereign power represents the head; the laws and customs, whose instruments are the judges and magistrates, are the brains (which are the nerve centre and the seat of the understanding, the will and the senses); commerce, industry and agriculture, which provide subsistence for all, are the mouth and stomach; the public finances are the blood, which a wise economy, acting as the heart, uses to distribute nourishment throughout the body; the citizens are the body and limbs, by which the machine moves, lives and works, and which cannot suffer hurt in any part without the sense of pain being at once transmitted, assuming that the creature is healthy, to the brain.

"The life of both consists in the *ego* common to the whole, the reciprocal sensitiveness and the internal harmony of all the parts. Should this system of communication stop, should the formal unity disappear, and the neighbouring parts cease to share one another's life while remaining neighbours, the man dies and the State dissolves.

"The body politic is, then, a moral being with a will, and this General Will which tends

What concerns us here, however, are the political conclusions to which the "organicist" system leads. We find ourselves once more watching the flight of a boomerang: a doctrine formulated with a view to restricting Power becomes almost at once an explanation of and justification for Power's extension.

Spencer was a Victorian Whig, whose creed throughout his literary life was the abridgment of Power's sphere of action. He owed much—far more than he was ever willing to admit—to Auguste Comte, but he was exasperated by the conclusions which the latter drew from the process of social differentiation.

Comte had said:

> The degree of intensity of the regulating function, so far from diminishing with the advance of man's evolution, becomes, on the contrary, more and more indispensable . . . each day, as a necessary result of the vast subdivision in operation of human Labour, each of us, in many respects, automatically rests the very continuance of his own life on a crowd of unknown agents, who could, either by folly or malignity, often seriously affect masses of people . . . the various particular functions in the social economy, being naturally bound up with an increasing Whole, must all tend by degrees to become subject in the end to the general direction of the furthest flung agency in the entire system—an agency marked as to character by the incessant action of the Whole on the parts.[22]

Spencer takes him to task for this forecast:

> M. Comte's ideal of Society is one in which government is developed to the greatest extent—in which functional activities are far more under public regulation than now—in which hierarchical organization with unquestioned authority shall guide everything—in which the individual life shall be subordinated in the greatest degree to the social life.

And he opposes to it his own thesis:

> That form of Society towards which we are progressing, I hold to be one in which government will be reduced to the smallest amount possible, and

---

ever towards the preservation and well-being of the whole and the parts, which is the source of laws . . . etc."

22. *Philosophie positive,* Vol. IV, pp. 486, 488, 490.

freedom increased to the greatest amount possible—one in which human nature will have become so moulded by social discipline into fitness for the social state, that it will need little external restraint, but will be self-restrained—one in which the citizen will tolerate no interference with his freedom, save that which maintains the equal freedom of others—one in which the spontaneous co-operation which has developed our industrial system, and is now developing it with increasing rapidity, will produce agencies for the discharge of nearly all social functions, and will leave to the primary governmental agency nothing beyond the function of maintaining those conditions to free action, which make such spontaneous co-operation possible—one in which individual life will thus be pushed to the greatest extent consistent with social life; and in which social life will have no other end than to maintain the completest sphere for individual life.[23]

### 6. The Problem of Power's Extent in the Organicist Theory

In this controversy the problem of Power's extent is frankly posed. Comte and Spencer agree in seeing in Power a product of evolution, an organ—for Spencer a biological organ, for Comte a figurative—whose final cause or end is the coordination of social diversity and the union of the parts.

Is it correct that, as society evolves and the organ of government adapts itself to its end, the latter must direct with increasing rigour and in greater detail the actions of the members of society? Or is the contrary true—must it loosen its grip, find fewer occasions for intervening, and abate its exactions?

His preconceptions led Spencer to deduce from his organicist hypothesis the conclusion, already latent in his mind, of Power's diminution. He deduced it the more eagerly when, after observing in his youth a drop in the curve of Power, he saw it in his maturity start to climb again—a movement which in his old age caused him great disquiet.[24] The

---

23. Spencer, *Essays*, Vol. III, pp. 72–73.

24. He was to write later in *Professional and Industrial Institutions:* "In the middle of this century there had been attained, especially in England, a greater degree of Liberty than there had ever been since nations started to form. . . . But the movement, which to so large an extent broke the despotic régime of the past, came to a certain limit from which it has begun to go back. New sorts of restrictions and constraints have been gradually imposed in place of the old sorts. Mankind has substituted for the domination of powerful social classes the rule of official classes who will become just as powerful and more so, and who, in the end, will be just as different from the imaginings of socialist theories as the rich and

coincidence of this ascent with the development of democratic institutions furnished sufficient proof that Power is not abated by installing the people as sovereign. Spencer had thought to show that such an abatement was in the natural order of evolution and progress.

For that purpose he made use of the antithesis of military to industrial societies made by Saint-Simon;[25] he translated into physiological terms the contrast drawn between them. True it is, he said, that, for the purpose of its external activity of warring against other societies, the social organism effects an ever more total mobilization of itself, collects its forces with an ever greater intensity, and achieves these results by way of a centralization and a growth of Power. But its internal activity, on the other hand, which develops by means of the diversification of functions and the ever more effective adaptation to one another of parts which subdivide and particularize themselves ever further, does not require one central regulator; it develops on the contrary a number of regulative organs of its own, which are separate from the governmental organ (such as the markets in raw materials or securities, bankers' clearing houses, trade unions, and associations of all kinds). And this thesis was supported by detailed arguments borrowed from physiology, in which he harked back to the same duality—the same concentration on the one hand and the same ordered dispersion on the other.

But this vision of society as an organism which he did so much to accredit was to be turned against himself.

Huxley, the biologist, could immediately make objection:

> If the resemblances between the body physiological and the body politic are any indication, not only of what the latter is, and how it has become what it is, but of what it ought to be, and what it is tending to become, I cannot but think that the real force of the analogy is totally opposed to the negative view of State function.[26]

---

proud hierarchy of the middle ages was from the poor and humble missionaries from which it sprang."

25. [Saint-Simon, Comte de (1760–1825), the founder of French socialism. In opposition to the feudal and military system, which had been re-established with the restoration of Louis XVIII, he advocated an arrangement by which the industrial chiefs should control society.]

26. Huxley continues: "Supposing that, in accordance with this view, each muscle were to maintain that the nervous system had no right to interfere with its contraction, except to prevent it hindering the contraction of another muscle; or each gland, that it had a right to secrete, so long as its secretion interfered with no other; suppose every separate cell left

It is not for us to determine whether Spencer's or Huxley's interpretation of "the political tendencies of the physiological organism" was the more correct. What matters is to note that the full adoption of the organicist viewpoint has militated exclusively on the side of justifying and explaining the unlimited growth of the functions and apparatus of government.[27]

Lastly, Durkheim, in a work which created in time a school[28] and is an amalgam of Hegelianism and organicism, laid down that the scale and functions of the governmental organ had necessarily to grow with the development of societies,[29] and that the strength of authority was bound

---

free to follow its own 'interest' and *laissez-faire* lord of all, what would become of the body physiological?

"The fact is that the sovereign power of the body thinks for the physiological organism, acts for it, and rules the individual components with a rod of iron. Even the blood corpuscles can't hold a public meeting without being accused of 'congestion'—and the brain, like other despots whom we have known, calls out at once for the use of sharp steel against them. As in Hobbes' *Leviathan*, the representative of the sovereign authority in the living organism, though he derives all his powers from the mass which he rules, is above the law. The questioning of his authority involves death, or that partial death which we call paralysis.

"Hence, if the analogy of the body politic with the body physiological counts for anything it seems to me to be in favour of a much larger amount of governmental interference than exists at present, or than I, for one, at all desire to see." (In the essay *Administrative Nihilism* written in reply to Spencer, and republished in the volume *Method and Results*. London: 1893.)

27. See, among many others, Lilienfeld: *Die menschliche Gesellschaft als realer Organismus* (Mittau: 1873). Society, he says, is the highest class of living organism. Alb. Schaffle, *Bau und Leben des sozialen Körpers*, 4 vols., published 1875–1878, where the author laboriously works out, organ by organ, the comparison of the physiological body with the social body. This did not deter Worms from again pursuing the same line of thought in *Organisme et société* (Paris: 1893). Or, again, G. de Graef, *Le Transformisme social, essai sur le progrès et le regrès des sociétés* (Paris: 1893): "In the history of the development of human societies, the regulative organs of collective power perfect themselves progressively, creating a more and more powerful co-ordination of all the social agents. Does not the same thing happen in the hierarchy of all living creatures and is it not the degree of organization achieved by them which gives them their place in the scale of life? So with societies, the degree of organization is the common measure, the measure of progress; in the history of civilizations there is no other criterion of their respective and relative worth." Novicow may also be cited: *Conscience et Volonté sociales* (Paris: 1893). The thesis had much success in socialist circles where Vandervelde became its enthusiastic exponent. Its best and most recent exponent is the biologist Oskar Hertwig: *Der Staat als Organismus*, 1922.

28. *De la Division du travail social* (Paris: 1892).

29. "It is utterly unsystematic to regard the actual dimensions of the governmental organ as something morbid and due to a concurrence of accidental circumstances. It is on all accounts a normal phenomenon, and one related to the very structure of the higher societies,

to increase by reason of the pressure of feelings shared in common.[30] At a later date he was to go further and claim that even the religious feelings were only the feelings of belonging to society—the obscure premonitions that we are working out a being which is our superior. And in the end he was to assert that, under the names of gods or God, the real object of our adoration has never been other than society.[31]

## 7. Water for Power's Mill

We have now passed in review four abstract conceptions—four families of theories, so to speak, of Power.

Two of them, the theories of sovereignty, explain and justify Power by a right which it derives from the sovereign, whether God or the people, and which it may exercise by reason of its legitimacy or due origin. The other two, to which we have given the name of organic theories, explain and justify Power by its function or its end, which is to assure the moral and material cohesion of society.

In the first two, Power appears as a centre of command in the midst of a multitude, in the third as a crystallizing fire, or perhaps as a zone of light from which enlightenment spreads, and, lastly, in the fourth as an organ within an organism.

In those of sovereignty the right of command is seen as absolute; in the organic the function of command is seen as growing.

Different as they are, there is not one of them from which the

---

since it advances regularly and continuously to the extent that societies approximate to this type," etc., etc., pp. 201–202.

30. "Whenever there appears a governmental structure of wide authority, the reason must be sought, not in the position occupied by the rulers, but in the nature of the societies ruled. We must examine what beliefs they hold in common, and what common sentiments there are which, becoming incarnate in a person or a family, have given him or it so much power," pp. 213–14.

As in Durkheim's thesis, which is in that respect inspired by Hegel, society starts from a strong moral solidarity, to return by a way of a process of differentiation to an even completer solidarity; it follows that authority, after a period of enfeeblement, must in the end acquire new force.

31. Cf. *Les Formes élémentaires de la Vie religieuse* (2nd ed., Paris: 1925): "The faithful are right to believe in a moral force which restrains them and from which the best in themselves is derived: this force exists: it is Society . . . the deity is but the figurative expression of Society," pp. 322–23.

justification for an absolute form of Power cannot be, and at some time or another has not been, derived.

The two first, however, because they are founded on a Nominalist view of society and on the recognition of the individual as the only reality, are somewhat allergic to the complete absorption of man: they allow the idea of subjective rights. Lastly, the first of them all, by implying an immutable divine law, implies also an objective right, the observance of which is imperatively ordained. In the more recent theories, on the other hand, the only objective right there can be is that which society forges and can modify at will, and the only subjective rights are those which it deigns to grant.

It looks, then, as if the various theories, viewed historically, broaden down in such a way that they become more and more advantageous to Power. A more easily observable phenomenon in each theory is its own evolution. Though in origin their purpose may be to place obstacles in Power's path, yet in the end they serve it, whereas the opposite tendency, of a theory advantageous in origin to Power becoming its enemy, is quite unknown.

The conclusion is, then, that Power possesses some mysterious force of attraction by which it can quickly bring to heel even the intellectual systems conceived to hurt it. There we see one of Power's attributes. Something it is which endures, something which can produce both physical and moral effects. Can we yet say that we understand its nature? We cannot.

Away then with these fine theories which have taught us nothing of the essential, and on to the uncovering of Power. Let us try, first of all, to be in at its birth, or at least to intercept it at as near a point as we can to its distant beginnings.

# BOOK II

~

# Origins of Power

The continuity of human development has been such that most, if
not all, of the great institutions which still form the framework of
civilized Society have their roots in savagery, and have been handed
down to us in these later days through countless generations,
assuming new outward forms in the process of transmission, but
remaining in their inmost core substantially unchanged.
—FRAZER, *The Early History of Kingship*.

# IV.

◞

# The Magical Origins of Power

TO UNDERSTAND THE NATURE OF POWER, let us learn first how it was born, what it at first looked like, and by what means it got itself obeyed. This approach is, intellectually, a natural one, especially for the modern intelligence, which has been shaped by evolutionist thought.

But the undertaking, once begun, is seen to be full of difficulties. The historian makes but a late appearance, in a society which is already highly developed: Thucydides is contemporary with Pericles, Livy with Augustus. The confidence due to him, so long as he deals with periods near his own and for which a whole variety of documents is available, is on a diminishing scale with every step he takes back to the city's founding. For those earlier periods his sources can be but oral traditions; these have, from generation to generation, suffered distortion, and his own version is that which suits his time. Thus it was with the myths of Romulus or Theseus. Eighteenth-century criticism, with its narrowly rationalist outlook, took them for poetical falsehoods; at the end of the nineteenth century, on the other hand, they were put under the microscope, and philology was brought in to help in elaborating ingenious interpretations of them—interpretations often fantastic and always dubious.

Can archaeology help us? It has done an amazing work! It has unearthed buried cities and breathed life into forgotten civilizations.[1] By its help,

1. Some idea of this undertaking of winning back for man his past appears in M. Marcel Brion's book: *La Résurrection des villes mortes* (2 vols. Paris: 1938).

millenaries, which for our ancestors contained nothing but Biblical characters, have been peopled with powerful monarchs; and the blank spaces in the map around the country of the Israelites have been filled in with mighty empires.

But what the pick has revealed to us have been the blooms of civilizations which were like our own, stemming like ours from a millenary development.[2] The gradually deciphered inscriptions are the codes and records of adult governments.[3] And if below the layers of debris which attest wealth and power we dig to traces of a more primitive life, or if we turn the soil—Europe's is a poor one for the purpose—for indications of our own beginnings, what we find are clues only as to the way men lived and not as to how they were governed.

We are left with one last resource—the ethnologist.

Herodotus and Tacitus attest the fact that in all ages the civilized have been curious about the uncivilized. But, while enjoying the thrill of tall tales, it did not occur to them that they might be receiving in the process enlightenment about their own origins. They regarded travel stories as so many romances, the miraculous quality of which might be legitimately enhanced by the introduction of headless men and other bogies.

The Jesuit Father Lafitau was perhaps the first man to bethink himself of looking for traces of the way we have travelled in the customs and practices of savages; light, he thought, could be thrown on the process of social evolution by comparing what he had observed of the Iroquois Indians with what the Greeks had reported of the oldest folkways which had come down to them by tradition.[4]

2. It is well established that there is not *one* civilization of which we represent the most advanced form, but that different societies have, in the course of human history, developed different civilizations, each of which reached a certain blossoming, sometimes much inferior to our own, at others equivalent to ours and in some respects superior. This conception is by this time so well known that I need not, I think, enlarge on it.

3. On this subject, Dykmans writes as follows: "As soon as we can discern for certain the first social groupings in Egypt, notably in the figured pictures appearing on predynastic paddles, we find ourselves confronted with organized cities, which are protected by ramparts, governed by panels of magistrates and given over to profitable maritime trade with the Syrian sea-board. . . . We know nothing of anything that preceded this period near to the dawn of history: the process of evolution, lasting for many thousands of years, from the origins of Society to cities like this, to the earliest confederations and to the first kingdoms, is buried in the depths of pre-history." Dykmans: *Histoire éco. et soc. de l'ancienne Égypte* (Paris: 1932) Vol. I, p. 53.

4. "I admit that, if the writers of antiquity have supplied me with information for the support of certain fortunate conjectures of mine about savages, savage customs have supplied me with information for the easier understanding and explanation of several matters on

It was only long after that the idea grew that primitive societies are in some degree retarded witnesses of our own processes of evolution. The first step was to recognize that all living organisms were related to each other and that the various species stemmed from a common trunk. This opinion, popularized as it had been by Darwin's book,[5] was then boldly applied to social organisms; search was made for the common trunk—the simplest type of primitive society[6]—from which the various civilized societies developed, and the various savage societies were seen as so many stages on the road of a development along which every society known to history had passed.

In the first flush of Darwinian enthusiasm no one doubted that the evolution of the clan into the parliamentary democracy could be traced as surely as the evolution of the ape into the man in a lounge suit. The discoveries and hypotheses of Lewis H. Morgan[7] caused Engels to draw his pen; with it he told all in a treatise entitled *The Origin of the Family, Property and the State*.

It is the fate of every science that, in the wake of the wonderful perspectives opened up by the earlier discoveries, the multitude of researches complicates and confuses the landscape. The daring and authoritative reconstructions of Durkheim are now derelict. It is no longer treated as proved that there was only one primitive society; now, on the contrary, it is readily admitted that different groups of men have from the beginning presented different characteristics, which, as the case might be, either caused them to develop differently or prevented them from developing at all. The vogue of fifty years ago, of looking in Australia for the very archetype of a backward community and finding there the explanation of our religious feelings, has gone by the board. But such a flow of reason

---

which the writers of antiquity touch." Lafitau, *La Vie et les mœurs des sauvages américains, comparées aux mœurs des premiers temps* (Amsterdam: 1742) Vol. I, p. 3.

5. In 1859.

6. The notion of a *primitive society* was formulated by Spencer in the following terms: "The conceptions of biologists have been greatly enlarged by the discovery that organisms which, when adult, appear to have scarcely anything in common, were, in the first stages, very similar; and that, indeed, all organisms start with a common structure. . . . If societies have evolved, and if that mutual dependence of their parts which cooperation implies, has been gradually reached, then the implication is that, however unlike their developed structures become, *there is a rudimentary structure from which they all set out*." *Principles of Sociology*, Vol. III, para. 464.

7. Morgan expounded his theory in 1877 in a book which had a resounding success: *Ancient Society or researches in the lines of human progress from savagery through barbarism to civilization*.

and research has not receded without leaving on the beach a considerable mass of materials. Let us see what we can pick up there.

## 1. The Classical Conception: Political Authority the Child of Paternal Authority

The first authority to enter our lives is the paternal. Must it not also be the first in the life of society? From antiquity down to the middle of the nineteenth century all authorities have agreed in seeing the family as the first society—as the primary cell from which the social structure afterwards grew, and paternal authority as the first form of command and stay of all the others.

"The family is the natural society," said Aristotle, and cites in support some of the earliest writers: "In it, said Charondes, all eat from the same bread; all of them, said Epimedes of Crete, seek warmth at the same hearth."[8] "The most ancient of all societies, and the only natural one, is the family," asserts Rousseau,[9] and Bonald too: "Society was in the beginning family and then State."[10]

Everyone thought that society was an aggregation of families:

> The primary partnership made up of several households for the satisfaction of not mere daily needs is the village. The village according to the most natural account seems to be a colony from a household, formed of those whom some people speak of as fellow-sucklings, sons and sons' sons.[11]

Over this assemblage, there is, again according to Aristotle, a natural ruler, "for every household is under the royal rule of its eldest member."

From this expanded family we arrive at the political society, which is reached by the same process of generation; for families, like men, reproduce themselves, until there is reached a "family of families," over which the natural ruler is a sort of "father of fathers."

Bishop Filmer in his *Patriarcha*[12] availed himself of this metaphor: Does not the Old Testament tell us that the children of Jacob lived

---

8. Aristotle, *Politics,* Book I, chap. i.

9. *Du Contrat social,* Book II, chap. ii.

10. *Pensées sur divers sujets.* Bonald also wrote: "Every proprietary family forms on its own a naturally independent domestic society." *Législation primitive,* Book II, chap. ix.

11. Aristotle, *op. cit.*

12. *Patriarcha, or the Natural Rights of Kings* (London: 1684).

together and made up a people? And while families grew into nations the patriarchs took the form of kings. The other and quite opposite supposition is that the heads of the various patriarchal families met on a footing of equality and formed an association voluntarily. As Vico puts it:

> In the heroic state of Society, the fathers were the absolute monarchs of their families. These monarchs, who were as between themselves naturally equal, made up the ruling assemblies and came, by a sort of instinctive feeling of self-preservation, to unite together their separate interests and link them to the hamlet which they called their country.[13]

According to which of these two hypotheses is adopted, the conclusion is reached that the "natural" government is either the monarchical or the senatorial. But from the time that Locke utterly smashed up Filmer's fragile structure,[14] the earliest political authority was considered to be the senate composed of fathers of families, using the word "families" in the widest sense.

Society must, therefore, have presented two degrees of authority, which were quite different in kind. On the one hand is the head of the family, exercising the most imperious sway over all who were within the family circle.[15] On the other are the heads of families in council, taking decisions

13. Vico, *La Science nouvelle,* translation of Princess Belgioso (Paris: 1844) p. 212.

14. *An Essay Concerning Certain False Principles,* which is the first of his two essays on government.

15. In 1861 the English jurist, Maine, gave a vivid picture of this patriarchal family which was universally regarded as the initial society. Maine had not been taught Roman law: and so, when he first made contact with the ordinances of earliest times, the contrast between them and modern jurisprudence came as a great intellectual shock to him, and he had a sudden vision of the mode of life which they implied. He then came to recognize that the *patres* of primitive Rome were simply the jealous proprietors of a group of men to whom they gave laws. The father had power of life and death over his offspring, punished them as he pleased, got his son a wife, and exchanged with some other father one of his daughters for one of the other's sons. He could take back the daughter he had given in marriage, drive out his daughter-in-law, exclude from his group any member who disobeyed him, and bring into it anyone he chose by a form of adoption which had the same legal results as legitimate birth. Chattels, beasts, and men—everything in the group belonged to him and obeyed him in virtue of his position; he could as easily sell his son as a head of cattle; the only rights and the only hierarchy were those of his introduction, and it was lawful for him to put in as chief of the group in his own stead the lowest of his slaves. Maine, *Ancient Law: its Connection with the Early History of Society and its Relation to Modern Ideas* (London: 1861).

in concert, tied to each other only by consent, submitting only to what has been determined in common, and assembling their retainers, who have, outside themselves, neither law nor master, to execute their will.

Here to hand is an illustration of the patriarchal family, from an example which has been thrown up by modern ethnology. Among the Samos of Yatenga[16] the patriarchal family may be seen in its pure form. There, in fact, we find families of more than a hundred souls living in the same abode around a common ancestor. All who live inside one of these vast quadrangular dwellings own the sway of the head of the family. He directs the labour and assures the livelihood of all who live under his roof. As it grows, the family splits off into separate dwellings in which a "head of the dwelling" holds acknowledged rule. Henceforward it is he who directs the work, but without derogation to the *religious* authority of a head of a family. The memory of their common origin survives with particular force among the Silmi-Mossis in the same region, who, though they number 5,627 in all, are divided up into no more than twelve large families. For practical purposes, no doubt, they are divided and subdivided into sub-families and dwellings, but it is the head of the huge family who owns the Ancestral Dwelling; he it is who offers sacrifice for them all, and who is entitled to give in marriage all the female children, even though in practice he confines himself to approving what the heads of the sub-families propose.[17]

What light, it may be thought, these observed instances throw on the

16. In the bend of the Niger. According to L. Tauxier, *Le Noir du Yatenga* (Paris: 1917).

17. The strength of family feeling, as found among the Silmi-Mossis, is perfectly compatible with the advance of the process of physical disintegration; indeed, the average number of persons which a dwelling (*zaka*) contains is only eleven or twelve. The Mossis are leading people of the district, and in the canton of Koussouka, for example, they number 3,456 persons, divided into 24 families; they live in 228 dwellings, which gives about 15 people to each.

The head of the family, or *boudoukasaman,* keeps only his own dwelling under his undivided authority, but as head of the family he performs the duties of priest and judge, and it is his prerogative to give in marriage the daughters of the family. When he dies he is succeeded by his younger brother, who in his turn is succeeded by the next brother in order until the whole line is extinct, when the succession comes back to the eldest son of the eldest brother. This rule of succession is very understandable; it tends to keep at the head of the family its most focal member. The head of a dwelling is called a *zakazoba.* For a part of the year the members of the dwelling owe him the best of their time on two days out of three, and for more than half the year, seven months out of the twelve, he provides for their sustenance. There are both family fields and small private fields. Cf. Louis Tauxier, *op. cit.*

possible nature of the Roman *gens!* How perfectly we now understand that a society so constituted had for its natural government the assembly of the tribal heads who enjoyed a sacred eminence, no doubt assisted by the more important heads of sub-families!

## 2. The Iroquois Period: The Negation of the Patriarchate

The classical conception of primitive society as resting on the patriarchate, which we have described, was rudely shattered round about 1860, almost concurrently with the Darwinian upheaval.

This revolution I call here the "Iroquois period," to mark the fact that its impetus came from the discovery made by a young American ethnologist, Morgan by name, who lived for several years among the Iroquois.

After demonstrating to start with—what had already been observed by Lafitau—that inheritance is with them maternal and not paternal, he noted next that their words for denoting the parents have a different connotation from ours—that with them the word "father" covers a paternal uncle as well, and the word "mother" a maternal aunt as well. At first he regarded these as mere peculiarities of the Iroquois, but, on finding the same phenomena occurring among other North American tribes, it occurred to him that he might be on the track of a family structure which was quite other than patriarchal.

At the same time that, with the help of the Smithsonian Institution and even the federal government, he was conducting an inquiry into the words denoting family relationships in use in every society scattered over the face of the globe, a Bâle professor published a remarkable book[18] based on ancient Greek texts and monuments of antiquity.

His point of departure was a passage of Herodotus:

> There is a curious law among the Lycians under which they take the name not of their father but of their mother. Ask a Lycian to what family he belongs, and he will answer you with the genealogy of his mother and her ancestors; the children of a free woman married to a slave are considered to be of noble rank; but if a male citizen, however illustrious his rank, marries a concubine or a foreigner, the children of the marriage are excluded from public honours.

18. Bachofen, *Das Mutterrecht: Eine untersuchung über die Gynoikokratie der alten We nach ihrer religiösen und rechtlichen natür* (Stuttgart: 1861).

Bachofen, with inexhaustible patience, then got together a whole number of analogous indications derived from peoples of antiquity, with a view to demonstrating that the custom of the Lycians, so far from being an exception, was the relic of a general rule. In other words, the affiliation of a child must have been uterine.[19]

From every side there arose the idea that uterine affiliation preceded the paternal.[20] A plethora of observations were soon to show it at work in a number of societies, in the form of the children of a marriage belonging not so much to the wife as to those who give the wife in marriage, viz., her father and, above all, her brothers. So that it would be more accurate to talk to avuncular inheritance.

The fact of the same word "parent" denoting a whole group of people was taken to prove that marriage must have been by groups: for instance,

19.  In the first flush of his discovery, the Bâle professor even went so far as to claim that Power must have belonged to the grandmother, who was the counterpart of the patriarch, and that the first great revolution in human affairs was the overthrow of the matriarchate. The memory of this overthrow was, he suggested, preserved in the myth of Bellerophon, who slew the Chimaera and overcame the Amazons. This hypothesis tickles the imagination but has not proved acceptable to the scientific world.

20.  It is noteworthy that in 1724 Father Lafitau had observed the phenomenon of uterine affiliation among the Iroquois and noted that this fact made the woman the centre of the family and nation. He had even then established the resemblance with what Herodotus had reported of the Lycians, but more than a century and a half had passed before anyone profited by his discerning observations. "It is," said Lafitau, "in the women that the nation, the nobility, the genealogical tree, the order of the generations and the preservation of families rightly consist. The women wield all real authority; the land, the fields and the entire harvest belong to them; they are the backbone of counsel and the arbiters of peace and war; they control the public treasury; slaves are their perquisite; they give in marriage; the children belong to them, and *the order of succession is founded in their blood*. The men, on the other hand, are entirely cut off and confined to themselves; their children are strangers to them; on their death none succeeds; none but a woman continues the house. But if in a particular house there are none but men, then, no matter what their number, their family suffers extinction; and although the formal choice of chiefs is made from among them, they do not labour for themselves; their only purpose in life seems to be to be the agents and helpers of the women. . . .

"It must be understood that the manner of marriage is such that the husband and wife do not leave their own families and huts to set up a separate hut of their own. Each stays put; the children of the marriage are the women's who bore them, and they are numbered among the hut and the family of the woman, and not those of the husband. The husband's goods are not kept in the wife's hut, to which he is himself a stranger, and in the wife's hut the daughters precede in succession the male children, who receive there no more than their subsistence! And so is verified the statement of Nicolas of Damascus about inheritance among the Lycians and what Herodotus told us about their nobility; the children being in dependence on their mothers, their importance turns on the importance of their mothers. . . .

my maternal uncle (or for that matter anyone else) is also my father because my mother must at one time have been as much his as my father's, for the reason that she was in her time the wife of a whole series of brothers (or of a whole series of men). In the same way my maternal aunt is also my mother through having formed with her a part of a group of women who were in married intercourse with a group of men. And this phenomenon of group marriage has been seen actually operating among certain peoples.[21]

These were the two bases on which, once Morgan's great inquiry had been published,[22] was founded more than one ambitious and hazardous reconstruction of the past history of human society.[23]

These reconstructions, built, destroyed, and reconstructed again as they were, stirred up researches from which one thing clearly emerged: that in a number of societies the family was not patriarchal, that the patriarchal family could not in consequence be the formative element of them all, and that therefore the paternal authority could not be the point of departure of every government

The way is now clear, therefore, for a new conception of the origins of Power.

### 3. The Australian Period: The Magical Authority

McLennan, in 1870, had been the first to observe that primitive groups have a cult of some particular plant or animal: it is their totem. On this observation of his, confirmed as it was by subsequent observation in Australia of the most primitive tribes of savages so far encountered, a new theory was erected.

It is at root a conception, formed by observation, of primitive mentality. The reason why Vico could seriously imagine the "fathers" discussing matters of common interest and deliberately creating the "fatherland," and why Rousseau could picture an assembly, deliberately and after a

The women do not exercise political authority but they transmit it," as Lafitau explains. *Op. cit.*, Vol. I, pp. 66 *et seq.*

21. Cf. notably the Urabanna of Central Australia. Spencer and Gillen, *The Northern Tribes of Central Australia* (London: 1904) pp. 72–74.

22. *Systems of Consanguinity and Affinity of the Human Family*, Vol. XVII of the *Smithsonian Contributions of Knowledge* (Washington: 1871).

23. Giraud-Teulon, *Les Origines de la famille. Questions sur les antécédents des sociétés patriarcales* (Geneva: 1874). And, above all, Lewis H. Morgan, *Ancient Society* (New York: 1877).

careful weighing of the advantages of liberty against the dangers of isolationism, concluding a social pact, was that in their time the nature of primitive man was shrouded in darkness.

All is now changed; the plumed paladin and the naked philosopher, those eighteenth-century hallucinations, have no existence for the ethnologist of today. The savage's body is, as he knows, exposed to such sufferings as through the organization of society we are spared; his soul is shaken by such terrors as would make our most horrible nightmares seem but passing dreams. The reaction of the human flock to all dangers and terrors is like that of animals: they gather closer, they curl themselves up, they give each other warmth. They find in numbers the principle of strength and safety for themselves.

So far, then, from man having given willing adherence to the group, his very existence is only in and by the group; for this reason the severest punishment on him is banishment, which casts him out defenceless from his brothers to the mercy of men and beasts.

The life of the group is, then, of a rigorously collective kind, and it is only by incessant vigilance that it maintains itself against the many dangers to it which are in nature. Death, disease, misfortune, all these are proofs of a pervading malignity. For the savage ascribes nothing to chance. Whatever evil befalls him comes of evil purpose: and a small misfortune is but a warning from this purpose of the approaching deployment of its full power. Therefore he must make haste to appease it with appeasing rites.

Whatever comes, whether an exceptionally long winter exhausts the group's store of food or a torrid drought wipes out cattle and men alike, be it famine or epidemic or merely a child breaking its leg, nothing comes by chance. It follows that the appropriate behaviour and ceremonies can forestall every misfortune.

But who, except the Elders, knows what must be done? And among the Elders those only who have magical perceptions. Those, then, are the men to rule, for they alone can teach the way of coming to terms with the invisible powers.

### 4. Frazer's Theory: The Sacrificial King

Certain observed facts have given to this idea of the intercessory government a tremendous impetus. The king must have been—and if necessary the appropriate man must have had the office forced on him[24]—

24. Frazer cites this testimony from the King of Étatin (Southern Nigeria): "The whole town forced me to be head-chief. They hanged our big juju (or fetish), the horns of a

someone who was qualified less to rule men's wills than to prevail upon the will of the invisible powers and secure their favour. His function was the appeasement of the evil purposes, if necessary by the sacrifice of himself in focusing them on his own person. It was also his business to encourage the forces of fertility. For instance, a very old song comes from Easter Island in which the growth and multiplication of potatoes, ferns, lobsters, and so on are ascribed to the virtue of the king. In winter there is a rigorous taboo on deep-sea fishing; when it starts again, the first tunnies to be caught must be brought to the king. Only after he has eaten them can the people use this source of food in safety.[25]

This widely spread custom of first-fruits is very likely the mark of the mistrust felt in olden times for food which had not first been essayed. The king's action is that of a man who takes on himself the risk: then he says to his people: "Now you may eat."

In some places, again, he must deflower the virgins, and the memory of this has been preserved in what history of the popular-serial type calls *le droit de seigneur*. There is no doubt that the act of deflowering passed for dangerous and was never, as the case of Australia shows, performed by the husband; rather it is the occasion of a rite in which other men "render the wife harmless" before she goes in to her husband. Here too was the principle of kingly intercession.

It does not strain the imagination to suppose that a king whose duties are to tame ceaselessly the evil powers, to replenish the number of good things and maintain at the same time the strength of the tribe, is likely to be put to death if he is a failure, or that any decline in his powers will be thought disadvantageous to his tribe. Thus, among the Shilluks of the Sudan, it is the duty of the king's wives to report any lowering of his virility, whereupon the now useless king lays his head on the knees of a virgin, and is buried alive with her.[26]

These facts are sufficient proof of the existence of magical kingships.

---

buffalo, round my neck. . . . It is an old custom that the head-chief here shall never leave his compound. . . . I am the oldest man of the town, and they keep me here to look after the jujus, and to conduct the rites celebrated when women are about to give birth, and other ceremonies of the same kind. By the observance and performance of these ceremonies, I bring game to the hunter, cause the yam crop to be good, bring fish to the fishermen, and make rain to fall. To make rain, I drink water, and squirt it out, and pray to our big deities. If I were to go outside this compound, I should fall down dead on returning to this hut." Frazer, *Early History of the Kingship*, p. 118.

25. Cf. Alf. Métraux, *L'Île des Pâques* (Paris: 1941).

26. Gaetano Casati, *Ten Years in Equatoria* (2 vols., London: 1891).

They do not go the whole length of proving what Frazer thought could be proved, that kingship arises, and can only arise, on a basis of magical power.

## 5. The Invisible Government

The further ethnological studies go, the more certain it seems that primitive societies do not fall into any of our three categories, monarchy, aristocracy, and democracy. Neither the behaviour of individuals nor the action of the community is determined by either one man or several men or all the men; they are prescribed by powers which overarch society—which certain men are able to interpret for their fellows.

We are given a picture of primitive peoples meeting in assemblies. But it takes an inflamed imagination to conceive of democracies of savages. It is a ludicrous error to suppose that meetings were held by the tribe for the purpose of debating the pros and cons of a particular course of action and that in the end the majority view prevailed. Their meetings were not deliberations at all: they were rather a species of black masses celebrated with the object of inducing the god to declare his will.

Take the history of the least religious people the world has seen—the Romans: even among them, as we read, sacrifice and the consultation of the auspices preceded the opening of a debate. To us in our time this practice appears only as the ceremonial prelude to a sitting. But it is certain that in the earliest times the holocaust, and the examination and interpretation of the entrails, were the sitting. Its sacred character limited the assembly to certain times and places. G. L. Gomme, an Englishman, set about discovering these places:[27] these ancient assizes were, he found, always held out of doors, and a sacrificial stone stood in the middle of the gathering of the Elders. These were the men who had exorcized the most evil of spirits and had qualified themselves the best to understand the sibylline responses of the god. We must picture the sacrificial stone and the gathering of the Elders as forming the spiritual centre from which political decision radiated—decision which wore the dress and carried the authority of a religious oracle.

The Elders, as the natural interpreters of the god, endowed him with their own attachment to ancient usages. Our distant ancestors were ever conscious of the miracle of equilibrium required for the continuance of

27. G. L. Gomme, *Primitive Folk Moots* (London: 1880).

life at all. It could be achieved only by the pious transmission of certain secrets. A priceless legacy indeed was the science of the metallurgist who first assured the tribe of an efficient armoury, and precious were the rites which accompanied the forging of metal! Even the least omission from the ordained series of motions was hazardous!

Humanity's march lay in those days across an unknown country strewn with ambushes; in one narrow path, to which the Elders were the guides, was its security. That path it followed, in the Elders' footsteps, fusing in one divinity and custom.

An example given by Sumner Maine[28] shows how great is the repugnance felt by uncivilized peoples to government by deliberative decisions. While he was a civil servant in India, the government constructed irrigation channels with a view to providing the village communities with water: it was left to the communities to distribute the water. What happened? Once all was in train and the delicate task of apportionment had been done, the villagers decided to forget that a human authority had allotted to each his water! They persuaded themselves into the fictitious belief that their portions of additional water had been assigned them by a very ancient custom, at the back of which lay a primitive ordinance![29]

If archaic societies felt like that, it is easy to understand the position held by the Elders. Such is the strength of their authority in Melanesia that Rivers[30] actually saw them there cornering the women, with the result that one of the commonest marriages was between a grandson and the discarded wife of his paternal grandfather. Also, as he observed, a younger brother would, if his elder brother could find no better use for one of his granddaughters, marry her.

Every act of life has its appropriate rite, and of those rites the Elders are the repositories. The assurance of a good harvest lies not in the work of men's hands and in their manner of husbandry, but in the rites. The impregnation of the female is achieved not by the sexual act, but by the spirit of a dead man who enters into her and is born again as a child.

Would any young man question the authority of the Elders when, but for them, he would never attain manhood? Before he can be numbered among the warriors, he must submit to a rite of initiation at the hands

28. [Sir Henry Sumner Maine (1822–1888), English comparative jurist and historian, whose best known work, *Ancient Law*, was published in 1861. His fundamental idea was to make patriarchal power the germ of society.]

29. Sumner Maine, *Village Communities* (London: 1871).

30. Rivers, *The History of Melanesian Society* (2 vols., Cambridge: 1914).

of the Elders.[31] When the time has come, the adolescents are cut off, imprisoned, starved, beaten; then, the ordeal endured, they get the name of men. The adolescent well knows that, should the Elders refuse him this name, he would remain a child for ever. It is in fact from the name "that there comes to him his share in the power infusing the group viewed as a single whole."[32]

## 6. The Rule of the Magician-Elders

Among primitive peoples the royal road to political rule is an understanding of the will of the occult powers and a knowledge of the times in which and the conditions under which they will be favourable.

The Elders are the natural repository of this branch of knowledge. But some are nearer to the gods than others, so near that they can even induce their actions. There is no question here of the divine will being moved by prayer, but rather, one might almost say, of its hand being forced by certain rites or incantations which obligate the god.

All primitive peoples believed in the existence of this magical power. Take the Romans: the men who drafted the Twelve Tables included in them, even at that date,[33] a prohibition against a man's lifting into his own field by magic the grain sown in another's! The Druids were credited by the Celts with the power of surrounding an army with a wall of air, that could be surmounted only at peril of immediate death. The evidence collected by Frazer proves that in various parts of the globe men have been deemed capable of either precipitating rain or checking its fall.[34]

Could anyone fail to base all his hopes and fears on those who wield powers like these? Or to desire above all things, if they are transmissible, to come by them? There lies the explanation of the amazing crop of secret societies among savages. The inner circle is formed by those of the Elders who are most deeply versed in the occult sciences, and to them the whole tribe is subject.[35]

31. Hutton Webster, *Primitive Secret Societies* (New York: 1908).

32. V. Larok, *Essai sur la valeur sacrée et la valeur sociale des noms de personnes dans les sociétés inférieures* (Paris: 1932).

33. [The date of the Twelve Tables was 451–449 B.C.]

34. Cf. *The Golden Bough,* Vol. I, Part I: "The Magic Art and Evolution of Kings."

35. On the secret societies in Africa, there is a good appreciation by N. W. Thomas in the *Encyclopedia of Religion and Ethics;* see the article "Secret Societies."

In the Bismarck Archipelago, apparitions of the divine monster, called the Dukduk, awaken at intervals the state of religious panic which holds society together. Before any trace of the new moon's crescent can be seen, the women hide themselves, for they know that it is death to see the god. The men of the tribe gather on the shore; there to the beating of drums they raise their voices in song—as much to conceal their own fears as to do honour to the Dukduks. When dawn comes there are seen on the water five or six canoes, tied together to support a platform: upon the platform flutter two ten-foot-high beings. At the moment of this contraption coming to shore, the Dukduks jump forth onto the beach, whereat those present scatter in terror: woe to the impious man who should touch these monsters—death by the tomahawk would be his fate. The Dukduks revolve around each other in a dance which they accompany with shrill cries. Thereafter they disappear into the undergrowth, where a house, crammed with presents, has been made ready for them. When evening comes they reappear, the one armed with staves and the other with a club: the men, drawn up in line, let themselves be beaten by them till blood is drawn and faintness supervenes—sometimes even to the death.

Are the two Elders who are dressed up as Dukduks aware that it is all an imposture? Do they do it for the sake of the natural advantages which thereby come to them, and to secure their rule over the society's life? Or do they really believe in the existence of the occult powers to which this play-acting of theirs gives sensible form? Who can tell? Do they know themselves? Whatever may be the answer, we have here a Power, religious, social, and political, other than which these tribes have none: it is centred in these play-actors.

Recruitment of the holders of this Power takes place by a careful system of co-option. Entry into the various degrees leading to the office of Dukduk cannot be hurried. A magic circle of the same sort, called the Egbo, has been found in West Africa. It is, say its finders, a degenerate one, because both entry and advancement are bought and sold. To rise by degrees to the innermost circle of the initiated costs a native sums which amount in stages to a total of £3000 in all. And in that way the rule of the magician-elders joins to its authority the forces of society. Their position is consolidated first by society's contributions in money, then by its support, and lastly by their depriving any potential opposition of the means wherewith to form itself.

The rule exercised by the magical Power is now a political rule, than which these primitive peoples know no other.[36]

Intimidation assures it the absolute submission of the women and children, blackmail gathers into it the whole of the collective resources of these communities. It imposes social discipline, it ensures observance of the oracular precepts which it gives forth, and of the judgments which it pronounces: all this it does by means of superstitious terror. So much so that superstition could be commended by Frazer as the wet-nurse of the state.[37]

## 7. The Conservative Character of Magical Power

Fear is the principle at the root of magical Power; its role in society is the fixation of customs. The savage who should turn aside from the practices of his ancestors would draw on himself the anger of the occult powers. But the more conformist he is, the more they work for him.

That is not to say that magical Power never innovates. The people may receive from it a new set of rules for the conduct of life, but these, once they have been promulgated, are integrated in the ancestral heritage; they are accorded, by a fiction which is characteristic of savage mentality, a special antiquity, and the new ways are no more called in question than the old. We may say that what Power wins, it wins conservatively. All individual variations of behaviour are checked, and society maintains itself in the same shape. To the group, magical Power acts as a cohesive force for the preservation of acquired social characteristics.

Before we leave it, let us note that the aftereffects of a form of rule which must have endured for tens of thousands of years will not disappear with its fall. The peoples will still view innovation with a certain horror, they will still feel that uncustomary behaviour calls down a divine punishment. The Power which comes to replace the magical Power will take over from it a certain religious prestige.

It came down to us from the earliest times, this superstitious feeling which, taking on a new form, will ascribe to kings the power to heal

---

36. G. Brown, *Melanesians and Polynesians* (London: 1910) writes (p. 270) of the islands of Samoa and the Bismarck Archipelago as follows: "There is no government apart from the secret societies, and the only revenue collected is that which comes from the tributes which they exact and the fines which they impose. The only laws there are the statutes which they pass."

37. J. G. Frazer, *The Devil's Advocate* (London: 1937).

scrofula or to calm epilepsy; so it is too with this fear, so often met with in history, of the royal person.

It is tempting to suppose that, with the liquidation of monarchies, all religious association went out of a now depersonalized Power. Very true it is that there is nothing holy about the people who now govern us! But our modes of feeling are more stubborn things than our modes of thinking, and we have transferred to the impersonal state some trace of our ancient reverence.

There are philosophers[38] who have given their minds to the phenomenon of disregard of laws and have sought out its causes. Much more surprising, however, is the opposite phenomenon of respect for laws and deference to authority. History never lacks instances to show us of vast masses of men submitting to a yoke which is hateful to them, and lending unanimous and willing aid to keep in being a Power which they detest.

The explanation of this strange veneration is in the unconscious worship which men still offer to the prestige of a remote titulary.

And so disobedience—deliberate, proclaimed, and placarded disobedience—to the laws of the state has still about it something of a defiance hurled at the gods, and provides, too, a test of how great their power really is. Cortes threw down the idols on the island of Columel to prove to the natives, by his impunity, that their gods were false. When Hampden refused to pay ship money at Charles I's behest, his friends trembled for him: but his escape was proof that celestial thunderbolts were no longer wielded by the Stuart king: the king fell.

Ransack the history of revolutions, and it will be found that every fall of a regime has been presaged by a defiance which went unpunished. It is as true today as it was ten thousand years ago that a Power from which the magic virtue has gone out, falls.

Power the most ancient has therefore bequeathed something to Power the most modern. We have met for the first time with a phenomenon which will become clearer and clearer as we continue. However brutal the means by which new orderings of society take over from the old, the former bear for ever the impress of the latter.

---

38. Cf. in particular Daniel Bellet, *Le Mépris des lois et ses conséquences sociales* (Paris: 1918).

# V.

⁓

## The Coming of the Warrior

THERE IS NO CERTAIN PROOF THAT OUR SOCIETY once passed
through the stage which any particular savage community is now seen to
have reached. Progress is now no longer represented as a single road along
which backward societies act as milestones. The present conception is,
rather, of groups of human beings moving on towards civilization by
roads which are quite different, with the result that most of them get held
up in culs-de-sac in which either they stand still or, on occasion, perish.[1]

It would not be claimed today that totemism was a stage of religious
and social organization which was traversed by every society without
exception. On the contrary, there are, it seems, only certain regions of
the earth to which it belongs.[2] Nor is it true that uterine affiliation
preceded everywhere the paternal. This line of thought is contradicted by
the survival of uterine affiliation among some societies even after they
have reached a relatively advanced stage of civilization; whereas in others
the patriarchal family may be seen already achieved while they are still in
a state of the crudest barbarism.

---

1. The theme of civilization running a course has been notably handled by Arnold
Toynbee, A *Study of History,* 5 vols. to date. Oxford.

2. "Totemism has not been found, at any rate as a live institution, in any part of North
Africa, Europe and, with the solitary exception of India, Asia. Neither has it ever been
proved beyond the possibility of reasonable doubt that it existed in any of the great human
families which have played the most distinguished rôle in history, the Aryans, the Semites
and the Turanians." Frazer, *The Origins of the Family and the Clan.*

The conclusion seems to be, then, that human societies, having made their appearance on the earth's surface independently of one another, could from the start adopt different structures—structures which have, perhaps, determined their future greatness or their undying mediocrity.

What is certain is that those which, whether naturally or by their own efforts, were the first to be organized patriarchically, which were the least inclined to people the universe with evil purposes or freed themselves soonest from these fears, come before us as the real founders of states and as the truly historical societies.

The extent to which exaggerated mystical fears inhibit every untried action and tend to block all innovation and all progress, needs no underlining,[3] and it is certain that the patriarchal way of life favours social development as the avuncular certainly does not. The result in action of the latter is that the children of its young women become the property of a social group which cannot multiply except in proportion to its young women. Whereas in the former it is the children of its young men who become the group's property, and the rate of its growth greatly increases if these young men can, whether by war or in any other way, make a store of wives.

Clearly then the patriarchal group will quickly become stronger than the avuncular, and at the same time more united. This has given rise to conjectures that some matriarchal societies had the patriarchal way of life thrust on them by their most powerful members, and that the groups so formed swallowed up the others whom they ground into a proletarian powder. But, however different their social structures may have been, it seems certain that all primitive societies answer to our description of the ritual rule of the Elders. Rule of that kind was necessary to guide men's uncertain footsteps past nature's ambushes. But, for society to take wing

---

3. Levy-Bruhl illustrates this fear with a report of the striking testimony of an Eskimo shaman: "We do not believe, we fear. We fear the spirit of the earth who raises storms, and whom we must fight to snatch our livelihood from earth and sea. We fear the moon-god. We fear want and hunger in our oppressive snow-huts. . . . We fear disease which is ever about us. . . . We fear malignant spirits, of the air, of the sea, of the earth, which can help evil-doers to wrong their fellows. We fear the souls of the dead and of the animals which we have killed.

"That is why our fathers received from their fathers all the ancient rules of life which are founded in the wisdom and experience of generations. Though we know not the how and why, we keep these rules so as to live protected from evil. And we are so ignorant that anything unusual frightens us." *Le Surnaturel et la nature dans la mentalité primitive* (Paris: 1931), pp. 20–21.

again, the old rule with its unchanging essence must be overthrown or, more accurately, discarded. What we may call the first political revolution was precisely that process. What was the cause of it? Beyond all question, war.

## 1. Social Consequences of the Warlike Spirit

The hypotheses about the "natural man" formulated by both Hobbes and Rousseau are one and all rejected by anthropology. He is in fact neither so brutal nor so innocent as they made out. Indeed, within the limits of the small circle to which he belongs, he displays a good measure of sociability, though anyone, no doubt, who is outside his circle is a stranger, which is as much as to say an enemy.

Is it, however, inevitable that societies living in isolation from one another should come to blows? Why should they? Their place is a small one on continents which are vast.[4] Do peoples fight one another when they are living completely independent lives? Fichte thought not, and in his thought the creation by each nation of its own self-sufficiency was the royal road to perpetual peace.[5]

In the cold light of reason the conclusion is that the co-existence on the earth of various savage groupings does not necessarily result in either peace or war between them. What do we learn from the Central African and Central Australian fields of observation? What did our predecessors learn from the North American field? That some peoples are pacific and others bellicose. The face is there, primary and irreducible: there are no circumstances to explain it. A people either has the will to power or it has not.

The presence or absence of the will to power brings in its train vast consequences. Take the case of a pacific people. It renders respect and obedience to those who understand how to disarm and mollify the forces of nature, knowing that to them are due abundant harvests and multiplying cattle. But take on the contrary a bellicose people, which is less submissive to the decrees of nature. Violence will furnish it with whatever it lacks of women or cattle. We may be sure that there the first man in consideration is bound to be the warrior-purveyor.

---

4. Eugène Cavaignac, in the first volume of his *Histoire Universelle* (Ed. de Boccard), indulges in some interesting speculations about the population of the world in prehistoric times.

5. Fichte, *L'État commercial fermé* (1802), French ed. Gibelin (Paris: 1938).

All history is that of man's rebellion against his original state, of his efforts to secure for himself more goods than are within his immediate reach. One form, and an uncouth one, of this rebellion and effort is the foray. The same instinct, perhaps, in early times caused war and now induces global exploitation. Be that as it may, it is beyond doubt that the principal authors of material civilization are the peoples who are marked by the spirit of conquest.

War is the cause, whatever else, of far-reaching social disturbances.

Let us suppose that the Elders of the tribe have celebrated all the rites and furnished the warriors with amulets which give immunity. The battle is then joined, and there now ensues a primitive form of scientific experiment. The strongest and the bravest proves the victor—not the man who carries the most charms. And before this harsh experience of reality the spurious reputations melt away. The man who returns in glory is the best warrior: his place in society will thenceforward be new and different.

War is the overthrow of the established hierarchy. Consider the case of those Australian savages[6] whose only form of wealth is their serving-maids. So precious a commodity are women that they can be had only by barter. And so powerful and selfish are the Elders that none but themselves may dispose of the girls of their hutment, whom they in fact barter, not for the benefit of the young men of their tribe, to get them wives, but purely for their own; thus the number of their own concubines increases while the young men have to go without. To make matters worse, these ancients, fearing reprisals, do not allow the young men to go out on armed forays for women. The latter, therefore, have to do without women, and count themselves fortunate should they find some elderly female whom no one else wants any more, to maintain their fire, keep their drinking vessels full, and transport their luggage from camp to camp.

Suppose now that a gang of these young men gets together and sets out on the warpath while the old men are palavering.[7] The warriors return generously provided with wives, and their status—not only their

6. Cf. P. Beveridge, "Of the Aborigines Inhabiting the Great Lacustrine and the Riverine Depression, etc." in the *Journal and Proceedings of the Royal Society of New South Wales*, XVII (1883).

7. Lafitau draws us pictures of private expeditions of this kind among the Iroquois: "These small parties are only composed as a rule of seven or eight people of a village; but this number is apt to be swollen by men from other villages who join them . . . and then they may be compared to the Argonauts." Lafitau, Vol. III, p. 153.

material but their moral status—is at once transformed. If the foray leads to war, so much the better for them, for strong right arms will go up in price in times of peril, and the longer the war the more complete will be the displacement of authority. Honour to the combatants! The bravest become the most sought after and form an aristocracy.

But we must not think of this process as a rapid one. Primitive military campaigns are brief and thinly scattered affairs. Between whiles the prestige of the Elders picks up, and the cohesion of the warriors fails to hold.

The course of events varies greatly according to whether the society is, or is not, patriarchal. If it is, then the sons' exploits profit the fathers by strengthening their credit. If it is not, then the opposition between the Elders and the warriors becomes more sharply defined; the one is the party of obstruction, the other of movement; the one is for fossilizing the behaviour of the tribe, the other for regenerating it by contact with the outside world. Where the Elders grew rich by monopoly of the tribal wealth, the new aristocracy grows rich by pillage: that is its contribution to the community's life, and there perhaps lies the secret of its political triumph. The bravest are also the best placed for practising the aristocratic duties of hospitality and largesse. Through the tribal feast they gain entry even into the secret societies and become their masters. They are, in a word, the parvenus of primitive societies.

## 2. War Gives Birth to the Patriarchate

Even if the possibility of the patriarchate ever having been a primitive institution is not admitted, its rise is easily explained in terms of war.

Agreed that, for natural reasons (in that the part of the father in the procreation of children was not at first understood),[8] the child was universally the property of the male members of the mother's family. But there is no maternal family with which the victorious warriors, returning from a raid with a booty of women, have any account to settle. The children will be theirs, and their multiplication will bring them wealth and strength. And here is the explanation of the transition from the avuncular family to the paternal.

The same explanation goes for the absolutist authority of the father; it comes, to put it shortly, from conquered women. And in that way war

8. An ignorance often encountered by ethnologists.

builds the bridge between one social regime and another. Notable philologists claim, moreover, to have found two strata of cults: the terrestrial cults of an agrarian and matriarchal society, later overlaid by the celestial cults of a warrior and patriarchal society.[9]

### 3. The Warrior Aristocracy Is Also a Plutocracy

We are in the region of guesswork. But what is certain is that, with the patriarchal family in being and war in progress, warlike courage becomes a principle of social distinction and a cause of social differentiation. War brings wealth and brings it in unequal shares.

In a society of this kind, in what does wealth consist? Not in the land, for its extent is, relatively to the small population, almost infinite. To some extent, in food stocks, but these are soon exhausted—the important thing is to keep them continually replenished. In tools, certainly, but tools are no use without men to handle them. At a relatively advanced stage, in cattle; but animals need men to guard and take care of them. Wealth, then, consists in having a large labour force—wives at first, slaves later.

War pays both these dividends, and pays them inevitably to the bravest fighters. It is they who come off best; it is they who have the largest families. The hero procreates on a scale which is in proportion to that of his successes.

At a later date, after the institution of monogamy, losses in war tend to extinguish the breed of warriors—our feudal nobility, for instance, is now extinct. Consequently, in our time, we have got used to seeing societies replenished by high birth rates among people of low position. But in earlier times the reverse was the case. It was the warrior families which multiplied. How many legends in how many languages tell us of the "hundred sons" of the gallant knight!

To the natural channels of increase others were soon added. Primitive people are so acutely aware of the importance of numbers to strength and wealth that the first thing the Iroquois warriors do, on returning from an expedition, is to proclaim the number of their dead.[10] The great

9. Cf. G. Dumézil, *Mitra-Varuna* (Paris: 1940) and *Mythes et dieux des Germains* (Paris: 1939). The author's ingenuity unearths in several myths a warrior-god who overthrows and changes the social arranging of the magician-god.

10. "Arrived near the village," says Lafitau, "the troop stops and one of the warriors utters the cry of death: 'Kohé,' in piercing and dismal tones which he drags out as long as possible and repeats as many times as there are dead.

thing is to replace them, and for that purpose use is made of the prisoners, who get incorporated into the families that have suffered losses.[11]

The practices of polygamy and adoption tip the balance strongly in favour of the clans which have won distinction in war. The weak and the flabby cannot breed at the same pace. They are but as dust against the mighty pyramidical structures of the clans, and constitute the lower and most isolated groups of men in society. Here we see, no doubt, the makings of the first *plebs*.

All quarrels—other than those which arise inside a clan and do not affect the outside world—are caused by each of two families espousing in a clash the interests of its own members; it follows that these isolated or nearly isolated men, the weak and flabby, cannot indulge in them at all against a strong clan. Being in need of protection, they join on to some powerful group and become its clients. And so society becomes a federation of clans, of social pyramids of greater or lesser strength.

The invention of slavery enriches them still further. Invention is the right word, for there is no doubt that more backward peoples had no conception of it. The idea of a stranger living among them had never entered their heads. If he could not be assimilated—adopted into a family—then his place was outside, and his fate was banishment or death. The first industrial revolution, comparable to the coming of the machines, took place when it occurred to men to spare the lives of their enemies and exploit their labour.

Who owns the slaves? The victors, whose aristocracy thus becomes a plutocracy as well. And from that time wars will be carried on, or at least the essential parts in them will be taken, by this plutocracy alone. For wealth furnishes new munitions of war, such as the chariot, which only a rich man can make ready. They seem a different order of beings, the rich, fighting from their chariots: they are the nobles. So it was in the

---

"However complete their victory is and whatever gain it has brought them, the first feeling to which they give expression is that of grief." Vol. III, pp. 238–39.

11. As soon as the prisoner whose incorporation has been determined enters the hut to which he is to belong, "his bonds are taken off and all the dismal flummery which gave him the appearance of a victim doomed to the sacrifice; he is washed with warm water to remove from his face the colours painted on it and he is properly dressed. Then he is visited by the relations and friends of the family where he has gone. Soon after, a banquet is served to the whole village to give him the name of the person whose place he is taking; the friends and comrades of the dead man also give him a feast, in the name of the dead man and to do him honour—and from that moment the prisoner enters on all his rights." Lafitau, *loc. cit.*

Greece of Homeric days. Besides the testimony of the poems themselves, Aristotle tells us that those were the times, both militarily and politically, of the "cavalry."

In this way war came to create a monopolistic caste of men who were at once wealthy, warlike, and politically powerful; the Romans called them the patricians, the Greeks the eupatrides.

The rest of society formed up inside the cadres of the clans, so that it came to resemble a line of human pyramids; at the top of each is the chief of the clan, lower down are the clients, and at the bottom are the slaves. Each is a little state, in which the man on top is government, law, and justice. Each is also a citadel of religion, with its own cult.

### 4. The Government

Society has grown. We are already far away from the primitive group which was, we are told (according to observations made in Australia)[12] of a strength of from fifty to two hundred persons under the authority of the Elders. What we now have are swollen clans, each one of which may be as strong as a whole primitive group. What now hangs together is the great patriarchal family, and no longer what may be derisively called the primitive "nation in miniature." But as between these families, what is the link?

We find ourselves confronted at this point with the same data on the problem of government as confronted the classical writers. While failing to recognize the existence of a political prehistory, they made no mistake about the point of departure of political history. And we fall back, naturally enough, on their solutions: the senate of the chiefs of clans, which is the confederative cement of society, and the king, who is its military symbol.

Our brief excursion into the dark ages has, however, prepared us to appreciate that the nature of these governmental organs is not a simple one.

It goes without saying that a chief for purposes of war there must be, and that his position is strengthened according as wars are frequent and his military successes unbroken; it is natural, too, that negotiations with foreigners should be conducted in the name of this redoubtable warrior,

---

12. A. Knabenhaus, *Die Politische Organization bei den Australischen eingeboren* (Berlin and Leipzig: 1919).

who, we may easily see, gets institutionalized to some extent and receives, while war is on, an absolute authority, the memory of which comes down to us from the Romans in the absolutism of the *imperium extra muros*.[13]

It is, moreover, logical to suppose that this chief, who in the ordinary way has at his disposition only the resources of his own clan, will have to reach agreement with the other chiefs of clans or be helpless: hence the necessity of the senate. But it is impossible to regard any institution as a mere piece of working machinery. All of them stand charged at all times with an electricity which has been transmitted to them by the past, and which is kept alive by the feelings handed down to the present. So it would be wrong to regard the senate as merely an administrative council in which each represents his own. It reproduces also some of the mystical characteristics of the council of magician-elders.

Even more complex is the problem of the king.

## 5. *The King*

This problem is too vast for us to handle in detail, and we make no claim to hold the solution of it. There seems, roughly speaking, to be in kingship a fundamental dualism.

Among certain peoples there are actually present, and among others there are traces of, two distinct personages, both of whom correspond generally to our idea of king. One is essentially a priest, officiating at the public ceremonies and conserving the strength and cohesion of the "nation";[14] the other is essentially chief freebooter, leader of forays, director of the nation's strength.[15]

It is noteworthy that kingship, as we understand it, is not the apanage of the warrior-chief solely in virtue of that capacity.[16] He is honoured

13. [This *imperium* included the power of life and death. It was assumed outside the walls along with the sacred weapons and the red garb forbidden inside the city. War, in fact, transformed the consular *potestas* into an *imperium*.]

14. We shall, with apologies, often be using the word "nation" in an inexact sense, to denote a social community ruled by a single political authority.

15. The Indo-European peoples would seem always to have given sovereignty two faces, as is illustrated by those fabulous personages Romulus and Numa: the young and vigorous leader of foray and the wise and aged friend of the gods. They would even seem to have carried this dualism into their Pantheon as shown by the double personality of Mitra-Varuna. (Cf. G. Dumézil, *Mitra-Varuna*. Paris: 1940.)

16. Cf. William Christie McLeod, *The Origin of the State Reconsidered in the Light of the Data of Aboriginal North America*.

and saluted; he receives tribute of trapped game that he may, from his place of honour at the banquet, praise in return the skilful hunter; he is acknowledged to have a good eye for danger or opportunity; he calls together the council of state—but he is only a man among men.

For him to be more than that there must be joined to his office of *dux*, as we may call it, the office of *rex*, which is religious in character. The *rex* is he in whom the ancient magical power and the ancient ritual office are subsumed and gathered up. At every point he is the slave of rigorous taboos. He cannot eat this, must not look at that; all about him is veneration, but his office is in truth precatory and expiatory, and himself but the prisoner and the victim of his mystic role. We glimpse dimly the *dux* usurping this place of honour; what he takes of it, however, are the prestige-advantages which the position carries—not its shackles.

There lies the explanation of the double character of the kingly Power of history—a duality which it has transmitted to all succeeding Powers. It is at once the symbol of the community, its mystical core, its cohesive force, its sustaining virtue. But it is also ambition for itself, the exploitation of society, the will to power, the use of the national resources for purposes of prestige and adventure.

### 6. The State or Public Thing

However it may be with these conjectures, it is sure that at a certain point of historical development we meet with the ambitious king who aims at extending his own prerogatives at the expense of the chiefs of clans—"the absolute monarchs of their families," as Vico calls them—and is jealous of their independence.

Inevitably the battle is joined. Among some peoples it is relatively easy to follow its course, and among them, as it happens, the king's armament of mystical prestige is small. That is why, no doubt, he comes off second best in Greece and at Rome: but in the East the issue is far different.

Let us examine first of all what is at stake.

Without the chiefs of clans the king is powerless, since it is they alone who bring him the obedience of the groups which they control; the groups themselves are impervious to the royal authority.

What is the objective of the king bound to be?

To deprive the magnates of this solid basis of power, which forces him to bring them into the government, and then, having broken their ranks, to acquire for himself the direct control of all the forces of which they dispose. To carry out this programme he seeks and receives the support of the plebeian horde which passes its uneventful life outside the proud pyramids of aristocracy; in some cases, too, he is helped by crushed and frustrated elements from within these pyramids.

A victory for the king will be followed by a complete reclassification,[17] by a new-found social independence for the humbler members of the community, and by the erection of a governmental machine which will make every individual directly amenable to Power. A defeat for the king will put back the social reclassification, will save for the time being the social pyramids, and will place the direction of public affairs in the hands of the patricians, who will form an oligarchic republic.

Mark this well: by its own inner logic the same impulse embarks Power on two courses—the diminution of social inequality, and the raising and centralizing of public authority.

### 7. Kingship Becomes Monarchy

The chances of success for the royal purpose are least in a community which is relatively small, and in which the cohesion of the patrician classes is that much closer. But a society tends to grow, at first by confederation and later by conquest. We have the examples of Rome, Sparta, and the Iroquois to show us that confederation comes naturally enough to warrior peoples. The effect of confederation is to introduce into the newborn "nation" an element of heterogeneity, which gives the joint rulers, of whom there were two at Sparta, two among the Iroquois, and in early times two at Rome, a certain accrual of influence. Inevitably they are linked together, as when, at the start of a war, they celebrate the various rites of each constituent society. They are, as it were, the crystallizing factor in the mythological process, the factor which unites the cults and marries the gods of different societies.

The societies of Greece and Rome, however, were not[18] either large enough or heterogeneous enough or religious enough to provide the kings with a spiritual arm wherewith to assure their triumph. In the East events are harder to discern. But it seems that there the kings were more obeyed, at first by reason of the accentuation of their religious character, and later by the sweep of their territorial conquests.

When vast annexations of several societies are effected by a small

17. Cf. the classification ascribed to Servius Tullius.
18. At the moment of their royal crises.

conquering nation, the chief of the latter has always offered him a wonderful opportunity of absolutist power. Within the city's walls there was but a small population to hear his call to rise against the patricians; but the subject peoples, vanquished at a time when national sentiment was still unformed, can give him all the help he needs. One instance of this is Alexander, who formed a guard of young Persians when his Macedonians mutinied. Another is that of the Ottoman Sultans, who recruited from the Christian peoples beneath their rule the corps of janissaries which brought them despotism at home and strength abroad.

By means of conquest and of the openings which the diversity of the conquered gives him, the king can now shake off the aristocracy, of which till then he had been little more than the president; he turns monarch. Sometimes he turns more even than that. In the confused mass of conquerors and conquered the cults of the different groups get confused— those cults which are in every group the privilege of a patrician elite.[19] For to have relations with the gods is one way of securing their complicity, and there is no sharing out a private alliance of that kind.

If, therefore, the king offers to the mass of his subjects a god for all, he is conferring on them an immense favour. The modern critic who thinks that the rulers of Egypt imposed on their humiliated subjects the cult of a god who was more or less themselves, is quite wrong. What happened was, on the contrary, that, basing themselves on the sentiments of their time, they gave the mass a newfound right and dignity, by including them with the nobles in a common cult.[20]

Such are the political and religious devices by which the monarch can erect a whole apparatus of stable and permanent government, complete with a bureaucracy, an army, a police, a tax code, and everything else which is connoted for us by the word "state."

### 8. The Public Thing Without State Apparatus

The apparatus of a state is built by and for personal power.

For the will of one man alone to be transmitted and exercised throughout a wide kingdom, transmission and execution must both be systematized

19. "From the point of view of religious rights," says Lange, "the *Plebs*, even after it has already won political rights, stands on quite a different footing to the people of the thirty *curiae*. The idea that a plebeian could take the part of priest and make sacrifice to the gods seemed sacrilege to the patricians." A. Berthelot, *Histoire intérieure de Rome*. Vol. I, p. 57.

20. Much light has been thrown on this by the fine work of J. Pirenne, *Histoire du droit et des institutions de L'ancienne Égypte* (4 vols. Brussels, starting in 1932).

and given the means of growth—in other words, bureaucracy, police, taxation. For monarchy this state apparatus is the natural and necessary instrument. But on society, too, its influence down the centuries is so great that, when at long last the monarch has vanished without disturbing it, its motive power will still be conceived of only as one will, though it is now the will of an abstract person who has taken the monarch's place. The mind's eye will see, for instance, the nation deciding and the apparatus of state executing its decisions.

Thinking thus, we find an ancient republic hard to understand; for there all action turns on a concourse of wills, whether the need is for decision or execution, and there is no state apparatus.

It is remarkable that even such thinkers as Rousseau and Montesquieu should have lumped together modern states and ancient cities without marking the essential point of difference between them.

The republic of old had no state apparatus. It needed no machinery for imposing the public will on all the citizens, who would have had none of such a thing. The citizens, with their own wills and their own resources—these latter small at first but continuously growing—decide by adjusting their wills and execute by pooling their resources.

It is for this very reason, that everything turns on the adjustment of wills and the pooling of resources, that the ancient republic bears the name of "public thing."

## 9. Ancient Republics

We have seen how the king of a warlike society of clans could not take action without the help of the chiefs of clans, and we realize how natural it was for him to aim at concentrating all power in himself—a purpose which was bound to end in his breaking the power of the clans with the help of outsiders and plebeians of every kind, both native and captive.

The clannish aristocracy suffers, inevitably, from a split mind. While seeking to maintain its status of near-independence of, and near-equality with, the king, it cherishes also the position of superiority and authority which it holds in relation to other elements in the community. Thus, Alexander's comrades in battle refused to prostrate themselves before him, while behaving with crushing arrogance to their latest victims in war and to their Greek associates.

It is this frame of mind which must have set on foot the revolution which extinguished the monarchy in both Greece and Rome. To take these revolutions for egalitarian in the modern sense, as some have, is to show a profound ignorance of the social structure in ancient times. Their object was to hold in check two associated phenomena—the political elevation of the king, and the social elevation of the *plebs*. This they did in the interests of a social hierarchy.

We can see this clearly in the case of Sparta, a city which, more than any other, preserved its primitive characteristics and thus enables us the better to appreciate their essentially aristocratic nature. What a paradox it is that Sparta of all places should have received so much admiration from the men of the French Revolution!

At Sparta there is nothing but the victorious warriors. These style themselves the "Equals"—with reason, for their desire is to be equal with one another and with nobody else. Below them are the slaves who minister to them, the Helots, who cultivate the fields for them, and the "dwellers-round," who are free but have no political rights.

This social constitution is a typical one, and that of Rome in the early days of the republic is just like it. The "people" has driven out the king. But "people" in those days meant exclusively the patricians, the men who belonged to the thirty *curiae*, or groups of noble clans—groups which were represented as such in the Senate (the assembly of the "fathers"). Even the word *patria* connotes, as Vico has pointed out,[21] the interests in common of the "fathers" and the noble families which they rule.

## 10. Government by Folkways

We do not find anywhere in the ancient republic a directing will so armed with its own weapons that it can use force. There were the consuls, I may be told. But to start with there were two of them, and it was an essential feature of the office that they could block one another's activities. On occasions when they wanted to impose their joint will, what means had they to hand? Only a few lictors; right through her republican period Rome never knew the means of public coercion and had for force only the people themselves, who could at need answer the summons of the leaders of society.

Only those decisions were possible on which there was general agreement, and, in the absence of any state apparatus, their execution depended solely on the cooperation of the public. The army was but the people in arms, and the revenues were but the sums gifted by the citizens,

21. The word *patria*, with the word *res* underlying it, denotes in effect "the interests of the fathers," Vico, ed. Belgioso, p. 212.

which could not have been raised except by voluntary subscriptions. There was not, to come down to the essential point, an administrative corps.

In the city of old, no public office is found filled by a member of a permanent staff who holds his place from Power; the method of appointment is election for a short period, usually a year, and often by the drawing of lots—which was called by Aristotle the true democratic method.

It thus appears that the rulers do not form, as in our modern society, a coherent body which, from the minister of state down to the policeman, moves as one piece. On the contrary, the magistrates, great and small, discharge their duties in a way which verges on independence.

How was a regime of this kind able to function at all? Only by great moral cohesion and the inter-availability of private citizens for public office.

A certain code of behaviour had become so much second nature to the members of the community, thanks to the discipline of the home and the teaching of the school, and the code received such strong support from public opinion, that a mass of human beings became virtually indistinguishable. This happened especially at Sparta. Xenophon, in his Constitution of Sparta,[22] stressed education above all else, as making for cohesion and a workable regime. The government of societies like this was, as has been truly said, the work of the folkways.

## 11. Monarchical Heritage of the Modern State

The really decisive moment in the early history of a people is that of the crisis between the king and the chiefs of clans; it is then that, according to the issue of the conflict, differences in political character are formed such as will never be completely erased. Entanglement in constitutional theories of notions formed by contrary experiences—republic or state, citizen or subject—is due entirely to failure to appreciate the importance of this fork in the road.

Whenever the chiefs of clans have won, the resulting political arrangements have been regarded as a society maintained jointly by the citizens for the advancement of their common interests—a *res publica*. The flesh and bones of this society are the individuals who make it up, and it takes visible form in their assemblies—the *comitia*. In time, those who were not

22. Ed. François Ollier (Lyon: 1934); see also the remarkable work of the same author, *Le Mirage spartiate*.

of the society at first are promoted to membership and take part in its life; and with them the assemblies expand—the *comitia centuriata* and the *comitia tributa*. But when it is a case of opposing the whole of the community to an individual member or to a foreign community, then the title invoked is this concrete reality, the *populus*, and the interests which concern it, the *res publica*. No one speaks of the state, and there is no word to denote the existence of a fictional person separate from the body of citizens.

If, on the other hand, the king wins, he becomes the man who is above all and rules all (*supra, supranus, sovrano*). The members of society are so many subjects (*subditi* = subjected). As and when the sovereign bids them, they lend him the aid of their resources; and the benefits which he brings them they enjoy.

The community's focal point, its manifestation in the flesh, is the king on his throne. It is he who decides for and acts for the people, developing for this purpose an apparatus which consists solely of himself and his minions. Around this skeleton the flesh of society, its men, ranges itself. And the tie to which the community responds is one of a feeling, not of being associated in common, but of being possessed in common.

Such is the manner of the formation of that complex idea, the state. The republic, that is clearly "we," we Roman citizens, looked at in the *milieu* of a society which we are forming for our common ends. The state, that is the sovereign commander of ourselves, who are its body servants.

That in the end the king disappears in a political revolution makes no difference; for his work remains, that of a society formed about an apparatus which is society's master, never to be discarded. A natural result of the existence of this apparatus, and of the relations established between it and the subjects, is that the modern man can never know citizenship in the ancient sense, when each decision and its execution was the work of all, when all took an active share in every side of public activity. True it is that every four years democracy will put him on a throne and give him the right of dispensing place and orientating policy; but the fact remains that for the rest of the time he is the *subject* of the apparatus which, if it is any consolation, he has helped to set going.

We see then that the monarchical period established in the body of society a distinct organ: this was Power, which has its own life, its own interests, its own characteristics, its own ends. It needs studying under this aspect.

# BOOK III

# Of the Nature of Power

# VI.

## *The Dialectic of Command*

THE SPECTACLE PRESENTED BY MODERN SOCIETY is that of an immense state apparatus—a veritable complex of moral and material controls by which individual actions are conditioned and around which private lives take shape. This apparatus grows with the growth of social needs, while its diseases infect both the life of society and the lives of individuals. The result is that, when we consider the sum of the services it renders us, the bare idea of its disappearance throws us into such a fright that an apparatus in such close communion with society naturally seems to us to have been made *for* it.

Society, we see, has furnished it with the human elements which compose it, and its strength seems, therefore, only a centralized and mobilized fraction of society's strength. In a word, it is *within* society.

If we look for the motive force which animates this Power, we find at work on it a crowd of influences situated at different points of the social compass; these influences, being in unceasing strife and combination with one another, assume at times the form of great waves which force the ship of state on to a new course. It is a convenient substitute for the analysis of this diversity of influences to consolidate and integrate them into one will, and call it the General Will or the Will of Society. And, since it is as its instrument that Power functions, Power must, one would think, have been forged by it.

Such is Power's dependence on the nation and so great its need to make its activities conform with the nation's necessities, that we are almost driven to the conclusion that the organs of command have been built up consciously, or unconsciously secreted, by society for use in its service. That is why jurists identify the state with the nation: that state, they say, *is* the nation personified, and organized as it needs to be for the government of itself and for dealing with others. There are great attractions in this view: unfortunately, it leaves out of account a phenomenon which is met with only too frequently—the seizure of the state apparatus by a particular will which uses it to dominate and exploit society for egoistical ends.

Once it is admitted that Power may forswear its true reason and end, and as it were detach itself from society to form far above it a separate body for its oppression, then the whole theory of Power's identity with society breaks down before this simple fact.

## 1. Power in Its Pure State

At this point nearly all who have written on the subject look the other way. A Power which is both illegitimate and unjust is off their intellectual beat. This feeling of repugnance, while it is understandable, has to be overcome. For the phenomenon is of too frequent occurrence to give any chance of life to a theory which does not take account of it.

It is clear enough how the mistake arose: it was from basing a science of Power on observations made, as it is history's business to make them, of Powers whose relations with society were of one kind only; what are in fact only its acquired characteristics were thus mistaken for Power's essence. And so the knowledge acquired, while adequate to explain one state of things, was quite useless in dealing with the times of the great divorces between Power and society.

It is not true that Power vanishes when it forswears its rightful begetter and acts in breach of the office which has been assigned to it. It continues as before to command and to be obeyed: without that, there is no Power—with it, no other attribute is needed for it to be.

It is not, therefore, the case that its substance was ever fused with the nation; it had a life of its own. Neither did its essence lie in its rightful reason and end. It can live, as it has shown, as command and nothing more. We must see it as it is if we are to grasp its inner reality, the thing without which it cannot be: that essence is command.

I shall, therefore, take Power in its pure state—command that lives for its sake and for its fruits—as the basic concept from which I shall set out to explain the characteristics developed by Power in the course of its historical existence; those characteristics have vastly changed its appearance.

## 2. Reconstruction of the Phenomenon by Synthesis

At the start of this undertaking it is necessary to clear away all misconception, whether it proceeds from the emotions or from the reason.

No reasonable explanation of political phenomena in the concrete is possible if the reader—as in these days, alas, he is but too prone to do—runs away with one piece of the argument, either to justify with it his own emotional approach or to attack it in the name of that approach. Suppose, for example, that he extracts from the concept of pure Power an apology for aggressive egoism as a principle of organization, then, in seeing even the germ of such an apology in this concept, he is guilty of wishful seeing. And the same is true if he reaches the conclusion that Power, being evil in its root, is therefore basically evil in action, and supposes it to be the author's intention to show this.

Let it be understood that our starting-point is a clearly defined abstract concept, our object being to discover the complex reality by way of a logical approach conducted in successive stages. What is essential to our purpose is not that this basic concept should be "true," but that it should be "adequate," in the sense of being able to furnish a coherent explanation of every fact submitted to observation. That is the way of approach in all sciences; all stand in need of certain fundamental concepts, such as the line and the point, the mass and the energy.

But we must not be expected—here is the second source of misconception—to copy the stern discipline of those exact sciences, to which, in that respect, political science will always be incomparably inferior. Even thought of apparently the most abstract kind is much dependent on the imagination: political thought is altogether governed by it. In politics the method of the geometrician would be but an artifice and a deception. We can make no affirmation about either Power or society without having before our eyes apposite historical instances. Therefore, our attempt to reconstruct the course of Power's transformation lays no claim to a dialectic which is independent of history or of the method of historical synthesis. Rather, we have tried to disentangle historical Power's complex nature by considering the age-long interaction of causes which have been ideally simplified.

Finally, let it be understood that we are concerned here only with Power in large formations.

Power in its pure state consists, as we have said, in command, a command which has an independent existence.

This notion offends the widely disseminated feeling that command is but an effect, an effect of the humours of a group of men whose needs drive them into submission to rulers.

This idea of a command-effect breaks down. When choice has to be made between two hypotheses neither of which admits of proof, the sensible thing to do is to choose the simpler. It is easier to imagine one man or a few men having the will to command than all men having the will to obey, to conceive of one or a few with the love of domination than of all possessed by the inclination to obedience.

Submission to a discipline is a product of the reason and is, therefore, of its nature later in time than the love of domination, which is instinctive. Submission is, politically, always a relatively passive factor; it may be doubted whether by itself it is creative at all, even whether the general need for and expectation of an authority can bring one into being.

But that is not all. The idea that the rulers have been willed into ruling by the ruled is not only improbable. If regard is had to the larger formation, it is also contradictory and absurd. For it implies that a formation in which a command is set up had needs and feelings in common—was in fact a community. Whereas, as history shows, communities of any size owe their existence to one thing only—to the imposition of one and the same force, and one and the same command, on divergent groups.

Power in its root-principle is not and cannot be an emanation and an expression of the nation, because there was no such thing as nation until various separate elements had lived long together under the same Power. Beyond all question, Power came first.

### 3. Command as Cause

This is the true relationship between them, but it has been obscured by the nationalist metaphysic prevalent in the nineteenth century. The historians of that time had had their imaginations so dazzled by striking instances of nationalist sentiment that they projected into the past, even into the distant past, the happenings of the present. They came to regard the sentimental groupings of their time as having an existence anterior to their own recent appearance. History becomes a novel about the personified nation, who, like a heroine of melodrama, always raised up at the critical moment the champion she needed.

Rapacious conquerors, like Clovis or William of Normandy, became, by a quaint transformation, the servants of the will-to-be of the French or English nations.

From one point of view history, like art, was greatly the gainer; at last it had found a unity of action, a continuity of movement and, above all, a central figure, all of which had been missing before.[1]

But it was literature, not history. The "collective conscience"[2] is, it is true, a phenomenon of very great antiquity; but the narrow geographical limits of this conscience must not be forgotten. In no other way could those limits be put back but by the fusion of distinct societies; the work of fusion was the work of command.

It is making a fateful mistake to suppose, as so many writers have supposed, that the major political formation, which is the state, was the natural product of human sociability. It seems a natural enough supposition, for society, which is a natural entity, is just such a product. But a natural society is a small thing. And for a small society to become a large one a new factor is necessary. For that there must be fusion, and this in the great majority of cases comes, not from the instinct of association, but from that of domination. The large formation owes its existence to the instinct of domination.[3]

In early times the nation did not raise up leaders for itself for the good reason that, until leaders had already appeared, there was not, either in

---

1. History attracts only in so far as it is the history of *someone*. Hence the lure of biography. But people of flesh and blood die, and interest dies with them. Therefore it must be brought to life by the substitution of another person. That is what gives to the recital the appearance of a series of episodes without emotional connection—*plenums* separated by *vacuums*. All is different since people took to writing the history of the personified nation. That was the artistic novelty of the nineteenth century. It is noteworthy that no one has succeeded in giving universal history, which is, intellectually, so much more significant, the same new impetus as has been given to national histories.

2. The expression should be taken metaphorically, and not in the meaning attached to it by Durkheim.

3. We may note that an undertaking of conquest generally begins with a process of federation (the Iroquois, the Franks, and the Romans are all federations, if legend is to be believed). But when once this process has mustered sufficient force, then unification begins and is completed by a process of subjection. So that there is in fact a core of conquerors and a protoplasm of conquered. That is how the state first looked.

fact or in feeling, a nation. Let us have no nonsense, then, as to the compelling and coordinating energy which creates nations being some ectoplasm or other risen from the depths of men in the mass. The history of large formations tells a different tale: their first and original cause is just that energy, behind which we cannot go. As if to prove the case more completely still, the energy generally comes from outside the formation.

### 4. Command as It First Looked

Conquest, and nothing but conquest, gives birth to large formations. Sometimes the conquerors are a component society within a group, but usually a warrior band from outside it.[4] In the first case one township takes command over many townships, in the other, one small people takes command over many peoples. Whatever the distinctions which the course of actual history forces us to draw, there can be no doubt that it is to these ancient phenomena that the notions of a capital city and a nobility owe in part their psychological content.[5]

The instruments chosen by fate to carry out this "synthetic activity," as Auguste Comte calls it, are of the most ferocious. The modern states of Western Europe, for instance, have to allow as their founders those German tribes of which Tacitus, notwithstanding the prejudice of the over-civilized man in favour of the barbarian, has left us a terrifying picture. The Franks, from whom the French take their name, were no better than those Goths whose roving career of pillage and devastation has been described for us in the striking pages of Ammianus Marcellinus.

The relative nearness to us in time of the Norman founders of the Kingdom of Sicily and of the companions in adventure of William the Bastard makes all doubt as to their real characters impossible. We have often seen them in the imagination—the greedy horde embarking at St. Valery-sur-Somme and then, arrived at London, having the country carved up among themselves by a victorious bandit chief, seated on his throne of stone. Strictly speaking, no doubt, they do not rank as unifiers

---

4. Even when the unification is brought about by a society within the group, it is generally a society on the periphery—usually the most barbarous.

5. That is naturally not to say that a nobility is always composed of a conquering band: history gives such an idea the lie. But it is noteworthy that a nobility which has a quite different origin, such as that of France in the eighteenth century, shows (cf. Boulainvilliers) rather a propensity to claim a warrior origin, thus showing that there is often a confused recollection of the existence in early times of a class distinction founded on this basis.

of territories, but they came to supplant others who had done the work of unification for them and were very much like themselves.

The Romans, those illustrious unifiers, were not in the beginning very different. On that score St. Augustine cherished no illusions:

> What are thieves' purchases but little kingdoms? for in thefts, the hands of the underlings are directed by the commander, the confederacy of them is sworn together, and the pillage is shared by the law amongst them. And if those ragamuffins grow but up to be able enough to keep forts, build habitations, possess cities, and conquer adjoining nations, then their government is no more called thievish, but graced with the eminent name of a kingdom. . . .[6]

## 5. Command for Its Sake

It follows that the state is in essence the result of the successes achieved by a band of brigands who superimpose themselves on small, distinct societies; this band, which is itself organized in a society as fraternal and as full of thieves' justice as you please,[7] behaves towards the vanquished and the subjected as Power in the pure state.

Power of this kind can make no claim to legitimacy. It pursues no just end; its one concern is the profitable exploitation of conquered and submissive subjects. It lives off the subject populations.

The meaning of William's division of England into sixty thousand knightly fiefs is just this: that henceforward sixty thousand groups of men will each have to support by their labour one of the conquerors. There lies the justification, the only one visible to the eyes of the conquerors, for the continued existence of the subject populations at all. If they could not be made useful in this way, there would be no point in leaving them alive. And it is well worthy of note that, where the conquerors are more civilized and do not treat the conquered so, they will yet, without having intended it, end up by finally exterminating populations which are no use to them: thus it has happened in both North America and Australia. The natives fared better beneath the rule of the Spaniards, who enslaved them.

History, with whom there is no shuffling, shows no instance of a spontaneous relationship between the victor members of the state and the vanquished, other than that of exploitation.

6. *The City of God*, Book IV, chap. iv.

7. The ancient writers said truly that there must be a law running among pirates to enable them to perpetuate their outrages effectively.

When the Turks had established themselves in Europe, they lived off the tribute paid them by the non-Mussulmans, whose difference of dress betrayed them as not belonging to the conquering race. It was a sort of annual ransom, the price extracted from those who could have been killed for being allowed to live.

The Romans acted in the same way. They made war for its immediate gains of precious metals and slaves: the more treasure and the more ravaged victims that followed in the consul's train, the more applauded was his triumph. The essential feature of the relationship between the capital and the provinces was the gathering of tribute. The Romans regarded the conquest of Macedonia as marking the date from which it had become possible to live entirely off the taxes paid by the conquered provinces.

Even Athens, democratic Athens herself, regarded the payment of taxation as unworthy of a citizen. Her coffers were filled by the tributes of her allies, and the more demagogic leaders increased their popularity by increasing the weight of these charges. Cleon raised them from six hundred to nine hundred talents, Alcibiades to twelve hundred.[8]

The parasitic domination of a small society over a collection of other societies—that is everywhere the mark of the big formation, the state. Whether the domestic economy of that small society is, as at Rome, republican, or, as at Athens, democratic, or, as at Sparta, egalitarian, in each the relations of the victors with the vanquished show us an exact picture of command for its sake and for its fruits.

## 6. Pure Power Forswears Itself

What a hideously immoral phenomenon, you tell me. Wait a little. For here is an admirable case of time's revenge: the egoism of command leads to its own destruction.

The further that the dominant society, urged on by its material appetites, extends the area of its domination, the more inadequate its strength becomes to hold down the growing mass of subjects, and to defend against other appetites an ever richer booty. That is why the Spartiates, who offer the perfect example of the exploiting society, limited their conquests.

8. Cf. A. Andreades, *Le Montant du budget athénien aux cinquième et quatrième siècles avant Jésus Christ*.

Again, the more the dominant society increases the weight of the charge which it imposes, the greater the desire it excites to shake off its yoke. Athens lost her empire by increasing the weight of the tributes which she extracted from it. It was for fear of that happening to them that the Spartiates took from the Helots a moderate rent only and allowed them to grow rich. The Spartiates knew how to discipline their egoism of domination. Among them, egoism acted as might's conductor to right, as it was put by Ihering.

But domination, no matter how prudently administered in practice, had its term. In time the master gang thinned out. Its strength faded, so that in the end it could no longer hold out against foreign armies. Its only resource then was to inject strength into the subject mass. But it was too late: at the time that Agis armed the "dwellers-round" and changed their status, there were but seven hundred citizens left, and Sparta was in its dying agony.

The instance of Sparta poses the problem which confronts Power in its pure form. Founded as it is on force, it has to keep up this force by maintaining reasonable relations with the mass which it dominates. Those who dominate are compelled by the most elementary prudence to strengthen themselves with associates recruited from among the subject ranks. According as the dominant society takes the form of a city or a feudal state (Rome was the former, Norman England the latter), the act of association takes the form either of extending the city's franchise to the new allies or of conferring knighthood on the serfs.

In the case of the cities a particularly strong repugnance is felt to this necessary process of reintegration of strength. This is shown by the opposition offered at Rome to the proposals for enfranchising the allies made by Livius Drusus, and by the ruinous war which the Republic had to endure before giving way.

That is the way in which the relationship of domination established by conquest is kept up: the Roman Empire was the empire of Rome *over* its provinces, the Kingdom of the Franks was the reign of the Franks *in* Gaul. In this way a political structure arises in which the superimposition of the society which commands upon those who obey is maintained: a relatively recent example of it is the Venetian Empire.

## 7. Establishment of Monarchy

So far we have treated the dominant society as if it were itself undifferentiated, but that, as the study of small societies shows us, is not the case. All the time that this dominant society is exercising over the subject societies a command which lives for its own sake and for its fruits, there is, in the interior of the dominant society itself, a command struggling to assert power over it. That command is the personal or royal power. Sometimes, as at Rome, it has fallen and vanished before the period of external conquests begins. Or sometimes, as in the case of the Germans, "the king" has still to be played at the time that external conquests start. Or finally, as in the case of the Macedonians, he has by that time already been played and the game won.

If this royal power is in being, the collection of an empire gives it a wonderful chance, not only of consolidating its conquests, but of breaking, at the same time, the half-independent, half-equal status of its partners in them.

What does it have to do? The king ceases to regard himself as the leader of a victorious band, the *rex Francorum*, upon whose united aid he must rely to maintain a power of constraint; instead he manipulates to his own advantage a part of the resources latent in the conquered formation, and employs them against either the rest of the formation or his own associates, whom he proceeds in this way to reduce to the level of subjects themselves. That, in its most brutal form, is what the Ottoman sultans did. From having been the chief men in a military feudal system, they became absolute monarchs when once they had made themselves independent of the enfeoffed Turkish chivalry; this they did by building up a new body-guard (*yeni cera*, or janissaries) from Christian children, who, owing them everything and loaded with privileges, proved an obedient instrument in their hands. For the same reason they chose their officers of state from Christians.

Command remains in principle the same: it is still, as always, force. But now the force has left the hands of the conquerors as a whole, and has come to rest in those of the king as a man, who can now employ it even against his old companions in arms. The larger the part of these latent resources on which the king can lay his hands, the more authority will he have.

He achieves much merely by attracting into his personal service some of the subjects, whom the contrast between the situation now within their grasp and the tyranny which so far they have endured will deeply affect. But he does better still if he can attach to his person the general body of the subjects by lightening such of the burdens laid on them as do not redound to his own advantage; the battle against the feudal system then opens. And in the end he crowns his efforts if he can manipulate to his own advantage the traditions of each of the groups which compose the whole; this Alexander did by giving himself out to be the son of Horus.

Not everyone had the advantage of being taught by Aristotle, but what Alexander did was so natural that he has had many imitators since. Henry I, the Norman King of England, married a daughter of the old Saxon royal family. The son of their marriage he made the fulfilment of a prophecy: the last of the Anglo-Saxon kings, Edward the Confessor, had promised his people that, after a succession of usurpations, a child would reign who should mend all. Here was that child.[9]

### 8. From Parasitism to Symbiosis

We see, systematically set out, the logical way of the establishment of what may be called "national monarchy"—it would still be an anachronism to use the word "nation." Power, as is clear at once, has not changed a jot: it is still what it always was, a system of command for its own sake and for its fruits.

The monarchy owes its existence to a twofold triumph: a military one, of conquerors over subjects; and a political one, of the king over the conquerors. The reason why one man can govern alone a vast mass of men is that he has forged the instruments which enable him to be, strangely enough, stronger than anyone else; those instruments are the state apparatus.

The subject mass is in the nature of a "boon" off which he lives and by means of which he maintains his state, sustains his instruments of compulsion, rewards loyalty, and pursues such ends as his ambitions suggest to him. But it would be no less true to say of this system of command that it owes its establishment to the protection which it has afforded the vanquished, its compulsive force to its skill in winning followers and making obedience popular, and, lastly, the resources which it draws from the people to the prosperity which it brings in its train.

Both explanations exactly fit the case. Power took shape and root in habits and beliefs, but it developed its apparatus and multiplied its instruments through knowing how to turn the circumstances of the time

9. Marc Bloch, *Les Rois thaumaturges*, published by the Strasbourg Faculté des Lettres, 1922.

to its advantage. But it could only so turn them by serving society. Its pursuit of its own authority never ceases, but the road to authority is through the services which it renders.

No one supposes, when he sees a forester pruning a copse to help the trees to grow, or a gardener hunting for snails, tending young plants under glass frames, or exposing them to the health-giving heat of a conservatory, that these things are done from a feeling of affection for the vegetable kingdom. And yet care for it he does, much more so than cold reason would suppose. This affection, however, is not the motivating reason for his pains; it is rather their necessary accompaniment. Reason would ban all affection from these labours of his. But the nature of man is such that his affections are stirred by the pains he gives himself.

And so it is with Power. Command which is its own end comes in time to care for the common good. Those same tyrants who left behind them in the shape of the Pyramids the proof of a horrifying egoism, also regulated the course of the Nile and fertilized the fellah's fields. Western monarchs have the best of logical reasons for encouraging national industry, but the encouragement becomes in time a pleasure and a passion. What had been a one-way flow of services from the City of Obedience to the City of Command tends to be balanced by a counter-current, even when the subjects are in no condition to claim benefits as of right. To speak in metaphor again—the plant of Power when it has attained a certain growth cannot continue to draw nourishment from the subject soil without putting something back into it. Then comes its turn of giving.

The monarch is not in the least the creature of his people, set up to satisfy their wants. He is rather a parasitic and dominating growth which has detached itself from the dominating group of parasitic conquerors. But the need to establish his authority, to maintain it and keep it supplied, binds him to a course of conduct which profits the vast majority of his subjects.

To suppose that majority rule functions only in democracy is a fantastic illusion. The king, who is but one solitary individual, stands far more in need of the general support of society than any other form of government. And, since it is human nature for habit to engender affection, the king, though acting at first only from concern for authority, comes to act with affection as well and in the end to be motivated by affection. The mystical principle of the *rex* has come again.

Power has, by a wholly natural transition, moved from parasitism to symbiosis.

The monarch is, as is obvious, at once the destroyer of the republic of conquerors and the builder of the nation. This explains the conflict of judgments which were passed on, for instance, the Roman emperors; they were condemned by the republicans at Rome and approved by the subject peoples of outlying provinces. And so, at the start of its career, Power pulls down the exalted and exalts the humble.

### 9. Formation of the Nation in the Person of the King

The material conditions under which a nation lives are the product of conquest: it is conquest that builds an aggregate out of disparate elements. But the nation is not at first a whole, since each constituent group is conscious of its separate life. How can a common consciousness be formed? The sentiments of all must have a common point of attachment. Who is to be this centre of crystallization for national sentiment? The answer is the monarch. By an unerring instinct he presents himself to each group as the substitute for and heir to its old chief.

Take Philip II: we smile now at the almost interminable list of titles which he bore. We see in it only vanity. We are quite wrong—it was necessity. Being the master of several distinct peoples, he had to present to each an aspect which was familiar to each. Similarly a king of France had to take the title of Duke in Brittany and of Dauphin in the Viennois. And the same thing held everywhere.

The string of titles is but the counterpart of the various aspects he wears. In time, these aspects fuse, and spiritual divergences get resolved in the corporeal unity of the royal person. This process of fusion is of capital importance, for by it the throne becomes the place where emotional clashes are stayed and national sentiment formed. The thing in common between the Bretons and the people of the Viennois is that he who is duke of the one is dauphin of the other.

In a sense, therefore, it is on the throne that the nation is based. Men become compatriots by reason of their allegiance to one and the same person. And now we see why it is that peoples formed in the monarchical mould inevitably regard the nation as a person; they think by analogy from the living person through whom a common sentiment has been formed.

The Romans were without this conception. The idea of a supposititious being living outside and above them did not enter their imaginations. They conceived of nothing but the *societas* which they formed. And the subject peoples did not belong to this *societas* unless they were admitted to it—herein lay the burning question of the franchise. The Romans did themselves no good by taking over the religious ceremonies of the vanquished and transporting them to Rome—for the subject peoples never came to have their spiritual home at Rome, or to regard it as their moral base. Never, that is to say, until the appearance of the emperors, who offered themselves to the adoration of each separate people in the image of what each wanted to adore. It was through the emperors that the aggregate became a whole.

### 10. The City of Command

Let us now assemble everything that goes to the command of a large formation at different stages of its existence.

In the early days of a state, the collection of people within it attains only at intervals to a unified existence. We see gathered in their assemblies the Gothic or Frankish conquerors; we see the Roman people sitting in conclave; we see the king presiding over his court of Norman barons. In them we see the lords of all, an elite in visible form superimposed upon the mass, a Power existing for its own sake and for its fruits.

Let us now jump forward in time. The place of assembly, be it field or forum or chamber, at times crowded and at times empty, has gone; there is now a palace, surrounded by a collection of buildings in which a variety of dignitaries and functionaries carry on their business. He who commands is now the king, helped by his permanent servants, his *ministeriales*, his ministers. A whole new city has sprung up, the City of Command—the place of dominion, the hearth of justice, the haven of the ambitious.

Should we be right in saying that this city has a significance quite different from that of the old assembly of lords and masters? that the new tribe of dignitaries and functionaries are not masters at all, but servants? that they are servants of the king, whose will is in accord with the needs and desires of the people as a whole? that what we now see is, in short, a working apparatus placed in the hands of a social will?

We should not be wrong, but we should not have said all. For the master's will, however closely it has been adapted to society, is still the master's will. And the apparatus is no passive instrument. It consists of men, men who have taken the place, by slow stages, of the old rulers, and they have succeeded to a position so similar to that of the old, that they have taken over some of their characteristics as well, so much so that in time they will leave the apparatus behind them, acquire wealth and nobility, and come to regard themselves as the posterity in title to the conquering race: to this development Saint-Simon and Boulainvilliers[10] are witnesses.

We must not therefore cease to regard Power, now that it is composed of the king and his administration, as a ruling elite; the difference is that it is now better equipped to rule, the more so that, besides ruling, it renders vast and indispensable services.

## 11. Overthrow of Power

All these services, betokening as they do so admirable a solicitude for the mass of mankind, almost forbid the idea that, in its essence, Power is still the dominating egoist that we at first postulated.

Its behaviour is quite changed, for now it dispenses the blessings of order, justice, security, prosperity. Its human content is quite different, for now it is made up of the most competent elements of the subject mass.

This great transformation scene is entirely explicable by reference to the tendency of command to persist as such, which it can only do by drawing ever closer its ties with the people beneath it, by widening the scope of its services and the recruitment of its elite, and by a harmonization of wills.

The effect is that Power behaves for practical purposes as if it had exchanged its essential nature, which is egoist, for an acquired nature, which is social. But at the same time it gives proof of a tendency to oscillation; sometimes this merges it completely with its asymptote, when it seems altogether social, and then again swings it back to its starting-point, when it becomes egoist once more.

It seems paradoxical, but the charge of domination now begins to be heard against a Power which has become in intention profoundly social.

10. [Henri Boulainvilliers, Comte de Saint Saire (1658–1722), French political writer. An aristocrat of the most pronounced type, attacking both absolute monarchy and popular government, he was also at great pains to prove that the right of the nobility to rule was founded on conquest, because the nobles, as he said, were descended from the conquering Franks, while the subjects were the sons of the conquered Gallo-Romans.]

This complaint can only take shape when Power has finished its work of spiritual unification and the nation has become a conscious whole. The more keenly this unity is felt, the greater becomes the opposition to Power as being not an emanation from the nation but something imposed on it. By a coincidence which is not at all unusual in social history, men become conscious of Power's alien character just at the moment when it has become closely national. In the same way a working class will come to think itself oppressed at the very time when its burdens are being lightened. For a fact to bring to birth an idea—which is brought about by the thing observed being brought within the limits of conventional thought—its happening must have been near in time to the idea. The same condition holds true if a fact is to serve as a basis for an idea's being attacked for not being what it purports to be.

So, then, this alien arbitrary, exploiting Power, which exists for its sake and for its fruits, gets overthrown. Yet at the very moment of its overthrow it had ceased to be either alien, arbitrary, or exploiting. Its human content had been entirely changed, its exactions were no more than what it required for its services: the maker of the nation had become its instrument—so far, that is to say, as it lay in Power's nature to become it, so far as a transformation of command is possible without its ceasing to be.

## 12. The Two Ways

I make no claim to have traced here the historical evolution of Power, but rather to have proved by a logical demonstration that the hypothesis of a Power based on "pure" force and "pure" exploitation carries with it the implication that such a Power must necessarily try to come to terms with its subjects and adjust itself to their needs and aspirations; that, although inspired by a "pure" egoism, and with no other end than itself, it will notwithstanding come, by a predestined road, to advance the interests of the community and to pursue social ends. In lasting it becomes social; it must become social to last.

The problem then arises of how to eliminate what is left of its primitive nature, how to deprive it of all possibility of reverting to its original mode of conduct; how, in a word, to make its essence social. There are two possible ways; of these, the one is logical but seems impracticable, the other seems easy but does not do the work required of it.

It is, to start with, generally agreed that Power which is born of domination and lives to dominate ought to be destroyed. The next step is for us who know ourselves for compatriots and proclaim ourselves for fellow-citizens to form a *societas*, for the joint management of our common interests; in this way we shall get ourselves a republic in which there is no longer a sovereign personage, whether in fleshly or ideal form, and one will no longer holds sway over the wills of all—where nothing can be got done except by an effective *consensus* of wills. We shall then have dispensed with any state apparatus formed in a centralized hierarchy and consisting of a coherent elite; we shall have gotten instead a large number of independent magistracies which the citizens will take it in turn to fill— thereby going through phases of both command and obedience, whose alternation Aristotle made the essential feature of the republican form of government. That would indeed be the complete overthrow of the monarchical type of constitution. But tendencies of that kind, though in fact they show themselves, do not carry the day. What does carry the day is the simpler idea of preserving whole the monarchical state apparatus with one solitary difference—the substitution of the ideal personage, the nation, for the fleshly personage, the king.

The City of Command still stands. All that we have done has been to drive out the occupant of the palace and put in his place the representatives of the nation. The new arrivals will quickly find in their newly conquered habitation the memories, the traditions, the symbols, and the means, of domination.

### 13. The Natural Evolution of Every Apparatus or Rule

To give our investigation strictly logical form, we will, for argument's sake, suppose this legacy removed. We will suppose that the revolutionaries, while recognizing the necessity of having a coherent state apparatus, a City of Command, want nothing of the old apparatus and of the old city. We will suppose them building a wholly new Power, a Power established by and for society, whose representative and servant it is by definition. This new Power, too, I say, for all its origin, will in time elude the intentions of its creators and tend to an existence for its sake and for its fruits.

Every association of men shows us the same spectacle. When once the social end ceases to be continuously pursued in common[11] and becomes

---

11. As happens, for instance, in an association of pirates, where there must be a chief, but where no active body emerges over against a passive generality.

the permanent charge of one differentiated group, to be interfered with by the rest of the associates only at stated intervals—when once this differentiation has come about, then the responsible group becomes an elite, which acquires a life and interest of its own.

It withstands on occasion the mass whence it came. And it carries the day.[12] It is hard in reality for private persons attending a meeting, taken up as they are with their own concerns and without having concerted among themselves beforehand, to feel the confidence necessary to reject the proposals which are cleverly presented to them from the platform, and the necessity for which is supported by arguments based on considerations of a kind to which they are strangers.

There, too, we see the reason why the Roman people was able for so long to pass its laws on the public square: an examination of the procedure followed shows conclusively that their effective part consisted merely in ratifying what had been jointly determined by the magistrates and the Senate.

In our times the same methods are exactly reproduced at annual general meetings of shareholders. How could the managing class, strong in competence and briefed to withstand opponents, fail to grow convinced that they are a people apart, that only in their hands can the interests of society be safeguarded and that, in brief, society's strongest interest is to preserve and cherish its elite of managers?

## 14. The Governmental Ego

If these phenomena occur, as they do, in every association, they cannot fail to press with peculiar intensity in political associations.[13] There is no need to suppose that the persons chosen to govern are not in general perfectly representative men, exactly resembling their subjects. But when once they have been summoned to the exercise of sovereign authority,

12. "Every established body of men," says Spencer, "is an instance of the truth that the regulative structure tends always to grow in strength. The history of every learned society, of every society whatever its end, shows how its general staff, being permanent either in whole or in part, directs its affairs and determines its actions without meeting much resistance." H. Spencer, *Problems of Ethics and Sociology*.

13. "If then this supremacy of the rulers in established bodies of recent origin, composed of men who have, in many cited cases, the free choice of affirming their independence, how great will the supremacy of the rulers become in bodies established long ago, already become vast and highly organized, and which, instead of regulating only a part of the life of the whole, regulate its whole life." Spencer, *loc. cit.*

their wills take on, as is observed by Duguit, a new character and a different force.

> Those who act in the name of the sovereign authority and express a sovereign will are set above the rest and act in regard to them by way of command, and by no other way. Those whom the sovereign addresses are bound to execute the order which he gives them, not because of what is in the order but because it comes to them from a will which is naturally superior to their own.[14]

It is then the case that the exercise of the sovereign authority engenders a feeling of superiority which in effect turns these "likes" of the ordinary citizen into his "unlikes." But yet, you say to me, they act only as his agents and trustees. You think so! From his experiences as a deputy in the 1848 Assembly, Proudhon drew this lesson:

> It is no use saying that the elected person or the representative of the people is only the trustee for the people, its delegate, its advocate, its agent, its interpreter, and so forth; notwithstanding this sovereignty which belongs, in theory, to the mass, and the formal and legal subordination to it of its agent, representative or interpreter, it will never come about that the agent's influence and authority will not be greater than his principal's and that he takes trusteeship seriously. It will always be so: in despite of principle, *the delegate of the sovereign will be the master of the sovereign*. Sovereignty on which a man cannot enter, if I may so put it, is as empty a right as property on which he cannot enter.[15]

Standing thus above the mass, to which the difference in their positions has made them different psychologically, the managers are drawn together among themselves, all being under the influence of their situations and functions: "All those," said Spencer, "who make up the organization of government and administration, join up together and draw apart from the rest."[16] They form an elite, as has been emphasized by Rousseau, who noted both the social inevitability and the moral consequences of its happening:

> . . . that the governing élite may come into being and have a life of its own which distinguishes it from the rest of the State; that all its members may

14. Léon Duguit, *Souveraineté et liberté* (Paris: 1922) pp. 78–79.
15. Proudhon, *Théorie du mouvement constitutionnel au XIXe siècle* (Paris: 1870) pp. 89–90.
16. Spencer, *Principles of Sociology*, para. 444.

act in unison and answer the end which it exists to pursue, for this it must have its private ego, an *esprit de corps* shared by its members, and a force and will of its own which make for its preservation.[17]

## 15. The Essential Duality of Power

The point could not be better put, that society, in setting up an apparatus for its service, has brought to birth a small society which differs from itself and has, inevitably, its own sentiments, interests, and personal wills. Anyone wishing to regard the nation as a moral being, endowed with a collective conscience, and capable of exercising a general will, must see in Power what Rousseau saw—*another* being, with *its* conscience and *its* will, drawn on by natural egoism to the pursuit of its private advantage. Striking evidence can be produced as to this egoism:

> It is true [remarked Lavisse, the historian] that the public authority in France, under whatever régime, the republican as well as the rest, has its own, narrow, egoistical ends. It is, I will not say a côterie, but a consortium of people who, having attained authority originally by an accident, are thenceforward concerned not to lose it by an accident. National sovereignty is undoubtedly a lie.[18]

As to the sentiments animating the consortium, we have the testimony of the great Bolingbroke:

> I am afraid that we came to court in the same dispositions that all parties have done; that the principal spring of our actions was to have the government of the State in our own hands; that our principal views were the conservation of this power, great employments to ourselves, and great opportunities of rewarding those who had helped to raise us, and of hurting those who stood in opposition to us.[19]

Candour of this kind is rare among those who command.[20] But it expresses accurately the view taken by those who obey. Forewarned by

---

17. *Du Contrat social,* Book III, chap. i.

18. Ernest Lavisse, in an article in the *Revue de Paris,* January 15, 1899.

19. Bolingbroke, *Letter to Sir William Windham.*

20. [Cf. Halifax, *Maxims of State*: "Parties in a State generally, like freebooters, hang out false colours; the pretence is the public good; the real business is to catch prizes; and wherever they succeed, instead of improving their victory, they presently fall upon the baggage."]

their intuitions and educated by their experience, the people regard as turncoats those who leave them to enter the City of Command. In a son of a peasant turned tax-gatherer, in a trade union secretary turned minister, his old associates detect one who has suddenly become a stranger to them. The reason is in effect that there is a climate of authority which changes men; the inmates of Power are, in consequence, as much and as necessarily the guardians of its house as are opium-takers of their den.

The subjects, feeling that government is not being conducted exclusively for their benefit, charge the regime, be it monarchy or republic, with a vice which belongs to human nature: there is, inescapably, egoism in Power.

We posited at the beginning a Power whose essence was egoist; we saw it acquire a social nature. We have now reached the position of positing a Power whose essence is social and seeing it acquire an egoist nature. This convergence of rational sequences brings us to the irrational conclusion of the whole matter: in the make-up of Power in the real, two natures are necessarily found in association. In whatever way and in whatever spirit it has been established, Power is neither angel nor brute, but, like man himself, a composite creature, uniting in itself two contradictory natures.

## 16. Of the Egoism of Power

It would be absurd to claim to have identified in every historical Power a combination, whether in the same or in different proportions, of two chemically pure substances, egoism and the social sense.

Every nascent science—and political science is, heaven knows, immature enough!—has to make use of abstract ideas. But it should not be lost sight of that these ideas are in fact so many syntheses of pictures supplied us by the memory; these pictures will always colour the ideas, creating associations which will only be shaken off—and then imperfectly—by long habit. Therefore, great care is needed in the handling of abstract ideas, which must be kept imprecise so as not to exclude the admission of further pictures. I go so far as to say that they should remain undefined until an adequate inventory has been taken of the actual things perceived to which they should provide the common denominator.

If, for instance, we base our idea of Power's egoism on the picture supplied us by the king of the Bantus, for whom ruling is, in essence, nothing more than swimming in wealth and eating enormous meals—so

that the same word, *fouma*, serves to denote both ruling and eating[21]—
if, under the influence of this picture of an obese chieftain swollen with
fat, we start looking for his exact equivalent in the modern world, we
shall not find it: in these days the exercise of Power does not take the
form of a preoccupation with overeating, and the ministers who abuse
their offices to enjoy and enrich themselves are the exceptions.

Is that to say that a careful scrutiny will disclose nothing in common
between the Bantus' way of doing things and our own? They heap up
tribute in the form of food, we pile on taxes. The king eats his revenues,
but he is joined in this by his dependants and those who help him in
governing—the equivalent of our administrative corps and our police
forces. So that there is a group of "tribute-eaters" with a vested interest
in the enlargement of the tributes, a group into which the governed, who
pay the imposition—here again the same word, *louba*, denotes governed
and taxpayers—strive to break, so as to exchange the position of nourisher
for that of nourished. Would anyone be so bold as to assert that nothing
of the same kind happens in our society?

But there is more to it than this. The king employs a considerable part
of the tribute in grants of largesse, bestowed by way of banquets or
presents, to those whose support consolidates his authority, whereas their
defection would endanger it. Do we not see modern governments as well
using the public funds to endow social groups or classes, whose votes
they are anxious to secure? Today the name is different, and it is called
the redistribution of incomes by taxation.

It would beyond question be wrong to say that Power levies taxation
today firstly for the benefit of its own machine and then to gain supporters
by boons or *beneficia*. But all the same does not this egoist interpretation
of taxation come as a necessary corrective to the social concept of it which
is usually taught? Is it quite true to say that the pace at which taxes grow
does no more than keep faithfully in step with the growth of social needs?
That the only reason for multiplication of posts is extension of services,
and that services are never extended to excuse the multiplication of posts?
Is it absolutely certain that the motive for largesse to the public is always
the care for social justice and never the interest of the governing faction?

The picture of the public official, of a man completely disinterested and
wedded to the public interest, who is indeed one of the least materially
minded human types to be found in our society, rises at this point to

21. H. A. Junod, *Mœurs et coutumes des Bantous* (2 vols. Paris: 1936) Vol. I, p. 381.

reproach us for these suggestions, yet what confirmation of them there is every time that Power changes hands and is used by the victorious party after the Bantu fashion, as a banquet at which the new arrivals fight for places and throw the scraps to their supporters![22]

Let us take note—without at this place developing the point—that the egoist principle comes to life again in its most barbarous shape every time that Power changes hands, even when the professed object of the change has been the triumph of the social principle. And let us reach this provisional conclusion: that it would be as incorrect to form an exclusively egoist picture of Power as to form an exclusively social one. A stereoscopic view combining these two pictures presents a truth which is very different.

### 17. The Noble Forms of Governmental Egoism

We must not form too narrow and squalid a conception of governmental egoism, a term which only denotes the tendency to live for itself which we have seen to be an inherent feature of Power. But this tendency shows itself in more ways than in the utilization of Power for the advantage of those exercising it. The pleasures which the holding of it brings are, except to spirits of an irretrievable squalor, quite different from that of gorged cupidity.

Man, in love with himself and made for action, rises in his own esteem with every extension of his personality and multiplication of his faculties. The leader of any group of men whatsoever feels thereby an almost physical enlargement of himself. His nature changes with his stature. The personal prudence and avarice which we associate with egoism are rarely seen in him. His restricted gestures take on an amplitude: he has, as the ordinary man truly puts it, "lordly" virtues and vices. He is the man of destiny.[23]

Command is a mountain top. The air breathed there is different, and the perspectives seen there are different, from those of the valley of

22. [This statement of the case is, no doubt, truer for France and America than for England. In America, notwithstanding some recent legislation, the spoils system still operates over a wide area. In England, too, there is a substantial field of ministerial appointment which seems unlikely to narrow.]

23. "To be the centre of action, the active focus of a crowd, to raise himself above whole peoples and ages, to be in command of History so as to bring his own people or family with their ends to the front of events: that is the historical and unconscious élan of each individual with a historical vocation." Spengler, The Decline of the West.

obedience. The passion for order and the genius of construction, which are part of man's natural endowment, get full play there. The man who has grown great sees from the top of his tower what he can make, if he so wills, of the swarming masses below him.

Are the ends which he sets before himself for the weal of society? Possibly. Are they in conformity with its desires? Often. And so the leader easily convinces himself that his one ambition is to serve the whole, and forgets that his real motive-spring is the enjoyment of action and expansion. I have no doubt that Napoleon was sincere when he said to Caulaincourt, "People are wrong in thinking me ambitious—I am touched by the misfortunes of peoples; I want them to be happy and, if I live ten years, the French will be happy."[24]

This memorable assertion well illustrates the claim invariably made by command which makes itself its end, that its one and only aim in life is to serve social objectives. The lie is not, it is true, always as flagrant, nor the contradiction always as glaring. And how often it happens that the turn of events gives some plausibility to the lie, for social ends are achieved, and it is of no interest to history whether they were the real motive-spring of the men of Power![25]

The egoism of Power and its social sense leave us, you say, in inextricable confusion. We are lost in a maze. Not at all. We have reached the goal: we stand in the presence of Power as it is, as all history has fashioned it. From now on they will strike us as futile and puerile, these endlessly renewed claims to be creating a Power from which all trace of egoism will be purged away.

The mind of man, in love with a simplicity which it finds nowhere in nature, cannot be convinced that the duality of Power is of its essence. Ever since the divine dreamings of Plato, themselves stemming from earlier Utopias, the search has gone on for an entirely virtuous government and one which lives only for the interests and the wishes of the governed.

For thinkers this illusion has done no more than thwart the creation of a political science worthy of the name; but, reaching the multitude, the disposer of Power, it has become the fruitful cause of the great disturbances which desolate our age and threaten the very existence of civilization.

The vices and abuses seen in the Power that is in being are not actively

24. *Mémoires de Caulaincourt.*
25. This theme has been admirably developed by Hegel.

restrained by the citizens, as knowing that such vices and abuses are inherent in the nature of Power. Civically passive, but emotionally active, they take these vices and abuses for the stigmata of a bad Power which should be overturned to make place for another Power which shall be infinitely just and beneficent. Away, then, with the egoisms, which, by long practice, have come to adapt themselves to society and have learned that, to attain their own satisfaction, they must first satisfy the needs of the generality by putting to the service of the public good the whole force of their private passions!

The road is now clear, the fool has said, for a spirit which is altogether social, a spirit with which the aspirants to Power claim to be overflowing. Even if they spoke truth, it is still unproven that the abstract and ideal conception of the general good which they bring with them would be any improvement on the practical and empirical understanding of the body of society which was possessed by their old-established predecessors. And, even if they should become completely stripped of egoism, even then something, as we shall see, would be lacking to Power. But, in sober truth, pretensions of this kind are always unjustified. Disinterested feelings may stir some of the conquerors of Power, but with them are mingled, both in the conquerors themselves and in their following, ambitions and appetites. Every change of regime and, to a lesser extent, every change of government is, as it were, a reproduction, on a more or less reduced scale, of a barbarian invasion. The newcomers wander about the power house with feelings in which curiosity, pride, greed, all have a place.

The credit which they then for the first time enjoy enables them to make full use of this formidable machinery, and even to add to it some further controls of their own. In time yet another faction will, by promising to make a better use of it, force its way in turn into the City of Command, which it will find already embellished by its forerunners. So that the hope, always renewed, of stripping from Power all trace of egoism results only in forging ever vaster means of compulsion for the next egoism.

Therefore, that is not political science which does not recognize the essential duality of Power: the egoist principle cannot be purged out of it. We have seen the natural ways in which it adapts itself to the social interest; also, no doubt, there are artificial ways, but they form part of the art of politics—and that is another story.

We may rest content with having made some advance in knowledge of Power in the concrete.

# VII.

# *The Expansionist Character of Power*

IF THERE IS IN POWER'S MAKE-UP an egoistical urge combined with the will to serve society, it is a natural supposition that, the weaker the former, the stronger will be the latter: perfection of government would consist in the complete elimination of the egoistical principle. The chimera of elimination has been unceasingly pursued by minds whose limited range is only equalled by their good intentions. They do not realize that the nature of man and the nature of society combine to make any such project chimerical. For without the egoistical principle Power would lack the inner strength which alone enables it to carry out its functions.

The duality is irreducible. And it is through the interplay of these two antithetical principles that the tendency of Power is towards occupying an ever larger place in society; the various conjunctures of events beckon it on at the same time that its appetite is driving it to fresh pastures. Thus there ensues a growth of Power to which there is no limit, a growth which is fostered by more and more altruistic externals, though the motive-spring is still as always the wish to dominate.

## *1. Egoism Is a Necessary Part of Power*

It is, no doubt, a flattering picture, this of a managing elite motivated exclusively by benevolence. The rulers themselves are so susceptible to it that they profess to dislike the discharge of public duties, which they claim to have undertaken from nothing but a sense of duty. But so much devotion, even if it was genuine, would not be to society's advantage. Any advantage there was would come to it only from minds of a purely speculative type, whose presence in public life has often been desiderated. A government of that kind fails—apart from one other very serious disadvantage to which we shall revert—from a lack of red blood, of which the governed quickly become conscious.

In the order of nature everything dies which is not sustained by an intense and brutal love of self. Power, in the same way, can only maintain the ascendancy necessary to it by the intense and brutal love which the rulers have for their authority. It has, alas! to be agreed that tenderness of heart, going to the length of self-denial, spells self-inflicted death to Power. Instances of this are the case of Lamartine[1] and the ever memorable one of Louis XVI. In an illuminating passage[2] Tocqueville has shown us the monarchy turning into its own prosecutor for its crimes, and calling down on itself a wrath from which it has no wish to protect itself. It lacked the will to live: "Go and tell the Swiss not to fire."

History rejects the heroes proffered it by poetry, the generous Carlos, the tender Alexius, the debonair Charles Edward. They were dear to their contemporaries, and even today sensitive spirits shed a tear for them. But, as Luther said, "God has not given rulers a fox's tail but a sabre." In other words, a certain feeling of superiority, a certain taste for domination, a certain assurance of rightness, and an imperious temper are appropriate qualities in rulers. The "Roi d'Yvetot," the good little king of Béranger's song, was like no king that ever kept his throne.[3]

Our era, too, has experimented in debonair rulers. Notwithstanding their amiable qualities, or perhaps because of them, history has swept them away with her broom. The life of Frederick the Great is in this

1. [Lamartine (1790–1869) was the leading member of the provisional government set up in February 1848. The reference here is to the failure of that government to cope with the disturbances of June 1848—a failure which led to the supersession of Lamartine by Cavaignac.]

2. Tocqueville, *L'ancien régime et la Révolution*, Book III, chap. v: "Comment on souleva le peuple en voulant le soulager."

3. [The town and territory of Yvetot was long a semi-sovereign principality, and the Lord of Yvetot was popularly styled "Roi d'Yvetot." Béranger's well-known song, with that title, was published in 1815.

Don Carlos (1545–1568), son of Philip II of Spain. Of weak intellect, he was confined, and possibly murdered, by Philip. Schiller, Alfieri, and Otway wrote plays about him.

Alexius Petrovich (1690–1718), son of Peter the Great. A gentle, emotional dreamer, he was little to the taste of his father, who in the end had him done to death.]

respect an object lesson. The amiable young man that he was! But had he so remained, he would have gone the way of the Czarevitch Alexius. Then he mounted the throne, and an astonished Europe saw a very different person.

A truce, then, to seeking in rulers virtues which are foreign to their condition!

Power takes life from those who exercise it, it is warmed and nourished unceasingly by means of the enjoyments which it procures them. The keenest of these enjoyments are not those infantile delights of luxury and vanity which dazzle the popular imagination, irritate the small shopkeeper and thereby demonstrate to him the egoism of Power. The banquets portrayed for us by the Burgundian chroniclers, the state processions, the luxury which encompassed a Charles the Bold, a Julian II, a Lorenzo de' Medici, a Francis I, or a Louis XIV, those epicures of wealth—that is what annoys the public. Yet we may feel grateful for their prodigalities, to which we owe the Van Eycks and Michelangelos of this world, as well as the Sistine Chapel and Versailles: the wasteful habits of princes have proved the most precious treasure of humanity.

To be completely acquitted of egoism by the generality, rulers need only affect a studied austerity and a strict economy. As if the real pleasures of authority were not quite other!

In every condition of life and social position a man feels himself more of a man when he is imposing himself and making others the instruments of his will, the means to the great ends of which he has an intoxicating vision. To rule a people, what an extension of the ego is there! The ephemeral delight given us when, after a long illness, our limbs return to their duty can alone give us some small idea of that incomparable pleasure of radiating daily impulsions into an immense mass and prompting the distant movements of millions of unknown limbs. It can be savoured in the shadows of a cabinet by a grey-haired and black-coated official. The thoughts he thinks keep pace with the orders he gives. He sees in his mind's eye the canal being dug along the line which his pencil has traced on the map, the boats which will shortly give it life, the villages springing up on its banks, the profusion of merchandise heaped high on the quays of his dreamtown. It is not surprising that Colbert, on coming to his desk in the morning, rubbed his hands for joy, as the tale is told by Perrault.[4]

---

4. [Perrault, who was Colbert's secretary, is the author of a well-known book of French fairy stories.]

This intoxicating pleasure of moving the pieces on the board of the social game breaks out continually in Napoleon's correspondence. Is it merely attention to detail that makes him, even in time of peace, prescribe the route that each troop of soldiers is to take across his vast empire, determine the number of muskets to be stored in each armoury, how many cannon balls there shall be in each place, or how much cotton shall be imported into France and through what customs houses—the way which it shall follow and the time which it shall take to come from Salonika? Far from it: when he regulates the vast traffic of men and goods, he feels, as it were, the coursing of an infusion of new blood which supplements his own.

In this way the people ruled becomes in some sort an extension of the ruler's ego; his sensations of pleasure in them are at first positive and then reflex—that is to say, the pleasure is no longer simply that of moving so many pieces, but has become a deeply felt consciousness of whatever affects any one of them. At that point the egoism of Power extends to the whole people, and its identification with them is complete. It was, in olden days, the monarchic principle which had to double the parts of a directing egoism and of an identification of itself with the social mass. And in this way the institution of monarchy, so far from merely subsuming the interests of the mass into those of one man, became sensitive to every wound received by every little cell. A secure hold on Power and its descent in a regular line assured the maximum of identification of egoism with the general advantage. Whereas, contrariwise, a transient or precarious hold on Power tends to make of the nation merely the instrument of a personal destiny, of an egoism which resists absorption in the whole.

The more quickly the holders of Power succeed each other, the less completely can their egoism be extended to a body which is but their mount of a day. Their ego stands more apart and takes its enjoyments in more vulgar fashion. Or else, if their egoism can be projected outwards at all, it stops at a formation, such as a party, with which it can stay in long association. So that the nation gets ruled by a succession of men who have identified their egos not with it but with parties in it.

It is the public service which is the repository of that sublimated sort of egoism which is the preservative of Power. Permanent officials bring to the maintenance and enlargement of their offices, which in their innermost hearts they regard always as a piece of their property, and which they have often inherited, the diligence of a lifetime. The social virtue of monarchy, which consists in identifying the ego with society, finds a pallid reflex in hereditary officialdom, or in the "great seminaries," which secure by other means the same continuity of sentiments.

## 2. From Egoism to Idealism

Once the necessity of there being a Power in society is admitted, it has to be agreed that it needs a preservative; this it gets from the affection felt by the rulers for their own functions, which in time they confound with their own personalities. By means of these functions they project what each feels himself to the far extremities of the body social. This concrete and visible phenomenon has given birth, by unconscious processes of thought, to the widespread theory of the nation-person, of which the state is the visible expression. The only element of truth in it is psychological: for those who are identified with the state, the nation is in effect the expression of their persons.

We must beware of the consequences which follow if we push this train of thought to its logical conclusion. If the governmental ego really could spread itself out over the mass of its subjects in such a way as not only to control all their activities but also to receive back from them every impress it bears, the traditional political antinomies would be finally resolved: to inquire whether the impulsive force should come down from Power in the shape of authoritative commands, or should ascend to it from the body social in expressions of the general will, would be a vain question, seeing that these commands would, *ex hypothesi*, have been fully adapted to that will: the only problem left would be the philosophical one of which came first.

Starting from the egoistical nature of Power, we should reach the conclusion that this egoism, even if given full rein, could desire for the future only what the needs of society demanded. This theory, absurd as it is, would be hardly more so than that which was for years the staple food of political economy. For if, left to themselves, the egoisms of individuals are bound to produce the best of all possible worlds, why should not the same apply to the egoisms of governments?

Political science needs purging of sophistries of this kind, all of them due to the same mistake of giving an indefinite extension to a truth which is valid only within certain limits. Reason and observation alike permit the conclusion that the lengths to which the egoism of men of high place carries them in their self-identification with society are all the greater if their hold of Power is stable and of long date. The notion of legitimacy is an expression of this truth. Legitimate Power is one in which Power's interests and those of society have reached an accommodation through getting used to each other.

But neither logic nor experience permits us to say that instinctive feeling can ever operate so as to make this accommodation complete. Here is the sunken reef on which have foundered all those doctrines both of ancient and modern times which taught that complete egoism could be the foundation for complete altruism. If it is true—what has never been strictly proven—that a man's maximum good results from thinking only of the good of others, it is a matter of observation that in practice he is incapable of inducing his egoism to the distant point at which these fruitful consequences begin.

In the case of even the most legitimate rulers, egoism continues to occupy a half-way house; it still gives out anti-social manifestations in sufficient quantities to render, should they be emphasized, the egoistical instinct suspect to the public, and make them unmindful of the services to society which, incontestably, egoism provides. The altruism for which the public calls is not a subconscious by-product but a conscious principle of government.

But as soon as Power is conceived as being exclusively the agent of the common good, it must form a clear picture for itself of what this common good is. While Power was egoist, the vital necessity under which it lay of reaching every day a daily accommodation with society, itself sufficed to form in it pictures of public requirements which, though confused, were born of actual contacts. But as soon as Power, under the spur of altruism, has a vision of the entire community and what medicine it needs, the inadequacy of the human intelligence to such a task appears in its fullness. What the judgment pronounces then shows itself a blinder guide than what the senses indicate—to put it another way, touch is superior to vision.

It is a noteworthy fact that all the greatest political mistakes stem from defective appraisals of the common good—mistakes from which egoism, had it been called into consultation, would have warned Power off. Take, for example, the revocation of the Edict of Nantes. Louis XIV was far too well aware of the value of the eminent services rendered to his authority by the clever mechanics who were his subjects,[5] the admission

5. It may be seen, either in the second and third chapters of my elementary course of economic history, *L'Économie mondiale au vingtième siècle*, or in my short study, *L'Or au temps de Charles Quint et de Philippe II*, that in the sixteenth and seventeenth centuries monarchy looked on an economic advance almost exclusively as a contribution to military power.

of talented persons into France had been pursued as a policy by the monarchy for too long and with results which were too fruitful,[6] for the King not to have taken into account the enormous disadvantages to himself of a step which would have the effect of throwing the best French citizens into the arms of the Dutch enemies and the English rivals of France. If, notwithstanding this, he took so disastrous a decision, it was through the impulsion of a false conception of the common good and of his duty as ruler. In his funeral oration Massillon expressly says so: "You specious reasons of policy, in vain you presented to Louis the timid counsels of human wisdom: the body of the monarchy enfeebled by the emigration of so many citizens, the course of commerce retarded either by the loss of their labour or the secret removal of their wealth, neighbouring nations becoming the protectors of heresy and ready to fly to arms in its defence. Dangers but strengthened his zeal. . . !"[7]

If it is yet possible to stand sufficiently away from the all-engulfing catastrophe of our own time, so as to pass a historical judgment on it, it seems to furnish an analogous instance. A healthy egoism would, in the absence of other motives, have dissuaded an ambitious Power from racial persecutions which were bound, as it knew, to excite universal indignation, and which, as it admitted itself, helped to throw into the scale of its enemies the immense weight of a nation which disposed of unlimited resources. Have we not here, too, a case in which an arbitrary vision of what society ought to be has hurled the Power seeing it into the crudest blunders—blunders from which the instinct of self-preservation would have saved it?

It is not true to say that Power redeems its egoism by pursuing ends which it considers social; for society is a complex structure, and, when it comes to ways of improving it, bogus science and ideological passion are blind and cruel guides—and not a whit less cruel for the people itself being privy to the errors committed.

6. Cf. the monumental labours of Boissonnade, *Le Socialisme d'état en France au temps des Valois et Colbert*.

7. Massillon, "Oraison funèbre de Louis XIV," *Œuvres* (ed. Lyon: 1801) Vol. II, p. 568. [Nothing in the career of Massillon (1663–1742), who in his day rivalled Bossuet as a preacher, suggests that there was the faintest tinge of irony in this passage—even though a man is no more on oath in a funeral oration than in a lapidary inscription! The funeral oration on Louis XIV is best remembered for its opening sentence: *"Dieu seul est grand."* D. W. Brogan, in his review of this book, gives some reasons for doubting whether Louis was in fact as single-minded as Massillon made out.]

Power, egoist though it is, can render immense services to society; it can also do untold harm in its attempts to render them. But only by intellectual analysis can we distinguish in it the two strands which the course of its actual life makes inextricable.

The egoism which gives it life and the ideal which it claims to be realizing are inseparable features of it, as the personalities of the great giants of Power show; they can no longer tell whether it is themselves or their peoples that inebriate them—they take everything and believe that they are giving it.

In the successive stages of Power's existence the joint action of these two characteristics serves to inflate it: the one gives it cash, the other tenacity.

### 3. The Egoistical Stimulus of Growth

To the extent that command is a species of egoism it tends naturally to grow.

Man, says Rousseau, is a limited creature,

> his life is short, his pleasures know bounds, his capacity for enjoyment is always static, and it is no good his raising himself in his own imagination, for he continues to be small. The State,[8] on the contrary, being an artificial body, knows no fixed bounds; the greatness which belongs to it is unlimited, and can always be increased by itself.[9]

And the egoisms which shape it and give it life expand its conquests.

The spirit of conquest has had both its shocked accusers and its apologists; the latter praise it for its work of consolidation and reconsolidation of small political entities—a work which has resulted in the creation of vast formations which are, to their minds, the necessary condition of a more perfect division of labour, of more efficient social cooperation and, in short, of an advance of civilization.[10]

The outward growth of Power has excited much comment, the inward growth astonishingly little. Insufficient attention has been given to the

8. Giving it the sense of people, nation, political formation.

9. Cf. the fragment entitled "Que la guerre nait de l'état social," in an appendix (p. 309) to the Dreyfus-Brissac edition of *Du Contrat social* (Paris: 1896).

10. Spencer, *Principles of Sociology*, Vol. III, paras. 438, 451, 481.

fact that any Power whatsoever looks on the mass it rules as an investment from which it can draw the resources needed by it for its purposes, or as a block of stone to be fashioned as it sees fit. To resume the likening of a nation to an individual, but without forgetting that it is really only the rulers who so look at it, the head aims continually at pressing more services from the body, and the brain at increasing its conscious control of the limbs. This characteristic of Power shows itself in concrete ways: in the increased budgets of which it disposes, and in the spawning of regulations which it imposes and of officials who see to their execution. Limiting ourselves to outward signs, have we ever seen a Power which, unlike the others, was not impelled by an inner urge to grow? That is not to say that every Power has been equally successful, or that the steady growth of expenditure, of legislation, and of officialdom is due to nothing but the impulse of Power. My point is that this impulse is immanent in every Power whatsoever.

The impulse is nourished by all the egoisms, great or small, noble or sordid, which, taken together, make up the egoism of Power. The perspectives which open before the great man are invisible to Tom and Dick as they come and go on their daily tasks. From them he must draw, whether by permission or constraint matters not, the means he has need of. The ruler of poor quality dreams no such exalted dreams: but he lets all the nuts in the machine go loose, and from their slackening will come the uncontested need for new levies and a further supply of public servants. At the bottom of the governmental ladder, the official, silently and inperceptibly, breeds the official, and brings his cousins and dependants into the offices of state.

The history of the West, from the time of Europe's fragmentation into sovereign states, shows us an almost uninterrupted advance in the growth of governmental Power. The only way of failing to see it is to fix exclusive attention on the forms which Power takes: a picture of pure fantasy is then formed, in which monarchs appear as masters to whose exactions there are no bounds, to be succeeded by representative governments whose resources are proportionate to their authority, until in the end democracy succeeds and receives from a consenting people only what it chooses to give to a Power which is its servant.

These are imponderables. But there are also ponderables—the dimensions of armies, the weight of taxation, the number of officials. The measurable scale of these implements provides an exact index of the growth of Power. Begin at the reign of Philip Augustus.[11] Without taxation to maintain him, the king lives, like other landlords, off his own estate. Without an army at his command, he keeps a meagre bodyguard who feed at his own table. Without officials, he depends for the discharge of public business on ecclesiastics whom he employs and on servants whom he appoints. Even his public treasure, as well as his private fortune, has an ecclesiastical home and is left in the hands of the monks who act as his bankers. Though I am his subject, my path never crosses that of this head squire; he demands no tax from me, claims from me no military service, and passes no law which can possibly affect my life.

By the end of the reign of Louis XIV, what a change is here for my countrymen! After a struggle lasting for centuries, the people has been brought to fill the royal coffers at regular intervals. The monarch maintains out of his revenues a standing army of two hundred thousand men. His intendants make him obeyed in every province, and his police harry the malcontents. He gives out laws and sets his dragoons at those who do not worship God in what he considers the right way; an enormous army of officials animates and directs the nation. Power has imposed its will. It is now no longer one small dot in society but a great stain at the centre of it, a network of lines which run right through it.

An infliction, you say? Is not the revolution which overthrows the king going to pull down his structure, attack his apparatus of command, which it will partly at any rate destroy, and reduce the taxation paid by the people? By no means; instead it will introduce the conscription which the monarchy long desired but never had the strength to realize. True it is that Calonne's budgets will never be seen again; but the reason simply is that they will be doubled under Napoleon and trebled under the Restoration. The intendant will have gone, but the prefect will have taken his place. And so the distension grows. From one regime to another, always more soldiers, more taxes, more laws, more officials.

I am not saying that the impulsion of Power is the only operative cause of all this; I do say that none can read history without being continuously conscious of its presence. Sometimes the impulsion relaxes, as when Charles V, on his death-bed, renounced all the taxes which he had with

11. Known to us through the splendid researches of F. Lot and R. Fawtier in *Le premier budget de la monarchie française 1202–1203*. [Philip Augustus was King of France from 1180 to 1223.]

so much trouble imposed and maintained, and which had made possible the victories of his reign. Almost at once, however, they were reimposed, though the doing of it required much bloodshed.[12]

Pauses there are, even retreats, but these are but incidents in the progress through the centuries of Power's distension. It is true, no doubt, that Power could not make this progress but for the very real services which it renders and under cover of the hopes aroused by its displays of the altruistic side of its nature.

### 4. The Social Justifications for Power's Growth

When Power makes a demand for resources for itself, it quickly wears down the complacence of the subjects. A thirteenth-century king might crave a grant for dressing his eldest son, amid seemly rejoicings, in knight's armour. But if too soon after he bethought him to giving his daughter in marriage and asked the provision of a suitable dowry, he would meet with a very bad reception.

To raise contributions, Power must invoke the public interest. It was in this way that the Hundred Years' War, by multiplying the occasions on which the monarchy was forced to request the cooperation of the people, accustomed them in the end, after a long succession of occasional levies, to a permanent tax, an outcome which outlived the reasons for it.

It was in this way, too, that the Revolutionary Wars provided the justification for conscription, even though the files of 1789 disclosed a unanimous hostility to its feeble beginnings under the monarchy. Conscription achieved fixation. And so it is that times of danger, when Power takes action for the general safety, are worth much to it in accretions to its armoury; and these, when the crisis has passed, it keeps.

It has, moreover, long been a matter of observation that the egoism of Power profits by public insecurity:

> War [exclaimed Omer Talon] is a monster whom there is a conspiracy not to throttle, so that it may continue always as the opportunity of those who abuse the royal authority, enabling them to devour such property as is still left in private hands.

It is impossible to exaggerate the part played by war in the distension of Power; but war is not the only set of circumstances in which it can invoke the public interest to strengthen its grip on the nation. Its role is

12. Cf. Léon Mirot, *Les insurrections urbaines*.

not merely that of defender of its subjects against other Powers which are like unto itself; it claims also to protect them against forces which are *different in kind.*

The mistake of not seeing in society more than the one Power, i.e. the governmental or public authority, has an astonishingly wide vogue. Whereas in fact the governmental is but one of the authorities present in society; there exist alongside it a whole host of others, which are at once its collaborators, in that they help it in securing social order, and its rivals, in that, like it, they claim men's obedience and inveigle them into their service.

These non-governmental authorities, to which we give the name *social authorities,* are no more blessed with an angelic nature than is Power itself. If they all were so blessed, there could be, depend on it, nothing but perfect harmony and cooperation between them. But it is not so: however altruistic one of these authorities, such as the paternal or the ecclesiastical, is intended by nature to be, human nature imparts to it a measure of egoism: it tends to make itself its end. Whereas, conversely, an authority which is by nature egoist, such as the employer's or the feudal lord's, is sobered by time, and develops by unequal stages the spirit of protection and kindness. Every authority is, by the law of its nature, essentially dualist. Being ambitious, each separate authority tends to grow; being egoistical, to consult only its own immediate interest; being jealous, to pare down the role of the other authorities. There thus ensues an incessant strife of authorities. And this strife provides the state with its main chance.

The growth of its authority strikes private individuals as being not so much a continual encroachment on their liberty as an attempt to put down the various petty tyrannies to which they have been subjected. It looks as though the advance of the state is a means to the advance of the individual.

Here is the main reason for the endless complicity of subjects in the designs of Power; it is the true secret of Power's expansion.

### 5. *Power as the Repository of Human Hopes*

Mankind passionately desires to escape the dooms of his destiny and his condition, and this wish of his is, when transformed into action, the origin of all progress. But it is also the basis of that vulgar[13] form of

---

13. In contrast to the mystical prayer which asks for strength to accept.

prayer which asks the intervention of the invisible powers in our private affairs.

Is it not natural that prayers of this kind, directed as they are to practical ends, should be addressed also to a visible authority, which is no less powerful to destroy the author of our oppression or of the wrong done us, no less rich for the ample fulfilment of all our wishes, and no less sovereign for the transformation of our entire lives?

The sceptre is, as it were, a magic wand which can work miracles for us: *"Si le roi voulait . . ."* But these miracles can only come about in so far as Power is not kept within the leading-strings of a strict rule of law. If it lacks the ability to temper justice with expediency and to grant boons unexpectedly, its fairy enchantments quickly fade. Hence it is that institutions of moderate tempo become, in Lamartine's vigorous phrase, "a bore."

Though the hurtfulness of arbitrary Power be proved and reproved a thousand times, arbitrary Power will always start up anew. To shake it off, men must grow tired of paying too dearly for a chance, which is too small, of the arbitrary ruler playing their game, just as we weary of a lottery in which we have gone on losing over a long time. But arbitrary Power is for ever lifting its head again; it returns to life by means of its promises, the irresistible attraction of which paves its way for it. The wider the gap between man's awakened desires and the realities of his existence, the more clamorous are the passions which summon and fetch him the magician.

Nor is Power the repository only of egoistical hopes; it is that of altruistic or, more accurately, socialist hopes as well. That is a miserable philosophy which explains all human behaviour by the simple motive of egoistical interest. It is given the lie both by the unceasing formation in speculative brains of visions of a better order and by the influence of these visions on men who have nothing personally to gain by the change. Any account of the various social transformations which neglected the determining influence of these visions would be an entirely false one. Yet, they too, no less than the grossest, most muddled expectations, are grist to Power's mill.

In the realm of nature there is nothing able to satisfy the human spirit's primitive passions. In love with his own experiments, with the simple relationships and direct causations his brain can grasp, and with the artless plans which he is wise enough to construct, man wishes that the whole created world may show itself built not only with the same instruments as he possesses but also by the same turns of skill as he has mastered.

Rejoicing as he does in all that can be brought to uniformity, he is for ever being disconcerted by the infinite variety which nature herself seems to prefer, as instanced by the chemical structure of organic bodies.

It is an agreeable game, imagining how man, if he had the power, would reconstruct the universe—the simple and uniform lines on which he would do it. He has not that power, but he has, or thinks he has, the power of reconstructing the social order. This is a sphere in which he reckons that the laws of nature do not run for him,[14] and there he tries to plant the simplicity which is his ruling passion and which he mistakes for perfection.

So soon as an intellectual imagines a simple order of things, he is serving the growth of Power. For the existing order, here as everywhere, is complex and rests on a whole mass of supports, authorities, sentiments, and adjustments of the most varied kind. If it is sought to make one spring do the work of so many, how strong must be the force of its recoil; or if one pillar must support henceforward what many supported, it must be of the stoutest! Only Power can be that spring or that pillar— and what a Power it must be! Simply because speculative thought tends to neglect the usefulness of a crowd of secondary factors which make for order, it leads inevitably to the reinforcement of the central authority, and never more surely than when it is unsettling every kind of authority, the central included; for authority there must be, and when it rises again it is, inevitably, in the most concentrated form open to it.[15]

### 6. Thought and Power, the Philosopher and the Tyrant

Much misapprehension exists as to the true relations between thought and Power. Thought has only to be the habitual critic of the existing

---

14. Comte observes well of this thing we call "evil," that, while not daring to hope to eliminate it from the natural world, we entertain every hope of eliminating it from the social world: "By reason of its greater complexity, the political world cannot fail of being worse regulated than the astronomical, physical, chemical or biological worlds. Why is it then that we are always ready to rise up in indignation against the radical imperfections of the lot of man under the first heading, but take all the others with calmness and resignation, even though they are not a whit less marked or shocking? The reason for this strange contrast must, I think, primarily be that up till now positive philosophy has been able to develop our innermost feelings as regards the laws of Nature only as regards the very simplest phenomena whose study was relatively easy and had to be completed first." *Cours de Philosophie positive* (1839) Vol. IV, pp. 152–153.

15. As Tocqueville truly observed in the case of the Revolution, a line of thought which criticizes as irrational, treats as inconsiderable, and helps to overthrow not only political authority but also the social and spiritual authorities making for order, prepares *ipso facto*

order and established authority for her passion for order and authority as such to be completely overlooked.

Rich in ideas of the beautiful, the harmonious, and the just, thought is bruised and revolted by all social reality. Here, it says, are cities spread out at random giving equal offence both to the eye and to the nostril; within them is a swarm of ugly, stupid, and unhappy beings; here stupidity darkens counsel, and stingy greed and squalid evil make holiday; are they to be found here, the royal homes of nature's king who has been made the reflex of the divine intelligence? How, from the depths of this sewer, can thought fail to evoke an ideal city, in which the severe beauty of the citizens would match the majestical quality of the buildings? It was in the slums of Naples that Campanella,[16] the Dominican, had his dream of a City of the Sun, which should carry on its walls no lascivious scrawlings, but geometrical figures and pictures of the animals and plants catalogued by science and of the instruments created by human ingenuity; its life to be presided over by the Supreme Metaphysician.

In this way, under the stimulus of the "divine tenderness which feels both loathing and love, which transforms and raises what it loves,"[17] the speculative man builds his perfect society, his Republic, his Utopia, whence all disorder and injustice have been banished.

Take a look, however, at the way in which the master builders of Paradises, the Platos, the Mores, the Campanellas, set about it. They get rid of the clashes by getting rid of the differences:

> Let the citizens never know [said Plato] and let them never desire to learn what it is to act independently and not in concert, and let them never form

the ultimate triumph of political authority, which is bound to rise again, over the social and spiritual authorities, which are under no such natural necessity. Hence political authority grows, unencumbered by checks and balances.

"The central edifice was found in ruins and restored; and, as at the very time that it was rising again, everything that had in former days served to check it remained in ruins, there was seen to rise suddenly from the entrails of a nation which had just overthrown royalty a power wider, more specific, more absolute than had been exercised by any king." *De la Démocratie en Amérique,* Vol. III, pp. 308–09.

16. [Campanella, Tomaso (1568–1639), a Dominican monk, who was kept in prison at Naples for twenty-seven years by the Spanish authorities for supposed complicity in a political conspiracy. His *Civitas Solis,* the work here referred to, was written in prison and produced in 1623. It is a cold and abstract variant of More's *Utopia,* with the same Platonic background.]

17. Nietzsche, *The Will to Power* (Fr. ed.) Vol. II, p. 283.

the habit of so acting; rather, let them all advance in step towards the same objects and let them have always and in everything but one common way of life. . . .[18]

Property is held in common: the magistrates will give to each citizen his share of what he needs. Clothing is uniform, meals are taken in common, lodging is in common, and Campanella shows us the magistrates distributing the inhabitants, for periods of six months, among the various dormitories, and having the name of each put up over each bed. The magistrates assign to each his task, and their consent, revocable at any time, is necessary to any course of studies. More divides up the lives of his Utopians between work in the fields and professional work in the cities, the latter, unless the magistrates decide otherwise, to be for each man what his father did before him. No one might leave his house without a permit specifying the date of his return. And Plato was for prohibiting all foreign travel, except on account of the public service: he imposed on the citizens on their return the duty of expounding to the rising generation how vastly inferior to their own were the institutions of other lands.

Such are the rules of the ideal republics dreamed of by the philosophers, the vision of which could bring enchantment to our ancestors at a time when they were obvious fantasies and in no danger of being realized. We in our time, as the storm-clouds draw nearer, look more closely at them; we look for liberty there and do not find it. These dreams are, one and all, of tyrannies, of straiter, heavier, more oppressive tyrannies than any that history has yet shown us. In all of them, order is secured at the price of universal registration and wholesale regimentation.

That is where thought leads us with no bit and bridle! And the imaginings are most revealing as to its natural bent. Thought delights in order, because thought is intelligence; and it conceives of order as simple, because thought is human. Whenever it strives to realize order, it displays the sombre savagery of a Savonarola or a Calvin; more often, however, it seeks and summons to its aid the man of action, its temporal arm: we see Plato, for instance, expecting his laws to be enforced by the tyrant of Syracuse.

Is that a paradox, the association of the philosopher with the tyrant? By no means. Authority can never be too despotic for the speculative

18. Plato, *The Laws,* Book XII.

man, so long as he deludes himself that its arbitrary force will further his plans. Proof of this is the attraction, seen time after time, which Russian despotism has had for the intellectuals. The approach of Auguste Comte to Czar Nicholas is but a repetition of Diderot's waiting for Catherine the Great to promulgate by ukase the Encyclopaedist dogmas.[19] Disillusioned with the weapon proper to itself, persuasion, the intelligence admires those instruments of Power which are swifter in action, and Voltaire found it in him to admire Catherine's ability "to make fifty thousand men march into Poland to establish there toleration and liberty of conscience."[20] And so the credulous tribe of philosophers works in Power's behalf, vaunting its merits right up to the point at which Power disillusions it; whereupon, it is true, it breaks into cursings, but still it serves the cause of Power in general, by placing its hopes in a radical and systematic application of its principles, being a thing which only a capacious Power can achieve.

Benjamin Constant[21] mocked with good reason at the unphilosophical preference of the learned for authoritarian methods:

> Every great development of the unlawful use of force, every recourse to illegal measures in times of crisis, has been, from one century to another, related with respect and described with complacence. The author, sitting peacefully at his desk, looses off arbitrary power in all directions and tries to make his style reflect the dashing quality which he approves in measures; he

19. [In a broadcast review of this book, Mr. Max Beloff compared the attraction of Catherine for Voltaire and Diderot with that of Stalin for the Webbs.]

20. This astounding letter in which Voltaire applauded the oppression of Poland is well known: "There is a woman who is getting herself a great reputation: it is the Semiramis of the North who is making fifty thousand men march into Poland to establish there toleration and liberty of conscience. It is a unique event in the history of the world, and will, I warrant you, go far. I am proud of being somewhat in her good graces: I am her challenger as regards and against everybody. I am well aware that a few trifling offences are imputed to her on the subject of her husband [whom she caused to be murdered], but those are family matters in which I do not concern myself; and besides it is not a bad thing to have a fault to put right, because it makes necessary great efforts to drive the public into esteem and admiration; and anyhow her wretch of a husband would never have done any of the great things which my Catherine does every day." Letter to Mme du Deffand, 18th May, 1767. *Œuvres*, Vol. XLV, pp. 267–68.

21. [Constant de Rebecq, Henri Benjamin (1767–1830), French writer and politician, from whose writings there are many citations in this book. A consistent advocate of Liberal principles and freedom of the press, and an intimate of Mme de Staël. His political writings, all short and pithy, are collected in two volumes entitled *Cours de politique constitutionelle*.]

sees himself, just for a moment, dressed in authority by reason of his praising its abuses; he warms his speculative life at the fire of all the demonstrations of force and power which serve to decorate his periods; in this way he finds a sort of pleasure in Authority; he repeats at the top of his voice the fine phrases—safety of the people, supreme law, public interest; he is lost in admiration of his own profundity and stands amazed at his own energy. Poor fool! His words are addressed to men who ask nothing better than to hear them, and who, having heard, will take the first opportunity of trying his theory out on him.[22]

Thought, dreaming of an order which is at once too simple and too rigid, seeking to realize it too quickly by measures which are too drastic and too radical, is in a perpetual conspiracy on Power's behalf: even in giving battle to the actual incumbents of authority, it is still working for authority's enlargement. For it puts into society's head visions which cannot take concrete shape but by an immense effort in the opposite direction to that of the natural course of things—an effort of which only Power, and a big one at that, is capable. So that in sum thought furnishes Power with quite the most effective justification for its growth.

As a self-proclaimed egoist, Power encounters the resistance of all the particular social interests with which it must have dealings. But let it call itself altruistic and give itself out for the executant of an ideal, and it will acquire such an ascendancy over every concrete interest as will enable it to sacrifice them to the fulfilment of its mission and crush every obstruction to its triumphal march.

22. Benjamin Constant, "De l'Esprit de conquête et d'usurpation." Œuvres, Vol. I, p. 249.

# VIII.

~

# *Of Political Rivalry*[1]

HISTORY IS THE REGISTER OF THE STRIFE of authorities. Always and everywhere man takes possession of man to bend him to his will and adapt him to his designs; so that society is seen to be a galaxy of authorities which arise, grow, and fight each other.

Between authorities which are different in kind, as is political authority from that of either the family or the squire or the priest, collaboration and conflict go on simultaneously. Between authorities which are similar in kind and unlimited in their scope,[2] the natural state of things is war. In the eyes of a man who lives exclusively in his own time, which may by happy chance have been a peaceful one, war seems but an accident; but to him who contemplates the unfolding of the ages war presents itself as an activity of states which pertains to their essence.

Look at the map of Europe, not in the static form in which the political geography of any given period presents it, but rather as the moving picture which has been showing down the centuries. Observe how the parts coloured pink or blue or yellow, signifying the state to which each belongs, now spread out at the expense of one or more of the others, and now contract under neighbourly compression. Now a tentacle is put out towards the sea, now alignment is formed along a river, or a mountain

1. [This chapter appeared in January 1943, in the review *Suisse contemporaine.*]

2. "The State," said Rousseau, "being an artificial body, has no predetermined limit . . . the inequality of man has had limits set it by Nature, but that of societies may grow unceasingly until one of them absorbs all the others."

150

is taken in the stride, or a foreign body is engulfed and absorbed. At long last the particular octopus loses its vitality; a day arrives when it becomes the prey of another's appetite, and disappears.

The picture evoked by these shifting colours is that of the crawling of amoebas observed under the microscope. That, heaven help us! is history.

## 1. Is War Alien to Modern Times?

Before the nineteenth century this sort of cannibalism was the principal subject matter of historical studies. From that time on our learned men have looked elsewhere. They thought, not without reason, that in modern times the spirit of conquest pertains, never to peoples, but only to their rulers; and they were rash enough to assume that the course of political evolution was that of the subordination of rulers to their peoples. War, therefore, was a thing of the past, the themes of the present were quite other, of man throwing off the yoke of social despotisms and, with the help of science, skill, and combination, making himself master of the earth's resources.

Bringing this modern eye to bear on the centuries that had passed, it seemed to man as if the wars which had given lustre to monarchs and left as their legacy to students the names of innumerable battles were but so many adventitious happenings which had cut across the main and essential lines of human development.

The real history was much more truly this development than the tale of military escapades! For the development gave a picture of a continuous advance in one direction—the integrated exploitation of the world's resources for the benefit of man in association with his fellows.

This was the end to which the peoples of the world, now the masters of their fate and the clear-eyed graduates of education, would march henceforward in conscious unison. Each separate Power, being now the servant of its nation, would press on this advance. If by any chance there were any further clash of arms, it could but be as by a deplorable collision between the cars driven by the various states; the fault was that of inexpert drivers or—but this would be quite exceptional!—of crazy and morbid ambitions.

But is the will to aggrandizement nothing more than an aberration of rulers? If it is so, how is it that the rulers most covetous of territory have also been the most astute to organize their peoples? Of such were Peter the Great, Frederick II, Napoleon, Bismarck—perhaps we must add the name of Stalin. Can it be doubted that the genius of statesmanship proves itself both in expansion and in administration, and that Power administers to conquer and conquers to administer? The instinct of growth is proper to Power; it is a part of its essence and does not change with its changing forms.

For Power is still command, with the passions proper to command, of which the first is to expand the area which is beneath its rule. Maybe this passion will lie dormant for decades, but its awakening is in the order of things. For like attracts like: authority attracts the authoritarian, and empire the imperious.

The quality of conquest is as much an attribute of Power as is infection of the bacillus; both have their periods of torpor, from which they awake to renewed vigour. After an interval of calm, the modern tyrannies were to find to their hand such resources as had been beyond the hopes of their ancient models, just as the sleeper in Wells' tale found when he awoke that, while he was asleep, his wealth had marvellously multiplied.

At the very time when, as it was claimed, violence had been banished from history, it was making its presence felt as much as ever. But this was happening in distant parts, where savage or technically backward peoples were being incorporated cheaply. The splashes of colour denoting the various states hardly changed in Europe but spread out overseas, and were soon confronting each other on fresh continents, multiplying in the process their frontiers, their disputes, and in the end their battlefields.

The wealth amassed by private persons was building up for the state immense resources for war. Metallurgical factories were going up which could, when the time came, be used for the construction of enormous guns. Savings were pouring into the banks which would defray the expenses of the war. Why was Germany developing production in the Briey basin, and England smiling at the grip of her great companies on the world's oil fields, and Russia covering herself with a network of railways? These activities all looked peaceful enough, but were in reality a process of accumulating trump cards to play in the unceasing game of power.

Lastly, the democratic advance itself put arms in the armouries of governments. Powers which are seen by all to be strangers to the peoples they rule cannot sweep them along into making really great sacrifices; where, on the other hand, they are intimately linked to their peoples, they can get more out of them, as was shown by the astonishing amount of force put at the disposal of successive authorities by Revolutionary and

Imperial France, the reason being that she conceived these authorities to be bone of her bone.

The upshot is that those very phenomena which seemed to give promise of an era of perpetual peace[3] were in fact building up for the various Powers material and psychological munitions of war, such as far surpassed in intensity and scale anything seen before.

## 2. A Self-Militarizing Civilization

Was it not conformable, you say, with the laws of history that a great society, such as is the Western World of our day, forming in itself a slice of civilization, should become demilitarized as its development proceeded? Had not this phenomenon been seen to happen in the Roman world? The longer this civilization lasted, the less inclined did its members become to take up arms. The military calling, which had been in early days the natural vocation of every adult man—as among all the primitive peoples, such as the Iroquois, the Zulus, the Abyssinians, it is seen to be—became in the end a specialized and discredited profession.

This process of progressive demilitarization showed itself in the number of Roman effectives available. The still uncouth City which Hannibal came over to attack numbered a mere million men at the time that it put in the field against him at Cannae an army of more than 85,000 men. But when its armies clashed at Pharsalia, the Republic, though by then it was spread out over the whole of the Mediterranean basin, could not put in the field more than 65,000 men in all. When Tiberius strained every nerve to avenge the legions of Varus, he could send the future Germanicus but 50,000 men. Marcus Aurelius seems to have had not many more in his attempt to finish off the secular quarrel with the Parthians. When Julian checked the Alemanni near Strasbourg, he had 13,000 men, and Belisarius was given 11,000 by Justinian to win back Italy from the Goths.[4]

Such is the natural evolution of a people which is rising in the scale of civilization. It is also the explanation of that people's culminating impotence in the face of the invasions of the Goths and Vandals, who were

3. [It was remarked by Leibniz that the only place in which the words *pax perpetua* had any relevance was a cemetery.]

4. Figures taken from the well-known treatise of Hans Delbrück: *Geschichte des Kriegskunst*, 4 vols., 1900–1920.

but small nations in arms, numbering but a few tens of thousands of men; the smallest province in the Empire, had its inhabitants still been trained to arms, could have wiped them out. Assuredly, Alaric could have no more taken the Rome of old than Genseric the Carthage of old.

The path followed by our own civilization is in the opposite direction; it is leading it to a catastrophe just as total but of quite a different kind.

At Poitiers, which was the decisive battle of the fourteenth century, about 50,000 men were engaged, and about the same number fought at Marignan. Only very few more, some 65,000 it is said, fought at Nordlingen, the decisive battle of the Thirty Years' War. But come to Malplaquet in 1709 and Leipzig in 1813: the figures there are 200,000 and 450,000 respectively.

In our time we have improved on that. The 1914 war killed or mutilated five times as many men as were under arms in Europe at the end of the Napoleonic Wars.[5] And in this present war (1939–1945) there is no counting the people involved. We are ending up where the savages began.

### 3. The Law of Political Rivalry

Why is it that we are retreating from civilization instead of advancing towards it like the Romans?

One difference between their world and ours leaps to the mind: theirs was monist, ours is pluralist. In its human content ours is perhaps less diversified than the Roman, but it is split up among several governments, each one of which, as Rousseau says, "feels itself weak as long as there are stronger ones than itself; its safety and preservation demand that it make itself stronger than its neighbours."

Rousseau continues:

> As its size is purely relative, the body politic must institute comparisons to get to know itself; it is dependent on what is around it and it must take an interest in everything that goes on there. It would be useless for it to try to stay as it is and keep within its own shell; it becomes weak or strong according as its neighbour expands or contracts, grows stronger or weaker.

This natural jealousy between Powers has brought to birth one rule which is familiar enough—states pay dearly if they forget it even

5. According to the Abbé de Pradt there were 3,000,000 men under arms in 1813–14. The war of 1914–18 killed 8,000,000 and mutilated 6,000,000, according to *L'Enquête sur la production,* by Edgar Milhaud (Geneva: 1920 and following years).

momentarily: that every annexation of territory by one Power, by increasing its sources of supply, compels each of the others to look about for a like extension with a view to redressing the balance.

There is, however, another way of growing stronger which is much more to be feared than any acquisition of territory: that is the advance made by any one Power in exploiting the natural resources of its own national domain. If it increases the draft which it makes on the strength and wealth of its people and contrives to get this increase accepted, it then changes the relationship between its own sinews of war and those of its neighbours; it becomes, if its capital is small, the equal of great Powers, and if it is large it brings hegemony within its reach.

If in the time of Gustavus Adolphus, Sweden's place in the world of politics was out of all proportion to the country's importance, the reason was that this great king had made the activities of the nation subservient to his designs, to an extent never before seen. Prussia, too, in the time of Frederick II, could not have kept at bay a coalition of three great monarchies, each one of which could have obliterated her, but for the similar intensive exploitation of her capabilities. And, to conclude, France at the time of the Revolution gained in a single bound frontiers which Louis XIV had been unable to reach, for the reason that the more total Power then in control had drawn more deeply on the national resources.

Burke, writing in 1795, understood this well:

> The State [France] is all in all. Everything is referred to the production of force. It is military in its principle, in its maxims, in its spirit and in all its movements. ... Were France but half of what it is in population, in compactness, in applicability of its force, it would be too strong for most of the States of Europe, constituted as they are, and proceeding as they proceed.[6]

Every encroachment by Power on society, whether it has been made with a view to war or for some totally different purpose, gives that Power an advantage in war.[7] Evidence of this is supplied by the two German

6. *Letters on a Regicide Peace* (Letter II).

7. It is no use bringing up against me the cliché about the despotic power of Xerxes going down before the liberty of the Athenians. When I refer here to a larger, more total Power, I mean a Power which demands and obtains relatively more from its people. It is certain that in this respect the Power in the Greek cities over the citizens was far in excess of that of the Great King over his subjects. For instance, the Ionian cities which were subjects of the Persian monarch had only to pay him a small tribute which was often remitted them; apart from that they were self-governing. I am not here concerned to discuss an Asiatic despotism, which took very little from its subjects, but the modern type of

invasions of France, made within a quarter of a century of each other. The debacle of 1940, which took the place of the miracle of the Marne in 1914, was probably the result less of the enfeeblement of France than of the accretion of German strength brought about by total mobilization of her energies. Further evidence of it is supplied by the very different destinies awaiting the Russian armies in the two wars, a difference which was due entirely to the conquests wrought in the interval by the Power inside that vast domain.

The lesson is that no state can remain indifferent to another state's wresting from its people more of their rights. It must make a corresponding draft on its own people's rights, or else pay dearly for its neglect to put itself on a level. So France had already lost the war of 1870 because, through failure to impose military conscription as her neighbour had done, she could only put in the field against the Prussians armies which were much inferior in numbers.

The most pressing and best known aspect of the phenomenon is the race in armaments. But the race in armaments is but the shadow and the reflex of a much more serious development—the race in totalitarianisms. A Power which interferes with its people only in certain respects cannot increase its warlike potential beyond certain limits. To pass them, it must revolutionize those respects and give itself fresh prerogatives.

### 4. Advance of Power, Advance of War
### Advance of War, Advance of Power

Thus it happens that the great steps forward in the process of militarization are linked up, whether as effect or cause, with the great steps forward of Power.

Sometimes the reason is that a political revolution suddenly strengthens Power and so makes possible a scale of armaments which was previously impossible. That happened when Cromwell built up without difficulty a naval power for England which was beyond the dreams of Charles I; or when the French Revolution instituted conscription—a thing which the servants of the monarchy would not have dared propose.

Sometimes the need to attain military equality with a formidable rival

---

despotism which takes from them immense quantities—and the more efficiently the more it keeps away from the haughty externals of despotism of the Asiatic type.

can be invoked to justify an advance of Power, as in France in Charles VII's[8] time, or in the United States today.

We see, then, that, as every advance of Power is useful for war, so war is useful for the advance of Power; war is like a sheep-dog harrying the laggard Powers to catch up their smarter fellows in the totalitarian race.

This intimate tie between war and Power is a constant feature of European history. Each state which has in its turn exercised political hegemony got itself the wherewithal by subjugating its people more completely than its rivals could subjugate theirs. And to resist absorption by their predecessors in hegemony, the other Powers of the continent were bound to get on a level with them.

If a feudal monarchy succeeded in getting financial aids from its vassals at more and more frequent intervals and could thus increase the number of mercenaries in its employ, the others had to copy it. If in the end these aids were consolidated into a permanent tax for maintaining a standing army, still the movement had to be followed, for, as Adam Smith remarks:

> Once the system of having a standing army had been adopted by one civilized nation, all its neighbours had to introduce it; security reasons made it inevitable, for the old militias were quite incapable of resisting an army of that kind.

But once the monarchy could rest on a standing army, it was in the way to impose taxation arbitrarily—in other words, to make itself absolute. And from that time it must also battle its way towards military conscription, of the menace of which Montesquieu was already conscious.

Military conscription, towards which the monarchies were making more or less timid advances, was inaugurated by Revolutionary France. And to it she owed her victories, most of which were won by overwhelming superiority of numbers. Right up to 1809, the French armies retained this superiority in all their battles. Gneisenau[9] formulated the only possible answer: "The Revolution has deployed in its entirety the national strength of the French people. . . . The other European States must draw on the same reserves with a view to restoring the ancient balance of Europe."

Such being the way in which political rivalry works, attempts at the

8. [Charles VII, King of France from 1422 to 1461. Joan of Arc was one of his subjects. He created a standing army supported by a permanent tax.]

9. [Gneisenau (1760–1831), one of the Prussian generals of the War of Liberation. Chief of Blücher's staff at Waterloo.]

limitation of armaments are, it is clear, a vain thing. Armaments are merely an expression of Power. They grow because Power grows. And yet those parties are loudest in demanding their limitation which, with unperceived inconsequence, are the most ardent supporters of Power's expansion!

Power is linked with war, and a society wishing to limit war's ravages can find no other way than by limiting the scope of Power.

## 5. From the Feudal Army to the Royal Army

The social regime which imposes the narrowest limits on the extent of a nation's involvement in war is the aristocratic regime, the reason being that no other regime is equally allergic to the expansion of Power. Such a regime wears, it is true, an essentially militarist air because the business of the ruling class is war. But then, war is the business of no other class. At Sparta, for instance, the disproportionately small number of soldiers compared to the population as a whole is striking, and in Western Europe the establishment of feudalism was the signal for a drastic cut in the size of armies. The number of Charlemagne's effectives is not reached again until the seventeenth century. The need to hold in check the Saracen or Hungarian cavalry, and to take up new positions as speedily as the Norman pirates in their light craft, led to the introduction of the cavalry era—but only the cavalry of the feudal lords, of which the king could not rightly call more than one troop his own. At that time the people took no part at all in war—were unaffected by it, except for those over whose plots of land it passed—and the memory of those days is preserved in the cry often uttered by the people today: "Those who want war have only to make it themselves and leave us alone."

There are big differences between the army of a landed aristocracy, which is naturally incoherent and undisciplined by reason of the diversity of the contingents forming it, and that of an urban aristocracy, to which, contrariwise, community of interests and education and the intimate ties of custom lend a peculiar strength. Troops of the latter type are superior to mercenaries, whereas troops of the former are bound to go down before paid regular troops, as was seen at Crécy and Nicopolis. The *ortas*, or companies, of janissaries were the expression of a Power which was much more extreme than any of its contemporaries in the West, who were to prove unable, right up to the end of the seventeenth century, to offer effective resistance to it. The English army—a paid army, from the

Prince of Wales down to the lowest archer—was the expression of a monarchy which could already get from its vassals and commons regular subsidies,[10] and was soon to get its hands on the national output of wool so as to provide itself with foreign exchange;[11] lastly, it could harness to its service the largest capitalists of the period, those of Florence.

In the history of France, the Hundred Years' War represents the attempts of the royal Power to get on an equal basis with the enemy Power. Numbered among them are the requests for subsidies made by Philip VI and John II to successive assemblies which were sometimes general and sometimes regional. So too are the taxes imposed for the ransom of John II, taxes which Charles V continued to levy and to which his victories were due: the taxes suppressed, the English fortunes revived again.

The significant thing that came out of the Hundred Years' War was the institution of the permanent poll-tax (taille) wherewith to maintain the orderly companies, that is to say a standing and paid force of cavalry (1444). In this way the result of the first great conflict of arms in Western society was to strengthen Power.

## 6. War, Midwife of Absolute Monarchy

And all the wars in all the centuries in which European states fight each other will have the same results. In the sixteenth century and for a part of the seventeenth Spain was the leading Power in Europe, buttressed with the gold of the New World and, above all, with the army forged for her by Gonzalo of Cordova, "the Great Captain." The Ordinance of 1496 instituted even at that early date a kind of conscription. One out of twelve of all subjects between the ages of twenty and forty-five were bidden to the service of the state. Those bidden became soldiers. That was the origin of that "redoubtable Spanish Infantry," in time to be celebrated by Bossuet.

The development of absolute monarchy in both England and France is linked with the efforts of their respective dynasties to resist the dangers from Spain. James I owed his wide powers to the Armada. Richelieu and

10. Cf. Carl Stephenson, "Taxation and Representation," in *Haskins Anniversary Essays* (Boston: 1929) and James Field Willard, *Parliamentary Taxes on Personal Property, 1290–1334* (Cambridge, Mass.: 1934).

11. Cf. Baldwin Schuyler Terry, *The Financing of the Hundred Years' War* (London: 1914).

Mazarin could raise high the prerogatives of the state because they could invoke unceasingly the peril from abroad.

Fontenay Mareuil gives us some idea of how large a part was played by military exigencies in liquidating the ancient forms of government and paving the way for absolute monarchy:

> To save the realm it was absolutely necessary that the king should have in it an authority which was sufficiently absolute to enable him to do whatever should seem good to him; for since he was dealing with the King of Spain with his large country in which he takes what he wants, it is only too certain that had our king had to assemble the States-General, as is generally done, or to depend on the benevolence of the Parliament for getting all that he needed, it would never have been got.[12]

Richelieu, finding that the entire military effectives of France had been reduced to 10,000 men by Marie de' Medici, raised them to 60,000; then, after having kept up for many years the war in Germany by means of subsidies to the Swedes and others ("putting," as he reported to the king, "his hand in the purse rather than on the sword"), when the exhaustion of the Swedes and their defeat at Nordlingen obliged him to step in, he did so with 100,000 foot-soldiers and 20,000 cavalrymen—armies on a scale unknown to France for eight centuries.

Heavy taxation was needed to sustain this effort; its collection could not be delayed by regard to forms, nor made subject to the consent of the taxed. Oblivion overtook the lesson taught by Comines.[13] "What king or nobleman is there on earth who has power to lay on his subjects a penny piece of taxation without the grant and consent of those who have to pay—except by tyranny and violence?"

Tyranny of this kind was justified in France by the "unceasing purpose to stay the progress of Spain."[14]

### 7. Powers in International Rivalry

But while Richelieu, with an eye on victory in the political battle, was violating all rights and destroying all institutions which obstructed the

12. *Mémoires de Fontenay-Mareuil* (éd. Petitot) Vol. II, p. 209.

13. [Comines, Philippe de (1445–1509), French statesman and historian. His memoirs, in seven books, have been called the earliest example in French literature of the "history" as distinguished from the "chronicle." Unlike the chroniclers, Comines cared little for show and spectacle, but made many acute comments on men and affairs.]

14. *Mémoires de Richelieu* (éd. Petitot) Vol. IV, p. 245.

state's power to tax, he was causing his rivals, all of them anxious to maintain their own positions, to take similar measures.

Olivarez in Spain strove to make effective the maxim that "the good of the nation and the army transcends every law and every privilege."[15] In England Charles I lost patience with Parliament's refusal and levied ship-money illegally, thereby calling out Hampden's resistance. Hampden's trial took place near the end of 1637; in 1639 Normandy revolted against Richelieu in an attempt to stop the levying of all taxes imposed since the death of Henry IV. In 1640 revolution broke out in Catalonia for the preservation of the traditional privileges and liberties. The Fronde, in its relation to European events, is but one of many reactions to the onward march in step of all the competing Powers towards domestic absolutism.

The Fronde did not succeed in undoing the work of Richelieu, by which was formed, according to de Retz, "in the most legitimate of monarchies, the most scandalous and dangerous tyranny that has ever existed."[16] As a result, the power of Louis XIV came to dominate Europe. Whereupon the other European states naturally started to invoke in their turn the need to check the course of France's advance.

The envy felt for Louis XIV by other princes is at the root of their usurpations of authority over their peoples. But the menace of his hegemony gave them a perfectly honourable pretext for imitating him.

### 8. Conscription

Achievement of the right to search its subjects' pockets for the wherewithal to maintain its enterprises had been the first great victory of Power in modern times. At first, in the time of the English Parliaments, the States-General of France, and the Cortes of Spain, taxation had been dependent upon the consent of the taxed. Then it became arbitrary, a step which marked an immense advance of Power.

But another, and for the waging of war still more important, advance had still to be achieved: to lay hands on the very bodies of Power's subjects, to swell the armies. Nothing was more alien than this to the genius of aristocratic societies; it is natural to them to be defended only by the aristocrats. That is the interest, the office, and the privilege of aristocracy. It is as warriors that they make themselves, taken as a whole,

---

15. Instructions given to the viceroy sent to Catalonia.
16. He is speaking as pamphleteer rather than as historian.

indispensable to the monarch who is their chief and to the common people who depend on them. As champions of the one and protectors of the other, they gain both the good opinion of the nation and the respect due to their position, and they are no less able to defend national interests against the foreigner than their own interest against encroachment from above and agitation from below.

The employment of mercenary troops had already cut into this monopoly of the profession of arms.[17] It perished when military service ceased to be the preserve of the nobility and was extended to the entire population. As we shall see,[18] kings have always yearned for universal military service; it provided them, so far as internal order was concerned, with the means of throwing down the barrier to state encroachments presented by the aristocratic order. And in respect of external order it brought them a prodigious accretion of resources.

The only way in which Gustavus Adolphus had been able to maintain his armies in Germany had been by securing that in every commune of Sweden the inhabitants periodically selected some of their number for the king's service. Louvois made a proposal to keep up to strength in the same way the French regiments whose wastage could not be made good by voluntary recruiting. It was, as he explained at the start, only for the purpose of local defence that thirty-five regiments, aptly called territorial, were being formed. But his initiative encountered so much opposition that he had to substitute for the selection of recruits a drawing by lot for them. What peasant distrust had felt coming soon came: these regiments acted as depots which could be drawn on to make good the numbers in regiments on active service.

Such were the timid beginnings of the militarization of entire peoples.

It was in Prussia that the new system first spread its wings. A kingdom of recent formation, it possessed neither population nor wealth on any scale, nor had it any territorial cohesion. Its various provinces had varying histories and lacked unity. Frederick William made it his aim to maintain

---

17. "Before Philip Augustus," writes Boulainvilliers, "the only soldiers in France were the holders of fiefs; but this king, having engaged in wars of which the barons disapproved, started the practice of hiring troops, and from this time on our kings have always had with them hired cavalry, both in France and in Germany; but there was no dilution of classes in the army until the time of the rebellions in Flanders, when it became apparent that there were among the common people men as fearless and as intelligent as in the ranks of the nobility. After that came the wars with England in which service in hired companies became a common thing." *Essai sur la noblesse de France.*

18. Chap. ix.

an army which should be composed of the finest soldiers that could be recruited throughout the length and breadth of Germany—and Europe. To each of his regiments he allotted a portion or "canton" of Prussian soil. Each canton furnished its regiment with the recruits needed to fill its ranks. These conscripts, who went by the name of "cantonists," served in the first instance only for a few months, but they were recalled for a few weeks every year and joined up in time of war.

Such was the import of the famous rescript of 1733. Military service, the status of reservist, mobilization in time of war, all were the work of Prussia. The small resources of men and money possessed by Prussia in its early days caused an ambitious Power to mobilize the strength of the nation to a point hitherto unknown. And Prussia, though it was still small by the side of France, notwithstanding the consecutive accretions brought it by its glorious victories, had under arms on the eve of the Revolution 195,000 men, as against 180,000 in France. It was a great advantage of the Prussian system that these 195,000 men cost only some forty-five millions, which was less than half the cost of the less numerous French army.

These figures, 180,000 French soldiers, 195,000 Prussians, 240,000 Austrians, sufficiently explain France's passivity towards the close of the monarchy, which remained deaf to the appeals reaching it from Holland in 1787 and Belgium in 1789—thereby missing its chance of closing once for all that "open door to the enemies of France," its northeast frontier.

The audacity which succeeded to this pusillanimity made ample amends! Harebrained and politically inexperienced rulers plunged the country into war with not one but both of the leading military Powers on the continent, who were joined by Spain, England, and Piedmont. How did France of the Revolution come to sustain the shock? She was saved in the first hour by the dubious conduct of Brunswick. But after that? After that she put in the field much more numerous armies than those of the coalitions combined; to do it she needed a Power whose absolutism was far different from that of the ancient monarchy, a Power which could proclaim: "From now on until the enemy has been chased from the soil of the Republic, every Frenchman is *permanently required* for service in the armies."

## 9. The Era of Cannon Fodder

This decision of the Convention of August 23, 1793, was followed by measures giving effect to it. In 1794, 1,169,000 men figured on the French military registers.

A new era in military history now opened, the era of cannon fodder. Not a single general of the *ancien régime* would ever have dared expose his troops in serried columns to the enemy's fire. Folard, who had proposed it, had been unable to get a hearing. The extended order of battle saved lives but brought no clear-cut decision. Whereas the generals of the Revolution and the Empire spent without counting the cost; Power could now draw for them on the whole French nation. And history was to record that these massacres were the start of the decline of the population and vitality of France.

Jourdan's law of 1798 gave formal shape to the system of requisitioning men. Service was obligatory for men of between twenty and twenty-five years of age, who formed the first five classes, numbering a million men; the law decided how many of them should be taken, and the conscripts were drawn by lot. Every year the oldest class could be recalled and a younger one called up. Napoleon was to employ this system: at first he took 80,000 men in each class, but, when he was making ready for the Russian campaign, he called up 120,000 men of the 1810 class, and after the disasters there he called up 150,000 men of the 1814 class besides bringing back 300,000 men of the classes on which he had at first economized. In all, from September 1805 to November 1813 he took from France 2,100,000 men in addition to the soldiers of the Republic who had been kept with the colours.

How could the rest of Europe ever have fought him if it had not had recourse to like measures? Many governments only consented with reluctance to measures which smacked of barbarism. But adopted they were, and Napoleon was crushed beneath the weight of numbers.

The advantage at first derived by France from intensive exploitation of her human potential was lost as soon as her competitors took to imitating her. The numerical balance of forces suggested the likelihood of crushing the French in 1793 or 1794. The French *levée en masse* prevented it. But when once the same methods had been adopted by all, France gained nothing by this postponement of the fatal day.

## 10. Total War

Germany, however, learned nothing from this experience. Alone of the victorious Powers who forced France to give up the system by means of which she had desolated Europe, Prussia retained an analogous but aggravated system, which prepared the way for the victories of 1870. Their success frightened Europe so much that every continental country followed Germany's example and introduced military conscription. The splendid result of this was that in 1888 Europe's armies on a peace footing were the same in numbers as at the height of the Napoleonic Wars—3,000,000 men. The public expenditures of the European states, which came to 170 million pounds sterling in 1816, reached 868 millions in 1898. In every country military expenditure took the lion's share.

At length the storm broke, with results which we know. The dead numbered 8,000,000, the mutilated 6,000,000. Taking the belligerent countries as a whole, 8 per cent of the male labour force was destroyed; in France and Germany the figure was 10 per cent.

And what was gained by so much destruction? The issue of the war would have been the same even if the armies engaged had been no larger than the professional armies of the seventeenth century. Just as Revolutionary France, notwithstanding her intensive utilization of the national resources, finally succumbed to a coalition which could bring to bear a far superior human and economic potential, so it was with the Germany of William II; her resistance broke down against such a combination of national forces as made it certain that, sooner or later, the balance of resources would be tilted against her.

Thus it was demonstrated a second time that the advantage in the political race given by the growth of a state's requisitions on its people is but an ephemeral one; rivals are thereby incited to take like measures, and the growth results merely in hateful burdens in time of peace and in a frightful aggravation of the hecatombs and ruins of war.

Had there to be a third demonstration? Our hearts fail us at the very thought of reckoning the price in human lives and cultural heritages destroyed.

It was the blockade of Germany in the First World War that gave birth to the doctrine of total war.

For the German state, as for its individual citizens, the satisfaction of needs is limited not only by the disposable funds available but also by the physical products of the limited areas controlled by the German armies. The measures necessitated by this situation become progressively systematized. In time of war all production must be planned by the state so as to get thereby the maximum war potential which is compatible with the need to maintain a minimum standard of life for the population. Thus the whole nation becomes a weapon of war wielded by the state; and the proportion engaged on warlike tasks is limited only by the need to keep it alive.

This total identification of the nation with the armed forces seems only to have been envisaged towards the end of the First World War. Progress in this direction was at first tentative, and the doctrine finally emerged from policies which kept, even to the end, an uncoordinated and empirical air. The idea was nourished round the hearth of German nationalism, which bequeathed it to the National Socialist movement. Once in power, that movement embarked on such a reconstruction of the German economy as made it come to look like a man-of-war. Its purpose was battle, with every man of the crew at his station, either as combatant or as victualler of the combatants. The magazines were filled with shells, but the victualling of the crew had not been neglected on that account.

Up to then the state, in the event of war, had requisitioned from the life of the nation only so much of its strength as was needed to sustain its warlike undertaking. But now, in time of peace, the state made ready the total utilization of the national resources for war.

The first encounters in the Second World War had exactly the issue that could be expected in a fight between a cruiser and Atlantic liners which were equipped with guns but on board which stewards were still serving sluggish passengers.

The outcome was different when Germany attacked a country, to wit Russia, in which, for twenty years, men had had their tasks assigned to them by the public authority.

Political rivalry had its usual consequences, and England and the United States had soon to copy the German methods of war. These are the two countries in which the private person has been most successful in maintaining his rights against the state. The United States had not instituted military conscription until the time of the Civil War and had abolished it when once the danger was past. Even in the First World War England had created a national army only after long hesitation, and the right of the state to constrain the subject was regarded as so questionable that the refusal of conscientious objectors to serve was admitted. Under stress of need Power had, it is true, swallowed up the nation's substance by borrowing and inflation, but it had afterwards taken on itself to restore what it had so taken by putting back the currency, pounds or dollars, to its old parity. In time of war no other means than those derived from its extraordinary credits had been employed by the state to divert production to its requirements.

It may be observed, however, that in the years immediately preceding the Second World War the state had made some notable addition to its empire, especially in the United States. The struggle against Germany witnessed its triumph. For the first time in history a President of the United States looked on the mass of his fellow-citizens as "human potential," to be used as might best serve the prosecution of the war!

Thus we see how, ever since the Middle Ages, to keep their places in the political race, states have been increasing the sacrifices which they demand of their nations. Whereas the Capetian kings made war with a few seignorial contingents whose service was for no more than forty days, the popular states of today have power to call to the colours, and keep there indefinitely, the entire male population. Whereas the feudal monarchs could nourish hostilities only with the resources of their own domains, their successors have at their disposal the entire national income. The citizens of medieval cities at war could, if they were not too near to the actual theatre of operations, take no notice of it. Nowadays friend and foe alike would burn their houses, slaughter their families, and measure their own doughty deeds in ravaged acres. Even Thought herself, in former times contemptuous of these brawls, has now been roped in by devotees of conquest to proclaim the civilizing virtues of gangsters and incendiaries.

How is it possible not to see in this stupendous degradation of our civilization the fruits of state absolutism? Everything is thrown into war because Power disposes of everything.

Industrial rivalry would go the same way as political, if masters exercised unlimited rule over their men. However humane they might be by nature, they would be forced to exact ever greater efforts from the subject mass below them—under the vital spur of keeping abreast of a rival's efforts.

This hateful consequence of rivalry is checked only because trade union opposition sets a limit to what the masters can exact.

Why does the modern state meet no organized resistance?

The *ancien régime* met with such resistance, which was offered it by the representatives of the various elements in the nation who fought in line against Power. But in the modern regime these elements have become Power, and the people are left in consequence without a champion. Those who are the state reserve to themselves alone the right to talk in the name of the nation; an interest of the nation as distinct from the interest of the state has no existence for them. They would crush as sedition what the monarchy would have received as remonstrance. Under the pretext that Power has been given to the nation, and from refusal to see that there are here two bodies which are and must ever be distinct, the nation has been delivered over to Power.

BOOK IV

# The State as Permanent Revolution

# IX.

# *Power, Assailant of the Social Order*

POWER IS AUTHORITY and makes for more authority. It is force and makes for more force. Or, if a less metaphysical terminology is preferred, ambitious wills, drawn by the lure of Power, expend unceasingly their energies in its behalf that they may bind society in an ever tighter grip and extract from it more of its resources.

The process is not uninterrupted, but the checks and recoils which it receives have not prevented the advance of the state through the centuries, as is sufficiently proved by the history of taxation, the history of armies, the history of legislation, and the history of police forces. It is clear enough that the fraction of society's wealth appropriated by public authority is a growing one, as is the fraction of the population which it mobilizes. It regulates private activities more and more closely, and watches more and more narrowly those who are its subjects.[1]

The sight prompts two questions: What has made possible Power's advance? And why has the advance been so little observed?

Its success in achieving an ever further direction of individual activities, and in appropriating for itself an ever larger part of the strength subsisting

---

1. Its spectacular acceleration in our time has made us particularly sensible of this process, which has now reached countries where it was hardly observable before. Thus, even before the Second World War, taxation in the United States had risen in three-quarters of a century (1860–1938) from 4.3 per cent of the national income to 22.7 per cent (cf. Simon Kuznets, "Taxes and National Income," *Proceedings of the American Philosophical Society,* Vol. LXXXVIII, No. 1). So, too, conscription has for the first time become a permanent feature in England.

in society, is not at first realized. Every increase of state authority must involve an immediate diminution of the liberty of each citizen; every augmentation of the public wealth means an immediate lopping of the revenues of each. So obvious a danger should, one would think, have the effect of uniting all in an almost unanimous opposition, by which Power's advance would be surely stayed.

Why is it that the opposite happens and that we see Power pursuing its triumphal way over all the pages of history?

It had to remain largely invisible, and not to let alarm arise at its becoming an ever larger creditor for obedience and services. But that raises a further mystery. Why is it not clear as crystal to everyone that the private citizen is falling ever more deeply into the public authority's debt for those commodities? And what is the explanation of the fact that, right down to our own time, the movement of history has in general been interpreted as a progressive liberation of the individual?

The reason is that there are in society, in addition to the state and the individual, social authorities as well, which also claim from the human being their due of obedience and services. And the diminution or disappearance of his obligations to a social authority may affect his life and stir his interest more than the aggravation of his obligations to the political authority.

Every social authority rests on a basis of services and dues, and naturally, therefore, a struggle ensues between the different authorities for possession of the services and dues available. What assists the advance of the state is this: that it is at war with others of man's masters, the abasement of whom tends to be more regarded than its own elevation. Only in an ideally simple society, in which there were no social authorities, would matters proceed differently.

When a particular society lies somewhere near this abstract prototype, as in communities of yeomen with nearly equal holdings, then Power encounters the maximum of opposition. Not only does it not expand, but it cannot even maintain its position as a separate entity in the body of society. It stays in, or returns to, the condition of being something open to all, and the members of society take turns in the function of command, the scope of which they are careful to guard from all accretion.

But the form of society is in general far different from this. It is an inextricable blend of juxtaposed formations, inside which are ties of dependence and relationships formed by exploitation. Or again it is a hierarchy, a system of inequality, a struggle of classes, as Plato saw it to be: "Every people, no matter how small it is, is naturally divided into two peoples, the rich and the poor, who make war on each other."[2]

The court at which Power holds sway is, therefore, a complex one. The situations, the interests, and the aspirations of men are many and various, and for that reason Power meets not only with opposition but with support as well.

Who are its supporters? Who its adversaries?

## 1. Power's Conflict with Aristocracy and Alliance with the Common People

We can see at once that if, in society, the behaviour of groups, large or small, is governed by various authorities, then those authorities are bound to conflict with Power, which seeks to govern the behaviour of one and all: as their prerogative keeps back its own, its own aims at breaking theirs. Those who are subjected to the rule of the various princes of society have no fear of the advance of the state, for they lose no liberty thereby. At the very worst they lose one command and get another. Conversely, Power, in search of resources, attacks the princes of society who got in first. For what purpose are wealth and strength but to hold in disposition a mass of human labour and energies? A rich man is one who can draw benefits from this mass. A strong man is one who can harness these energies to impose his will. The word "wealth" calls up the idea of a retinue of servants, "strength" that of an army of soldiers.

Always and everywhere the labour of men is put to use, and the energies of men are tamed. Power, which needs them for itself, must therefore start by detaching them from their first overlords. The leaders of groups, the masters of resources, the gatherers of tithes, the employers of labour, are all despoiled by it, but their servants get no more than a change of masters. Thus, in the time of its expansion Power's predestined victims and natural enemies are the powerful—the men with payrolls, and all those who wield authority in society and are strong in it. To attack them Power need feel for them no conscious hostility; with animal instinct, it overthrows what irks it and devours what nourishes it.

All command other than its own, that is what irks Power. All energy, wherever it may be found, that is what nourishes it. If the human atom which contains this energy is confined in social molecule, then Power

2. *The Republic,* 422 E.

must break down that molecule. Its levelling tendency, therefore, is not in the least, as is commonly thought, an acquired characteristic which it assumes on taking democratic form. It is a leveller in its own capacity of state, and because it is state.[3] The levelling process need find no place in its programme: it is embedded in its destiny. From the moment that it seeks to lay hands on the resources latent in the community, it finds itself impelled to put down the mighty by as natural a tendency as that which causes a bear in search of honey to break the cells of the hive.

How will the common people, the dependants and the labourers, welcome its secular work of destruction? With joy, inevitably. Its work is that of demolishing feudal castles; ambition motivates it, but the former victims rejoice in their liberation. Its work is that of breaking the shell of petty private tyrannies so as to draw out the hoarded energy within; greed motivates it, but the exploited rejoice in the downfall of their exploiters.

The final result of this stupendous work of aggression does not disclose itself till late. Visible, no doubt, is the displacement of many private dominions by one general dominion, of many aristocracies by one "statocracy."[4] But at first the common people can but applaud: the more capable among them are, in a continuous stream, enrolled in Power's army—the administration—there to become the masters of their former social superiors.

It is the most natural thing, therefore, that the common people should be Power's ally, should do its work in the expansion of the state—a process which they facilitate by their passivity and stir up by their appeals.

## 2. Is Power a Social Conservative or a Social Revolutionary?

To represent Power as being of its nature dedicated to casting down social authorities and robbing them, as being inevitably thrown into

3. I find this thought recurring in Tocqueville. It even forms the principal theme of Vol. III of his *Démocratie en Amérique:* "Every central authority which follows its natural instincts likes and favours equality; for equality more than anything else facilitates the working of this sort of authority, and extends and assures it." *De la Démocratie en Amérique,* Vol. III, p. 483.

4. To "aristocrat," by which I mean a man who is in his own right leader of a group in society with an authority which does not come to him from the state, I place in antithesis "statocrat," being a man who derives his authority only from the position which he holds and the office which he performs in the service of the state.

alliance with the common people, is to run counter to accepted ideas. But to find in it a revolutionary smacks of paradox. For a thoughtful mind the least breath of paradox acts as a warning that he must retrace his steps and plot his road anew.

I have against me here not only the popular view, but also that of men like Montesquieu and Marx. The nobility, says the former, is impelled to defend the throne; the state, affirms the latter, is an instrument for the domination of one class by another. Who, they say, is the real beneficiary of the protection of the laws, the decisions of the courts, the interventions of the police? Those in possession, whose position is legitimized, guaranteed, and protected by the public authorities. And who, unless the victims of the social order, will look on Power as an enemy? The proletarian, having no interest in property, stands in inevitable fear of the policeman, who is its guardian.

History, surely, is full of the cruelties inflicted by Power on those who have aspired to shake off an aristocratic yoke. What need to catalogue the massacres of Jacqueries or the shooting down of strikers? Besides, these men go on; Power, acting thus, was only filling its necessary role. For how could a feudal king have mustered an army if the barons whose duty it was to bring him each a contingent had not received obedience in their own domains? And how could the industrialists have paid their taxes if their workers had stopped work?

And look, they will say further, at the extent to which the state is of its nature conservative of acquired rights. Even in our days, when it is in the hands of the representatives of the greatest number, and is for this reason compelled to pull down social authorities, it may yet be seen supporting with one hand what it attacks with the other; it still gives sanction to the right of inheritance even when, in one law after another, it destroys the substance of the bequest.

The example is well chosen. We see here the state playing two roles at the same time, guaranteeing the established order by its organs and undermining it by its legislation. What I am saying is that it has always filled this double role. True it is that the judiciary, the police, and, at need, the army do cause acquired rights to be respected. And if the state is viewed as a collection of institutions, as so much machinery, it is abundantly clear that these institutions are conservative in character and that the machinery works in defence of the existing social order.

But we have already proclaimed our intention of not studying the state as an "it," but of finding in it a "they." As machinery, it plays its conservative role automatically; as a living thing with a life of its own, thriving and developing, it can but thrive and develop to the detriment of the social order. Look at it in its Being, and it is the protector of the privileged. But look at it in its Becoming, and it is the inevitable assailant of the master class, a word under which I comprise every form of social authority.

In the course of history kings have welcomed more and more people to their courts, which became more and more brilliant. Is it not obvious that these courtiers and "officers" were stolen from the feudal lords, who thus lost at one fell swoop their retinues and their administrators? The modern state nourishes a vast bureaucracy. Is not the corresponding decline in the staff of the employer patent to all?

Putting the mass of the people to productive work makes possible at any given moment of technical advance the existence of a given number of non-producers. These non-producers will either be dispersed in a number of packets or concentrated in one immense body, according as the profits of productive work accrue to the social or to the political authorities. The requirement of Power, its tendency and its *raison d'être*, is to concentrate them in its own service. To this task it brings so much ardour, instinctive rather than designed, *that in course of time it does to a natural death the social order which gave it birth.*

### 3. The Troughs in the Statocratic Waves

This tendency is due not to the form taken by any particular state but to the inner essence of Power, which is the inevitable assailant of the social authorities and sucks their very lifeblood. And the more vigorous a particular Power is, the more virile it is in the role of vampire. When it falls into weak hands, which give aristocratic resistance the chance to organize itself, the state's revolutionary nature becomes for the time being effaced.

This happens either because the forces of aristocracy oppose to the now enfeebled statocratic onslaught a barrier capable of checking it, or, more frequently, because they put a guard on their assailant, by laying hands on the apparatus which endangers them; they guarantee their own survival by installing themselves in the seat of government. This is exactly what did happen in the two epochs when the ideas of Montesquieu and Marx took shape.

The counter-offensive of the social authorities cannot be understood unless it is realized that the process of destroying aristocracies goes hand in hand with a tendency in the opposite sense. The mighty are put down—if they are independent of the state; but simultaneously a statocracy is exalted, and the new statocrats do more than lay a collective hand on the social forces—they lay on them each his own hand; in this way they divert them from Power and restore them again to society, in which thereafter the statocrats join forces, by reason of the similarity of their situations and interests, with the ancient aristocracies in retreat.

Moreover, the statocratic acids, in so far as they break down the aristocratic molecules, do not make away with all the forces which they liberate. Part of them stays unappropriated, and furnishes new captains of society with the personnel necessary to the construction of new principates. In this way the fission of the feudal cell at the height of the Middle Ages released the labour on which the merchant-drapers rose to wealth and political importance.

So also in England, when the greed of Henry VIII had fallen on the ecclesiastical authorities to get from their wealth the wherewithal to carry out his policies, the greater part of the monastic spoils stuck to the fingers of hands which had been held out to receive them. These spoils founded the fortunes of the nascent English capitalism.[5]

In this way new hives are for ever being built, in which lie hidden a new sort of energies; these will in time inspire the state to fresh orgies of covetousness. That is why the statocratic aggression seems never to reach its logical conclusion—the complete atomization of society, which should contain henceforward nothing but isolated individuals whom the state alone rules and exploits.

Here, then, we see the general character of the action of Power on society, and how the struggle of Power for more power intervenes in the struggle of classes. It must be examined more closely. First, we shall illustrate by three examples the problem which is posed for Power by the constitution of society in watertight autonomous cells. Next, we shall demonstrate what is the final objective of the statocratic offensive. Then, in another chapter, we shall present the statocratic offensive in action, throwing into relief the stages of its development, the factors which help

5. Cf. my short study on *L'Or au temps de Charles-Quint et de Philip II* (Paris: Sequana, 1943).

it, the obstacles on which it stumbles, and the extraordinary exertions required of it to overcome those obstacles.

### 4. *Power and the Cell of the Clan*

The great societies which are called "political" do not, as Hobbes supposed, spring forth ready armed, leaving to Power the subsequent task of establishing order in a crowd of individuals. On the contrary, they are the result of the coalescence, whether by violence or by consent, of smaller and much more ancient societies which are called, in the case of the Indo-European peoples, clans.

Clans are coherent, orderly formations, obeying their own authorities. All that the political authority need do, therefore, to superimpose itself on these primitive groups, is to establish cohesion and order *between* them.

The City of Athens, says Fustel, "must have borne a close resemblance to a federal State. The wider political association had not only left intact the internal constitution of each clan—it had not even modified it. This sort of huge family, while becoming an integral part of the City, still kept up its ancient cults, its customs, its laws, its festivals, its internal jurisdiction. It remained under the rule of its patrician chieftain, and continued to form a small monarchical State in which the rule of the City did not run."[6]

Even the murder of one member of a clan by another did not involve the intervention of Power. It was the business of the responsible chieftain to punish the crime as he saw fit. The king's concern was only with murders in which the murderer and his victim belonged to two different groups. And even then his role was a pacificatory one. He did not punish an act at which the only people entitled to be angry were the dead man's clansmen. He strove to prevent the pursuit of vengeance destroying the harmony between the groupings, and to that end exacted from the murderer's family such reparation as might satisfy the avengers.

Power of this kind, then, has business only with the heads of groups, between whom it arbitrates and to whom it gives commands. Its authority does not run within the group itself. Nineteenth-century writers took for legend the revolution unleashed at Rome merely by the rape of Lucretia.

6. Fustel de Coulanges, article on "Attica Respublica" in the *Dictionnaire des antiquités* of Daremberg.

But the event is not an improbable one, for, when Norway was at a similar stage of civilization, the king, who had made unwelcome intrusion into someone's home, found the hands of all the freemen raised against him; they sought to kill him, and on his escape forbade him ever to return to the country.

In this shape Power is little more than a sort of chairmanship exercised by the bravest, the richest, and the most respected chieftain over the others. Political society is but a congeries of social pyramids which touch only at their summits. The army, as may be seen in the *Iliad,* is no more than an assemblage of private contingents. In historical times, the *gens Fabia* may still be seen launching on its own a military expedition. The king is in consequence constrained to unceasing consultation with his peers, for they alone can supply him with the troops he needs. Must it not be a standing temptation to him to substitute for his mediatory authority an immediate one, to claim direct obedience from the members of the clan? But in that case he poaches on the preserves of the Elders and comes into conflict with them. And by the same stroke of policy he becomes the ally of all those who seek to escape from the harsh rule of the patriarchate.

To break the cadre of the clans is, therefore, of the first importance to kings. Their resistance is the reef on which kings are shipwrecked; but the Power which succeeds them, although but a mandatory of the aristocracy of the clans, carries on the work of breaking the clans, because that work is essential to the development of Power. That is why the classifications of the people, attributed to Solon and Servius Tullius,[7] assume so capital an importance in Greek and Roman history. They mark the break-up of the natural groups, the members of which were now divided up into categories, to be in their individual capacities soldiers, taxpayers, and electors.

Power's war with the cell of the clan is never over. It continues through all history. With admirable perspicacity Maine[8] hung his exposition of the evolution of Roman law on the thread of the successive recoils of the

7. [Servius Tullius, sixth King of Rome, from 578 to 534 B.C. His famous classification of the freeholders, here referred to, though subsequently adopted to some extent as the basis of the political system, was in origin much more exclusively military than would appear from the text. Its object was to grade the fighting men in classes by reference to their equipment, and therefore by reference to their wealth. In doing so, no regard was paid to the old clan divisions.]

8. [Sir Henry Maine. See footnote 28 in chapter IV.]

*patria potestas*. In the beginning the legislator did not have to concern himself at all with the son, the daughter, and the slave, for these fell within the exclusive jurisdiction of the father. Step by step they all became subject to the law: the state had broken through into a world from which it was at first excluded, and had claimed as subject to its own jurisdiction those who had in former days been subjects of the father alone.

### 5. Power and the Baronial Cell

We have just been seeing political Power concerned to break a "clandom" which preceded it in time. Let us now see how it behaves in regard to a clandom which is its contemporary. It may be said in effect, paraphrasing Shakespeare: "Monarchy and feudal aristocracy are two lions born on the same day."

There was something of an act of piracy about the foundation of the European states. The Franks who conquered Gaul, the Normans who conquered England and Sicily, and even the Crusaders who went to Palestine, all behaved like bands of adventurers dividing the spoil. What was there to divide? First of all, the ready cash. Afterwards there were the lands; no deserts, these, but furnished with men whose labour was to maintain the victor. To every man, then, his share in the prize. And there we have the man-at-arms turned baron. This is shown by the evolution of the word *baro,* which in Germany meant "freeman," and in Gaul denoted the name of the class.

There remains for seizure the apparatus of state, where there is one: naturally it is the share of the chief. But when a barbarian like Clovis found himself confronted with the administrative machine of the Late Empire, he did not understand it. All he saw in it was a system of suction pumps bringing him in a steady flow of riches on which he made merry,[9] with no thought for the public services for which these resources were intended. In the result, then, he divided up among his foremost companions the treasure of the state, whether in the form of lands or fiscal revenues.

In this way civilized government was gradually brought to ruin, and

---

9. Fustel de Coulanges says of the Merovingian kings: "Almost all of them seem to have considered royalty as a fortune and not as a function. It was for that reason that they shared it out among themselves like an estate. They measured it in terms of lands, taxes, and valuables." *Les Transformations de la royauté,* p. 26.

Gaul of the ninth and tenth centuries was reduced to the same condition as that in which William of Normandy was to find the England of the eleventh.

There was imposed the system of barbarian government known as government by retainers. Let Charlemagne use as the *points d'appui* of Power the influential men who were already on the spot,[10] or let William create his own influential men by a share-out of big fiefs in England—it was all one. The important thing to note is that the central authority appoints as its representatives in a given district either the chief proprietors of the soil who are there already or those whom it sets up in their place.

By a slant common to the barbarian mind, or rather by an inclination which is natural to all men but in barbarians encounters no opposing principle, these influential men soon confound their function with their property, and exercise the former as though it were the latter. Each little local tyrant then becomes legislator, judge, and administrator of a more or less extensive principality; and on the tribute paid by it he lives, along with his servants and his men-at-arms.

Power thus expelled soon returns, however, under the spur of its requirements. The resources at its disposal are absurdly out of proportion to the area which depends on it and to the population which calls it sovereign. The reason is that the manpower has been taken over by the barons. What was in other days a tax is now a feudal due. The only way out is to rob the baronial cell of its withheld resources. That is why monarchy establishes townships on the confines of the baronial lands; they act as cupping-glasses, drawing away the best elements in the population. In that way the barons will get fewer villeins and the king more bourgeoisie, who will be grateful for the franchises conferred on them and will help the king in his necessities from their purses. For this

10. Charlemagne made himself quickly obeyed throughout a vast empire by making the agents of his authority the notables whom he found on the spot: "Let each chief," said he, "exercise a restraining influence on those below him, to the end that these latter may obey the imperial commands and precepts with ever more willing hearts" (Marc Bloch). In this way state power, for practical purposes non-existent, uses as its intermediary the different feudal authorities and borrows from them their very real force. In a situation of that kind, there is no other way of restoring in a few years the authority of the state. But, as soon as the personal ascendancy of Charlemagne was no more, the authority of the Carolingians showed itself to be fragile and as having no strength proper to itself. The Capetian kings built more slowly and by quite other means; they established by progressive stages, in opposition to the notables whom they at first employed, agents of Power who should be that and nothing else.

reason, again, the monarchy, through its lawyers, comes between the barons and their subjects; the purpose is to compel the former to limit themselves to the dues which are customary and to abstain from arbitrary taxation.

In this way the monarch curbs the exactions of the barons with one hand, but with the other serves his own turn. His demands for grants-in-aid become more and more frequent; that is to say that, instead of subsisting solely on the workers who are directly subject to him, he lives more and more on those who are subject to the barons.

The memoranda of the States-General are full at one and the same time both of requests to the king that he curb the exactions of the barons and of protests against the progressive extension of his own exactions.

No doubt the attitude of Power grows more and more protective, but the reason is that Power gets greedier and greedier. Its battle with the feudal cell is essentially that of a creditor with a second charge who tries in every way to release the debtor from a debt which is in front of his own: the motive is not generosity but the desire to have his own debt served.

We cannot but admire the ways, hidden even from itself, in which Power attains its ends.

It is well known that wars multiply the grants-in-aid demanded by the king, and how these grants, which were at first exceptional, became in the course of the long conflict between England and France more and more frequent, until in the end Charles VII was able to establish the permanent poll-tax, on top of which came the super poll-tax, a foundation for the ensuing structure of taxation.

What is less well known is how this continuous advance in demands for public taxation was made possible by an increasing recoil in the collection of feudal dues. The back of the worker would have been broken had one set of taxes been imposed on top of the other; but in fact one took the place of the other, which gradually became less burdensome by reason of monetary devaluations.

The reasons for these devaluations have been misunderstood, just as their effects have been underestimated. The French kings were not counterfeiters by habit, in the sense that, with a view to facilitating payments, they passed into circulation clipped currencies to which they gave the same nominal value. The course of events was different. To further their imperial ends, and above all to meet their military requirements, they had to have supplies of precious metals. Their way of attracting them to the mints was to raise the price offered for gold and silver marks.[11] In that way there was an inflow of gold and silver, but, as the price of the mark in pounds had risen,[12] and in order not to incur a loss by the transaction, they had to mint and put into circulation additional pieces with a higher nominal value. That is the real way in which devaluations operate: their rhythm follows that of the state's requirements.

An aristocracy lives on the fixed dues paid it by the peasantry; therefore the effect of each devaluation was to impoverish it and enrich the peasantry. In the course of four centuries the silver content of the pound fell progressively to an eighteenth of what it had been before the Hundred Years' War. It is easy to see what inroads this single cause[13] made in the baronial revenues. No doubt the feudal lord was able to compensate the attenuation of his revenues by raising the dues payable, so long as he was the absolute master of the men under his jurisdiction. But at first the meaning of the phenomenon escaped him. And when at last he did try to make adjustments, the king's courts had already become powerful enough to prevent him. The result was that, at the time that the monarchy ended, the notables, though their estates were enormous, were drawing from them relatively small revenues and had been reduced to begging for pensions.[14]

In this way Power, even where it has no such intention, merely by the slant given to it by its nature, puts down the mighty and frees those who were subject to them: by closing the door on one form of exploitation, it opens it to its own.

## 6. Power and the Capitalistic Cell

If the aristocracy of the clans preceded the city state of old, and if the feudal aristocracy was the twin brother of the Gothic type of monarchy,

11. A unit of weight.

12. Philip the Fair, for instance, for his war with England, and later for his Flemish war, which was made notable by the disaster at Courtrai, was in such need of money wherewith to pay his mercenaries that the price offered for a silver mark rose in successive stages from 2 pounds 18 sols to 8 pounds 10 sols, according to Dupré de Saint-Mur (*Essai sur les monnaies*). It was naturally not possible to put the same amount of silver as before in a coin of the same nominal value; naturally also the coins already circulating took on a higher nominal value.

13. After deducting the depreciation of silver in terms of goods consequent on the opening of the mines in America.

14. The analogy with what we see happening in our own day to the owners of house property is a striking one. The state has forbidden them to raise their rents to correspond

the capitalist aristocracy came after the birth of the modern state. It grew in its shadow and may fairly be called its child. But its parent chases it with an appetite worthy of old Saturn.

By forcing men out of the closed formations of which they are in the beginning integral parts, Power creates the essential condition of a mercantile economy: they are now entered on the roll in both columns, as producers and consumers.

So long as Power is fighting its battle with the *notables*, who keep men in the fetters of a personal dependence on themselves, it views with favour the rise of a class of *rich*, who seem to it to derogate nothing from its own authority, being as they are without a subject group which takes its law from them and disregards that of the state. That is the reason why the celebrated classifications of Servius Tullius and Solon, conceived as a means of putting down the aristocracy of the clans, had the effect of exalting the rich. The kings, who are the most set on destroying the feudal baronies, are also the best friends of the merchants, the bankers, and the master manufacturers.

A shipowner is not the chieftain of a gang of sailors whom he abstracts from Power's clutch, but rather an employer of labour who, on the contrary, makes them available to Power when the time comes for it to require them; in this way is explained the favour shown by Francis I, to take one instance, towards Ango. A banker is not after political power—he is after wealth. His function is to build a sort of store-house on which, when the time is ripe, Power will draw to transmute this wealth into strength.

A mercantile aristocracy, then, so far from abstracting anything from the state's resources, makes potential additions to them which will, when circumstances so require, be realized. This is the only aspect under which, for many years, Power saw the money power.

But in the end the overthrow of every other social domination of whatever kind left financial domination master of the field. At that stage it was seen to be the formative source of fresh cells. That showed itself clearly enough in the case of the industrial employers. Not only was the employer the law in his factory, but quite often he would put up nearby a township for his workers in which he had the position of prince. A point was even reached, as in some of the states of the U.S.A., at which

---

with depreciations in the currency, with the result that their incomes no longer bear any relation to the real or replacement values of their properties.

the manufacturer, owning as he did the land on which the factory had been built, allowed on it no other police than his own.

In its jealousy of any and every command, however small, which was not its own, Power could not tolerate such independence. Moreover, as in every other battle which it had fought with aristocratic formations, it soon found itself appealed to by the underlings. Then it made its way not only into the employer's township but into his workshop as well; there it introduced its own law, its own police, and its own factory regulations. If its earlier aggressions against closed aristocratic formations were not our old friends, we might be tempted to see in this one nothing more than a result of the popular character of the modern state, and of socialist ideas. These factors played, no doubt, their part, but no more was needed than that Power should be itself—a thing naturally tending to shut out the intervention of all other authorities.

The financial cell is less visible to the eye than the industrial cell. By its hold on money, and above all by its disposal of vast amounts of private savings, finance has been able to build up a vast structure and impose on the ever growing number of its subjects an authority which is ever plainer to the view. On the empires of finance also Power made war. The signal for battle was not given by a socialist state, the natural enemy of the barons of capital. It came from Theodore Roosevelt, himself a man of Power and therefore the enemy of all private authorities.

In this way a new alliance was sealed—an alliance no less natural than that of the Power of early days with the prisoners of the clan-cells, than that of the monarchy with the subjects of the feudal barons—that of the modern state with the men exploited by capitalist industry, with the men dominated by the financial trusts.

The state has often waged this particular war half-heartedly, thereby marking the extent to which it has turned its back on itself and has renounced its role of Power. And renunciation was in this case favoured by the internal weakness of modern Power; the precariousness of its tenure encouraged its phantom tenants to betray it in favour of the financial aristocracies.

But Power has natural charms for those who desire it for use. It was as certain that anti-capitalists would come to occupy the public offices of the bourgeois state as it was certain that anti-feudalists would come to occupy those of the monarchical state.

Not that they were the real artisans of the capitalist downfall. They were not responsible for the growing diversion at the source of the rivulets of savings which fed capitalist authority. The growth of savings banks, the accumulation of their earnings in an enormous bank which was larger than any capitalist bank, their enlargement by funds of a social character, the employment of the deposits of commercial banks in government issues, everything, in short, which has put the bulk of the national wealth at Power's disposal, was done without thought of socialist purpose.

It was because of the state's needs, and from no anti-capitalist design, that there was developed that efficient weapon, the income tax, which is associated with the names of Pitt and Caillaux.

In the end, calling it socialization or nationalization, the state strives to make its own all the great castles of the economic feudal system, the railway companies, the electricity distributing companies, and so on. Only those who know nothing of any time but their own, who are completely in the dark as to the manner of Power's behaving through thousands of years, would regard these proceedings as the fruit of a particular set of doctrines. They are in fact the normal manifestations of Power, and differ not at all in their nature from Henry VIII's confiscation of the wealth of the monasteries. The same principle is at work; the hunger for authority, the thirst for resources; and in all these operations the same characteristics are present, including the rapid elevation of the dividers of the spoils. Whether it is socialist or whether it is not, Power must always be at war with the capitalist authorities and despoil the capitalists of their accumulated wealth: in doing so it obeys the law of its nature. Whether it is socialist or whether it is not, it cannot but present itself as the ally of those who are under the dominion of the capitalist. Philanthropy, it is true, plays a part in this alliance. But the sure instinct for the distension of the state necessarily turns this philanthropy to the glory and strength of Power.

One particularly interesting feature of the war waged by Power in our own time has been that, up to now, it has fought only one of the two categories of social authorities which made their appearance in the second half of the nineteenth century: its enemy has been the capitalist forces, not the syndicalist.

These two authorities have evolved on almost parallel lines. In the beginning both were associations in the true sense—between masters who knew each other and men who knew each other. Helped by the folly of legislatures, both grew to Gargantuan proportions, and with that took on new forms. They then became associations in the fictive sense, in which an apparatus of command gave rule to the associates, of whose control it became much more independent than political commands have succeeded in becoming of their peoples. Will political Power, after beating capitalist feudalism with the help of syndicalist feudalism, now round on its ally?

If it does not, it will be the syndicalist feudalisms, and not itself, which will exercise the vast powers committed to it by individuals. And the state will then be the "public thing" of the syndicalist feudalisms.

In the alternative, as has happened in Russia, it will beat them down into subordination. This battle is now joined everywhere before our eyes.

Where does it all lead to, this unending war waged by Power against the other authorities which society throws up? Will the jaws of the great boa constrictor of human energies ever cease to close on all who in turn put these energies to their use?

Where will it end? In the destruction of all other command for the benefit of one alone—that of the state. In each man's absolute freedom from every family and social authority, a freedom the price of which is complete submission to the state. In the complete equality as between themselves of all citizens, paid for by their equal abasement before the power of their absolute master—the state. In the disappearance of every constraint which does not emanate from the state, and in the denial of every pre-eminence which is not approved by the state. In a word, it ends in the atomization of society, and in the rupture of every private tie linking man and man, whose only bond is now their common bondage to the state. The extremes of individualism and socialism meet: that was their predestined course.

Every historical society seems, by successive stages, to have dragged its slow length into a form of institutions in which all life is absorbed by, and all movement emanates from, Power. It is a despotic form; in it there is neither wealth, nor authority, nor even liberty, outside Power, which is in consequence the goal of all ambition; nor can its holders find shelter from the rivalry which breeds anarchy, except by buttressing themselves with divine status.

We feel much as Tacitus might have felt about this "imperial" ordering of society. But we must in honesty admit that at certain periods of history the desire of men is to live in tranquillity, even if to do so requires keepers. Sometimes it has happened that an unlimited and omnipotent sovereignty made small demands of its subjects, the reason being that it pursued no large ends, had no fanatical leanings, and feared no foreign rival. But even these conditions would not have sufficed in the absence of another and decisive one: which is that the strength of Power was in proportion to its extent.

When an energetic and persistent will exercises even the most extensive powers, custom after a time deadens the weight of the duties and inhibitions which it inflicts. Power's security, both internal and external, then makes possible a real alleviation of the burden, so that at certain periods of the Roman Empire, for instance, a very wide measure of personal liberty seems to have been effectively enjoyed.

Very different, however, is the case when the strength of Power is in inverse ratio to its extent—which is what we see today, when the political controls, which extend in all directions and leave nothing untouched, are liable to be given, whether simultaneously or successively, contradictory impulsions, and the master of a regimented society is not a single mind but a confused jumble. It is in such a case as certain as anything can be that, unless there is curtailment of the state's activities, the reins of government will in the end be brought together into one imperial hand, whatever name it takes and from whatever place in society it comes.

What, then, will an egalitarian society, in which the high command no longer resembles an excited crowd, look like? The Ancient Egyptian Empire, which Jacques Pirenne has strikingly depicted, may give us some idea.[15]

In an individualist society in which no family or social group exists, every public duty is performed exclusively by the State. First among them is that of assuring external security. To guarantee it the State disposes of an up-to-date military organization, which is distinct from the civil authorities and of which the king is the supreme head. The army is divided into tactical units which are placed under the command of regular officers; it is equipped, victualled and supplied by a commissariat service; the fleet, composed of large ships, is built in the shipyards of the State; the frontier forts are built by the military labour corps. In addition, the army is formed out of recruits; and the only security the Nation knows is that which it gets itself by supporting the burden of military service imposed on it by the State.

Internal peace is assured by the judicial body, which holds pride of place among all the administrative bodies. All justice emanates from the king, in whose name the various courts of first instance and appeal pronounce their judgments. The litigants may, it is true, resort to arbitration, which, however,

15. J. Pirenne, *Histoire du droit et des institutions privées de l'ancienne Égypte,* Vol. I, p. 204.

derives all validity and authority from the assurance that the State will execute its awards.

The social life, whose external and internal security is assured by the army and the judicial body respectively, rests on the service of the civil departments, which give to each and preserve for each his place in Society, of the land-survey, which is the foundation of all property rights, and of the registry of documents, which, by transcribing all conveyances and contracts, can assure at need respect for the pledged word and guarantee to each the free disposal of his own goods and rights.

The economic life largely depends on the service of the inland waterways. The ever more powerful State is ever more lavishly housed by the public works administration. The coordination of the various departments is the work of the chancery.

The offices of all these various services are spread over the country; in all parts of it officials of all grades write minutes on papyrus rolls, which are then collected and filed in the State archives.

In this way the administration makes itself not only the foundation but the very condition of existence in this individualist society; that society owes life itself to the supremacy of a State which guards, but, for that very reason, encroaches further and further.

And so, in the act of developing, the administration fastens closer and closer the grip of the State and multiplies incessantly the number and importance of its services and officials.

All these functions must be paid for. The State, it is true, possesses vast estates with enormous revenues. But the charges which it has to meet grow unceasingly. Not only does the administration itself cost more and more, but the growing authority of the State increases continually the prestige of the king, who, now canonized not only into a god but into the god of gods, surrounds himself with a Court the measure of whose luxury calls for an ever more numerous retinue of priests, courtiers, employees and servants. Thus the requirements of the State come to exceed by far the revenues of its estates. Recourse is then had to taxation.

The civil departments, the land-survey, the registry of documents, thanks to which each single Egyptian is secured in his property and in his rights, have the further effect of giving the State a very good idea of what each possesses and of levying taxation on it accordingly. The administration of the finances and the taxation service then assumes an importance second to none, for, if Egyptian Society, from the third to the fifth dynasty, is viable only by reason of its competent and complicated administrative machine, that machine itself lives only on the strength of the taxation yield. So that the fiscal weapon is seen as an essential feature of the Egyptian Empire under the fourth dynasty.

All Egyptians are equal before the Law, but this equality of their levels them all into an equal subservience to a more and more omnipotent State as represented in the king.

## 7. Zenith and Dismemberment of the State

There we see where the development of the state leads. The social hierarchy is in ruins; the individual members are like peas shelled from their pods and form a numerical whole composed of equal elements. The state is the beginning and end of organization; it must apply itself to the task with the highest degree of authority and attention to detail. But is that to say that there are now no longer any privileged persons? There are indeed; but as regards the state they are no longer privileged as men preceding its authority. They hold their privileges in and from the state.

> The *cultus* of the king, established as it was to assure the supremacy of the sovereign and to exalt him far above those ancient local cults to which in former times the territorial nobility had owed its power and its prestige, undoubtedly played a large part in destroying this ancient nobility; simultaneously, however, it brought to birth in the heart of the services of the Crown a new and non-hereditary nobility which, though owing everything to the king, was bound little by little to raise up against his authority a new social force of considerable strength.[16]

Bureaucratic omnipotence tends naturally to convert the holders of key positions in the vast administrative machine into a new variety of notables and nobles. So it happened in the late Roman Empire. The aristocratic families had been ground to powder by taxation. Those, on the other hand, often the freedmen of subject races, who occupied strategic positions in the wealth-absorbing machine, got from it immense fortunes not unmixed with personal regard. On this subject Rostovtzev says:

> The reforms of Diocletian and Constantine, by implementing a policy of systematic spoliation to the profit of the State, made all productive activity impossible. The reason is, not that there were no more large fortunes: on the contrary, their build-up was made easier. But the foundation of their build-up was now no longer creative energy, or the discovery and bringing into use of new sources of wealth, or the improvement and development of husbandry, industry and commerce. It was, on the contrary, the *cunning*

16. *Ibid.*

*exploitation of a privileged position in the State*, used to despoil people and State alike. The officials, great and small, got rich by way of fraud and corruption.[17]

We may be sure that this new race of barons will try to make their own the offices which bring them such advantages and to assure their transmission to their descendants. It will be the feudal system over again.[18]

Conqueror though it is of the aristocracy which took shape in society, the state will in the end be dismembered by the statocracy which it itself has borne. The beneficiaries of the state leave it, taking with them a veritable dowry of wealth and authority, leaving the state impoverished and powerless. Then it becomes the turn of the state to break down these new social molecules, containing as they do the human energies which it needs. And so the process of the state's expansion starts all over again.

Such is the spectacle which history presents to us. Now we see an aggressive state pulling down what other authorities have built up, now we see an omnipotent and distended state bursting like a ripe spore and releasing from its midst a new feudalism which robs it of its substance.

## 8. The Dynamism of Politics

Has this process of everlasting weaving and undoing no term or purpose? Apparently not. It is this making and unmaking of the state that gives social life its rhythm.

We do not demand of a chemist who has just described to us a chemical reaction that he should pass on it a judgment of value. Why, then, should the political analyst be expected to hold up one phase of this unending transformation scene as progress and another as decadence?

All that can be said is that contemporaries get the feeling of progress right through the period in which the state is building up, a feeling comparable to the sense of well-being which in an economic cycle accompanies the period of high prices. When the process nears its apogee, the more sensitive spirits are assailed by feelings of doubt and dizziness. It begins to be seen that this perfection of equality and this carefulness of organization are a work of men's hands and stand against the blasts of

17. Rostovtzev, *Social and Economic History of the Roman Empire* (Oxford: 1926) p. 475.

18. Rostovtzev shows them sinking the yield of their levies in landed estates, and erecting in the middle of their properties vast and luxurious fortified villas in which they reigned surrounded by their families, their slaves, a veritable court of armed retainers, and thousands of serfs!

natural laws only by a conscious effort of will, and that, on the first sign of slackening in the rulers, or at the first shock from the outer world, nuclei of resistance form among the powerless.

Then the question is heard again whether the egalitarian society, which is the handiwork of the despotic state, is more or less advantageous to the mass of the workers than a society of independent authorities. The question does not admit of an exact answer. For the condition of a man who is bound in shackles, whether they are those of a state or of an employer, turns much less on the nature of his particular master than on the degree of rivalry subsisting among all the masters; the condition of the Lancashire families engaged in the cotton industry at the time of intense rivalry for the world market was a miserable one. Those workers would have had everything to gain by entering the service of a state which was pacific. But when states are engaged in an operation of war, that one which is loudest in its appeal to popular principles demands of its citizens such an output as makes them sigh for the hardest private employer.

It is, by a lamentable conjuncture, always in warlike times that the state tries its hardest to take immediate hold on the labouring classes. In times of peace it is relatively content to leave them in the hands of private employers; for the state obeys the rhythm of its own needs.

Whoever does not wish to render history incomprehensible by departmentalizing it—political, economic, social—would perhaps take the view that it is in essence a battle of dominant wills, fighting in every way they can for the material which is common to everything they construct: the human labour force.

# X.

## *Power and the Common People*

IF THE NATURAL TENDENCY OF POWER IS TO GROW, and if it can extend its authority and increase its resources only at the expense of the notables, it follows that its ally for all time is the common people. The passion for absolutism is, inevitably, in conspiracy with the passion for equality.

History is one continuous proof of this; sometimes, however, as if to clarify this secular process, she concentrates it into a one-act play, such as that of the Doge Marino Falieri. So independent of the Doge were the Venetian nobility that Michel Steno could insult the Doge's wife and escape with a punishment which was so derisory as to double the insult. Indeed, so far above the people's heads was this nobility that Bertuccio Ixarello, a plebeian, was unable, in spite of his naval exploits, to obtain satisfaction for a box on the ear given him by Giovanni Dandalo. According to the accepted story, Bertuccio came to the Doge and showed him the wound in his cheek from the patrician's ring; shaming the Doge out of his inactivity, he said to him: "Let us join forces to destroy this aristocratic authority which thus perpetuates the abasement of my people and limits so narrowly your power." The annihilation of the nobility would give to each what he wanted—to the common people equality, to Power absolutism. The attempt of Marino Falieri failed and he was put to death.

A like fate befell Jan van Barneveldt, whose case was the exact converse. In the history of the Netherlands we come across this same conflict between a prince wishing to increase his authority, in this case the Stadtholder of the House of Orange, and social authorities standing in his way, in this case the rich merchants and shipowners of Holland. William,[1] commander-in-chief throughout thirty difficult and glorious years, was nearing the crown, and had already refused it once, as did Caesar and Cromwell, when he was struck down by the hand of the assassin. Prince Maurice inherited his father's prestige, added to it by victories of his own, and seemed about to reach the goal, when Barneveldt, having organized secretly a patrician opposition, put an end to Maurice's ambitions by putting an end, through the conclusion of peace, to victories which were proving dangerous to the Republic.[2] What did Maurice do then? He allied himself with the most ignorant of the preachers, who were, through their fierce intolerance, the aptest to excite the passions of the lower orders: thanks to their efforts, he unleashed the mob at Barneveldt and cut off his head. This intervention by the common people enabled Maurice to execute the leader of the opposition to his own increasing power. That he did not gain the authority he sought was not due to any mistake in his choice of means, as was shown when one of his successors, William III, made himself at last master of the country by means of a popular rising, in which Jean de Witt, the Barneveldt of his period, had his throat cut.

De Witt and Barneveldt were in the tradition of Cato; they stood for a commonwealth administered by the most considerable men in the community. The Princes of Orange were in the tradition of Caesar; to make themselves supreme they roused the mob. The poorest of scholars remembers those scenes of riot—Cato pulled down from the rostrum by an angry mob, and warning it in vain that it is silencing its superiors only to give itself a master.

The uses of demagogy to ambition are well known, but no study of Power's confederacies in violence with the common people is complete which does not draw attention to their amiable and permanent cohabitation down the centuries. What it took Caesar a few years to do took the

---

1. [William the Silent (1533–1584), Prince of Orange.]

2. Sir William Temple, that shrewd politician, wrote: "The credit and authority of Prince Maurice, which were at first founded on his father's but were soon raised by his own virtues and qualities and military success, had at that time reached such a height that several of the States-General, led by Barneveldt, a man of much talent and then enjoying great prestige, became jealous of the authority acquired by the prince and pretended to be afraid that he would attain in the end an absolute authority. They knew that his authority would grow

Capetian monarchy some four hundred years: but the task and the tactics were the same.

Aristocracy, always and everywhere, opposes the rise of a Power which disposes in its own right of sufficient means of action to make itself independent of society, those means being, essentially, a permanent administration, a standing army, and taxation.

The type of regime which answers to the aristocratic spirit is one in which the magistrates are entrusted by rotation to the most eminent citizens, an armed force is formed at need by the gathering together of the various social forces, and financial resources are collected, as occasion calls, out of the contributions of the leading members of the community.

The more concentrated and urban an aristocracy is, and the more tightly knit its common interests, the more effective will such a system be; the more spread out and landed it is, and the more divided in interest, the less effective will it be. In a constitution such as this lay the strength of Athens at the time of the Persian Wars, and that of Rome at the time of the Punic Wars; but in it, too, lay the weakness of Germany in the Renaissance.

Always and everywhere a concrete Power tends to form in the midst of these aristocratic republics; its success is measured by the build-up of its bureaucratic, military, and financial agencies; the cooperation of the common people is the stay of its advance, its victim is the aristocracy.

To this the history of France bears striking testimony.

## 1. The Feudal Commonwealth

Was it really Power that Hugh Capet got in A.D. 987? It was much more like the presidency of a loosely-knit aristocratic republic or, to speak more accurately still, of a federation of barons.

It is common knowledge that a long line of our kings took their most important political decisions only when they were sitting at court with their peers and that the same procedure marked the giving of judicial decisions. It would be a mistake to think that the monarch merely asked for the peers' advice.

This customary procedure was a reflection of the social constitution. To bring into being any public body of force meant a bringing together

---

with every day that the war, the conduct of which was in his hands, lasted, and they calculated that it would diminish in peace and leave them preponderant. This calculation inclined all this party of peace."

of numerous private forces, the result being that nothing could be undertaken without the consent of those to whom those forces belonged. What use would it have been to the king to decide on a war if the barons had not mustered their contingents? What use to condemn a notable if his peers were certain to refuse to cooperate in the execution of the sentence?

The king's court of those days corresponded to the board of directors of ours; its purpose was to handle matters which were within the competence of the commonwealth but not of one man.[3]

The weakness of Power of this kind was due to the process of decomposition which has been fully studied.

Gaul, no doubt, had yielded the Frankish chiefs important state demains, and even state workshops, together with regular revenues from forced contributions. But the chiefs divided up these properties and assigned the revenues to the Frankish nobles and the Roman bishops, whether from the native generosity of barbarians, or more probably from being compelled to buy up continually variable local loyalties, the demand for which was only too frequent because of their own dynastic quarrels.

No doubt the invaders obeyed their king's call to arms—such was the German custom—and even included in it the subject populations. But this service was unpaid, and the warrior, whose duty it was, had to equip and provision his contingent himself;[4] it therefore carried the implication

3. The very language of the ordinances sufficiently indicates that the decisions were reached in common; the *Stabilimentum Feudorum*, for instance, at the relatively late date of 1204, still starts in these words: "Philip by the grace of God King of France, Eudes Duke of Burgundy, Hervé Count of Nevers, Renand Count of Boulogne, Gaucher Count of Saint-Paul, Guy de Dampierre and several others who have unanimously agreed . . ."

The monarch is in this court only the president and does not always get his way. It embodies the principle—that, namely, of a commonwealth managed by the social princes—opposite to that of the state. It makes another appearance in the Latin kingdom of Jerusalem, where the sovereign could not touch either the person or the fief of a vassal except in virtue of a judgment of the feudal court—of, in other words, the entire community of vassals. In Spain, again, Alfonso IX swore not to proceed against either the person or the property of a vassal, until his case had been heard by the court. In England, too, Britten tells us that the court was judge in cases to which the king was a party; there the Mirror of Justice asserts that the court should be as much open to actions against the king as to actions against anyone else.

Cf. the paper given by A. J. Carlyle at the third session of the International Institute of Philosophy and Legal Sociology.

4. The Carolingians tried to maintain, or, more accurately perhaps, to re-establish, this ancient custom. The frequency of their ordinances on this subject seems to bear out that the "national" army could no longer be got together as easily as in the past. An ordinance

that he was rich enough to procure the arms needed[5] and had slaves enough to absent himself from home.[6] The class of freemen who fulfilled these conditions had been numerous in the time of Dagobert[7] but declined progressively from the eighth to the tenth century. The independent proprietor, seeing his freehold threatened with devastation by Norman or Saracen or Hungarian, placed himself and his possessions in the hands of some notable who could supply the king's inability to protect him. From this there emerged the establishment of feudal "police forces," consisting of mounted troops clad in costly cuirasses, at a price which only the most substantial men could support. There was not, then, a national army for the king to muster, but only feudal troops, for the loan of which he had to ask.

The reason for the king's inability to govern without the barons was that the wealth and energy of the country were their private property. They, naturally, came to occupy in the commonwealth positions of an importance which was in proportion to their own, bringing to those positions a greater authority than any they derived from them. So that the king was not so much served by an administration as kept in leading-strings by the "great officers" of the realm.

## 2. Power Asserts Itself

Power emerged from this primitive state of impotence by continuous and successive stages: for the organs lent it by the social authorities it substituted its own.

---

of 811 reminds the men that they must carry with them sufficient provisions to enable them to campaign for three months outside the country. It also lays down that they must be equipped for a six months' term of absence. The *Capitulare Aquisgranense* lays down the minimum requirements of armour, lance, shield, and a bow with two strings and twelve arrows.

5. In the miserable state into which the industrial arts had fallen, the lance and shield alone cost the price of an ox. The sword and dagger cost three large oxen and one fair-sized one. The cuirass, which was at that time no more than a leather jerkin on to which were sewn iron rings to form a breast-plate, cost as much as ten oxen. And the helmet and crest cost three. It took, therefore, a substantial fortune to get a complete suit of armour. Cf. Loi Ripuaire, quoted by Mlle de Lezardière in *Théorie des lois politiques de la monarchie française,* Vol. I, p. 391.

6. Charlemagne had to lay it down that the obligation extended only to the possessors of four furnished tables, corresponding to the twelve acres on which four families of serfs worked.

7. [Dagobert (reigned A.D. 631–638), first of several Merovingian kings of that name.]

At the top was the court, in which the divergent interests of the barons found expression. The king slipped into it some ecclesiastics, not any of the great bishops, who were as baronial as the barons, but humble priests who had in strict reason no place in what was really an assemblage of petty sovereigns. But their habit and their knowledge brought them respect: and their opinions supported the king's. Next, he introduced some lawyers of plebeian rank, who sat humbly on the steps of the benches reserved for the peers and upper barons—as Saint-Simon contemptuously records[8]—that they might be consulted when it was convenient to do so. Raised from nothing by the king, they gave advice, having for its inspiration the Roman law,[9] which was always favourable to the central authority. In the end the sovereign permitted them to express opinions, thus subverting the primitive constitution by which a man's importance in the state was in proportion to the strength which he wielded in society. At long last, the court became the parliament—the expression of none but the royal interest.

The fist of the state was an army made up of feudal contingents, each of which acknowledged only its immediate chief, the particular baron who had summoned it to his banners: a structure which was without cohesion, for the caprice of any one baron could at a stroke deprive it of an entire group of combatants: an undisciplined kind of coalition which could not, as was seen at Crécy,[10] be trained to orderly movements. The king soon put in their place a force of hired cavalry which he developed as far as his resources allowed. He would have liked to withdraw the commons from feudal authority and draw on them for a substantial force of infantry, a truly national army which would be under his orders. But all attempts in that direction failed until the last one, Charles VII's[11] free

8. *Mémoires* (ed. Boislisle) Vol. XXV, p. 204.

9. The monarchy was at first hostile to the Roman law, on which the Emperor rested his claims. It became friendly to it, once there was nothing to be feared from the Emperor, because it buttressed its own claims to absolutism.

10. When the two marshals sought to bring some order into the cavalcade and gave the order: "Halt banners," those in front obeyed, but those behind, being jealous of their honour, kept on riding forward, saying that they would not stop until they had reached the head of the army; "and when those in front saw that those behind were catching them up, they too rode forward—for each man was anxious to surpass his companion." But "as soon as they saw their enemies they all retreated at once, and in so disorderly a fashion that those who were behind were dismayed and supposed that those in front had joined battle and had already been discomforted." Froissart.

11. [Charles VII (1422–1461) ended the Hundred Years' War successfully for France in 1453.]

corps of archers, of whom nothing more would be expected after their rout at Guinegate (in 1479).

Infantry did not become capable of withstanding cavalry charges until the Swiss had revived the Greek tactical formation of the "hedgehog": and it was only then that, backed by plebeian mercenaries, the monarchy could make itself absolute.

The nerve centres of the political high command were at first the "great officers of state," powerful barons who supervised, controlled, and bridled the king, and on occasion turned against him. The king in his turn took every occasion of noiselessly removing these dangerous auxiliaries. That was what happened to the seneschal. This "officer of state" was charged with the oversight of the king's table, and, when that was served, with victualling the king's men-at-arms; this meant that it was he who also led them to battle and was their military commander. But, besides that, since the provisioning of the court fell in those days on the provosts who administered the royal estates, the seneschal, as was natural, controlled the provosts and superintended the estates.

When functions of this character had been concentrated in the hands of a baron who was already powerful in his own right, anything might be feared. It took a palace revolution to bring about the fall of Étienne de Garlande in 1127, and Philip Augustus did away with the office in 1191. Later, however, the constable, who carried the king's sword, was to prove, as is shown by the Constable de Bourbon's treason, no less dangerous.[12]

It was in the military sphere that the monarchy let itself be served longest by the great barons. In all others it may be seen having systematic recourse to plebeian servants.

What could be more essential to the royal authority than finance? And how could its management possibly be left to a powerful baron, such as the chamberlain, whose key denotes that the safe is in his keeping? For that reason the sovereign took for the effective administration of his

12. Once more, the word "treason" implies the idea of a state as the kings conceived it and as we conceive it. But the constable saw things differently: the realm in his eyes was a confederation of manors, at the head of which was Francis I. And one of the offices of the confederation was that of constable: but it was lawful for a confederate member to quit the confederation and rely on his own forces. Men thought thus throughout the Middle Ages. In the time of Francis I this conception no longer corresponded to reality in France, but it still corresponded to it in Germany, where the Empire has visibly taken on the character of a confederation of aristocratic authorities and where the central authority had been reduced to a shadow.

revenues humble ecclesiastics and mere bourgeoisie. Borelli de Serres has given us the names of these officials from the time of Philip the Fair in the late thirteenth and early fourteenth centuries: all of them are men of humble rank.

There we see it: plebeian counsellors, plebeian soldiers, plebeian officials; these are the instruments of a Power which seeks, more or less consciously, to make itself absolute.

### 3. The Place of the Common Man in the State

In popular imagination a monarchy keeps its employments for the nobles and excludes from them the common people. In fact the exact opposite happens; it endures the services of the great only so far as it stays under aristocratic tutelage; but it calls on the services of the common people so far as it aims at becoming absolute.

The most total Power that Europe in the days of the *ancien régime* ever knew was that of the Ottoman Turks. And where, if you please, did their *grand seigneur* find his most faithful soldiers and his surest servants? Not among the Turkish nobility, the companions of his conquests, of whose pride and turbulence he went in fear. He recruited his janissaries among the subject Christian races. To them, too, he went for his administrators, and even for his grand vizier. In this way he raised above the natural aristocracy a statocracy composed of men who had nothing and owed him everything.[13]

Our French kings moved on the same road. Some of them moved consciously, as in the case of Louis XI (1461–1483), who is shown us by Comines as being "the natural friend of the middle class and the enemy of the great who could do without him." The other kings followed instinctively the same course.

The natural requirements of Power made the fortunes of the common

13. For an ambassador coming, like Busbecq, from Europe, it was an astonishing sight to see a court in which there were no Turkish nobles but only officials: "There was not a single man in all this great assembly who owed his position to anything but valour and merit. The Turks attach no importance to birth; the consideration given a man turns only on the position occupied by him in the state. There are no disputes as to precedence: *the office gives the place.* In making his appointments, the Sultan pays no attention to either rank or fortune. . . . Those who receive from him the highest offices are more often than not sons of shepherds."

people. All those "little people," whom Dupont-Ferrier[14] shows us staffing the Treasury Court and the Taxes Court, no sooner found their niche in the state than they set about advancing their own fortunes along with their employer's. At whose expense? The aristocrats'. With a boldness born of obscurity they encroached progressively on the taxing rights of the barons and transferred to the royal treasury the incomes of the great. As their invasions grew, the financial machine grew larger and more complicated. That there might be new posts for their relations, they discovered new duties, so that whole families came to take their ease in a bureaucracy which grew continually in numbers and authority. Again, as more and more taxes were demanded from the people of the realm, the middle-class officials of the Taxes Court took the chance presented to secure the elevation of their provincial colleagues. Assessment and collection were at first entrusted to men chosen by the taxpayers; but these officials soon came to be appointed by the administration and continued in office from one tax to the next, spawning the while a whole hierarchy of underlings—deputies, clerks, registrars. So it was that everywhere the service of the state became the road to distinction, advancement, and authority for the common people.[15]

The judicial world went the way of the financial. The poor bachelors of law who were summoned to the king's court steadily pushed the barons out of it, gained assurance, put on a periwig, became the parliament,[16] and forced their way by degrees even into the baronial estates; this last they did by setting up as judges between the baron and his followers: in other words, by robbing him of his authority.

What a sight it is, this rise of the clerks,[17] this swarming of busy bees

14. G. Dupont-Ferrier, *Études sur les institutions financières de la France* (2 vols. Paris: Firmin-Didot, 1930 and 1932).

15. Maine noticed in British India a similar phenomenon, that of those responsible for the collection of the taxes becoming the leading men of the locality.

16. ["Parliament" has been used to translate *parlement* here and elsewhere in this book, but it requires to be noted that in France, from the end of the thirteenth century down to the Revolution, *parlement* signified, not a deliberative assembly, but certain superior and final courts of judicature, in which also the edicts of the king were registered before they became laws. The chief *parlement* was at Paris, but there were also twelve provincial *parlements*. The *parlements* had, by virtue of their judicial functions, some measure of control over the administration within their several provinces.]

17. On the eve of the Wars of Religion, Augustin Thierry wrote: "The Third Estate found itself, by a sort of prescriptive right which operated less completely against the clergy than against the nobility, holding nearly the whole of the offices in the civil administration,

who gradually devour the feudal splendour and leave it with nothing but its pomp and titles! Does it not leap to the eye that the state has made the fortunes of all these common people, just as they have made the state's?

They are bound by a passionate attachment to the offices the possession of which transforms their lives. When the King was mad and the Dauphin imbecile, and the Duke of Burgundy, flown with pride and popularity, had given Paris over to anarchy and butchery, it was Jean Jouvenel, King's Advocate, who, all alone, vindicated and retrieved the laws of the state.

Their love of office, though essentially conservative, has its aggressive side. In putting down the mighty they not only serve the state, they take their revenge at the same time. There are, as it happens, certain aristocratic interests which are also the interests of society. "The continuance of prosperity," said Renan, "needs to be safeguarded by institutions which, though admittedly they give a privileged position to some, form notwithstanding organs of the national life without which certain of its needs stay unsupplied."[18] There is no asking your plebeian official to understand the meaning of that. "The various small fortresses," adds Renan, "in which are stored the things that pertain to society, come to look like feudal castles." Against these feudal castles the men of the king tirelessly renew their attacks.

The historians of the Italian cities picture to us the bourgeoisie setting out on expeditions against the nearby châteaux, attacking them, and, once they had taken them, demolishing them stone by stone. Those who had been the barons were forced by the bourgeoisie to live, alongside themselves, the lives of plain citizens; and in this way the citizens extended the city's authority over the open country. The same memories of past humiliations and deeply felt jealousies, the same passion for the city—

including the highest, including even those which have since received the name of ministries. It was from the plebeian class, rising by way of university degrees and more or less numerous tests, that there came the Chancellor Keeper of the Seals, the Secretaries of State, the Master of Requests, the advocates and procurators of the crown, and the entire judicial body. Similarly, in the financial administration, the officials of every rank—superintendent treasurers, intendants, controllers, receivers general and particular—all belonged to the class of educated bourgeoisie who went by the name of 'gentlemen of the robe.' As for the jurisdiction of the seneschals, the bailiffs and the provosts of the king—if these offices were still held by gentlemen at all, the gentlemen must needs find substitutes and assessors to do the work." A. Thierry, *Histoire du Tiers État* (ed. 1836) pp. 83–84.

18. Renan, "La Monarchie constitutionnelle en France" in *La Réforme intellectuelle et morale de la France* (ed. Calmann-Lévy) pp. 249–50.

which is the City of Command—to which he belongs, impel the politician of the people to destroy every private authority, and anything else that bounds, limits, or stays the majesty of the public authority.

### 4. Plebeian Absolutism

Thus we see that the advance of the common people in the state is closely linked with that of the state in the nation.

The common people are to the state servants who buttress it; the state is to the common people the master who raises them.

In favouring the freeing of the serfs and limiting the right of the barons to exploit their underlings, the king thereby weakens his natural enemies. In encouraging the formation of a stratum of well-to-do bourgeoisie, an oligarchy of commoners and a mercantile class, he gets himself servants and assures himself support. In instituting the farming of taxes, he opens to this bourgeoisie the gates of the state. In allowing these taxes to become a heritable property, he links with his own fortunes entire families among the bourgeoisie. He encourages the universities, which provide him with his most effective champions. These maintain his cause, whether against the Emperor or the Pope, in brilliant theses, but, also and still more, they gnaw darkly and continuously at the foundations of baronial right. Augustin Thierry has, therefore, good reason to assert:

> For a period of six centuries, from the twelfth to the eighteenth, the histories of the Third Estate and royalty are indissolubly linked together. . . . From the coming of Louis the Fat to the death of Louis XIV, each decisive period in the advance of the various plebeian classes towards liberty, well-being, enlightenment and social importance, corresponds, in the list of reigns, to the name of a great king or of a great minister.[19]

During minorities, or when the sovereign was a weak one and took his orders from the nobility, as was the case with Louis X or Louis XVI, this advance was interrupted and a reaction took shape.

But, the greedier was the monarch of Power, the harder he hit the social princes and the further he pushed the work of emancipation. This was well understood by the Third Estate, and, at the States-General, its representatives—who knelt down to speak—were the most ardent

19. *Op. cit.*, p. 9.

supporters of Power. Sometimes, when their grievances had anticipated the wishes of the king, they incited him to speed his seizure of the baronial jurisdictions.[20] At other times they gave vigorous support to his authority, as at the first convocation summoned by Philip the Fair, and we even see them handing to the monarchy in 1614 an irrevocable mandate to do what it pleased,[21] such as might have emanated from the brain of a Hobbes and to which only a class with a vested interest in absolutism could ever have agreed.

The aristocracy was no less aware that the principal instrument of its progressive decline was the plebeian staff into whose hands Power was falling ever more completely. We have only to listen to Saint-Simon's[22] bitter cries against Mazarin. Saint-Simon well understood that at the time

20. When the process had already gone a long way, the Third Estate at the States of 1562 protested that the barons were exacting *corvées* and taxes in excess of their legal rights, and were haling their subjects "before judges who were their own liegemen"; it claimed that "for the future, in causes between barons and their subjects in which the former have a personal interest, the subjects should only be summoned before a *royal* judge of the province." How useful complaints of this kind were to the expansion of Power!

21. Here is the article which the Third Estate put at the head of its memorandum entitled "The Fundamental Law": "The king shall be entreated to promulgate in the assembly of his Estates, as a fundamental law to be known to and kept inviolate by all, that, as he is the recognized sovereign in his state, holding his crown from God alone, there is no authority on earth of any kind, temporal or spiritual, which has any power in his realm to take it from the sacred person of our king, or to dispense and absolve his subjects from the obedience which they owe him, on any cause or pretext whatsoever, and that all his subjects, of whatever quality and condition, will keep this law for true and sacred and as conforming to the word of God, without distinction, equivocation or limitation of any kind; it shall be sworn to by all the States deputies and after them by all the beneficiaries and officers of the realm, before entering on the possession of their benefices and the performance of their duties; all tax-collectors, regents, doctors and preachers shall be instructed to teach it and make it known; that the contrary opinion, that it is lawful to kill or depose our kings, to rise up in rebellion against them and to shake off the yoke of obedience to them for any reason whatever, is impious, detestable, contrary to truth and contrary to the constitution of the State of France, which is in direct dependence on God alone."

No doubt this declaration is occasional, and is in response to a campaign organized by the Jesuit doctors; in it may be felt the memory of the frightful disorders of the days of the League. But, whatever the particular reasons which inspired it, the declaration was made, and is unquestionably an unlimited and irrevocable mandate.

22. [Saint-Simon, Duc de (1675–1755), French soldier and diplomat, and the author of memoirs, published posthumously, which are such a masterpiece of their kind as to have caused Sainte-Beuve to rank him with Tacitus. After the death of Louis XIV in 1715 he sought, as one of the regents, to realize his favourite vision of France ruled by the nobles for its good; the vision quickly faded, and with it his influence.]

of the Fronde a revolution happened, not of the tumultuous sort at which the Frondeurs tried their hand, but rather an invisible one, which was accomplished by the minister who was Richelieu's heir and Louis XVI's tutor.

All his attention and care were devoted to abolishing in every possible way the distinctions of birth and to despoiling persons of quality of every sort of authority, for which purpose he tried to keep them away from affairs of state; to bringing into the administration people of as low extraction as his own; to magnifying their offices in point of power, distinction, credit and wealth; to persuading the king that as every nobleman was the natural enemy of his authority, he should prefer to them, to handle his affairs, men of no account, who could at the first sign of discontent be reduced to insignificance by having their employments taken from them as easily as the gift of them had raised them from insignificance; whereas the nobility, being already men of importance by reason of their birth, their marriage connections and often by their establishments, acquired through high office and ministerial patronage a formidable strength and became, for the same reason, dangerous to remove from office. That was the cause of the entry into public life of men of the pen and the long robe and of the destruction, still felt and seen, of the nobility at a rate which will seem a prodigy; the men of the pen and the long robe well knew the means of hastening this destruction, and made their yoke worse every day until a point was reached at which the greatest nobleman in the land became of no use to anyone and became in a thousand and one ways dependent on the vilest plebeian.[23]

And again, speaking of Mazarin, he said:

A foreigner coming from the dregs of the people, a man of no account and having no other gods than his own greatness and power, has no care for the state [i.e. nation] that he governs other than as he is himself affected. He despises its laws, its genius, its interests; he disregards its rules and forms; *he thinks only of subjugating and confounding all, of contriving that the all shall be the common people.*

Let us stop to admire how the invective of a great writer flourishes in the soil of truth. To subjugate and confound all, to contrive that the all shall be the common people, therein is the real genius of a monarchical administration. Historians of the sentimental school have sometimes

23. Saint-Simon, *Mémoires* (ed. Boilisle) Vol. XXVII, pp. 6, 7.

regretted that royalty became absolute, while at the same time rejoicing that it installed plebeians in office. They deceive themselves. Royalty exalted plebeians just because it aimed at becoming absolute; it became absolute because it had exalted plebeians.

It is always utterly impossible to build an aggressive Power with aristocrats. Care for family interests, class solidarity, educational influences, all combine to dissuade them from handing over to the state the independence and fortunes of their fellows.

The march of absolutism, which subdues the diversity of customs to the uniformity of laws, wars against local attachments on behalf of a concentration of loyalties on the state, douses all other fires of life that one may remain alight, and substitutes for the personal ascendancy of the notables the mechanical control of an administration—such a system is, I say, the natural destroyer of the traditions on which is founded the pride of aristocracies and of the patronage which gives them their strength.

Resistance is, therefore, the business of aristocracies.

## 5. *The Aristocratic Reaction*

Philippe Pot[24] has come in for much praise by reason of the reproaches he hurled at the monarchy for the despotic character which had just been impressed on it by Louis XI. His defence of the rights and liberties of the nation is often quoted; what is often forgotten is that he was speaking in the name of the nobility.

The Duc de Montmorency, who, as Governor of Languedoc, undertook the defence of the ancient liberties against Richelieu and paid for it with his head—he too was acting the part natural to an aristocrat.

Bonald was not far wrong when he wrote:

> Nobility preserves subjects from oppression merely by its existence. A despotic Power is one which can change, destroy and overthrow as it pleases; a Power which can overthrow as it pleases is an unlimited Power. Nobility sets a limit to Power, for the monarchy cannot obliterate a nobility which lives beside it, is the child, like itself, of the constitution and is, again like itself, linked to society by indissoluble ties. . . .[25]

24. At the States-General of 1484; Louis XI, it may be noted, had died the previous year.

25. Bonald, *Théorie de pouvoir politique et religieux*, Book III.

The reason could not be put more shortly why it was that the unceasing movement of the monarchical Power towards uniformity and unification never attained its logical end—an end which the Revolution was to reach in a few months. The reason was that the monarchy had to reckon with an always resistant and often rebellious nobility, and that the kings, though in logic bound to destroy the nobles utterly, were held back from doing so by tradition, sentiment, and a failure to realize their own true historic role.

The main differences between the history of France and the history of England are almost entirely due to the very different ways in which their respective nobilities acted—as De Lolme[26] has perfectly understood.

The French aristocracy managed badly the day-to-day defence of itself; it proceeded by way of violent, disorderly, clumsy, and brutal counter-offensives, as when, in Louis X's reign, it hanged Enguerrand de Marigny and put to the torture Pierre de Latilly, Chancellor of France, and Raoul de Presle, King's Advocate.[27] It could not carry with it the Third Estate by making it understand that the only motive for freeing it from superiorities which time had sweetened was to subject it to the crushing domination of the state. If the two did find themselves working together, as at the start of the Fronde, the aristocracy soon lost the others' support through incapacity to give its revolt the appearance of a defence of the general interest; soon it was split itself by the greed of the rebels, each of whom was ready, if it was made worth his while, to make his private treaty of peace with the crown.

In short, it lacked the political sense, and knew no other way of recapturing lost positions than under cover of civil disturbances, such as the Wars of Religion or the Fronde—events which weakened authority and so allowed the nobles to resume in the general disorder their part of petty potentates whose return to the fold, when the task of pacification began, would have to be bought.[28]

26. [De Lolme, Dr. J. L., was a Swiss, who published in 1771 *The Rise and Progress of the English Constitution*.]

27. A. Thierry, *op. cit.*, p. 29. "The lawyers of the fourteenth century, who were the founders and ministers of the royal autocracy, came to the end common to great revolutionaries. The boldest perished in the reaction of the interests they had injured and the folkways they had violated."

28. Saint-Simon saw clearly how disturbances worked to the advantage of aristocracy: "All that Henry IV could do, with the support of his faithful nobles, was, after endless toil,

The English aristocracy knew better how to work together; the reason perhaps being that, whereas in France the Parliament passed into the hands of the lawyers and so became an instrument of the crown, in England it remained an organ of the social authorities and a rallying-point for their opposition. So well did it understand the art of giving to its resistance a plausible show of public advantage that the Magna Charta, to take one instance, though in reality nothing more than the capitulation of the king to vested interests acting in their own defence, contained phrases about law and liberty which are valid for all time.

Whereas the French nobles got themselves known to the people as petty tyrants, often more unruly and exacting than a great one would be, the English nobles managed to convey to the yeoman class of free proprietors the feeling that they too were aristocrats on a small scale, with interests to defend in common with the nobles.

This island English aristocracy achieved its master-stroke in 1689. With Harrington[29] rather than John Locke for inspiration, it riveted on the Power given the king whom it had brought from overseas limits so cleverly contrived that they were to last a long time.

The essential instrument of Power is the army.[30] An article of the Bill of Rights made standing armies illegal, and the Mutiny Act sanctioned

---

to get himself fully recognized for what he claimed to be, *by buying as it were the crown from his subjects* by means of treaties and the millions in money which they cost him, *the vast establishments and the assured places for Catholic and Huguenot leaders*. Nobles with places so assured, and who yet felt much disappointed after the positions which each had dreamt of for himself, were a difficult team." *Op. cit.*, Vol. XXVII, p. 9.

29. [Harrington, James (1611–1677), English political philosopher. Of his main work, *Oceana*, in which he expounds an ideal constitution for England, it has been said that "it contains many valuable ideas but is irretrievably dull." The key to his system is rotation in office. One of the valuable ideas is that when all property is concentrated so is all power.]

30. Charles I, for instance, had he disposed of a small well-trained army, would have broken the mass levy of the Covenanters who descended from Scotland under Leslie's command. He would not have been compelled to summon a Parliament before which he had to appear as a suppliant after haughtily dissolving its predecessor. He had to give way to the English in the vain hope of getting the means to subdue Scotland, and then, when the English spurned him, to ask help from the Scots themselves. From one capitulation to another, the unhappy king lost both his strength and his honour. What was needed to save him from this career of humiliations? An army. And what did Cromwell need to build on the ruins of the monarchy an authority without break or limit? An army, one which he forged in the name of Parliament and then turned against Parliament, a noteworthy instance of the disloyalty of troops to institutions and principles, and of their devotion to persons. And how else was Charles II's Restoration achieved than by Monk's army?

courts-martial and imposed military discipline for the space of only a year; in this way the government was compelled to summon Parliament every year to bring the army to life again, as it were, when it was on the verge of legal dissolution. Hence the fact that, even today, there are the "Royal" Navy and the "Royal" Air Force, but not the "Royal" Army. In this way the tradition of the army's dependence on Parliament is preserved.

Under the Stuart kings Parliament was summoned at irregular intervals and always voted subsidies for several years, sometimes indeed for the entire period of the reign. It continued to grant William III the right to collect the customs dues for the term of his life, but annual meetings of Parliament were needed to vote the annual supplies. Thus not only the army but the civil administration too were made dependent on the consent of Parliament: in other words, of the aristocracy of whom it was composed. De Lolme rightly discerned in this the foundation of English liberty.

The right, possessed by the English, of deciding themselves what taxes they will pay seems to be generally regarded as a guarantee of private property against the pretensions of the crown; but to look at it so is to ignore the best and most important part of this privilege.

The right which the English possess of measuring out the subsidies to the crown is in fact the safeguard of all their liberties, civil and religious. It is an infallible method of securing that they retain the right *of passing judgment on the conduct of the executive*; it is the rein by which the executive is held in check. The sovereign can, no doubt, dismiss at pleasure the representatives of the people but he cannot govern without them.[31]

The word "people" is here used in the meaning which the Romans gave to the word *populus*, that is to say, the aristocracy. At that time the aristocracy had a monopoly, which they were to retain until 1832, of seats in Parliament.

Already, in 1689, not all the blood of the aristocracy was blue. Men who had done well out of the Cromwellian confiscations, substantial merchants of the East India Company who had bought land cheap, Restoration wire-pullers, formed between them a high proportion of the whole. There was to be no pause in the flow of recruits to the aristocracy from big business. It was in essence a class of large landowners. The restrictions which it laid on Power are pregnant with historical consequence. The king, lacking the right of taxation, was led to borrow; the

31. De Lolme, *Constitution de l'Angleterre*, 1771.

lending class had seats in Parliament and watched over the administration of the debt. From this cause the public credit was born in England one hundred and twenty years before anything worthy of the name appeared in France. It was to have striking political results.[32]

The English aristocracy, perhaps because of the nabobs' infiltration into it, was so well in control of economic phenomena that it stopped dead every attempt at monetary devaluation, thereby assuring the stability of its income in terms of goods, and in the eighteenth century even raising its value, thanks to the downward movement of prices during that period.

Thus armed with power and wealth, the British aristocracy was, under the Hanoverian kings, to be the true master of the state. When at a much later date democracy raised its head, it was to find in England a Power quite surrounded by a network of aristocratic defences, whereas in France it seized at a stroke a Power which was an unrestricted monarchy. This fact explains the difference between the two democracies.

## 6. Bad Tactics and Suicide of the French Aristocracy

For France the eighteenth century was a period of aristocratic reaction, so badly handled, however, that, instead of resulting in the limitation of the monarchical Power, it ended by destroying monarchy and aristocracy alike, and by exalting a Power which was far more absolute than that of the "Great King" had ever been.

Saint-Simon shows us the upper nobility waiting for the death of Louis XIV to recover the ground which they had lost since Mazarin. How to do it? Was it a case of setting up against the king a moderating counter-authority? The dukes thought otherwise and aimed at laying hands on the state. Apt scholars of the plebeian officers of state, whose victims they

32. "Since the time that the expenses of war came to be met almost exclusively by public loans and could be met in no other way with any success, the strength of governments in their external relations can no longer be measured, as in antiquity, by the extent of their dominion, the number of their subjects and the spirit and discipline of their armies, but rather by the progress achieved in agriculture, industry and the arts, and by the size and fruitfulness of the public credit. The strongest government is that which can borrow the most, at the lowest rate of interest, for the longest term. So long as money is war's main sinew, the government of the richest people with the largest credit will find everywhere forces ready to serve it, allies inclined to help it and partisans interested in its success; it will be assured of the ability to dominate and enslave peoples without wealth, or to overthrow and destroy governments without credit." Ch. Ganilh, *Essai politique sur le revenu public* (Paris: 1823).

had been, their only idea of political action was to use the levers of state authority.

> My plan [says Saint-Simon] was to start installing in the ministry nobles with all the dignity and authority that belonged to them, thereby displacing the clerks and the lawyers; I planned to manage things prudently and gradually and empirically, so that bit by bit this rabble should lose all its posts which were not of a purely judicial character and be replaced in all its offices by seigneurs and nobles only; in this way the entire field of administration would have come under the nobility.[33]

This senseless project, seasoned by Fénelon's utopian ideas, had already entered the head of the Duke of Burgundy. It implied to start with a mistake as to the composition of the aristocracy; it was no longer composed exclusively of the nobility, but included also the class of gentlemen of the robe, who had interests in common with the nobility— whom the nobility were now in their folly seeking to shut out. It implied, secondly, a non-comprehension of the aristocracy's historical role, which was, not to govern, but to act as bufferstop to the government. The examples furnished by Venice and England of government by aristocracy had turned French heads. But the composition and temperament of the Venetian nobility were quite different. It was not a collection of independent princes with separate interests which one prince had brought into subjection, but a body of notable citizens who had been elevated to the charge of public affairs. As for the English nobility, it had fitted itself into the government by means of a long *tête-à-tête* with it in Parliament.

The reaction that occurred in France in 1715 resulted merely in the disorganization of the state, through "the ignorance, idleness and frivolity of a nobility whom practice had made good for nothing but getting themselves killed."[34] The plebeian clerks, who had had to be kept on as the secretaries of the now preposterous councils, were noiselessly reinstalled as heads of the administration. But now Power had been weakened, to the profit of those competent folk, the gentlemen of the robe. In origin they were statocrats. Raised up in the shadow of the state, as they acknowledged,[35] they prided themselves, and with good reason, on having raised up the state:

33. *Mémoires* (ed. Boilisle) Vol. XXVII, pp. 8 and 9.
34. *Ibid.*
35. At the time of the 1770 conflict with the royal authority, the Parliament of Paris made representation to the king as follows: "The magistrates who make it up will always

*If the pride of the great vassals has been forced to humble itself before the throne of your ancestors, to renounce its independence, and to recognize in the king a supreme jurisdiction and a public authority which is superior to that exercised by themselves* . . .[36] these are all services, the most important doubtless ever rendered to the royal authority, which are due, as history testifies, to your Parliament.[37]

Strong in services rendered, the now wealthy heirs of Power's lawyer-servants claimed henceforward to control its actions,[38] and assuredly there was no other body of men in the country better qualified to hold Power in check.

If offices were bought, the control over the sales exercised by this body hedged in the appointment of a new magistrate with guarantees which ensured that no senate was ever recruited better. If the members of the Parliament were not elected by the public, they deserved on that account more of the public confidence, as being less its flatterers by design than its champions by principle. Taken as a whole, they formed a weightier and more capable body of men than those of the British Parliament. Was it right, then, for the monarchy to accept and sanction this counter-Power? Or did its dignity demand that it react against the pretensions of Parliament? That was the policy of one party, which called itself Richelieu's heir and was in fact led by d'Aiguillon, a great-nephew of the great Cardinal. But if the need was to smash now this aristocracy of the robe and extend the royal authority ever further, it had to be done as in former days to the plaudits of the common people and by employing a new set

---

recognize that they have no other title to their jurisdiction than as officers of your Majesty." (Representations read to the king on December 3, 1770.)

36. At this point the Parliament added: ". . . if the independence of your crown has been maintained against the attacks of the Court of Rome, whereas sovereigns nearly everywhere had bent their necks beneath the yoke of ultramontane ambition; lastly, if the sceptre has been passed down to the eldest son of the royal house by the longest and most prosperous succession of kings ever seen in the annals of Empires . . ."

37. Representations of December 3, 1770.

38. The clergy's remonstrances in 1788 show what a hold ideas of the limitation of Power had now taken: "The will of the prince may, if it has not been elucidated by his courts, be regarded as *his will of the moment*. It only acquires the majesty which assures it of execution and obedience if the explanations and remonstrances of your courts have first been heard in your privy council." The truth is that the idea that every expressed wish of the sovereign had not *ipso facto* sovereign force played a role of capital importance under the *ancien régime*. It was eclipsed momentarily, and then not completely, only at the height of Louis XIV's reign.

of plebeians against the present wearers of periwigs. Mirabeau saw as much, but d'Aiguillon's faction were blind to it.

That faction consisted of nobles who had been more or less plucked by the monarchical Power and were now getting new feathers by installing themselves in the wealth-giving apparatus of state which had been built by the plebeian clerks. Finding that offices were now of greater value than manors, they fell to on the offices. Finding that the bulk of the feudal dues had been diverted into the coffers of the state, they put their hands in them. And, occupying every place and obstructing every avenue leading to Power, they succeeded in weakening it both by their incapacity and by their feeble efforts to prevent it from attracting, as formerly, to its banners the aspirations of the common people.

In this way the men who should have served the state, finding themselves discarded,[39] turned Jacobin. In the cold shades of a parliamentary opposition, which, if it had been accepted, would have transformed the absolute monarchy into a limited one, a plebeian elite champed at the bit; had it been admitted to office, it would have extended ever further the centralizing power of the throne. So much was it part of its nature to serve the royal authority that it was to ensure its continuance even when there was no king.

39. Notably by the ridiculous regulation of 1780 which made a patent of nobility going as far back as 1400 a condition of belonging to the court. In this way the king was forced to live in the midst of an unadulterated nobility. And for what purpose? The purpose was pure greed, so as to have a monopoly of the favours and places which the king did not grant to those who were out of his sight.

# XI.

## *Power and Beliefs*

WHAT THE INQUIRING MIND FIRST SEES in any human formation are the emergent authorities which superintend its groupings and direct its activities. But soon it realizes that the rules and constraints of these visible authorities could not of themselves achieve harmony and cooperation among men.

The behaviour of individuals is much less influenced by the external forces pressing upon them than by an invisible director who determines their actions from within. Each man with a given position in a given society strays only in the most exceptional cases from a typical behaviour. This regularity is produced by a code of beliefs and moralities which is deeply embedded in the nature of man in society.

The ancients showed, by the importance which they attached to folkways, that they were well aware of this; if folkways were good, government was hardly necessary, and if they were bad, it was almost impossible.

So long as persons of every degree behave according to fixed rules which everybody knows, their actions under all circumstances can be predicted by their associates, and confidence reigns in human relationships. Conversely, a nonconformist behaviour upsets all calculations, makes every precaution necessary, stirs up acts of reprisal for its own wrongful acts of aggression, and, if the evil grows, unleashes in the end hatred, distrust, and violence.

The ancients had, therefore, good reason to keep the foreigner at a distance. His folkways were different, and it could not be known how he would act. No less logical was it to punish with the greatest severity behaviour of any kind which ran counter to the normal course of things. Under these conditions little government was needed, for education had done what was necessary to regulate actions.

Hence it is that Power, in so far as it aims at securing social order, finds in folkways, and in the beliefs which maintain folkways, its most valuable adjutants. But the egoism which is its essence impels Power towards an ever wider expansion. We have already seen it attacking, in the course of this advance, those very social authorities which aid it, taking position under cover of their demolition, and replacing the natural aristocracies by its own statocracy. In the same way, folkways and beliefs must be brought low, that Power may substitute for their influence its own authority and build its church on their ruins.

## 1. Power Restrained by Beliefs

The successive developments of public authority become incomprehensible if we think that the measure of its strength is to be found in its formal constitution.

Governments are in that case graded according to the number of the restraints put on their incumbents by checks and balances. And the most absolute government, the most arbitrary, the most free to do what it likes, is the one which encounters no organized obstruction.

This criterion, though the intellectually lazy find it highly convenient, is completely fallacious, for it disregards the domain of the moral sentiments, which is, whatever may be the case with their quality, an immense one. I am not referring here to the highest type of emotions, those of the individual conscience in search of the sovereign good; but rather to a society's attachment to its own modes of action and feeling, which make up, in the fullest sense, its *comme il faut*. The moral sentiments, so understood, obsess the body social and the conscience of the rulers themselves, who steer their course on them; that action is effective which runs with acquired habits and convictions, that action is ineffective which brutally offends them.

Therefore, the more stable and rooted are a society's habits and beliefs and the more predictable is its behaviour, the less freedom will Power have in action. It may indeed seem absolute even when it is only playing the part allotted it by folkways. But let it once run counter to the force of usage, and it will be found to be infinitely weak. And the more inflexible the usage, the less latitude has command.

There lies the explanation of the fact that there were ancient despotisms which, though endowed by custom and superstition with a luxury and cruelty which astonish us, were yet powerless to put through measures which seem simple enough to us. In some respects superstition maintained them, in others it checked them. For that reason the proposition so often met with in eighteenth century philosophy, that "superstition is the support of despotism," needs to be examined before it can be accepted. Before we are done with the subject, our ideas will be much clearer and quite different.

To the rationalist thinkers of the seventeenth and eighteenth centuries primitive man appeared as a completely free agent following the caprices of his own will. It was only when he had bowed his neck beneath the social yoke that forbidden fruits, defined as such by the law, made their appearance. And a pious fraud gave to this same law the semblance of a divine revelation. It followed that Power was the author of every prohibition and rule of conduct, with religion acting as Power's ghostly policeman.

Today's view of the subject is very different. The further we seek to know primitive men, the more struck we are, not by the extreme liberty of their behaviour, but, on the contrary, by its extraordinary strictness. In very backward societies the life of man consists of an extremely narrow cycle of actions which are always alike. Far from this regularity being the work of a lawgiver, it may be seen even in communities in which there is a minimum of government.

The savage derives an obvious satisfaction from conformity. To all attempts to impel him into an uncustomary activity he evinces a repugnance which soon reaches the point of panic. It is easily explained. Every novelty arouses emotions of indistinct fear. The "things that are not done" make up an enormous mass in which the distinctions with which we are familiar—the immoral, the illegal, the shocking, the dangerous—have not yet been drawn. The bad appears as an undifferentiated mass which blocks nearly the whole of a primitive man's field of vision. If we picture to ourselves everything which is physically possible as a map, the morally feasible forms but a narrow zone on it—hardly more, indeed, than a line. Or, to vary the metaphor, the morally feasible is a narrow track across an unexplored bog; it has been beaten by ancestors and may be followed in safety.

Even when a society of this kind has a despot at its head, we may feel sure that the extreme fixity of the folkways will force him to keep to the track. Far from being, as was so lightly supposed, the author of this social discipline, he is himself answerable to it.

Legislation is quite a modern idea; by which I do not mean that it belongs exclusively to our own time, but rather that it makes its appearance only at a very advanced stage in the evolving life of a society. To a society which is young it is inconceivable that a group of men, whoever they are, are in a position to prescribe rules of behaviour. The rules in existence constitute a categorical premise for all members of the society, however powerful or however weak.

These rules are buttressed by the entire authority of ancestors who inspire everywhere a fearful respect. It is not beyond the capacity of savages to explain their "laws," if that is the right word for them. Each of them is justified by a legendary tale which is linked to some mythical and superhuman ancestor.

A whole structure of such tales supports a structure of rites, ceremonies, and practices which are of an entirely obligatory character, and in regard to which the savage is infinitely less capable of insubordination than we are in regard to laws which are known to us to be of human origin and to be maintained by human constraints.

The less advanced a society is, the more sacred is custom, and a monarch who was imprudent enough to order something which did not conform to custom would, in doing so, break his own authority and risk his life.[1]

1. Ethnology provides a veritable harvest of illustrations of these propositions which are sufficiently evident anyhow. Here are some facts put together by Westermarck in *The Origin and Development of the Moral Ideas*, Vol. I, p. 162.

The Rejangs of Sumatra "do not acknowledge a right in the chiefs to constitute what laws they think proper, or to repeal or alter their ancient usages, of which they are extremely tenacious and jealous. There is no word in their language which signifies law, and the chiefs, in pronouncing their decisions, are not heard to say, 'So the law directs,' but, 'Such is the custom.' " (Marsden, *History of Sumatra*. London: 1811.) According to Ellis, "the veneration of the Malagasy for the customs derived from traditions, or any accounts of their ancestors, influences both their public and private habits; and upon no individual is it more imperative than upon the monarch who, absolute as he is in other respects, wants either the will or the power to break through the long-established regulations of a superstitious people." (Ellis, *History of Madagascar*. London: 1838. 2 vols.)

The King of Ashanti, although represented as a despotic monarch, is nevertheless under an obligation to observe the national customs, which have been handed down to the people from remote antiquity, and a practical disregard of this obligation, in the attempt to change some of the old customs, cost one of the kings his throne. (Beecham, *Ashantee and the Gold Coast*. London: 1841. Stuhlmann, *Mit Emlin Pasha ins Herz von Afrika*. Berlin: 1894.)

So great is the power of suggestion exercised by instances which are always like each other, to such an extent does the imitative instinct exclude all eccentric behaviour, that there is not even any need to make express provision for the case arising.

Such is the explanation of the peculiar nature of the sanctions operating in very primitive societies—as, for instance, in Greenland. In the periodic public assemblies which are the only governmental organ of the Eskimos, any man violating the public order gets himself denounced and tormented by "teases," who career about him chanting songs of derision. This public humiliation, singularly reminiscent of the habit in vogue among children of putting out their tongues at people, proves sufficient to put the delinquent, now reduced to desperation, to flight into the mountains, where he remains hidden until he has digested his disgrace. Moreover, if he has offended too deeply the feelings of the society, no other punishment is possible than his formal expulsion from the tribe; this is the custom among the Eskimos and among the Bedouins, and it makes its appearance also in the Bible.

## 2. The Divine Law

A rigorous conformity with meticulous rules is a characteristic feature of small primitive societies. But, as may easily be seen, complications arise when conquest, a phenomenon of comparatively recent date in human history, brings several communities with distinctive folkways under one and the same government. Each of them, of course, retains its own usages, but the resulting friction tends all the same to make originality possible and to release initiative. Moreover, any people, to conquer at all, must have partly freed itself from the underlying fear of setting in motion invisible forces which are everywhere present.

An innovating people, released from the sleep induced by thousands of years of servile imitation, rushes impetuously into every sort of original activity. At a later date a system of law steps in which opens up to it the various fruitful avenues of development, while those which would lead it on the path of its own destruction lose entirely their divine authority. In

---

"The Africans," says Winwood Reade, with special reference to Dahomey, "have sometimes their enlightened kings, as the old barbarians had their sages and their priests. But it is seldom in the power of the heads of a people to alter those customs which have been held sacred from time immemorial." (*Savage Africa*. London: 1863.)

its march towards civilization every people has had its divine book, which has conditioned its progress. In the case of the great historical peoples these books have been so admirable that even a man of small religion will tend to see in them an intervention of Providence. Contrariwise, their great suitability to the needs of society has caused them to be taken for monuments of human wisdom, to which, by a neat piece of trickery, a divine origin has been ascribed. This egregious mistake brings in its train another: that of supposing that Power is the author of law, whereas in truth it is subject to law, as appears from Deuteronomy, where the duty of the king is said to be to get himself a copy of the Law, to read in it all the days of his life, to observe faithfully all the commandments, and to depart from them neither to the right hand nor to the left.[2]

The lawgiver is not Power, but God, speaking through the mouths of men who were either inspired or, at least, deeply convinced. Any transgression offends not the social authority, but God. God, and not the social authority, punishes. Maine has observed[3] that in the most ancient texts of the sacred books of the Indians no provision is made for any punishment to be administered by the state; they merely advise the guilty man to punish himself by, for example, casting himself three times in the fire, or by handing himself defencelessly over to the malice of his enemies, that he may escape the yet more terrible punishment of God.

By reason of the strong feeling of solidarity among early peoples, the individual's impiety compromises the whole people's alliance with the supernatural legislative authority. The criminal must be excluded from the society for fear that his sin may be visited on the whole. "If thine arm offend thee . . ."

Men smite the transgressor because they fear that the divine vengeance will find them out if they tolerate the presence among them of one who has incurred it; they do not punish, but they cut off from themselves a guilty man whose presence puts them in jeopardy. So great towards God, so little towards man, is the accountability of the sinner, that society cannot and dare not pardon him. The Oedipus myth expresses this truth with incomparable force. Oedipus was a good king, and the public advantage required that a veil should be thrown over the crimes which he had in all ignorance committed. As though to make us more conscious of the social virtue of Oedipus, Sophocles shows us how Thebes, after

2. Deuteronomy xvii, 16–19.
3. *Dissertations on Early Law and Custom* (London: 1887) pp. 36–37.

his fall, was first racked with civil war between Eteocles and Polynices, and then oppressed by Creon, the tyrant. It would have been better, certainly, to keep Oedipus. But that was impossible. It vexed the gods to see on the throne one who had committed parricide and incest: therefore they loosed on Thebes the pestilence. Oedipus, his eyes gouged out, had to leave the city—to satisy whom? Not men, but gods.

When the captain of a Greek ship refused to receive a murderer aboard, it was not that the murderer filled him with horror, but rather that he feared that the divine vengeance would strike himself along with the guilty man, and even the boat which carried him.

Crime was God's business. For that reason, even at an advanced stage of civilization, judgment was committed to him. There are Polynesian tribes that embark the man under sentence of death on a canoe; if God so wills, He will bring the outcast to port. The ordeals which are an almost universal social phenomenon stem from the same principle. Even in our own Western society it was not so long ago that a man might prove his innocence by seizing after Mass a cross thrust in fire throughout the preceding night. If at the end of three days the resulting scar was healed, God had decided his cause for him.

In the sphere of law, God is legislator, God is judge, God is administrator.

## 3. The Law's Solemnity

It is only in the third of these roles that men may take a part; they may put to death—offer up, that is, as a sacrifice to God[4]—one whose guilt has been certified by a sure sign. At a later date they became bolder and took to giving judgment. But it is noteworthy that this role was more often taken by an assembly of the people than by an agent of Power, as is shown by the courts of peers of the Middle Ages and by the popular verdicts in capital causes at Rome.

Power in the role of legislator had still to appear. What seems to us to be the highest expression of authority, that of saying what should and what should not be done, of distinguishing the lawful from the unlawful, becomes an attribute of political Power only at a very late stage of its development.

4. *Supplicium*, the punishment of death, is linked etymologically to the idea of appeasing the gods (*subplacare, supplex*), as Ihering points out in *L'Esprit du Droit romain* (French ed.) Vol. I, p. 278.

This fact is of capital importance. For a Power which lays down the good and the just is, whatever form it takes, absolute in a quite different way from one which takes the good and the just as it finds them already laid down by a supernatural authority. A Power[5] which regulates human behaviour according to its own notions of social utility is absolute in a quite different way from one whose subjects have had their actions prescribed for them by God. And here we glimpse the fact that the denial of a divine lawgiving and the establishment of a human lawgiving are the most prodigious strides which society can take towards a truly absolute Power. So long as a supernatural origin was ascribed to law, this step remained untaken.

If God is the author of law, who else is there worthy to amend it? There must be a new law from Him. And so we find Christians calling the law brought by Christ the New Law, and the Mosaic Law, in so far as it dealt with points on which Jesus did not touch, the Old Law. St. Thomas so refers to them.

Up to that point the Mussulmans are in agreement. But they allow for a third revelation as well, that of Mohammed, which, with a constancy greater than our own, they still regard today as the one foundation of their law. When we read of the voyages of Ibn Batoutah we are struck to find him charged with the duty of doing justice in a country which is as far away as possible from his birthplace. Can we imagine an Abyssinian, newly arrived in France, being summoned to preside over the highest French court? His ignorance of French laws would alone make it impossible. But Ibn Batoutah knew the one law which ran throughout the Islamic world. Unity of belief brought unity of lawgiving, because there was no other lawgiver than God.

All the great civilizations were formed in the framework of a divine law given to society, a law which even the strongest will of all, that of the wielders of Power, was powerless to shatter or replace.

So it was with the least religious peoples in history, the Greeks and the Romans.[6] No doubt the principles of Roman law quickly lost any tincture of religious connotation. But their civil ordinances and institutions are, as Ihering has shown, the exact reproduction of ancient ordinances and institutions which had a sacred character.[7]

5. A more or less late stage according to the particular people and civilization. We know that at Rome the secularization of the law was especially precocious.

6. Ihering, *op. cit.*, p. 266.

7. *Ibid.*, p. 305.

The modern man, imbued as he is with the idea that laws are but man-made rules issued with a view to the convenience of society, will observe with some astonishment that, even at a late stage of civilization, Cicero began his treatise on the laws with a detailed dissertation on the ways of honouring the gods. Yet nothing could be more logical: respect for the laws is but one aspect of respect for the gods.

Cicero expounds the nature of law as clearly as anyone could wish:

> Our greatest philosophers have unanimously concluded that law is neither an invention of man nor anything at all resembling the rules of day-to-day life; rather it is something eternal which governs the universe by the wisdom in which its orders and prohibitions are conceived. According to these same authorities this primitive law is nothing other than the supreme expression of the spirit of God Himself, whose sovereign reason is the source of every precept, whether to do or not to do. From this law comes the nobility of that which the gods have given to mankind, which is in fact the reason and wisdom embodied in the man who has learnt to command what is good and prohibit what is bad.[8]

No doubt divine orderings and prohibitions do not cover the whole field of social requirements. The situations which arise make dispositions necessary to which Cicero makes disdainful allusion: "rules of day-to-day life" he calls them. But what a difference there is between the divine law and these human laws!

> As the seat of the supreme law is in this divine spirit who conceived it, it resides no less in the spirit of the man who is wise or perfect. As for the written laws, which speak with different voices on the same subjects and last but for a time, they bear the name of law rather from popular acquiescence than in their own right.

### 4. The Law and the Laws

There are, therefore, two sorts of laws. First there is what may be called the commandment, which is received from on high, either because a deeply religious people conceives it to have been issued to a prophet or because a people with greater confidence in the human intellect believes its seers to be capable of declaring it. In either case, God is its author. A

8. Cicero, *De Legibus*, Book 1.

breach of this law is an offence against Him. Punishment ensues, whether or not the temporal power takes part. And then there are the regulations, made by men to discipline the infinitely various modes of conduct which the growing complexity of society brings in its train.

The more attention is paid to the process of social evolution, the clearer this duality becomes. The man who slowly changes his habits will still remain faithful to certain modes of action and will still observe respectfully certain prohibitions. A stern imperative upholds these social constants. That is the domain of the absolute.

On the other hand, fresh activities and contacts throw up new problems, rendering necessary new patterns of behaviour. There must be new rules to meet new situations. How are these new rules to be formulated? For a truly religious people there is but one way. The divine law is the one foundation of morality and the sole basis of jurisprudence; as questions are put, the doctors of religion formulate the answers, basing themselves on the principles of the Book. In that way a nation, trusting to ecclesiastical jurisprudence, can do without a legislature at all. The Jewish people, for instance, could, even though dispersed, settle in this way the most embittered disputes. This example of practical legislation formulated in the absence of any duly constituted state seems not to have received the attention it should have from political thinkers. In the Islamic world the jurisprudence based on the Koran has played a similar role.[9]

In these instances, then, laws are not made. Interpretation of the law provides the necessary answers to all particular cases. Legislation becomes no more than a jurisprudence, and jurisprudence a casuistry.

The Oriental genius inclines to this solution; the Western does not. The latter tends to cantonize the divine law into its own sphere—that, namely, of actions which are absolutely obligatory or absolutely prohibited, and to assume that actions not specified by the law are a matter of indifference to it. Thus, in this open field individual energies and initiatives can gallop loose, subject to no other restraints than those which they impose on each other—restraints which take the concrete forms of war or litigation.

The further away from a primitive conformity that behaviours develop, the more they give rise to clashes; the growth of these clashes is the

9. It is significant that one of the most celebrated treatises on Mussulman jurisprudence was entitled *At Taqrib*, meaning "the drawing closer to God," and the commentary on it *Fath al Quarib*, meaning "the revelation of the Omnipresent."

visible reflex of society's evolution. The number of disputes grows as the pace of the transformation quickens. The harmony of behaviours is no longer a natural thing as in a static society, but must be continually restored anew. Therein is the need for particular (or judicial) decisions and general (or legislative) decisions, the rapidly growing volume of which places a superstructure on the law. They will form a human law as opposed to a divine law.

Take Rome, where the distinction between the two spheres is particularly clear-cut. Suppose a Roman to have taken a vestal for his mistress: as he has offended the gods, the king punishes the crime, acting as the instrument of the divine wrath. But suppose, on the other hand, he has killed a fellow citizen: as he has offended only the family of the victim, it is for the family to take justice into its own hands. But the murderer's family stands by him, until this vendetta threatens the integrity of the whole community; the king then intervenes as mediator, acting in behalf of the interests of society.

It cannot be too much emphasized that at the root of these two interventions two very different principles are at work, the one moral or religious and the other social or expedient. Nor should it be overlooked that the second principle comes into play only through a deficiency of the religious sense, by reason that the gods of Western man are conceived as having only a limited circle of interests. The Romans are, perhaps, the least mystical people ever seen on the face of the earth. And that is the reason why they so soon distinguished from the *fas*, which is what the gods enjoin, the *jus*, which is the work of men's brains.

## 5. The Two Sources of Law

From then on it is possible to discern two sources of law. On the one hand are categorical rules of conduct, making up an objective law which is religious in character. On the other we see human beings at strife confronting each other, and, in the interest of all, giving in the end reciprocal recognition to subjective rights, which form in bulk, if looked at from the outside, an objective law which is utilitarian in character.

The spheres of these two laws vary greatly according as any given society regards the divinities which it worships as egoist and wanting only burnt offerings, or as judicial and concerned for men to act in truly moral ways. We find the first alternative in its pure form among certain African tribes, where, we are told, "religion consists solely in ceremonial worship, and nothing but the neglect or omission of a rite can call down the anger of the gods."[10] This is an extreme case; but the fact remains that gods may be more or less "moral." The less moral they are, the larger is the sphere of a purely human law.

Nor is the line between the two spheres drawn once and for all. The food of human law is the course of life and the pressure of interests and passions. Ihering could even say that a subjective right was only a protected interest. We see that, as an interest hardens, it gets itself judicial cover because of the force which it generates. In a sense, human law is at any given time the existing state of a treaty which is subject to periodical revision by the stresses set up. A movement of that kind, which happens inevitably, has a natural tendency to encroach on the sphere of divine law; it encounters, unless faith is living and active, an opposition which is but passive.

Much more, ideas themselves are excited by this medley of interests and passions. Ideas are not the products of the study but are subject to influences of time and place. So it comes about that the conception held of what is the will of the divinities gets modified in the heat of the social battle and that the moral imperative suffers both infiltration and attrition.

Some elaboration of the theme is needed to demonstrate how differently the line can be drawn between the two spheres, and that they are not impervious to one another's influence.

A secularist people like the Romans merely reserves to the gods their sphere of law, while proceeding to elaborate its own.[11] It is sufficient to give the gods no direct offence. A deeply religious society, on the other hand, like that of the Middle Ages, makes the divine law the predominant partner. The more exalted the conception of God, the more completely must it give the answer to human problems. St. Thomas is thus able to affirm that everything is covered by the divine legislation:

> As, then, the eternal law is the idea in the mind of the supreme ruler, it follows that all schemes of government which are in the minds of inferior

10. Cf. A. B. Ellis, *The Yoruba Speaking Peoples of the Slave Coast of West Africa* (London: 1894).

11. "As in nearly all the governmental orders at Rome, but notably in the laws, there is invariably a clause declaring that nothing capable of violating the rights of the gods is included in the law. In this category are included violations of the sacrosanct orders; but it also covers the violation of any right whatsoever belonging to the gods by which what is probably intended first and foremost is the inviolability of the *res sacrae*. The law itself robs of their validity any measures falling under the ban of this provision; there is, therefore,

[sc. terrestrial] rulers stem from the eternal law. Now the schemes of government of inferior rulers are the whole body of laws whatsoever other than the eternal law. Therefore all laws, to the extent to which they partake of right reason, stem to that extent from the eternal law. . . .

Human law answers to the idea of law to the extent to which it accords with right reason; if it does so accord, then it is clear that it stems from the eternal law. But in so far as it is repugnant to reason, to that extent it is an iniquitous law; and in that event it is in the category not of law but rather of violence.[12]

Nothing could be more precise: the human, or positive, law must be written within the framework of the divine, or natural, law. St. Thomas elaborates it still further:

> The eternal law, in effect, contains no more than certain general precepts which remain always the same; man-made law, on the other hand, contains particular precepts to meet the various cases which arise.[13]

We see, then, that the growing complexity of society may demand ever more numerous prescriptions. All that St. Thomas requires of them is that the starting-point of them all should be the principles enunciated once and for all. The guarantees given to the individual by such a way of procedure are easily conceived. While he conforms to certain principles learned almost in babyhood, he enjoys an absolute security, for the law has no other foundation than these principles, and men no other rule of conduct, including even the men who exercise Power.

A society which acknowledges a law is not, of course, exempt from violation of it. Swayed by passion or flown with authority, its members frequently commit gross violations of it, and princes more than anyone else. St. Louis[14] would not be famous if all Christian princes had behaved like Christians.

---

no need to repeat them, it is enough to put the facts on record. But, even when the clause was omitted, legal provisions which were contrary to the claims of religion must have been regarded as non-existent." (Mommsen, *Manuel des Institutions romaines*. French ed. Vol. VI, Part 1.)

12. St. Thomas, *Summa theologica*, Ia, IIa, question 93, art. 3.

13. *Ibid.*, question 97, art. 1.

14. [Louis IX (1226–1270), a king whose object it was to reconcile all Christendom by a general crusade and to do justice (which he meted out under the oak of Vincennes) to everyone. A man of lofty religious morality, he sought to make it the rule of public, as well as of private, life, and to give the lie to the dictum that "politics is one long second-best."]

But the subject, even when he is suffering a wrong which is contrary to the law, can still regard the law as a dike which the wave of crime, though it has flooded it for the moment, will not carry away.

The abuse of authority is recognized for what it is even by its abettors. Thus, to disapproval from without is added vacillation within to compel a withdrawal. The Middle Ages abound in instances of royal recantations in which uneasiness of conscience has played a larger part than your rationalist historian thinks.

Law is thus seen to be a given frame; to it folkways conform and within it all behaviour, private or public, is fitted with greater or lesser irregularity. In the uncertainty of human affairs it gives to human calculations the highest degree of certainty which is possible.

### 6. The Law and Custom

Divine law must not be confused with custom. Custom is the crystallization of the whole of a society's habits. A people among whom custom is altogether sovereign endures the despotism of the dead. Law, on the other hand, while prescribing and fixing such habits as are essential to the preservation of society, does not bar the door to favourable variations: it acts, so to speak, as a discriminating filter.

The supremacy of a creed may no doubt result in riveting on a docile race the sovereign authority of doctors of the law who will aim at stabilizing for all time the whole of human behaviour. But up to now the personalities thrown up by the Western peoples have been too vital for such a yoke to be feared. Variations in behaviour have been produced under the vigorous impulsion of the will to authority. These the law did not condemn out of hand, but did provide criteria for settling the disputes arising from these novelties, and general principles for organizing aright these new behaviours.

Law and custom, though not identical in Logic, are so for practical purposes.

The feelings of veneration which are directed towards law handed down by ancestors extend also to their modes of action. "My father, who feared God, acted in this way." Traditional behaviour and institutions, even when they are without religious content, get somehow incorporated into religion: they resemble the booths which were in other days set up against the sides of cathedrals.

It is from beliefs and habits, and from nothing else, that are deduced the rules of law used in an evolving society to restore unceasingly that harmony which is for ever being troubled by the conflict of wills. This rule-making activity may take the form either of judicial decisions exclusively or of judicial decisions combined with legislation.

If the former, then "the wise men," having to confront problems of infinite variety, must devise ever more daring fictions with a view to bringing the problems under ever remoter precedents. But also law develops in step with life, and the most intricate systems of social rules are the successive emanations of a bundle of principles and habits which is the common heritage of the whole society; so much is this the case that the subtlest piece of reasoning by the "wise man" is first cousin to the proverbs quoted by the village centenarian.

When the regulation of novel modes of conduct is effected judicially, there ensue political and psychological consequences of importance. So far as society as a whole is concerned, the effective need to go back to ancient customs buttresses the sense of continuity, and so acts as a corrective to the progressive decline of the worship of ancestors. It is for the individual a high school of morals and vitality—not to be armed at every point by the appropriate law but to have to decide for himself what is his due and to have to win respect for it in judicial combat. For Power, finally, and that is what concerns us here, belief in a law outside itself is of first-rate importance.

Behaviours continue to change without prescription of them by Power, and the problems to which these changes give rise continue to be solved without its intervention. By long prescription human law acquires an authority proper to itself, comparable almost to that of divine law, to which it is linked by more or less close ties. Taken together the law makes a formidable whole: not only must Power respect it but even the men who exercise Power feel themselves caught in a vast network of obligations. The law is above them, and they can move only along its paths. So it was in early Rome, where the state, instead of using against the citizen any specific rights of police, had to bring an action against him, called the *actio popularis;*[15] so it was also in England, where, according to Dicey,

> what are called the principles of the constitution are certain inductions and generalizations based on particular decisions given by the courts in matters concerning the rights of specified individuals.[16]

15. Cf. Ihering, *L'Esprit du Droit romain* (French ed.) Vol. II, p. 81. Also Mommsen, *Manuel des Institutions romaines* (French ed.) Vol. I, pp. 364 *et seq.*
16. A. V. Dicey, *Introduction to the Study of Constitutional Law.*

There are, then, good grounds for seeing in the *corpus juris* a powerful instrument of social discipline which owes nothing to Power; it opposes Power and imposes itself on it; it both limits it and strives to control it.

## 7. The Development of the Legislative Authority

It is obvious that the part played by Power in society will vary greatly according as it does or does not make the laws, according as it prescribes the rules of behaviour or contents itself with enforcing respect for them.

When at a given moment of historical development we find Power making laws with the assent either of the people as a whole or of an assembly, and being unable to make them except with this assent, we are apt to interpret these rights of the people or assembly as a limitation on Power, as a decline from its primitive state of absolutism. But this primitive absolutism is pure myth. It is not true that mankind has emerged from a former state in which magistrates and monarchs dictated out of their own heads the rules of behaviour. They had not in truth a vestige of such a right, or, more accurately perhaps, of such a power.

It is, then, not the case that the people or the assembly deprived Power of the ability to make the laws by itself, for it never had this ability. We form a completely wrong idea of societies in their adolescent state if we think that one man or a few men, happening to wield effective authority, are thereby enabled to impose on their subjects behaviours which involve a breach with their accepted scheme of beliefs and customs. So far from that, we find that the rulers themselves are in thrall to the accepted scheme.

The assents of people or assembly, so far from fettering for the rulers a freedom to act which they never had, made possible an extension of governmental authority.

In the Middle Ages it was Power which summoned the English Parliaments and the French States-General. Its primary object was to raise taxes to which custom gave it no title. Even in 1789 it was again Power which summoned the States-General, that with the help of the people it might find the strength to break the resistance offered to the reforms which it deemed necessary.

The power to legislate is not an attribute which was taken from Power by the establishment of an assembly or by popular consultation. It is an addition to Power, of so novel a kind that without an assembly or without popular consultation it would have been impossible.[17] Note the slow, timid pace at which this power develops. At first there is nothing more than a restatement of custom.[18] Then, by slow degrees, innovating laws are introduced, which are, however, deliberately presented as returns to good old customs. Through the practice of legislation the idea gains ground little by little that the laws or law may not only be restated but created—by formal proclamation.

In a word, it is not to the caprice of some fabulous despot but to popular or representative institutions that we must ascribe the conception which makes a more or less late appearance in the history of every civilization, that it is lawful for a directing will to put in question at any moment the laws and modes of conduct of men.

For that to happen there had to be opposed to the divine authority, which had laid them down, the authority, not of a solitary monarch, but

17. Pollard has described very clearly the use to which the English kings put Parliament, with whose help they took powers which they had not had before. The king in Parliament could order what the king alone could not. "The crown had never been sovereign by itself, for before the days of parliament there was no real sovereignty at all: sovereignty was only achieved by the energy of the crown in parliament. . . . So sovereignty has grown with popular representation. . . ." A. F. Pollard, *The Evolution of Parliament* (2nd ed. London: 1934) pp. 230 and 233.

18. The idea of anyone whatsoever being able to make laws which are repugnant to custom is completely foreign to the Middle Ages. For instance, when St. Louis issues an ordinance (1246), in what language does he do it? He says that he has summoned to Orleans the barons and the notables of the country that they may determine what the custom of the country is, as now declared by the king and commanded by him for observance:

"Nos volentes super hoc cognoscere veritatem et quod erat dubium declarare, vocatis ad nos apud Aurel baronibus et magnatibus earundem terrarum, habito cum eis tractatu et consilio diligenti, communi assertione eorum, didicimus de consuetudine terrarum illarum, quae talis est. . . .

"Haec autem omnia, prout superius continentur, de communi consilio et assensu dictorum baronum et militum volumus et praecipimus de coetero in perpetuum firmiter observari." Cited by Carlyle, Vol. V, p. 54.

We here see legislation to be a matter of determining and authenticating custom. Hence the presence of the "barons and magnates," who are there as a jury of fact. It would therefore be a mistake to regard the assemblage of barons and king as a joint legislative body, of which the king in Parliament would be the modern equivalent. But it is easy to see that these meetings of the king and his *curia* to determine what is custom came in the end to be a means of dictating it. And it is easy to imagine how this happened. It was by giving out for customary and constant what was in fact new. Cf. in this connection what Maine said about the supply of water in India.

of society. The notion of society consciously elaborating the rules of conduct binding on all its members may make its appearance all the sooner, as noted already, if the divine authority played (as at Rome) a relatively minor part in the formulation of law; its triumph is assured by nothing so much as the rationalist crisis which occurs in the history of every civilization.

## 8. The Rationalist Crisis and the Political Consequences of Protagorism

In its youth every civilization fears supernatural powers, venerates its ancestors, is loyal to custom. If it conceives of a better state of things, it puts it in the past, and it is a sure sign of its progress that what it fears above all and tries to prevent is degeneracy.

Its life then runs into a contrary phase in which, trusting in its own lights, it sets about regulating men's behaviour in such a way as to produce the maximum of utility; never doubting its power to attain in this way an Age of Gold which is concealed in the future, and wholly taken up with the idea of its own improvements, it no longer takes thought for the preservation of its inheritance, and sometimes declines into corruption and dissolution at the moment when its hopes are at their most exaggerated. The line, or rather the zone, of division is drawn by the rationalist crisis.

There comes a time when, just because of the vitality given to it by its folkways, a people expands and comes into contact with a number of very different societies; at first it mocks them in derision, then it takes to examining more attentively beliefs and modes of conduct which are different from its own. "The just and the unjust are mainly a matter of geography. A change of three degrees in elevation shatters an entire jurisprudence."[19]

On the one hand, these contacts affect favourably minds which are capable of rising above outward forms and perceiving the underlying unity of laws, as was the case with the Jesuit missionaries in China; on the other, they are dangerous to baser minds, which, through failure to realize the inner coherence of the entire scheme of a society's beliefs and customs, regard themselves as free to adopt at random some way of life

19. Pascal, *Pensées* (Havet) III, 8.

or other, and then take to wondering whether any way of life is really necessary.

Finding that one of their beliefs is not universally held, they conclude that neither is it necessary, without stopping to think that as regards their own society it may be necessary. At this point, whether by correlation or coincidence, the pure intelligence itself starts to destroy its ancient handiwork. It had at first applied itself to defining the idea of the natural order, to understanding the rationality and the beauty of what is, and to proving that it is to man's moral and material advancement to range himself behind such admirable laws. Then it turns in its tracks and starts to put in question everything which it had previously affirmed.

In Greece, for instance, whereas the Pythagoreans had affirmed the divine origin and nature of law[20] and the immutability of customary laws, the philosophers started to represent laws as being purely the work of men's hands, which had been maintained by the device of a fictitious intervention from above.[21]

In that case not only are the laws subject to change—in this respect the philosophers did no more than justify the legislative practice already in vogue—but, in addition, there is in them no element of fixity, nothing of natural law or of objective morality. This is held proved by the fact that no single law has received men's assent in all times and in all places.[22] From this it is easy to deduce that there is no natural law, and that legislation and morals are merely things of convention and the products of human wills.

It is an attitude of mind which Plato has made familiar:

> As regards the gods, these men claim that they have no natural existence but are artifacts living by virtue of certain laws; that they are different among

20. Cf. A. Delatte, *Essai sur la politique pythagoricienne* (Paris: 1922).

21. So ran Critias's famous interpretation of them: "After the first human laws against obvious injustices had been invented, people took it into their heads, with a view to obviating the dangers caused by hidden injustices, to talk of a powerful and immortal being who sees and comprehends by his spirit whatever is secret, and punishes evil. These fictions coined by the first sages were directed to planting fear in men's hearts." Diels. fragm. 25.

22. On this point Pascal has copied and condensed an argument of Montaigne's: "They profess that justice does not reside in these customs but in natural laws which are known in every country. Assuredly they would be on strong ground if the venturesome chance which is the disseminator of human laws had met with at least one law which was universal; but the joke is that men's caprice takes such varied forms that there is no such law." *Pensées* (Havet) III, 8.

different peoples, according to the intention which each people had in establishing them; that the good is one thing in nature and another in law; that, in regard to justice, absolutely nothing is just by nature, but that men, always divided in feeling about it as they are, are for ever making fresh arrangements in regard to the same objects; that these arrangements are the measure of the just for as long as they endure, and originate in art and laws and not in nature.[23]

The rationalist crisis, as has been said, occurs in every society at a certain stage in its development. While its historical importance is generally recognized, its result tends to be wrongly interpreted because only the immediate consequences are regarded.

The prop of the throne, we are told, was superstition, and the effect of the rationalist onslaught is, therefore, to bring down Power by weakening the support given to it by beliefs.

We must look further. Community of beliefs was a powerful factor in social cohesion; it was the stay of institutions and the keeper of folkways. It assured a social order, complementary to and bulwark of the political order; its existence, as shown by the independence and sanctity of the law, discharged Power from a vast measure of responsibility and set up against it an almost impassable barrier.

Can we fail to note the coincidence of the breakdown of beliefs from the sixteenth to the eighteenth centuries with the elevation of absolute monarchies during the same period? Is it not clear that they owed their elevation to this breakdown? Is not the conclusion this: that the great period of rationalism was also that of enlightened and free-thinking despots,[24] all assured of the conventional character of institutions, all persuaded that they both could and should overturn the customs of their peoples to make them conformable to reason, all extending prodigiously their bureaucracies for the furtherance of their designs, and their police in order to smash all opposition?

The directing will is then credited with the power of reordering all things, the legislative authority is deployed, and the law, which has now ceased to be the master and guide of human ordinances, becomes henceforward a mere statute book.

History knows nothing apter to Power's enlargement. And the choicest

---

23. *The Laws,* Book VIII.
24. Cf. Robert Leroux, *La Théorie du despotisme éclairé chez Karl-Théodore Dalberg* (Paris: 1922).

spirits of the eighteenth century knew this so well that they aimed to bar the legislator's way with an irreproachable guide—the "natural religion" of Rousseau or the "natural ethic" of Voltaire. We shall see how these brakes functioned in the nineteenth century, and how in the end they ceased to work.

Logically, they were bound to go under. For, once man is declared "the measure of all things,"[25] there is no longer a true, or a good, or a just, but only opinions of equal validity whose clash can be settled only by political or military force; and each force in turn enthrones in its hour of triumph a true, a good, and a just which will endure just as long as itself.

25. [This aphorism is ascribed to Protagoras. Montaigne, in the *Apology for Raimond Sebond*, quotes Pliny on it: "As if he could take the measure of any other thing, who cannot take his own!" Montaigne comments on this: "Truly, Pythagoras stuffed us very nicely when he made man the measure of all things, who never knew even his own."]

BOOK V

# The Face of Power Changes,
# but Not Its Nature

# XII.

# *Of Revolutions*[1]

POLITICAL REVOLUTIONS, BEING VIOLENT CRISES in the careers of institutions, engage closely the attention of historians. The sudden blaze of lurking passions, the explosion and the incendiary propagation of principles which had been working underground, the rocket-like ascent into importance of new men, the play of characters in brutal and violent action, the monstrous outbreaks of the mob in which the serious faces of men about their business are soon no longer seen but only the terrifying visage of hate and animal cruelty—here indeed is matter to inflame the writer and to give the peaceable reader at his fireside the shudders!

These are the most written-up periods of history, but they are also the least understood. The spirit of man is still in its childhood, and learning raises a smile more often than it instructs him. Aware of the outward aspect of events, he thinks to find in it their meaning; he takes the onrush of the wave, which is under his eyes, for the movement of the sea, which demands the faculty of thought. He holds to the cry of "Liberty," which goes up in the beginnings of every revolution; he does not perceive that there never was a revolution yet which did not result in an accretion of Power's weight.

To grasp the true role of revolutions and to give these swift and

1. [In this chapter the meaning in French history of the word "parliament," explained in footnote 16 in chapter X, should be remembered.]

spectacular denouements their due place in the long march of history, we must turn our eyes away from the fascinating spectacle of their eruption; we must notice how the stream looked before it reached these rapids and in what shape we find it again when events have resumed their even pace.

Before the rapids, there was the rule of a Charles I, a Louis XVI, a Nicholas II. After them, that of a Cromwell, a Napoleon, a Stalin. Such are the masters to whom the peoples that rose against Stuart or Bourbon or Romanov "tyranny" find themselves subjected next.

The phenomenon is as startling as the usual interpretation of it is misconceived. How sad, it is said, that the revolution strayed from its natural course, that the anti-social extravagances of liberty called for a constraining force to discipline them, that these extravagances caused so widespread a ruin that there had to be a man to reconstruct! If this or that mistake had but been avoided! Ingenuity is freely expended in unearthing the exact moment at which licentiousness set in, in isolating the act that made the revolution sin, in naming the criminal.

*O pectora caeca!* What a misunderstanding is here of the revolutionary phenomenon! The Cromwells and Stalins are no fortuitous consequence, no accidental happening, of the revolutionary tempest. Rather they are its predestined goal, towards which the entire upheaval was moving inevitably; the cycle began with the downfall of an inadequate Power only to close with the consolidation of a more absolute Power.

### 1. Revolutions Liquidate Weakness and Bring Forth Strength

The beginnings of a revolution are of an indescribable charm. The event, while it is still in suspense, seems to open up every possibility. It holds promise for the unsatisfied dream, the despised system, the wounded interest, the disappointed ambition; it will mend all, fulfil all, and accomplish all; the joyous assurance of its youthful gait wins the hearts of all and attracts even those whom it directly menaces.

These happy hours are written ineffaceably in the memories of peoples, and they colour, for the eyes of posterity, the sequel which belies them. It is in their lyrical quality that men will look for the clue to the movement, it is from the old revolutionaries that they will ask for it; as though men knew what they did and did what they thought to do! They thought to fight oppression, to limit Power, to put an end to arbitrariness, to guarantee the life and liberty of each, to remove the exploitation of the people and compel its beneficiaries to disgorge.

They would like to build—a vain wish, for this has never been their destiny. Their historical mission has been performed when they have braved and flouted Power. Their impunity attests its weakness and gives the signal for a general assault on the helpless monster. The sluices of envy are opened and the bonds of appetite are struck off, against authority; it falls, and in its fall may be heard crashing around it the social authorities. Nothing remains but ruins for the wave to break on. New men ride on its crest; to ask of them what their programme is would be a scorn and derision. They are but sails filled with the wind of their time, shells that catch the sound of the tempest.

But at long last the sea of society is calm again. Now is the chance for those who then install themselves in what remains of the City of Command; they buttress it with fragments taken from the ruins of the social commands, they extend their Power with none to say them nay.

How can this fail to be the predestined and providential end of every such cataclysm—the liquidation of a weak Power, the erection of a strong one?

## 2. Three Revolutions

The English Revolution, the Civil War, began in the name of outraged property rights, in a resistance to a small tax on land called "ship-money." It was soon to impose on land a tax ten times as heavy. It was a protest against certain confiscations on the part of the Stuarts; soon it would itself not only plunder the Church systematically but, on political pretexts, seize as well a great part of property in private hands. In Ireland a whole people was dispossessed. Scotland, which had taken arms in defence of its own ways of life and government, saw taken from it all that it so highly valued.[2]

---

2. Clarendon records at the time of the Restoration: "The entire structure of the ancient government of Scotland had been so confounded by Cromwell, the country's laws and customs had been so overturned to the advantage of those of England, those, that is to say, that Cromwell had established, that hardly a trace had been left by him to indicate what Scotland's had been before. The power of the nobility had been so completely suppressed and extinguished that all claims to respect and distinction had now only so much validity as was conferred on them by the credit and offices bestowed by Cromwell." *Life of Clarendon*, by himself.

So strengthened, Cromwell could get himself the army for want of which Charles had fallen, and drive out the Parliament men to whom the king had had to submit. The dictator could found the naval power which the unhappy monarch had dreamt of for his country, and wage European wars for which Charles had lacked the means.

The French Revolution freed the peasantry from feudal burdens, but it forced them to bear arms and sent mobile columns in pursuit of the refractory; it suppressed *lettres de cachet,* but erected the guillotine in public squares. It denounced in 1790 the plan, which it ascribed to the king, of joining the Spanish alliance in a war against England standing alone; but it hurled the nation into a military adventure against the whole of Europe, and, by unprecedented requisitions, drew from the country resources on such a scale that it was enabled to accomplish the programme which the monarchy had had to abandon, the conquest of France's natural frontiers.

It has taken a quarter of a century for the Russian Revolution of 1917 to be seen in its true light. A far more extensive authority than that of the Czar has released in the country very different forces, by which it has recovered all, and more than all, of the territory which the Czarist Empire had lost.

Thus we see that the true historical function of revolutions is to renovate and strengthen Power. Let us stop greeting them as the reactions of the spirit of liberty to the oppressor. So little do they answer to that name that not one can be cited in which a true despot was overthrown.

Did the people rise against Louis XIV? No, but against the good-natured Louis XVI, who had not even the nerve to let his Swiss Guards open fire. Against Peter the Great? No, but against the weakling Nicholas II, who did not even dare avenge his beloved Rasputin. Against that old Bluebeard, Henry VIII? No, but against Charles I, who, after a few fitful attempts at governing, had resigned himself to living in a small way and was no danger to anyone. And, as Mazarin sagely remarked, had he not abandoned his minister, Strafford, he would not have laid his head on the scaffold.

These kings died not because of their tyranny but because of their weakness. The peoples erect scaffolds, not as the moral punishment of despotism, but as the biological penalty for weakness.

Peoples never rebel against a Power which squeezes the life out of them and grinds them underfoot. The savagery of such Power is feared, and it even happens that men find something admirable in its scourging of the great. What is detested is softness: firstly, by reason of that natural instinct which, when the rider is hesitant, turns the most obedient mount into an almost wild animal; secondly, because a soft Power is in reality, however good may be its intentions, the enemy of the people—it cannot in fact stop whatever has authority from grabbing wealth and making heavier its social yoke; lastly, because the law of rivalry summons peoples to an ever greater concentration of their strength in an ever more imperious hand.

### 3. Revolution and Tyranny

Revolutions rend the air with denunciations of tyrants. Yet in truth they encounter none in their beginnings and raise up their own at their ends. The principle of government which they overthrow is a worn-out one, inspiring but a modest respect, and with no more than faded authority left to it. The same causes which made possible its fall rendered it incapable of despotism.

In place of a nerveless scarecrow, popular agitation hangs out the banners of its own enthusiasm, and supplants a weary and sceptical set of rulers with the political athletes who have just emerged bloody but victorious from the eliminating contests of the revolution.

Are not men of that kind, acting in the name of a principle which evokes such fervours, certain to receive a fanatical obedience? Not only is Power given new life at its centre, but the direction given by it to the nation's course no longer encounters the obstacles set in its path by the social authorities—whom the whirlwind has swept away.

The further the liquidation of the aristocracy has been carried, the more complete will be the tyranny established by the revolution.

Cromwell's confiscations were, no doubt, immense; but the soil itself was not ground to powder—it was merely transferred in large blocks to new owners, often men who had grown rich in the service of the East India Company. For that reason social interests continued as a powerful conservative force. They kept in check the Levellers, inspired Monk, and, with the disappearance of the Commonwealth, applied themselves to limiting the authority of the state; for that they needed thirty years and a different dynasty, but their work was to endure for a century and a half.

In France the destruction of the aristocratic families by the suppression of privileges and the break-up of estates went much further. But inequalities of wealth were respected, and the spoliation of the Church and the pillage of Europe gave rise to new fortunes. And so were erected the capitalist barriers to the all-powerful state.

But the Russian Revolution seized all private property in whatever form. In that way the Russian state met with no other obstacles than that of the Nepmen, whose rise it had allowed, and then that of the Kulaks, whose independent means had seemed at first too small to be worth destroying. So it is that the English Revolution strengthened Power less effectively and durably than did the French, and the French less than did the Russian. Yet all three ran the same course. Only to outward view were they revolutions against Power. Their true effect was to give to Power a new vigour and poise, and to pull down the obstacles which had long obstructed its development.

## 4. Identity of the Democratic State with the Monarchical State

The state's underlying continuity through every change of form, and the growth given to it by those changes, are strikingly illustrated by the French Revolution. Violent as this upheaval was, it did not break the continuity of the evolution of the French state; rather it was a brutal liquidation of the obstacles which had by the end of the eighteenth century gathered in its path, and were hindering its advance.

Viollet understood this well:[3]

> The dominant feature of the historical evolution of the monarchy in its last three centuries had been a general tendency towards unification and uniformity. Everywhere liberty fell, authority rose.
>
> The Revolution resembled the violent breaching of an enormous dam which the weight of water carried away in one sweep. This rush of water was itself largely the sum of traditional and historical forces; therefore, and we cannot note it too closely, the genius of the *ancien régime* remained at the service of new ideas. That genius, authoritarian and centripetal in essence, triumphed with the Revolution and presided over its work of destruction, with a force multiplied a hundredfold. The heart of the past continued beating and living.
>
> Our concept of the omnipotent state, properly understood, is, therefore, the *ancien régime's* urge to rule erected into a doctrine and a system. In other

3. Cf. Paul Viollet, *Le Roi et ses ministres pendant les trois derniers siècles de la monarchie* (Paris: 1912). Quotations taken from the introduction, pp. 6, 7, 8.

words, *the modern state is no other than the king of earlier centuries; it continues triumphantly his relentless work of suppressing all local liberties, it is, like him, leveller and standardizer.*

If this truth is not yet generally accepted, the reason must be sought in the method adopted by most historians for studying the eighteenth century. From the *Télémaque*[4] to Madame de Staël's *Considérations sur la Révolution française* there was a prodigious outpouring of ideological assertions. Never was there such a flow of books and speeches, irony and argument, about politics. Our learned men, with infinite care and subtlety, have constructed genealogical trees for the ideas of the century down to their final flowering. They make stimulating studies. For the elucidation of history, however, it is less important to listen to what men say than to observe what they do.[5]

Action in politics is in the last resort administration. Let who will open the administrative dossiers from the reign of Louis XIV to that of Napoleon. The continuity of Power will then strike his eye; the obstacles which it encountered and the true direction of events will then stand revealed.

## 5. *Continuity of Power*

The officials of the monarchy had one constant policy: that of Richelieu and Mazarin; it consisted of the struggle, going back to Louis XI, against the House of Habsburg. The deep-laid schemes of Mazarin, adapted and realized by Louis XIV, had driven the Habsburgs from the throne of Spain. In both Spain and Italy Bourbons were installed in the place of Austrian princes. Vienna still had to be opposed, not from need to destroy a state that was no longer dangerous, but because, in opposing her, France became the natural rallying-point of the German princes, who feared the Emperor, and in that way not only prevented the union of Germany under the Habsburgs, who were no longer formidable, but also and above all its crystallization around an internal centre of resistance, Prussia, which would, it was certain, fill the role of protector from the moment that France abandoned it.

4. [*Télémaque* was Fénelon's famous "utopian" romance, published in 1699.]
5. ["We cannot," said Dr. Johnson, "pry into the hearts of men, but their actions are open to observation."]

In that policy, as simple as it was far-sighted, the French officials never wavered. But they could not maintain it, because noble wire-pullers, having made their way into the employments of ambassador and minister, worked against French policy, whether because vanity made them want to cut a figure or because, as in the case of Choiseul, they made of a foreign court a rallying-point for the defence of themselves and their faction against the incessant intrigues of Versailles.

If Marie Antoinette was hated as was no other queen of France before her, the main reason for it certainly was that she represented the Austrian alliance, which had brought on France the disasters of the Seven Years' War and driven her from the first rank of European Powers.

Now, what was the result of the Revolution on French foreign policy? The war against Austria. War against Prussia too, no doubt, but with Prussia there was no delay in coming to terms and seeking an alliance. And the war was pursued with the same enemy, the same plans, and the same objects as in the palmiest days of the monarchy. The officials triumphed, the continuity of the state was restored. "Ha! who could wish himself into thinking that the French Republic is not another Louis XIV?"[6] Was it due to chance? Not a bit. Burke records the anger which reigned in official circles on the morrow of the partition of Poland; it did not stop at insulting the sovereign. It was to the order of those circles that Soulavie, the pamphleteer, wrote his *De la Décadence de la Monarchie française,* in which he developed the principles of the ancient policy of France, "whose aim abroad was to raise up the small states and humiliate the Great Powers; whose aim at home was to raise up the power of the state and humiliate all subordinate authorities."[7]

### 6. Disparate Character of the Authority of the Ancien Régime

Fulfilment of the second part of this programme was no more successful than of the first, under the monarchy.

The royal authority had grown slowly by way of a prudent but unceasing advance; it subordinated, when necessary, principle to expediency. It held unequal sway over the different parts of the realm; for instance, it is true that no taxation was levied and assessed by its agents except in the electoral

6. The phrase is that of Yvernois, the pamphleteer, born at Geneva and an agent of the English.

7. Soulavie, *Mémoires du règne de Louis XVI* (Paris: anno X) Vol. I, p. 144.

districts, whereas, in the districts of the states, regional assemblies decided the sum which they would raise for the king and divided it up among the persons liable. These variations in the degree of his authority were met with again according to the "order" of the population to which the king applied. The contribution of the clergy retained the title of "gratuitous gift."[8] In addition to regional privileges and those attaching to rank, there were now added those of the agents of the state and freeholders of their offices, the principal of whom were the Parliament men, whose claim it was that their approval was necessary to give validity to the royal edicts.

In this way Power

> found itself checked at every turn by the respect which it had to pay to our rights and usages.
>
> When it asked its subjects for gratuitous gifts, taxes and grants in aid, it had, in order to get them, to make representation to the clergy of France and call them together.
>
> It negotiated for the entry into force of a fiscal edict with the Parliament.
>
> It asked for jurisdiction in the State of Languedoc.
>
> It commanded it in Burgundy.
>
> In Brittany it generally had to buy it, more or less indirectly.
>
> It took it by force of arms in the provincial administrations.[9]

The royal government had, therefore, to tread delicately. To buttress it, it was at all times necessary to counter simultaneously all the various centrifugal tendencies, while taking care never to unite their interests against the state.

This disastrous union of interests was brought about in the eighteenth century by a series of mistakes which were to bring about the fall of the monarchy.

### 7. Weakening of Power. Aristocratic Coalition.

A nobility of birth surrounded the king and acted as a screen which prevented the rise of the plebeian servants who had so ably served his

8. "I do not think so," answered Louis XVI to a suggestion of Necker's that it would be a good plan to get rid of the words *don gratuit*, "firstly, because this phrase is an old one and attracts connoisseurs of formulas; secondly, because it may be a good thing to bequeath to my successors a phrase which tells them that they must rely entirely on the affections of Frenchmen and not dispose of estates in a military manner."

9. Soulavie, *op. cit.*, Vol. VI, pp. 341–42.

ancestors. Louis XIV had strictly excluded the nobles from every political office, but now this crowd of courtiers, greedy of power and place, started to wage a continuous war against the king's ministers, each of whom had henceforward to raise his own faction to maintain himself in office.

The result was that the monarchical government no longer offered that stability, that aloofness as regards disputed matters, which were in principle its merits. Each party at court sought support in the country, and, for the sake of a momentary advantage, strengthened, as in the case of Choiseul and the Parliaments,[10] a partial interest. They even went for help to foreign Powers, and their ambassadors and agents played a part which had been forgotten since the days of the League.[11]

While authority vacillated, the Parliaments united against it the centrifugal forces. To keep the men of law in service to authority, as in their beginning they had been, all that was needed was that their ranks should be filled either from the bodies of poor clerks attached to the courts or, at the least, from a middle class between whom and the nobility there was a great social gulf. But hereditary offices, which had at first attached certain middle-class families to the interests of the state, had detached them from the middle class, and made of them a distinct caste, which constant intermarriage bound to the interests of the higher nobility. The Parliament men, who were at first statocrats, with no more status than their offices gave them, had become aristocrats, with an authority proper to themselves and interests which were distinct from those of the state. If an attempt was made to cut down the absurdly bloated number of officials, which got in the way of the dispatch of business, the Parliament men obstructed it. The reason was that the officials, like the Parliament men, had bought their offices (which had been created in lean times to bring in a revenue) and the Parliament men could not permit any attack on a form of property[12] which gave them their own importance. If an

10. [Choiseul, Duc de (1719–1785), Louis XV's chief minister from 1758 to 1770. He owed his rise to the Pompadour; his position was weakened by her death in 1764, and Madame du Barry was largely the means of his dismissal in 1770. One of the reasons for it was his support of the provincial parliaments against Maupéou, the Chancellor, who was his rival. A recent French historian has called him *"étroitement lié aux parlements, jansénistes."*]

11. [The League, in French history, was the organization formed in 1576 by the Duc de Guise to maintain the predominance of the Roman Catholic religion and exclude the Protestant princes of the blood from the throne. Civil war shortly ensued on its formation.]

12. When Maupéou, having put the Parliament to flight, set about suppressing a crowd of useless offices, it was to be for the middle class a veritable financial disaster. We read in the diary of a Parliament man under date of April 26, 1772: "It would be impossible to

attempt was made to spread taxation evenly over all the orders, with regard henceforward paid to nothing but ability to pay, the Parliament men, who themselves had fiscal privileges, made common cause with everyone else who had them. In view of the conflict looming inevitably between Power and themselves, they made themselves, they who were by tradition the enemies of local immunities, the paradoxical defenders of those very immunities.

They became in the end so strong that Maupéou's dismissal of them in 1770 amounted to a *coup d'état*. Such was the feebleness of authority at the time that some courtiers of the parliamentary faction were able to maltreat the Minister of Finance in the antechamber of the king itself.[13]

Behind the Parliament were the nobility, the clergy, the provinces, and the princes themselves. There was no king's party to be found. Or, rather, it was the people.

## 8. The Third Estate Restored the Monarchy Without the King

In 1788 the administration confronted everywhere forces which thwarted it. It had been reduced to the lowest level of impotence. The Revolution was suddenly to liberate it from all its adversaries.

The retreat of the monarchy had gone so far that it had had to throw to popular clamour its provincial intendants, who were the executors of the central government's will; they were succeeded by provincial assemblies—a move which was in the opposite direction to all French history. The Revolution, on the other hand, was to subject the entire

---

depict the desolation which reigns in most of the families of France by the appalling number of offices abolished—a number which grows daily. It is nothing but bankruptcies, filings of petitions, suicides, etc. Although last year there were 2,350 petitions filed and 200 suicides, the number of both will grow still further as things are going. . . ." *Journal historique de la Révolution opérée dans la constitution de la monarchie française par M. de Maupéou, Chancelier de France* (London: 1775) Vol. III, p. 69.

13. "Some days ago at Versailles, in the antechamber leading to the Œil de Bœuf, there was a group of young soldiers and noblemen who, on sight of the Abbé Terrai, conceived the idea of playing a trick on him, which took the form of squeezing his sides so hard that he cried out in pain and begged them to let him go; just at that time there arrived M. le Marquis de Muy, comptroller of the household of Madame la Comtesse de Provence; at that the ranks opened and, as the Marquis walked across unhindered, a voice called loud enough for the Comptroller-General to hear: we only make way here for honest people!" Under date March 29, 1772, in the *Journal historique,* quoted above.

country, more strictly and uniformly than ever before, to the will of Power.

The work of the Revolution was the restoration of absolute monarchy. The direction of the common people's aspirations had been understood by Philip the Fair: for that reason he—the first to do it—had summoned the Third Estate to the States-General. Nearly five centuries later the event still justified him; but Louis XVI was no Philip the Fair. And the restoration was to take place without a king.

Whoever examines in detail the tumultuous career of the revolutionary assemblies loses himself at first in the currents and countercurrents of ideas, and in the intrigues of factions who often use language only to mask their real intentions. But one thing is clear enough: that from the start the Constituent Assembly sacrificed the interests of just those privileged persons who had demanded the convocation of the States-General. A few sessions saw the destruction of privileges on which the kings had never dared lay hands. The suppression of the States-Provincial, which had been an object of royal policy for centuries, was the work of a moment. The vast possessions of the clergy were made over no less swiftly to Power, and the Parliaments, whose obstructionist tactics had brought about the convocation of the States-General, received a more summary dismissal than in the time of Maupéou.

The checks and balances were all swept away, and here, as Mirabeau saw, lay the king's great opportunity.[14] He wrote to him: "The idea of forming all the citizens into but one class would have pleased Richelieu, for an equality of this kind facilitates the work of Power."[15] Mirabeau saw himself filling the part and place of the great Cardinal, gathering the fruits of this stupendous lopping of heads.

But Louis XVI and the Assembly thought otherwise; so did history.

14. In a memorandum of remarkable lucidity he notes: "In the course of a single year liberty has triumphed over more of the prejudices impeding authority, *has wiped out more enemies of the throne,* and has obtained more sacrifices for the national prosperity, than the royal authority could have done in several centuries. I have always called attention to the fact that the obliteration of the clergy, the Parliaments, the state lands, the feudal nobility, the provincial jurisdictions and every species of privilege was a victory both for the nation and for the monarchy." Twenty-eighth memorandum for the Court, dated September 28, 1790, in *Correspondance de Mirabeau avec le Comte de La Marck,* in 3 vols. (Paris: 1851) Vol. II, p. 197.

Mirabeau clearly understood that the Revolution had worked for Power. But it was not Power in its traditional shape that was to know how to gather the fruits.

15. Letter to the king, July 9, 1790. *Corresp. avec le Comte de La Marck,* Vol. II, p. 74.

Attempts have been made, but in vain, to uncover the intentions of the members of the Constituent Assembly. True, they approved the separation of Power into an executive, left with the king, and a legislature, to be taken over by the representatives of the people. True, they also committed local administration to local elected bodies and in that way effected a further division of Power. But these dismemberings of authority, however great the importance attached to them by their authors, are without historical significance. For the Assembly's work, even as its final repentance shows, was, despite itself, the complete transference of Power.

It took away the legislative power from the king, and swore to take no more. Lalli-Tollendal[16] and Mirabeau[17] both descanted on what a menace the Assembly would be were it ever to take over the powers left with the king. "Yes, I assure you," cried Mirabeau, "I can think of nothing more terrible than a sovereign aristocracy of six hundred people." Yet it came, inexorably. And it is a sight for philosophers, that of the men, first of the Constituent and then of the Legislative Assembly, fighting against their fate, which they both dreamed of and feared.

To create a national assembly the first revolutionaries invoked the principle of the general will and claimed to be its mandatories. It is curious to observe how this principle carried them on its crest in so far as it assisted the foundation of a new Power, but went underground at the first sign of its causing that Power embarrassment. Since the national

16. In his report on the Constitution Lalli-Tollendal wrote on August 31, 1789: "It is asked whether the king, as part of the legislative body, will not be incessantly exposed to seeing all his influence broken by the union of all wills in a single national Chamber.

"If he then gives way, what limits are there to the authority of the Chamber? The people must be protected from tyrannies of every kind: England suffered as much from its Long Parliament as from any of its despotic kings. . . .

"Under Charles I the Long Parliament, so long as it continued to observe the constitution and act in concert with the king, redressed a number of grievances and passed a number of useful laws, but, when it arrogated the legislative authority to itself alone and excluded from it the royal authority, it was not long before it laid hands on the administration as well, and the result of this aggression and this concentration of powers was an oppression of the people worse than that from which it had been, as was claimed, delivered."

17. In the famous debate on the right to declare war, he explained his position as follows: "Authorities are exercised by men; men abuse an authority which is not sufficiently checked, and overstep its limits. It is in this way that monarchical government becomes a despotism. And that is why we must take so many precautions. *But it is in this way too that representative government becomes an oligarchy,* whenever, of two authorities made to balance each other, one gets the better of the other and, instead of checking it, encroaches on it." Speech on May 20, 1790.

will was the source of all authority, the king too, if he was to continue to hold a part of it, had to be, together with the Assembly, "a representative of the nation." But then the paradox arose of having elected representatives and a hereditary representative both functioning. And soon the king became no more than first functionary: but then, why should a mere functionary be irremovable? The opportunity was favourable, and they suppressed him; and now the executive and legislative powers were joined in the Convention. "As for the equilibrium of powers, we have in the past let ourselves be the dupes of its prestige . . ." exclaimed Robespierre, but now,

> what do we care for devices devised to balance the authority of tyrants? It is tyranny that must be extirpated: the aim of the people should be, not to find in the quarrels of their masters short breathing-spaces for themselves, but to make their own right arms the guarantee of their rights.[18]

In other words: when the Power was held by others, we favoured limiting it; now that we hold it ourselves, it cannot be too big.

So the Assembly became sovereign. But if it draws its authority from the fact that it expresses the general will, it is, of course, right for it to stay constantly subject to those who put it there. Not a bit of it! During its very first days[19] the "Constituents" threw off the imperative instructions which many of them had received from those who had sent them there.

Parliamentary sovereignty was substituted for popular, less because of the arguments of Sieyès than because of the will to power of the men who heard them. By all means let the people be an absolute sovereign in the hour of choosing its representatives, for in that way the representatives hold from it unlimited authority. But when it has conferred on them this authority, its role is finished and it is of no further importance: it is now the subject, and only the assembly is sovereign. Only the assembly is the place where the general will is formed,[20] and consultation with the people is no more than a species of cookery which boils down the entire nation

18. Robespierre's speech at the sitting of May 10, 1793.
19. Sittings of July 7 and 8, 1789.
20. "Our business here," said Sieyès, "is, not to count a democratic poll, but to propose, to listen attentively, and to change our minds *with a view to forming collectively a collective will*." Speech of September 9, 1789.

into a microcosm of six hundred persons who, by an exceedingly courageous fiction, are deemed to be the assembled nation itself.[21]

Yet this exalted sovereignty, which dared to send the king to the scaffold and rejected contemptuously the Girondins' proposal of appeal to the electoral assemblies, abased and humbled itself—before whom? Before the bands of unbridled fanatics who were welcomed at the bar of the Convention and whose crazy petitions were accepted as the expression of the popular will.

There have been great jurists who have expended an admirable ingenuity in reducing all these contradictions into constitutional theories. It passes my imagination how they can fail to hear with the mind's ear the cries of the street and the rattle of the tumbrils, and how they can put their trust in written words, which were either dashed down under the influence of hate or panic, or were pieced together in hours of compromise and weariness.

The logic of a revolutionary epoch is to be found, not in the Ideas, but in the facts.

The central fact is the erection of a new Power, that of the self-styled representatives who, in so far as they did not kill each other off, kept themselves in session from the days of the Convention right through the Directory and Consulate, and contributed their quota to the men of the Empire.

The true incarnation of this new Power was Sieyès. No one had played a larger part than he in the unfolding of the Revolution; having been a member of the Constituent Assembly, of the Convention, and of the Committee of Public Safety, a Director and a Consul, he prompted, no doubt, these words of Napoleon, which, had he been in a position to do so, he would have spoken on his own account: "The Revolution is closed; its principles are fixed in my person. The government in being is the representative of the sovereign people. There can be no opposition to the sovereign."

## 9. Napoleon's Prefect, the Child of the Revolution

The boundless authority of Napoleon was the goal towards which the entire upheaval had been proceeding from the day on which the ambition

21. "Decision," said Sieyès, "belongs to the assembled nation and cannot belong elsewhere. The people or the nation can have but one voice, that of the national legislature." Speech of September 9, 1789.

of Orleans or the vanity of Lafayette set it in motion. "One would say that *to create Napoleon I* was the uninterrupted design, daily and meticulously followed, of the men of the Revolution."[22] Everything converged on that end. Look, for instance, at the way in which the dictatorship of the prefects, which was to be a constant feature of French society, was in successive stages prepared.

The wish of the population was to be quit of the royal intendants and to administer itself by localities. The Constituent Assembly gave it apparent satisfaction by entrusting all departments of government to elected local assemblies. But simultaneously it destroyed just those historical units which had the ability and the will to govern themselves. The geometrical intelligence of Sieyès conceived the idea of cutting up the country into twenty-four equal rectangles, themselves divided into nine equal *communes,* which, by the same infantile geometry, spawned nine cantons each.[23] Though this crazy plan was not followed through, it remained the ideal of the creators of the *départements.* It was safe enough after that to give these artificial creations an autonomous existence! As though there were danger of such as they feeling the breath of a life of their own!

> The systematic spirit [said Benjamin Constant][24] at first went into raptures over symmetry. The passion for Power soon found out what an immense advantage this symmetry procured it. It nearly came to the point of denoting cities and provinces by numbers, just as numbers were used to denote legions and army corps: so great was the apparent fear of any moral idea being attached to whatever was done!

But before long even the wretched directories of departments were accused of retarding or checking the policies of the central authority. Billaud-Varenne condemned them in these terms:

> Unfortunate results of this kind will always be liable to happen so long as the directing nerve of the complicated organism of government is relaxed: it

22. E. Faguet, *Du Libéralisme* (Paris: 1903) p. 243.
23. Cf. Paul Bastid, *Sieyès et sa pensée* (Paris: 1939) pp. 388–89.
24. *De l'Esprit de conquête,* chap. xiii, "De l'Uniformité." *Œuvres* (éd. 1836) p. 170.

must be taut and, to be that, it must run uninterruptedly from the centre to the circumference, with but one intermediate support.[25]

The "intermediate support" was to be the Napoleonic prefect. To quote Benjamin Constant again:

The despotism which has replaced the demagogy, and *has made itself the residuary legatee of all the latter's works,* has continued very cleverly on the trail blazed for it. The two extremes were in agreement on this point because, at bottom, there was in both of them the will to tyranny. The interests and memories which spring from local customs contain a germ of resistance which is so distasteful to authority that it hastens to uproot it. Authority finds private individuals easier game; its enormous weight can flatten them out effortlessly as if they were so much sand.

### 10. The Revolution and Individual Rights

That the Revolution, however fine its language, worked for Power and not for liberty is strikingly proved by what happened to individual rights in the course of the upheaval which started in 1789.

Never was more striking—or, no doubt, more sincere—proclamation made of the intention to recognize that man, as man, had certain sacred rights. That was the great conception of the members of the Constituent Assembly; that is their title to fame. And in like manner the members of the Legislative Assembly and the Convention, and the Thermidorians, all alike, even Bonaparte himself, claimed to have dedicated and guaranteed these rights. And yet the Revolution, obeying the stirrings less of the ideas which it proclaimed than of the unseen principle of life which gave it motion, wiped out all the rights which it had claimed to exalt, and effectively disarmed the citizen of every sure guarantee against the Power to which it had bequeathed an unlimited authority.

Let us examine the facts.

The safeguarding of individual rights is the function of the judiciary.

---

25. Report on the course of government made in the name of the Committee of Public Safety by Billaud-Varennes, 28th brumaire, an II.

The hostility to local authorities dates back to the very beginnings of the Revolution. Sieyès, who understood where he was going better than the others, expressed himself violently on the subject on September 7, 1789. I quote his view in the following chapter.

Such was the ingratitude of the Constituent Assembly to the old Parliaments whose obstructive tactics had led to the summoning of the States-
General that it dismissed them summarily. It then rebuilt the temple of
justice on new foundations, that justice might be "all-powerful to succour
all rights and all individuals." Justice would now be completely independent
of Power. A citizen could not be prosecuted for an offence unless a grand
jury had returned a true bill. In that way, before a man could be handed
over to stand his trial, certain citizens, selected by chance and under no
other direction than that of a judge who took no part in their deliberations,
had to decide that there was a case for him to answer. Before whom
would he appear next? Before the Court of the Department, in which
another jury would pronounce his guilt or innocence. Yet even so, and
notwithstanding all efforts to cut it down, the part played by the judges
remained considerable. Very well, then, they must now be elected by the
people. In this way the citizen would be judged in future by the people
alone, and Power would be unable to punish the man whom his peers
should be disposed to acquit.

Could more complete guarantees be imagined?

But the Power which was born of the Revolution was young and
ardent, ambitious to shape society to its own fancy, impatient of all
opposition and quick to denounce it as a crime. It was soon to find that
the guarantees which it had itself granted were an embarrassment to it.
It claimed that the judges drew their inspiration, not from the laws worthy
of the name which the Constituent Assembly had at first formulated, and
which laid down general principles, but from occasional standards, aimed
at specific classes of citizens, and masquerading under the name of laws.
It attacked them for being too lenient. When, after August 10, 1792,
Danton became Minister of Justice, he frightened the judges by announcing
that he had attained high office by way of the breach of the Tuileries'
walls, that the cannon was now the *ultima ratio* of the people, and that
bloodshed would have been prevented if the functionaries had done their
duty—but these had prosecuted popular societies and outspoken writers,
while protecting non-juring priests. On the motion of a popular society,
Philippeaux demanded a clean sweep of the tribunals which had been
elected, two years before, for six years. "I can bear witness," he said, "that
in most of the tribunals a man need only be a patriot to lose his suit."
And from then on there was to be election after election. But the people's
choice would never be sufficiently to the taste of Power, which took to

purging the elected of the people after their election: the Directory, for instance, was to annul the elections in forty-nine departments.

Even the process of purging was not enough for the Terror. The Terror required revolutionary tribunals on the model of the Revolutionary Tribunal at Paris, which, unassisted by a grand jury, soon ceased hearing either witnesses or defending counsel, and, without leaving their seats, took to condemning accused whose names and alleged crimes had hardly been declared.

When this monstrous creation had been swept away, Power went back to ordinary judges but would not grant them independence. Tired by this time of annulling elections, it vested in itself in the year VIII the nomination of judges, and their promotion.[26] From that time on it preserved religiously a means of pressure which under the *ancien régime* it had not had, because in those days offices were for sale or inheritance.

The Parliaments of former days were like a federation of small republics in the midst of the monarchy; they were jealous of their liberty and were guardians of the Roman tradition. Whatever may have been the defects of the justice administered under the *ancien régime,*

> there was not to be found in it [says Tocqueville] that servility to authority which is the worst form of venality. To this deadly vice, which not only corrupts the judiciary but soon infects the body of the entire people, it was completely a stranger.[27]

Independent, majestic, and capable of withstanding the king himself, the judiciary influenced profoundly the character of the people.

> Judicial habits had become in many respects the habits of the nation. The courts had spread the idea widely that every dispute was subject to argument and every decision to appeal; they had made publicity customary and formality desirable, both of them things which keep servitude at bay.[28]

This independence has never reappeared: "The subordination of the magistracy to the government is one of the triumphs of the Revolution.

26. Cf. Jean Bourdon, *L'Organisation judiciaire de l'an VIII* (2 vols. Paris: 1941).
27. Tocqueville, *L'Ancien régime et la Révolution,* p. 171.
28. *Ibid.,* p. 173.

At the moment of proclaiming the rights of man, it destroyed their castle and paralysed their defenders."[29]

### 11. Justice Stands Disarmed Before Power

That was not the only respect in which "progressive" justice found itself worse equipped than in pre-Revolutionary days for the defence of individual rights.

In former days the Parliaments had had no scruple in citing before them agents of Power, or in launching proceedings against them in defence of the rights of private persons.

It is remarkable that the very men who claimed to have placed individual rights on an unassailable foundation attacked the Parliaments for having protected them even against the acts of the prince. Who talked this language? The men of the Convention? Not so; the men of the Constituent Assembly had already talked it. They applauded Thouret, one of their colleagues,[30] unanimously, when he hurled at the judicial authorities this reproach, which was in reality, as they should have seen, a commendation: "As the administrative authority's rival, it interfered with its actions, checked its operations and disquieted its agents." On January 8, 1790, the assembly issued an instruction by which every act of the tribunals and courts of justice tending to thwart or hold up the operations of the administration, being unconstitutional, was declared to be of no effect and to be powerless to check the various administrative bodies. On the August 24 following, a law made provision: "The judges are forbidden, on pain of forfeiture, to interfere in any way whatsoever with the operations of the administrative bodies or to cite administrators before them for anything done in the course of their duties."

When, as was to happen, the vigilance committees had covered the whole country with a network of informers, and the representatives on circuit had violated every principle of justice and humanity, the Convention hurled its thunders, not at them, but at the weak and timorous obstacles placed by the judges—whom the people had elected, do not forget—in the path of arbitrary cruelty.

The National Convention decrees . . . that it annuls all causes proceeding and judgments delivered in the courts against members of the administrative

29. Faguet, *op. cit.*
30. Sitting of March 24, 1790.

bodies and vigilance committees on complaints laid concerning requisitioned goods, revolutionary taxes and other administrative acts issuing from the said authorities with a view to the execution of the laws and decrees of the representatives on circuit.

The tribunals are again forbidden to take cognizance of administrative acts, of whatever nature they may be. . . .[31]

I have cited these passages at length because they establish the point that the Revolution took away from justice the duty which it had previously performed of defending the individual against the encroachments of Power. Also because they demonstrate that the cribbing and cabining of justice and the baring of the individual were the work, not of the Terror, but of the Constituent Assembly. Also because this condition of things has been bequeathed by the Revolution to modern society, in which these principles are still in action.[32]

Just as the Revolution crushed any bodies whose authority was capable of limiting that of the state, so it deprived the individual of every constitutional means of making his right prevail against that of the state. It worked for the absolutism of Power.

## 12. The State and the Russian Revolution

The Russian Revolution offers the same contrast, but still more pronounced, between the liberty promised and the authority realized.

It was not any particular Power, but Power itself, which was denounced and damned by the school of Marx and Engels, with a vigour nearly equal to that of the anarchists. In a justly celebrated pamphlet Lenin asserted that the Revolution must "concentrate all its forces against the might of the state; its task is not to improve the governmental machine but *to destroy it and blot it out.*"[33]

31. Decree of the 10th fructidor, an III.

32. If in practice it has been found possible to defend the right of the individual against Power, the fact is due to the tenure of Power—a precarious tenure, be it noted—by one class only, the bourgeoisie, whom education and interests caused to fear the abuse of authority and who elaborated the admirable jurisdiction of the *Conseil d'État*. But in this jurisdiction it was the state which consented to give judgment against itself; this graciousness on its part might come to an end the following day at the sole pleasure of a government which should want to exercise the absolutism conferred on it by that child of the Revolution, French law.

33. Lenin, *State and Revolution*. The italics are Lenin's. [*The* (London) *Times* of March 10, 1947, gives extracts from articles by Stalin and Vishinsky in a recent number of the

The state is in fact rooted in evil. Engels scoffed at its deification by Hegel:

> ... according to philosophy, the state is the realization of the idea; it is in philosophical language the reign of God on earth, the domain in which eternal truth and justice are realized, or should be. Hence comes this superstitious respect for the state, and for all that affects the state, a respect which finds a place in men's minds the more easily because they have got used from childhood to supposing that the general business and interest of society as a whole cannot be managed otherwise than as they have been managed up till now, that is to say by the state and by the subordinates whom it installs in office in due form. And people think that they have already made a positively dashing advance if they shake off the belief in hereditary monarchy to swear fealty instead to a democratic republic. But the state is in reality nothing else than an instrument for the oppression of one class by another, and it is more completely this in a democratic republic than in a monarchy.[34]

Since "the state is the specific organization of a force, the force destined to subjugate a certain class,"[35] its *raison d'être* will vanish with the oppressor: "Marxism has always taught that the suppression of the state must coincide with the suppression of classes."[36]

Engels said the same thing in a passage which is regarded by all Marxists as of fundamental importance:

> The proletariat seizes all authority in the state and at once transfers the means of production into state ownership. By that means it abolishes itself *qua* proletariat, it abolishes all class antagonisms and at the same time it abolishes the state *qua* state. The old society, which moved in the midst of class antagonisms, needed the state, because it needed at every period an organization by which the exploiting class could maintain its external conditions of production and could, above all, force the exploited class to remain in the conditions of servitude made necessary by this existing mode of production (slavery, serfdom, hired work). The state was the official representative and visible embodiment of the whole of society, but only in

Russian periodical *Bolshevik,* from which it appears that this feature of Marxist theory has now been officially disclaimed by the present rulers of Russia.]

34. Engels in his 1891 preface to Marx's *Civil War.*

35. Lenin, *op. cit.*

36. *Ibid.*

so far as it was the state of the class which itself represented in its time the whole of society: the state of the slave-owning citizens of antiquity, the state of the feudal nobility in the Middle Ages, the bourgeois state of our own time. But in the act of becoming the *effective* representative of the whole of society, the state renders itself superfluous; when once there have been repressed, along with the rule of the old anarchy of production, the clashes and excesses which resulted from it, there is no longer anything left to restrain, and any specific power of restraint, a state, ceases to be necessary.[37]

The passage is marked by a vigour of thought and clearness of expression which earn it its celebrity. It removes all possible doubt as to the true doctrine. So does this letter from Marx to Hügelmann, written at the start of the Commune:[38] "I say that the revolution in France should have made every endeavour not to transfer the bureaucratic and military machine into other hands, which has been the only result of revolutions to date, but to smash it." In this passage Marx seems to want the apparatus of constraint broken even while a revolution is still running its course, whereas Lenin, on the other hand, was to take the view that it was first necessary to make use of it "to repress the resistance of the exploiters and to sweep in the vast mass of the population—peasantry, lower middle class and half-proletarians—to building the socialist economy."[39]

In any case Power must, sooner or later, disappear. To the question "What is to replace the mechanism of the state when once it has been smashed?" Lenin replied:

Instead of the institutions set apart for a privileged minority (civil servants and military staff officers), the majority can itself carry out directly the duties of government, and the more the people itself takes over these duties the less will be the need for government. In this respect one of the steps taken by the Commune, to which Marx directs particular attention, is especially noteworthy: it suppressed all "expense" allowances, along with all pecuniary privileges of the civil service, and it reduced all official salaries to the level of the workers' pay. In this may be seen the best indication of the transition from middle-class democracy to proletarian democracy, of the transition from the democracy of the oppressors to the democracy of the oppressed. . . .[40]

---

37. Engels, *Anti Dühring*.
38. April 12, 1871.
39. Lenin, *op. cit.*
40. *Ibid.*

Compare now these principles with the formidable apparatus of constraint erected in Russia by the Revolution. The adherents of the Marxist doctrine can, if they like, denounce the betrayal of the Revolution's objectives. The enemies both of the doctrine and of the regime can, if they like, call pointed attention to the discrepancies. The partisans of the regime can, if they like, justify them by reference to the needs of a transitional period in which socialism is being built up.[41]

Our present concern is not controversy, but to find in a contemporary event of vast extent an illustration of what is in our view the law of revolutions: that they tend always to buttress Power by changing its agents and resuscitating its spirit.

A nation may get from a revolution a new strength, as the enfeebled France of Louis XVI got from the Revolution the energy to win her natural frontiers, and as Russia, which in 1917 met defeat, got from it the will to conquer in 1942; but let it never expect from it liberty. In the final analysis revolutions are made, not for man, but for Power.[42]

---

41. [All three parties have doubtless overlooked a truth enunciated by Gibbon: "From enthusiasm to imposture the step is slippery and perilous; the demon of Socrates affords a memorable instance how a wise man may deceive himself, how a good man may deceive others, how the conscience may slumber in a mixed and middle state between self-illusion and voluntary fraud."]

42. [Cf. what Tocqueville says about Marrast in his *Souvenirs* of the 1848 Revolution: ". . . *il appartenait à la race ordinaire des révolutionnaires français qui, par liberté du peuple, ont toujours entendu le despotisme exercé au nom du peuple.*"]

# XIII.

# Imperium *and Democracy*

HISTORY, WE HAVE SEEN, IS THE PICTURE of a concentration of forces growing to the hand of a single person, called the state, which disposes, as it goes, of ever ampler resources, claims over the community ever wider rights, and tolerates less and less any authority existing outside itself. The state is command; it aims at being the organizer-in-chief of society, and at making its monopoly of this role ever more complete. We have seen how, on the other hand, various social authorities defend themselves against it, and set their rights in opposition to its rights, and their liberties, which are often of an anarchic or oppressive character, to its authority. Unceasing war has been waged between these two forces, between the interest calling itself general and interests avowing themselves private.

Power has had its ups and downs, but, looking at the picture as a whole, it is one of continuous advance, an advance which is reflected in the stupendous growth of its instruments, its revenues, its armed forces, its police forces, and its capacity to make laws.

Next, we have seen the old Power cast out. But this revolution has not been followed by Power's dismemberment; far from it. What has perished in the upheaval have been the social authorities which obstructed its advance. And the spiritual authority, too, which gave it rules of behaviour, has suffered a great decline. But the complex of rights and powers which composed it has not fallen apart: it has only passed into other hands.

What is called the coming of democracy is really the conveyance of the established Power to new owners, or, if you prefer it, the conquest of the City of Command by new tenants. As this conveyance or conquest is accompanied by the annihilation or recoil of whatever forces oppose the *imperium,*[1] the position of Power in society is in the end more isolated and therefore more powerful.

The new Power, like the old, calls itself the "expression of society," in which it arouses less distrust than the old Power. We shall now see the consequences of this.

It would not, however, be correct to treat this political transformation as having been no more than the replacement of one sovereign by another. Had that been all, the incorporation in the concept of democracy, which, properly speaking, means no more than sovereignty belonging to the people and exercised in its name, of ideas such as liberty and law, in strict logic strangers to it, would be unintelligible. Their presence in this connection is instructive. Just as the presence of shells on a mountain-top attests that in former days the sea was there, so the emotional associations of liberty and law with democracy serve to remind us that something different and wider was intended by it than a mere change of sovereign. It represents a claim to have civilized and domesticated the Minotaur, to have converted this tyrant, whose appetites were formerly his only law, into a mere piece of machinery, purged of all emotion, the passionless executive of just and necessary laws, and incapable of laying a hand on individual liberty; a servant, in short, of those great and fair ideas, law and liberty.

This attempt, if successful, would deprive of their occupation the various social and religious forces which hold the state in check. The isolated position of Power in society would work harm to nobody, and even seem desirable. Was it possible for this attempt to succeed? Can the nature of Power be reformed?

The position occupied by it, the attraction inspired by it, the opportunities offered by it, the hopes aroused by it, alike contribute to impress on it certain permanent characteristics. Proof of this is seen in the ultimate end of all systems of ideas with a libertarian, "legalitarian," and democratic flavour.

### 1. On the Fate of Ideas

Does thought preside over the successive transformations of human communities? Hegel asserted it did, and changes in the form of a state

---

1. [The sovereign authority in a state.]

are for him only the shadows cast by the majestic march of ideas engendered by the world spirit which advances through an unceasing synthesis of opposites bred by itself. With Marx ideas are no longer queens but servants, the mere formal expressions of needs and feelings brought into being by situations: their effectiveness is not their own but has been lent them by the social impulsions which give them birth.

Marx was wrong to deny the creative quality of the spirit, but Hegel misunderstood the way in which the mechanism of politics works.

It is true that ideas are queens by birth: but they only gain favour when they enter the service of interests and instincts. Follow an idea through from its birth to its triumph, and it becomes clear that it came to power only at the price of an astounding degradation of itself. A reasoned structure of arguments, setting in motion a whole stream of logical correspondences between defined terms, does not as such make its way into the social consciousness: rather it has undergone pressures which have destroyed its internal architecture, and left in its place only a confused babel of concepts, the most magical of which wins credit for the others. In the result, it is not reason which has found a guide but passion which has found a flag.

The history of the democratic doctrine furnishes a striking example of an intellectual system blown about by the social wind. Conceived as the foundation of liberty, it paves the way for tyranny. Born for the purpose of standing as a bulwark against Power, it ends by providing Power with the finest soil it has ever had in which to spread itself over the social field.

## 2. The Principle of Liberty and the Principle of Law

To get an understanding of this catastrophic descent to earth, let us first of all restore the internal ordering of the ideas in question—an ordering which lies today in ruin and confusion.

The originators of democratic doctrine made liberty of man the philosophical basis of their whole structure, and they thought to rediscover that liberty as the political consequence of their activities. It marks the elevation of their minds that, out of the slow decay of the Christian cathedral—to the ruin of which they had, incidentally, made their own contribution—they should have sought to salvage the conception of man's dignity.

A man, whoever he is, has, in their eyes, ends proper to himself, towards which an inner urge directs him. He may be prevented from realizing them by two external causes: the crushing weight of physical needs and the aggression of his fellows, whatever form it takes. Association enables him to lighten the burden of need, and should guarantee him against the will of his neighbour. But association is a snare and delusion when it subjects him "to the inconstant, uncertain, unknown, arbitrary will of another man,"[2] his sovereign.

Our authorities allow in principle that a man on "entering into association" has accepted of his own free will certain rules of conduct which are necessary to the upkeep of the association. But he is obliged to obey those rules and nothing else; his only master and terrestrial sovereign is the law. "A free people," said Rousseau, "obeys laws and laws only, and it is by the force of the laws that it does not obey men."[3]

Let us pause a moment to salute the nobility of this conception, which has been debased less by its critics' attacks than by the use made of it by its avowed champions.

Liberty is the principle and the end of society: no other sovereignty is acceptable than the necessary and sufficient sovereignty of law. Such are the postulates, postulates which furnish immediate justification for the abasement and subordination of Power—which has henceforward no other right or reason for existence than to execute the law. The law is over all, and its authority, which protects man against man, contains Power within the limits of its proper functions. "The law should protect public and individual liberty against oppression by those who rule."[4] The intention informing these foundations is unambiguous: it is a matter of restraining Power.

Let us now see what ideas go to the making of the rest of the building.

Since the law is over all, the question of capital importance to decide is where the law is to come from and who is to enunciate the rule of right. The Middle Ages knew nothing of this difficulty; for them the law was fixed, the rule a premise. But from the time that the divine law was rejected as superstition, and custom as a mere routine, the law had to be *made*.

There had to be a legislative authority, which, as the fount of the

2. Locke, *Second Treatise of Government,* chap. iv.
3. *Lettres écrites de la Montagne,* Part 2, letter viii.
4. Declaration of Rights of 1793, art. 9.

supreme rule of life, would necessarily be supreme.[5] But what is this? Shall men prescribe the conduct of men? Has Power, now sunk to the status of "executive," been put in chains merely to raise up a new and prouder Power? The danger was clear enough. All our authorities were aware of it. As temperament and nationality dictated, they coped with it either empirically or philosophically.

### 3. The Sovereignty of the Law Results in Parliamentary Sovereignty

The remedy discovered by English thinkers was, as Montesquieu put it, of Gothic inspiration.

The country had had experience for centuries of assemblies which, though convoked by the monarch, always showed a tendency to limit his rights and refuse him the facilities for which he asked. Indeed, in times of trouble they had been seen to go to the length of giving him directives which narrowly limited his powers. This decided tendency to a negative attitude was mistakenly regarded as inherent in representation of the people as such, whereas it was in fact due to the special nature and status of these medieval assemblies.

What were they? In the beginning, gatherings of the privileged. Those sitting or represented there were at first those persons (the great barons) who had proved sufficiently powerful to assert their autonomy; next, they were that powerful entity, the Church, which had maintained such moral and temporal independence as was necessary to the fulfilment of her mission; lastly, they were the small communal bodies which, having received their liberties through their own initiative, had been granted by the king a power of decision proper to themselves.

The meeting of Parliament had, then, from the start this essential characteristic, that it was the convocation of authorities, great and small, to which the king could not give orders and with which he had to parley.

The English king in his Parliament, or the French king in his States-

---

5. "For," says Locke, "what can give laws to another must needs be superior to him; and since the legislative is no otherwise legislative of the society, but by the right it has to make laws for all the parts, and for every member of the society, prescribing rules to their actions, and giving power of execution, where they are transgressed; the legislative must needs be the supreme, and all other powers, in any members or parts of the society, derived from and subordinate to it." *Op. cit.,* chap. xiii.

General, constituted a congress of the various authorities in the nation: there the public authority encountered the private authorities, and the general interest, impersonated by the king, held parley with the sectional interests, which appeared either in person or by representatives.

In the dialogue which ensued between unity and diversity the nation was represented in two different characters—as a whole, as regards the interests gathered up in the sovereign, and as a collection, as regards the sectional interests represented by those present.[6]

An assembly of this kind was a necessity for a Power which could not dispose of property by force but had to make request of each private interest to make its own contribution to the public requirement. The attitude of the representatives to Power's requests was more or less negative. They did not give all that was asked, and they attached conditions to what they did give; an unreserved assent could be obtained from them only in the event of the clearest necessity. They were, moreover, tightly held by imperative mandates to the sectional interests whom they represented.

In raising taxation without having obtained it as a benevolence from these assemblies, men like Louis XIII and Charles I embarked on a revolutionary course: no longer did the general interest take account of private interests but proceeded to the disposal of property by force. Naturally public opinion, confronted with this absolutist revolution, favoured return to a regime of assemblies which guaranteed private interests. Reluctance to have the sovereign legislate without the concurrence of these assemblies was reasonable. His legislative career had begun only with them and by their consent, and for him to claim to exercise this dangerous authority by himself was an abuse. It could be restrained within just limits only if the consent of sovereign and assembly had both to be obtained, and of the latter it could safely be predicted that it would tend to a negative attitude and be reluctant to give more than the indispensable minimum.

When, however, the predominant position secured by the assembly over the sovereign had made it the sole repository of the legislative authority, as being the sole representative of the nation, the change that was bound to ensue in its character and attitude escaped attention. Instead of being a juxtaposition of different interests, represented by men who

6. The list of interests represented became incomplete, faulty, and distorted because changes in the representation lagged behind social transformations.

were tied to a strict mandate, it became a representation in whole of the whole nation;[7] it was bound to become this under a system of ideas which laid on it the task of making laws in the nation's name.

What the old constitution had guaranteed was that no proposition made by Power in the name of the public interest could become law without having obtained the assent of the various interests included in the nation. It would have been illogical for these various interests as such to have proposed laws, since the purpose of laws was to serve the public interest. The assembly could become, as it did, the propounder of laws only in virtue of the quite novel idea that it was representative of the nation, considered as a whole and in its general interest; this was the role that had formerly belonged to the king. The change, which affected the very essence of the assembly's nature, was marked by a new-found freedom of action on the part of the representatives in regard to their constituents, a freedom which the doctrinaires of the new system especially emphasized.[8] They were careless of the fact that Parliament, once it had been unified, emancipated, and made supreme as being the main, and tending to be the sole,[9] author of law, could not possibly maintain the same dispositions as had characterized it when it was disparate, bound down, and without authority proper to itself.

7. This principle, which was enunciated during the first sessions of the Constituent Assembly by Sieyès, was embodied in the Constitution of 1791 in the following form: "The representatives designated in the departments shall not be representatives of a particular department but of the whole of France." *Titre III de la Constitution,* chap. i, section 3, art. 7.

It was embodied in constitutional law. It is noteworthy that in the English Parliament, which had emerged by a slow evolution from a medieval assembly where each man had beyond a doubt represented those only who had sent him there, the same idea of the individual deputy representing nothing but the whole nation triumphed in the end.

8. At the sitting of July 7, 1789, of the Constituent Assembly, Sieyès rejected the medieval idea of an imperative mandate. French constitutional jurisprudence proclaims as null and void any imperative mandate which a deputy has accepted. The same views hold the field in England, but are there the fruit of a long process of transformation of the character of the representation.

9. As for England, Sir Edward Coke writes in his *Fourth Institute:* "Of the power and jurisdiction of the Parliament, for making of laws in proceeding by bill, it is so transcendent and absolute, as it cannot be confined either for causes or persons within any bounds. . . . It has a sovereign and uncontrolled authority for the confection of laws, their confirmation, their extension, their restriction, their abrogation, their renewal and their interpretation in all matters, ecclesiastical or temporal, civil, military, maritime or criminal; it is it that the Constitution of these realms invests with the absolute despotic power which must in all governments reside somewhere. All abuses, grievances, operations and remedies, which arise

Parliament was now the king's successor as the representative of the whole: it had taken over his mission and his requirements. Unlike him, however, it no longer had representatives of diversity to deal with, mandatories of particular interests which it must take into account.

In the ancient constitution the interest of the nation was represented in two ways, as a whole and as a collection of parts, the former disposed to ask and the latter to refuse. One of them now disappeared. It was not, as might have been expected, the king, for the legislative Power representing the public interest is merely his successor. No, what has disappeared has been the representation of the various interests included in the nation. What had been a body for the protection of private citizens is now one for the advancement of the public interest, and has been clothed with the formidable power of legislation.

In its new form Power had a much wider scope than in its old. The sovereign, when he was a king, was tied down by a higher code, which religion validated and of which the Church stood guardian; he was restrained as well by the various customary rules which, being rooted in popular sentiment, acted as makeweights to himself. But this code and these rules are of no avail against Power turned lawgiver, whose recognized right and duty it is now to be itself the source of codes and rules. "The English Parliament," it has been said by some wit, "can do anything except change a man into a woman."

It is quite certain that nothing of this sort entered philosophical heads. All of them were deeply convinced of the existence of a natural and necessary order, and the function of the lawgiver, as they saw it, was to disentangle the outlines of this order and to keep on recalling erring governments to observance of it. Locke considered, but only to condemn, the absolute and arbitrary capacity to make laws.[10] Blackstone considered,

---

ordinarily from the laws, are within the competence of this extraordinary tribunal. It can regulate or re-fashion the order of succession to the throne, as was done in the reigns of Henry VIII and William III. It can modify the established religion, as was done several times in the reigns of Henry VIII and his three children. It can change and even re-make the constitution of the realm and of the Parliaments themselves, as was done by the Act of Union and by the different statutes concerning triennial and septennial elections. It can in sum do anything which is not physically impossible." It is true that in the vocabulary of those days "Parliament" meant the concurrence of the king and two chambers. But the enfeeblement of the royal element has progressed so far that now "parliamentary sovereignty" means no more than that of the House of Commons.

10. "Though the legislative be the supreme power in every commonwealth, it is not, nor can possibly be, absolutely arbitrary over the lives and fortunes of the people. . . .

along with all the sages of antiquity and all the theologians, that human laws derive their competence only from their conformity to, or their coherence with, the divine law.[11]

But there is now no concrete sanction to safeguard this conformity or this coherence. We can do no more than hope that lawgivers will be men sufficiently imbued with this higher code to give them to us. And that, it is clear, depends in the last resort on the dominion of religious and moral ideas.

In the end, therefore, the principle of legality, intended as the absolute guarantee of each man's liberty, was to come to justify the absolute commission of that liberty to the discretion of a parliamentary aristocracy.[12]

That aristocracy becomes "the prince," and a more powerful prince than a king not in control of legislation ever was. One of two things may now happen. Either this "prince" succeeds in breaking loose from his constituents—as happened, for instance, with the Republic of Geneva in the eighteenth century—when he becomes absolute: though he may still be restrained from violating civil liberty by his recognition of a higher code, a code which is the source of his laws—as of the monarch's under the theory of divine right properly understood—and the regulator of his behaviour.

Or again, in the contrary event, the members of the assembly may become the mere instruments of parties, or the playthings of forces outside the assembly altogether, parties and forces which are the expression of sectional interests and are all the more dangerous to society for being as well the expression of philosophic heresies. As each of them seeks for itself an absolute dominion, a battle ensues, in which the stake is now not only Power, as in the dynastic conflicts, but *the laws themselves*, which will no longer be the constant reflection of higher truths but will chop

---

"The Law of Nature stands as an eternal rule to all men, legislators as well as others. The rules that they make for other men's actions must, as well as their own and other men's actions, be conformable to the Law of Nature, i.e. to the Will of God, of which that is a declaration. . . ." Locke, *Second Treatise on Government,* chap. xi, para. 135.

11. "This Law of Nature, being coeval with mankind and dictated by God Himself, is of course superior in obligation to any other. It is binding all over the globe, in all countries and at all times: no human laws are of any validity, if contrary to this; and such of them as are valid derive all their force and all their authority, mediately or intermediately, from this original." Blackstone, *Commentaries,* I, p. 41.

12. "To put it shortly, Parliament, which was conceived as the representative of the nation, has become its effective sovereign." Carré de Malberg, *La loi, expression de la volonté générale* (Paris: 1931).

and change with every fluctuation of fortune in the combat. In a regime of this kind there will be neither certitude in law nor guarantee for liberty.

## 4. The People, Judge of the Law

As a Genevan, Rousseau was warned of the first danger by the history of his native city. All his political writings, while written in exaltation of the principles of liberty and equality,[13] are at the same time an attempt to prevent them from issuing in parliamentary sovereignty. That he damns and denounces in many passages, and his proclamation of the inalienability of popular sovereignty is made with a view to obviating it.

It is of the greatest importance, nor is it difficult, to re-establish his meaning, which has suffered much tendentious distortion.[14]

The citizen must be free, and freedom turns for him on his obeying nothing but laws. If the laws are his master, then it is most important that there should be only such laws as are just and necessary.

Rousseau does not entrust the establishment of such laws to a body of self-styled representatives. Certainly not. The citizen is both the subject-matter and the end of law. So he must be its judge. A new law will impose on a citizen a new obligation: it belongs to him, and to him only, as the person obligated, to accept or reject this obligation. According to Rousseau's reasoning, each law is an amendment of the social contract: for it to be valid the parties to that contract must have assented to it.

This line of argument, if pushed to its logical conclusion, would make laws valid for those only who had voted in favour of them in the assembly

13. "There is, then, no liberty without laws, nor any place where any man is above the laws: even in the state of nature, man is only free thanks to the natural law which is over all. A free people obeys without servitude; it has leaders, not masters; it obeys law but it obeys laws only, and it is through the power of the laws that it does not obey men. All the barriers which are set up in republics to the authority of the magistrates are only set up to safeguard from the executive's aggressions the sacred enclosure of the laws; the magistrates are their servants, not their masters; their duty is to guard them, not to infringe them. A people is free, whatever its form of government, when it sees its ruler not as a man but as the instrument of the law. In a word, the fate of liberty is linked to the fate of laws, liberty rules or perishes with them; of that I am absolutely sure." Rousseau, *Lettres écrites de la Montagne,* Part 2, letter viii.

14. [For a fuller exposition of Rousseau's ideas, see the author's essay on "The Political Thought of Rousseau," appearing as introduction to his edition of *Du Contrat social* published by Constant Bourquin, Geneva, 1947.]

of the people. But a system of that kind would destroy the body social. He therefore presupposes that the primitive convention contained a clause by which the contracting parties had to obey laws approved by a majority.

The object of Rousseau's system was, it is clear, to restrict the number of laws, and also the extent both of the obligations imposed on the subject and of the powers conferred on the magistrates. It did not enter his mind to suppose that the people could make laws,[15] but he wanted to place it in their power to reject any which they thought unjustified. Theirs was in effect to be the same negative and eliminatory role as is played in practice by the referendum, a device which has been taken straight from the Rousseauesque principle.

Light is thrown on his ideas by the legislative technique of the Romans, who were always much in his mind. At Rome it was a member of the executive who proposed to the people a new law: he made them acquainted with its provisions and fixed a day three weeks ahead[16] for the popular verdict on it. To carry a law meant, in strict parlance, to put it forward.[17] Before voting day orators harangued the people in the forum either for or against the law. Only those who had come expressly participated in these debates, and the rule was, though it was often broken, that they must listen in silence. On voting day, on the other hand, all the citizens had to be present. The magistrate then put the question: "Are you in favour of this law?" and voting took place in one of the two constitu-

---

15. The laws are, properly speaking, only the conditions of life in society. The people, being subject to the laws, must be their author; only those who are associated together are entitled to regulate the conditions of the society. But how will they regulate them? Will it be by common consent or by sudden inspiration? Is the body politic endowed with an organ for the expression of its wishes? Who will confer on it the foresight necessary to draft its statutes and publish them beforehand? How could a blind multitude which often does not know what it wants because it seldom knows what is good for it, carry out unaided an undertaking as large and as difficult as is a scheme of legislation? Left to itself the people always wills what is good, but left to itself it does not always perceive it. The general will is always righteous, but the judgment guiding it is not always clear-sighted. It needs to be made to see things as they are, sometimes as they ought to seem to it; it needs to be shown the good road which it seeks, to be safeguarded from the seductions of private wills, to be made aware of places and times, to be taught to weigh the attraction of the immediate, concrete advantage against the danger of the latent and distant evil." *Du Contrat social,* Book XI, chap. vi.

16. To be precise, three nundines. (A nundine was a Roman market-day, recurring every eighth day.)

17. Mommsen, *Manuel des institutions romaines.*

tional ways provided (either by centuries or tribes).[18] The acceptance of the law by the people was, properly speaking, a contract entered into between the magistracy and itself: the word *lex*, incidentally, means contract.[19]

Not all the laws proposed by the magistracy—the government, if the word is preferred—were accepted. Therefore, the procedure could be described as a process of negation and elimination.

If we stop there, however, we shall be overlooking the rising tide of laws which were adopted by the people in the latter days of the Republic without having emanated from the executive. These were "popular resolutions,"[20] so called; they were taken on the initiative of the tribunes, who were persons outside the actual government, and they had been assimilated to laws in the strict sense by a lengthy process of evolution. With them it is no longer a case of the executive asking for an extension of its prerogatives or proposing to the people a new set of regulations: it is the people, roused thereto by its leaders, setting the executive in motion. The popular will no longer plays the passive role of a sieve, but the active role of an instigator.

If Rousseau had really held the views on popular sovereignty which have been ascribed to him, it is this last method of legislation which he would particularly have favoured. Now, a whole chapter of *Du Contrat social* is expressly consecrated to the tribunate.[21] And what he says about it is this: "The tribunate is not a constituent part of the city, and *should have no share either in the legislative authority* or in the executive."

> My wish would be [he says elsewhere][22] that, to check the interested and ill-conceived proposals and the dangerous innovations by which the Athenians came to grief in the end, each man should not have the power to propose new laws at will; that the right to do this should belong to the magistrates only; that they should make such careful use of it, that the people for their

---

18. [The reference here is to the *comitia centuriata* and the *comitia tributa*. The *comitia* were the meetings of the Roman people held for the purpose of electing magistrates and voting laws. The *comitia centuriata*, in which the voting was by the military formation of centuries, was the earlier and more patrician of the two. The *comitia tributa*, in which the voting was by tribes, elected the tribunes and was the assembly of the *plebs*. In it were passed *plebiscita*, or popular resolutions which had force of law.]

19. Mommsen, *op. cit.,* p. 352.

20. *Plebi scitum* means, simply, a popular resolution.

21. Book IV, chap. v.

22. *Discours sur l'inégalité*, dedication.

part should be so reluctant to give their assent, and that the promulgation of new laws should only be made in so solemn a fashion that everyone should have time to realize, in advance of the overthrow of the constitution, that it is above all the great antiquity of the laws which makes them sacred and venerable; that the people should quickly learn to despise those laws which they see changing every other day; and that they should get to know that a habit of neglecting ancient usages under cover of improving on them often puts right lesser evils at the cost of introducing great ones.

His conclusion is, therefore, this: that the people is "the source of laws" only in the sense that it alone gives them their validity and is also free to reject them; but not in the sense that every popular urge should, either directly or through the medium of representatives, be translated into law.

It was not his view that any sort of laws would do, that they might as well be the caprice of whatever set of interests or opinions happened to be predominant, but rather that, as their function is to increase the good of the whole, their intent should sufficiently show them to have had, as it were, an existence prior to their revelation by the legislator—the person, that is to say, who proposes them. And the general will is an infallible instinct which knows them for what they are.

The notion of a general will is something of a mystery and has given rise to much misconception: notwithstanding the care which Rousseau took to set over against it the will of all,[23] there is a tendency to see in it no more than the sum or mean of private wills. But it is not that at all: rather it is a will from which every subjective element has been purged, which has become, as Hegel would say, objective, and thereafter, by an inevitable process, aims only at the best. This will for the best lives in each of us, but is overlaid by our private passions, which are far stronger than itself. The effect of general discussion is, on Rousseau's supposition, to void and extinguish the private passions by throwing them into opposition to each other; and so, in the end, the passions are silenced, and the general will makes good its claim.

Rousseau's detestation of factions comes from his regarding them as so many coalitions of interests and passions by means of which the

---

23. He declares (Book II, chap. iii): "The general will is always righteous and always to the public advantage," but adds at the same time: "but it does not follow that the people's deliberations are always of the same worth." And further on he says: "There is often a big difference between the will of all and the general will."

elimination of interest and passion, necessary to the manifestation of the general will, is checked.

The presentation of a law to the people is, therefore, the occasion for a judgment to be passed by the feeling for right—always supposing that the conditions are favourable for its manifestation—on what it is sought to make positive law.

This conception of Rousseau's will perhaps become clearer by comparing it with the contemporary thought of Léon Duguit. That great jurist regards as laws in the true sense only such as conform to the rule of right, a rule which he conceives as imprinted on the social conscience. Borrowing Duguit's terminology, we might say that, in Rousseau's system, the object of presenting a law to the people is not only to save the citizen from being subjected to obligations to which he has not subscribed, but even more to ensure that the law is brought face to face with the social conscience and in that way with the rule of right.

### 5. Law as the People's "Good Pleasure"

That is how Rousseau put the coping-stone on the structure of his thought on law and liberty.

The uses to which his doctrine has been turned are a matter for amazement and provide a striking lesson in social history. All that has been taken over from it is the magic formula, popular sovereignty, divorced both from the subject-matter to which it was applicable and from the fundamental condition of its exercise, the assembly of the people. It is now used to justify the very spate of legislation which it was its purpose to dam, and to advance the indefinite enablement of Power—which Rousseau had sought to restrict!

All his school had made individual right the beginning and end of his system. It was to be guaranteed by subjecting to it at two removes the actual Power in human form, namely the executive. The executive was made subject to the law, which was kept strictly away from it, and the law was made subject to the sacrosanct principles of natural justice.

The idea of the law's subjection to natural justice has not been maintained. That of Power's subjection to the law has fared a little better, but has been interpreted in such a way that the authority which makes laws has incorporated with itself the authority which applies them; they have become united, and so the omnipotent law has raised to its highest pitch a Power which it has made omnicompetent.

Rousseau's school had concentrated on the idea of law. Their labour was in vain: all that the social consciousness has taken over from it is the association between the two conceptions, law and popular will. It is no longer accepted that a law owes its validity, as in Rousseau's thought, only to the formal consent of the people; law is now whatever the people wishes, or whatever it is represented as having wished. Law, he thought, should be confined to a generalized subject-matter.[24] Its majesty was usurped by any expression of an alleged popular will.[25]

A mere juggling with meanings has brought the wheel full cycle to the dictum which so disgusted our philosophers: "Whatever pleases the prince shall have force of law."[26] The prince has changed—that is all.

The collapse of this keystone has brought down the whole building. The principle of liberty had been based on the principle of law: to say that liberty consists in obedience to the laws only, presupposes in law such characteristics of justice and permanence as may enable the citizen to know with precision the demands which are and will be made on him; the limits within which society may command him being in this way narrowly defined, he is his own master in his own prescribed domain. But, if law comes merely to reflect the caprices of the people, or of some body to which the legislative authority has been delegated, or of a faction which controls that body, then obedience to the laws means in effect subjection to the inconstant, uncertain, unknown, arbitrary will of men who give this will the form of law. In that event the law is no longer the stay of liberty. The inner ligatures of Rousseau's system come apart, and what was intended as a guarantee becomes a means of oppression.

---

24. "When I say that the object of laws is always general, I mean that the law always considers subjects in the round and actions in the abstract, and never an individual man or one particular action. For instance, a law may provide that there shall be privileges, but it must not name the persons who are to enjoy them; the law may create several classes of citizens and even designate the qualifications which will give entry to each class, but it must not nominate for admission such and such persons; it may establish a royal government with a hereditary succession, but it must not select the king or nominate a royal family: in a word, anything that relates to a named individual is outside the scope of the legislative authority." *Du Contrat social*, Book II, chap. vi.

25. Carré de Malberg, speaking for France (*La loi, expression de la volonté générale*. Paris: 1931), and Dicey, speaking for England (*Introduction to the Law of the Constitution*), clearly set out that what gives a law force is, in modern jurisprudence, only the fact that the decision has been taken by the authority designated as the legislature. The legislature can pass any law on any subject.

26. [*"Quod principi placuit, legis habet vigorem."* Justinian, *Instits.*]

Government is by way of laws, and it is by laws that the transfer of Power to the legislative body has been effected. Their fusion once completed, a new Power, calling itself the expression of the popular will and presenting itself as the guarantor of individual liberty, will be seen separating itself by degrees from the legislative body, which is constitutionally unsuited to the work of command. The truth is seen to be that the entire logical structure of Rousseau's doctrine was destroyed by popular pressures, leaving behind it nothing but one simple association of words: popular sovereignty and liberty.

### 6. *The Appetite for the* Imperium

This distortion of doctrine, incomprehensible though it is to the dealer in ideas, seems natural enough to an observer of the social mechanism. It has been said that the reader determines the fate of the book: it is equally true that an idea gets its political meaning from the class which takes it over.

Suppose the case of a country in which the Power in being, the *imperium*, has been successfully challenged by the social forces, and has been enclosed in a limited circle of fixed duties, within which a patrician "people" keeps watch and ward on it. In it the system of individual rights has grown autonomously, and the ordinances of religion have retained much of their force. It will naturally follow both that the patrician "people" will make use of the principle of law to put a bridle on the vagaries of Power, and that the law will draw its inspiration from the system of rights which was formed in the womb of society. The function of the representative body will be that of vigorous control, and the legislation will be of a restrictive character. Such were, in effect, the features of English political life, so long as an aristocracy was in the saddle and the "people" was exclusively patrician.

Now suppose a country in which the Power has no history but has been built up from nothing, its only opponents being some localized authorities of more ancient date which for long derive advantage from an intenser loyalty. In it, moreover, a fundamental law is laid down, the guardians of which will be a judicial authority with a penchant for a traditional scheme of individual rights. It will necessarily follow that an improvised *imperium* such as this will for long remain weak; it will be held in check by a legislative authority which is itself checked by the *imperium* and both of them will be restrained not only by the provisions of the fundamental law but by the watchful jealousy of older authorities. So it was with the United States.

Far different is the case in countries where the Minotaur has already amassed vast forces, and has compelled the social makeweights to fight an ever more desperate defensive action. The *imperium* has there become so rich a booty and so great a stake that all desire and all ambition must be to lay hold on it. If a body is charged to regulate by laws the manner of the *imperium*'s exercise, its high position will seem to it of small account until it can lay its own hands on the great treasure-house of honour and authority. It will grow more faithless to its office of control, and more disposed to conquest, with every step it takes away from being representative of aristocratic interests on the defensive and towards being representative of popular interests on the march. It will thus follow that the legislative Power, which was called into being to exert popular control over the *imperium*, will tend more and more to take over the *imperium*. And, as there is in this country no autonomous scheme of individual rights, the faculty of legislation will be used with no higher rule to guide it than the class feeling of the legislative body soon to be sovereign. So it is with France.

Her political destiny was really settled for her by the concentration of Power effected under the Bourbon kings. From then on Power gleamed with so bright a radiance as to attract to itself all eyes. Those who could hope to be its new inheritors lived anxiously hoping. Those who could not lived in the expectation of profiting by a force whose miraculous virtues they much exaggerated.

For that reason the legislative authority in France has never been valued but as a near-by elevation to the City of Command, as a vantage-point from which the latter might be stormed. For that reason popular sovereignty has always been secretly taken by its "representatives" to imply the exercise by themselves of the *imperium*. It is the logic, not of ideas, but, in politics a more potent logic, of situations.

It was to the possession of Power by the representatives of the people that the Revolution came when it replaced the king's ministers by committees of the Convention. The same ownership of Power was brought in its train by the course of events which issued in the resignation of MacMahon in 1875.

## 7. Of Parliamentary Sovereignty

The evolution of the nineteenth century—an evolution which more or less continued into the twentieth—presents us with three important facts in regard to the *imperium*. The first is political: it is the conquest of the *imperium* by the parliamentary body, which exercises it through a committee, the cabinet, formed from within itself. The second is social: the parliamentary body becomes, slowly but surely, more and more plebeian. The third and last is moral: the general acceptance of the democratic principle, understood in the sense that it is the province of the people taken as a whole, not, indeed, to pronounce on laws—the true notion of which has been lost—but to govern. It is invariably assumed that this moral fact is the cause of the other two. But the opposite assumption is more probably the correct one.

During this period the parliamentary body came to play the same role as was taken under the *ancien régime* by the service of the king: it became, more and more, the social ladder of plebeians. As it steadily filled up with their ambitions—and there is in this respect a striking contrast between the Constituent Assembly and the Convention—its fingers itched the more to close on the executive power, the source of actual command.

To satisfy this ambition, popular sovereignty had, as was natural, to be invoked. Parliament, by a daring fiction, gave itself out for the assembled people itself: it was thus its function to make laws, for the laws were the people's. But it was its function also to govern: and it would be the people governing.

History may be ransacked in vain for a thinker who commended the sovereignty of an assembly, at once legislator and, for practical purposes, magistrate, to which, as the supposed incarnation of the interest of the whole, every private interest was subject, and which, as the sole begetter of the laws, the laws could not check. Rousseau kept his strongest invective for just such a regime:

> I can but marvel at the carelessness, the incuriosity and I will even say the stupidity of the English nation, which, after arming its deputies with supreme power, applies no brake for controlling the use which they make of it during the seven whole years that their commission lasts.[27]

Parliamentary sovereignty is not, then, the realization of an idea; rather it is the case of an idea having been adapted to fit the purposes of the parliamentary body hungering for *imperium*. The harmfulness in action of parliamentary sovereignty has been much exaggerated; but the extreme harmfulness of the intellectual system to which it has had to go for its justification has been completely ignored.

27. *Considérations sur le gouvernement de Pologne*, chap. vii.

It has been in actual fact, for a time at least, the government of an elite, bound by a real attachment to an exalted conception of law.

The Declaration of 1789 had imprinted on minds certain principles which from then on haunted the waking hours of a middle class with a legalistic outlook.

The violation of these principles during the Terror caused their value to be recognized, and, though legislation which was a contradiction of them met with no positive obstacle, they presented a framework which the action of the legislature had still to take into account.

Moreover, the choice of parliamentary representatives was for much of the time a good one. Montesquieu expressly said so: "The people has a great gift for choosing those to whom it must entrust some part of its authority."[28] The quotation generally stops there, and his meaning thereby receives an arbitrary extension. But there is no denying that the inhabitants of a sufficiently small constituency, just because they know the candidates, do naturally single out those who have recommended themselves to them by the worth of their lives, the number of their good services, and their exalted merits. In that way good assemblies are formed as long as the choice is made on no other principle. Popular habit, in truth, changes slowly. The people, bidden to choose men who were to be for all practical purposes its sovereign, preferred, as in former days, to nominate those who would defend its local interests against Power. It therefore tended to select such of the local notables as, from experience, it knew to be suited to this task. And these social authorities, as is the way of an aristocracy, added but little weight to political authority.

The separation of powers, though it could exercise only for a time its moderating function, did at least set up a friction by which parliamentary absolutism was slowed down. Moreover, this absolutism found a sort of check in the very numbers of the assembly: such a large body is naturally unsuited to steadfast and vigorous action. But this was a dangerous safeguard, for, while parliamentary sovereignty with its concentration of powers paved the way for an unlimited Power, its incapacity to use these powers itself summoned to the seat of this Power a formidable occupant.

## 8. From the Sovereignty of the Law to the Sovereignty of the People

Had my purpose been to study merely the bodily growth of the Minotaur—the growth, that is to say, of its rights, powers, and resources—

---

28. *Esprit des lois,* Book II, chap. ii.

my reference to democracy could have been limited to showing what it had effectively contributed to the transformation of the state; and then I should have omitted this chapter altogether. But the age of democratic Power is characterized by a misconception which is so favourable to the growth of the *imperium* that some light needed to be thrown on it.

It needed to be recalled that the democratic ideal was not in origin the substitution of the arbitrary will of a body or of a crowd for the arbitrary will of a monarch as the principle of rule. As was finely said by Royer-Collard: "The will of a single person, the will of many, the will of all, these are but variants of force of a greater or less degree; not one of these wills can, as such, claim either obedience or the smallest respect." As Clemenceau said later, ". . . had we expected that these majorities of a day would exercise the same authority as that possessed by our ancient kings, we would but have effected an exchange of tyrants."[29]

The stuff of men's dreams was that law should be sovereign, and not just any law but one which was compulsive in its own right. The guarantee of liberty lay in the sovereignty of the rule of right or law.

The advances in law and liberty for which democracy gets the credit were in fact the fruit of complex governmental machinery in which no human will, whether single or collective, was sovereign: to constitutional regimes of this kind the word "polity" was properly applicable.[30] These polities, being more or less shackled in their movements, came to be attacked on two counts; these were: their executive incapacity, and the fact that Power had in them no rational foundation.

Men called more and more loudly for the institution of popular

29. At the inauguration of the monument to Scheurer-Kestner, *Journal Officiel*, February 13, 1908. [Clemenceau's words echo nearly some spoken by Chatham on January 9, 1770: "Are all the generous efforts of our ancestors . . . reduced to this conclusion, that instead of the arbitrary power of a king we must submit to the arbitrary power of a House of Commons? If this be true, what benefit do we derive from the exchange? Tyranny is detestable in every shape; but in none so formidable as when it is assumed and exercised by a number of tyrants." (Cf. Acton: "It is bad to be oppressed by a minority, but it is worse to be oppressed by a majority. For there is a reserve of latent power in the masses which, if it is called into play, the minority can seldom resist. But from the absolute will of an entire people there is no appeal, no redemption, no refuge but reason!")]

30. [The word "polity" is here used in its Aristotelian sense, to indicate "constitutional government." For a full account of it see the *Politics* 1293b, where it emerges as a blend of oligarchy and democracy, but also is akin to aristocracy. (Perhaps the sort of alternating oligarchy of trained minds which governed England for much of the nineteenth century answers to an Aristotelian "polity.")]

sovereignty, with its absolutism; in other words, the complex of springs which played the part of shock-absorbers had to be made as simple as possible, and there had to be a concentrated Power, of a sensibility which would make it obsequious to the wishes of a day, and of a strength which could fulfil them. This cause was espoused both by the magistracy and by the legislative body, which saw in the proclamation of popular absolutism the way to magnify its own authority. It was not realized that this was the way of the renunciation of the rule of law—that rule so difficult in practice[31]—and of the abandonment of guarantees for liberty; that there was in truth going up a new Caesarism which was certain in time—*similia similibus*—to find its Caesars.

31. Rousseau fully appreciated the difficulty: "Putting law over man is a political problem comparable to that of squaring the circle in geometry. Solve this problem well, and the government founded on the solution will be good and free from abuses. But, until you have solved it, be sure that, *instead of enthroning laws, as you imagine, you are really enthroning men.*" *Considérations sur le gouvernement de Pologne,* chap. 1.

# XIV.

# *Totalitarian Democracy*

PROUDHON SAID TRULY[1] THAT POPULAR INSTINCT grasps the simple notion of Power more successfully than the complex notion of social contract. The explanation of the democratic principle's degeneration is psychological: conceived at first as sovereignty of the law, it triumphed only when it had come to be regarded as sovereignty of the people.

Its only effect was to transfer into other hands, those of the representatives of the people, the whole complex of rights, duties, and resources which had been built up during the monarchy for the behoof of the king.

The *imperium* took no diminution therefrom but an accretion. The traditional view of it, as a principle of authority which was, however necessary, the enemy of liberty, gave way to one in which it was regarded as the agent of liberty. From being, in other words, *one* will, and within certain limits a beneficent one, among others equally worthy of respect, it passed henceforward for the general will. From being but *one* interest in society, an eminent and essential one certainly, it became *the* interest *of* society.

We have posited that the transformation of Power took place in such

---

1. Cf. *La Révolution sociale démontrée par le coup d'état de 2 décembre* (Brussels: 1852) p. 17: "In the centralization envisaged by the Jacobins may be seen the influence of popular instinct, which grasps more easily the simple notion of Power than the complex notion of Social Contract."

a way as to disarm all suspicion of it. The credit then opened in its name has prepared the way for an age of tyrannies. This we are now going to see.

## 1. Sovereignty and Liberty

Viewed historically, liberty had been a status, acquired not without a struggle by certain men, maintained by an energetic defence, and guaranteed by privileges extorted from authority. Men aspired to make of it a right conferred on all, and thought to guarantee it by regulations of general extent. This idea, arbitrary simplification though it was of the most difficult problem in political science, was even so too subtle to penetrate the social consciousness, and was besides unsatisfying to the appetites of the new officeholders, who greatly preferred command to liberty.

The libertarian idea is, as such, indifferent as to the form which Power takes. Its principle is the recognition, or the assumption, that there is in every man the same pride and dignity as had hitherto been assured and protected, but for the aristocracy only, by privileges. Proclaiming as it does the sovereignty of each man over himself, its sufficient requirement is that every member of society should have a domain proper to himself in which to be his own lord. And, as corollary to this, that Power be confined within a zone of influence from which it never breaks out. This condition once realized, it is a matter of indifference whether the command remains monarchical and so assures itself of the advantages both of stability and of neutrality in the strife of interests; or whether it becomes aristocratic and benefits by an incessant rivalry of intelligent ambitions and well-grounded opinions; or, again, whether it becomes democratic. Even Rousseau shared this indifference: the choice between the various forms of government turned, in his view, on the size of the community, and if his own leaning was to aristocracy it was because it suited the moderately sized states of his choice.

But this indifference is not to the taste of ambitions dressed in the panoply of new ideas. Their objective would be outside their grasp were they to use the libertarian aspirations which escort them to Power, merely to usher in a limitation of the *imperium*. Their aim is, rather, the seizure of this *imperium*. They can no more tolerate a Power which is not theirs than they can admit limitations to one which is. Hence the idea that it is not enough for individual sovereignties to be guaranteed against Power: also and more, they must admit no Power which has not issued from themselves. If they are sacred, why should they accept a command which they cannot but distrust? On, then, with the good work of abolishing such a Power, and let the sum of private liberties set in its place a new authority, which of its nature cannot turn traitor to those who gave it life.

In this way, it is claimed, to the existing means of defence against Power, and to the established liberty, are added, for the individual's benefit, the right of taking part in Power and an established sovereignty. It is, unfortunately, an abandonment of the substance for the shadow.

It looks on the face of it as if the joint sovereignty of the citizens must be a greater which includes the less of liberty, which will in this way find its fixed and certain guarantee. The mistake is one which was exposed in advance by Montesquieu: "As it is a feature of democracies that to all appearance the people does almost exactly what it wishes, men have supposed that democratic governments were the abiding-place of liberty: they confused the power of the people with the liberty of the people."[2] This confusion of thought is at the root of modern despotism.

It is possible, with the help of prudently balanced institutions, to provide everyone with effective safeguards against Power. But there are no institutions on earth which enable each separate person to have a hand in the exercise of Power, for Power is command, and everyone cannot command. Sovereignty of the people is, therefore, nothing but a fiction, and one which must in the long run prove destructive of individual liberties.

It is difficult, it requires unceasing vigilance, to keep the libertarian principle alive, for the spirit of domination never slumbers. While admitting that Power cannot be dispensed with, and while allowing it the full use of its energies in its own sphere, the libertarian principle never ceases to distrust Power as being potentially an aggressor, and keeps a jealous watch on the frontiers of liberty. But, when once Power is based on the sovereignty of all, the distrust comes to seem unreasonable and the vigilance pointless: and the limits set on authority no longer get defended.

## 2. The Idea of the Whole Advances

The onlooker sees in society a vast crowd of individuals, each animated by his particular will; he sees that their diversity of characters, functions, and situations tends naturally to group them in various categories, each of which has an interest of its own—an interest which is, in regard to the

2. *Esprit des lois,* Book XI, chap. ii.

members of a category, general, and, in regard to society, particular. These individual wills, these sectional interests, are the rudimentary realities of social life. They live, no doubt, in constant warfare, but, given the observance of certain rules, that warfare is the breath of life of society.

The will and interest of Power have always taken a hand in this warfare. The will has always sought to seem infallible, the interest transcendent. But, so long as the regime was monarchical, in spite of the royal house's movement towards absolutism, they never fully succeeded. Democratic Power has other weapons. Its predecessor, being personified, was, patently, above but also outside the people. Democratic Power claims identity with them, yet, in the nature of things, remains above them.

The royal will was, and was known to be, that of a crowned head, his favourite, or his minister; it was in that respect as human and *personal* as that of anyone else. The will of democratic Power goes by the name of *general*. It crushes each individual beneath the weight of the sum of the individuals represented by it; it oppresses each private interest in the name of a general interest which is incarnate in itself. The democratic fiction confers on the rulers the authority of the whole. It is the whole that both wills and acts.

This personification of the whole is a great novelty in the Western world, and is a throwback to the world of the Greeks, from whom its inspiration comes. But the citizens of an ancient city state, being enclosed within its walls and having been conditioned by much the same education, showing in social standing differences that were but of degree, came much nearer to being a real whole than the people of an extensive nation, of various origins and traditions, and marked by a diversity of functions.

This whole is not a fact, for all the care that is taken to break down every private formation and tradition in existence.[3] It is a fiction, which it is sought the harder to accredit for being the title deed of Power.

It does not admit of doubt that the suppression or lightening of the *imperium*, and the ability to follow their private desires which people would have received therefrom, would have had a solvent effect on the

---

3. A care of which Tocqueville had been the terrified spectator: "The old localized authorities disappear without either revival or replacement, and everywhere the central government succeeds them in the direction of affairs. The whole of Germany, even the whole of Europe, presents in this respect the same picture. Everywhere men are leaving behind the liberty of the Middle Ages, not to enter into a modern brand of liberty but to return to the ancient despotism; for centralization is nothing else than an up-to-date version of the administration seen in the Roman Empire." Letter to H. de Tocqueville in *Œuvres*, Vol. VII, pp. 322–23.

men and territories once held together by the monarchical grip. And that
was what the *imperium's* new owners refused to tolerate. Sieyès expressed
himself on the subject[4] with the greatest vigour:

> France must not be an assemblage of small nations each with its own
> democratic government; she is not a collection of states; she is a single whole,
> made up of integral parts; these parts must not have each a complete existence
> of its own, for they are not wholes joined in a mere federation but parts
> forming a single whole. The difference is a big one, and one which is of vital
> importance to us. Everything is lost once we consent to regard the established
> municipalities, the districts, or the provinces as so many republics joined
> together only for the purposes of defence and common protection.

### 3. The Attack on Centrifugal Tendencies

Every Power is sure to attack centrifugal tendencies. But the behaviour
of democratic Power offers in this respect some peculiar features of a
striking kind. It claims its mission to be that of liberating man from the
constraints put on him by the old Power, which was the more or less
direct descendant of conquest. But that did not stop the Convention from
guillotining the Federalists, the English Parliament from wiping out, in
some of the bloodiest repressions of history, the separatist nationalism in
Ireland, or the government at Washington from launching a war such as
Europe had never yet seen to crush the attempt of the Southern States
to form themselves into a separate unity. Another instance would be the
action of the Spanish Republic in 1934 in opposing by force the movement
to Catalan independence.

This hostility to the formation of smaller communities is inconsistent
with the claim to have inaugurated government of the people by itself,
for clearly a government answers more closely to that description in
smaller communities than in larger.[5] Only in smaller communities can the

4. In the Constituent Assembly, September 7, 1789.

5. "All things considered," said Rousseau, "I do not see how it will be possible
henceforward for the sovereign to maintain among us the exercise of sovereignty if the city
is not a very small one." *Du Contrat social,* Book III, chap. xv.

And again: "Size in nations and large extent of states, these are the first and principal
cause of human misfortunes, and above all of the countless disasters which undermine and
destroy civilized peoples. Nearly all small states, republics and monarchies alike, flourish by
reason of being small, because then the citizens can keep a watchful eye on each other and
the leaders can see for themselves both the evil which goes on and the reforms which they

citizens choose their rulers directly from men whom they know personally. Only in them can justification be found for the encomium pronounced by Montesquieu:[6]

> The people is well fitted to choose. . . . The people knows well whether a man has often seen active service and what successes he has won: therefore it is well equipped to choose a general. It knows whether a judge attends to his duties; whether most people leave his court satisfied; whether or not he is corrupt: therein is knowledge sufficient for it to elect a praetor. It has been impressed by the magnificence or wealth of a certain citizen: this qualifies it to choose an aedile. These are all facts which make a public square a better-informed place than the palace of a king.

A further requirement is that there should be a public square or its equivalent, and that the choice of administrators should take place at the municipal level.

The desire to secure the fullest measure of popular sovereignty possible should, logically, lead to the same principles being followed in the formation of the higher authorities. At the provincial level, the population is already too large and too scattered to be effectively assembled, so that each candidate for a place may be known personally to everyone. For that reason the choice and control of regional administrators should be the work of representatives of the municipalities. And, for the same reasons, the choice and control of national administrators should be the work of representatives of the regions.

A system of this kind would assuredly be the best fitted to embody popular sovereignty, especially if the representatives were held in check by imperative mandates,[7] and were liable at any moment to be recalled by their constituents, even as the representatives attending at the Dutch States-General could be recalled by their provinces, and the representatives at the States-Regional by their townships.[8]

---

have to effect, and can get their orders executed almost under their eyes." *Gouvernement de Pologne,* chap. v.

6. *Esprit des lois,* Book II, chap. ii.

7. "The second method [of preventing the representative body from becoming oppressive] is to subject the representatives to an exact obedience to their instructions and to oblige them to give a strict account to their constituents. . . ." *Ibid.*

8. As Carré de Malberg put it: "Democracy, which is in the true sense government of the people by the people, is attained effectively by a federal organization of society; the members thereof are arranged in a hierarchy of groups by reference to community of interests, but it is understood by all that only the groups of the first degree will be the

But the new men whom the popular voice has made masters of the *imperium* have never shown any inclination to a regime of that kind. It was distasteful to them, as the heirs of the monarchical authority, to fritter away their estate on subordinating themselves. On the contrary, strong in the strength of a new legitimacy, their one aim was to increase it. Against the federalist conception Sieyès[9] was their mouthpiece: ". . . a general administration which, starting from a common centre, will reach uniformly to the remotest parts of the Empire—a body of laws which, though its elements are provided by the body of citizens, takes bodily form at as distant a level as that of the National Assembly, to whom alone it belongs to interpret the general wish, that wish which thereafter falls *with all the weight of an irresistible force on those very wills which have joined in the formation of it.*"

## 4. The Authoritarian Spirit in Democracy

So! On particular wills there falls, "with all the weight of an irresistible force," a "general wish"; the wish, from being the expression of the aforesaid particular wills, justifies the force. . . . Behind these phrases lies a reality, the irresistible nature of the "general wish"; lies also a lie, the generation of this "general wish" by the particular wishes.

So far from the people being the sole author of laws, it does not rest with it to pronounce even on the most general, those which affect most profoundly its way of life. Although there exists a method of popular consultation, the referendum, which has been tried out in Switzerland, democratic Power is careful not to have recourse to it.

In the moment of proclaiming the sovereignty of the people, it limits them exclusively to choosing delegates who will enjoy that sovereignty's plenary exercise. The members of society are citizens for a day and subjects for four years, a state of things which was damned in the strongest terms by Rousseau. In America, they choose both legislators and administrators. In Europe, only legislators, so that the latter are virtually masters of the administrators, and there is no separation of powers.

---

repository of the sovereign power; on those groups the executive agents appointed to the various groups will necessarily have to depend." *Contribution à la théorie générale de l'état,* Vol. II, p. 254.

9. In the speech already referred to.

In France the practice was for the electors to choose deputies, and these came by degrees to the point of choosing the ministers;[10] these in turn chose the public functionaries, notably the official who is in regional control, the prefect, and so on down to the official who in practice exercises the municipal authority, the teacher. That was how France was, in reality, governed in 1939. It was, in fact, quite unconstitutional for the ministers to be chosen by the deputies.[11] Municipal authority belonged, no doubt, to the local councillors, who tended, however, to get rid of it onto the teacher. That he exercised it ably and patriotically is not denied. The point is, however, that, even in positions where the onrush of Power did not dispense with them, the citizens dispensed with themselves.[12]

It comes to this: that the "Power of the people," so called, is in fact linked to the people only by an extremely slack umbilical cord—general elections;[13] it is, to all intents and purposes, a "Power over the people," a Power which is all the greater for getting its authorization from this cord.

The *imperium* could have wished no finer justification, the Minotaur could never have gazed on a face of things that seemed more propitious for his appetites. Power now crushed those provincial autonomies before which the monarchy had had to retreat. It obtained the financial resources which were refused to the king. It achieved conscription—conscription which had floated before Louvois' eyes as an impossible ideal. It discovered

10. The president of the republic, in whom at first was vested the power of choosing his ministers, was soon reduced to the position of choosing one only. And even he was chosen only in accordance with the advice received from the presidents of the two chambers and, before long, after consultation with party leaders. The votes of the Chamber became in the end an imperative direction to him. The vote taken by the Chamber when the minister presents his ministry to it is really a sort of negative election of the president of the council. And it has become customary for the speakers to pass in review, favourable or the reverse, the men chosen by the president for the different offices; unfavourable comment often causes the president to make changes in his cabinet.

11. [Since this was written it has become constitutional for the President of the Council to be elected by the Assembly, and his ministers are the delegates of sections of the Assembly.]

12. In the same way a tendency may be observed in the United States for the municipal bodies to entrust municipal administration to city managers. But here at least the surrender of power is not to the central administration.

13. So slack is it that it is possible for a legislature to govern, as was seen in France in 1926–1928, 1934–1936, and 1938–1939, in opposition to the clearly expressed wish of the electoral body. These changes of direction in mid-term had come to be a regular feature.

the secret of mustering the entire people for war—war which is the special business of Power.

## 5. *The General Interest and Its Monopoly*

A democratic regime ensures, so we are told, that the general interest is exactly represented by Power. From this postulate flows a corollary: that no interest is legitimate which opposes this general interest. For this reason every local or particular interest must bend the knee to Power, for is not the whole naturally to be preferred to the part? Nowadays it is a mere truism that "particular interests must be sacrificed to the general interest." It has been said so often that it no longer stays for an answer.

And of course no answer is possible if the very existence of society is at stake. But that is a case of infrequent recurrence. Whereas it often happens to the *imperium* that it comes up against a sectional interest whose resistance, even if it were successful, could not possibly endanger society. Yet this resistance is damned as egoistical; it is considered illegitimate, and the organ which gives it expression is regarded as an evil influence. Indeed the fathers of democracy held it for a fundamental principle that an organ of this kind had no right to exist; that Power which incarnated the general wish and interest could not suffer in society the existence of any group which embodied less general wishes and interests; that Power had by right both monopoly and solitude.

Since that time, "particular interest," the very name, has become a species of insult—a development of language which, on being examined, is seen to reflect the unceasing mobilization of public opinion against the community's constituent sections.

This *a priori* damnation of every particular interest as such is a most surprising phenomenon. The more advanced is a society, the more diversified is its functional and human content and the more numerous the categories which arise in it of their own accord. In the early Middle Ages there were some who commanded and fought, some who studied and prayed, and some who farmed and provisioned: here were three categories, of which one was menial. A little later there arose, at a level lower than that of the nobility and priesthood, a Third Estate of merchants, artisans, and lawyers. It was in those days freely admitted that the nobility as such had certain interests of their own which, though doubtless egoistical, were yet legitimate and such as might be opposed to the royal Power. And so it was too with the other orders.

Observation shows that the social categories of today are just as clear-cut as then and far more numerous. But the egoistical interests of any one of them are no longer thought legitimate or such as may be opposed to the democratic whole. For instance, a military officer who tried to win for subjective rights of his own the same respect as in former times the knights-at-arms won for theirs would be guilty of sedition. Yet, if each specialized group is necessary to society, no less necessary and respectable must be the conditions which allow it to fulfil its function. And the sacrifice of those conditions to a self-styled general interest is for society a defeat and not a victory.

It is the height of folly to rely on Power alone to bring about the conditions in which each category can play its part; the only result of that must be that Power fights with each of them in turn, falling on each minority with the whole weight of all the others whom it has at call; and it will oppress each in turn by the same methods.

## 6. Self-Defence of the Interests

The whole course of the evolution of democratic society has belied its monist principle. The various interests which found themselves no longer safeguarded took to defending themselves. The experience of centuries had shown them the way of defence: the formation of representative bodies. And these have been developed in the teeth of every interdict and persecution. They have won themselves rights by asserting them and fighting for them. These rights are naturally proportioned to the strength of each group's reaction.

This spontaneous formation of society into syndicates of interests, secret or professed, has been denounced and damned, but in vain. It is a natural phenomenon, acting as a corrective to the false totalitarian conception of the general interest.

These private authorities occupy all the same a somewhat uncertain position in relation to the political Power. The latter, invoking the general will, cannot endure that each fractional interest should rule autonomously in its own inviolable domain. And the interests, having no defensive position which they can take up to check the onrush of Power, have had perforce to act on the offensive. They have had, in other words, to get sufficient sway over Power itself to influence its actions and make them conduce to their own advantage. The result is the besieging of Power by particular interests which is seen at its most visible in the popular assemblies of America. There each great interest, whether it falls within the category of agricultural, industrial, or working-class, keeps at the federal parliament representatives of its own who fill the lobbies (from which they take their name) of the official buildings, and lay siege to "the representatives of the Nation." So well recognized is the phenomenon that it is often called "the third chamber."[14] There they are, armed with resources which are not hard to guess, for the express purpose of hindering or helping the passage of such laws as affect those who sent them. If they do not get their way, their associations start campaigns in the country which make the legislators pause.

Democratic Power recognizes no other authority in society than itself, and claims always to go just as far as the general will carries it—or as it claims it carries it. But this Power, if there is no stopping it, is on the other hand eminently open to be wooed and won.

Every Power tends to be the object of manœuvres of this kind, which are the more necessary the less limited it is, and the more effective the wider is its base. If it is a king, the interests can only win him over by setting in motion, by means of slow and systematic approaches, someone within the inner ring of his court. If it is an aristocracy, they must make use of family relationships and social contacts. In this way Power can be influenced or led.

But this is as nothing to what the interests can make of a democratic Power. In this case Power is conferred by the opinion of the majority. If, therefore, sectional interests know how to organize themselves and can but acquire the art of creating movements of opinion, they can enslave Power, they can degrade it, they can even seize it, to use it to their own advantage and benefit themselves at the expense of other groups or of society as a whole.

They make the participants in Power their slaves when they exact from them, at election times, precise pledges in favour of particular groups; they degrade Power when they force it to retreat before a well-orchestrated press campaign; lastly, they seize it when they sweep a party into power which is the expression and instrument of their particular needs.

In other words, particular interests, having been deprived of all means of defence, have been driven to an offensive activity which results in their

---

14. Donald C. Blaisdell and Jane Grevens, *Economic Power and Political Pressure*. Monograph 26 of the American inquiry: *Investigation of Concentration of Economic Power* (Washington: 1941).

oppression of other interests; these in their turn are thereby stimulated to stop, push, or conquer Power by similar methods. Authority then becomes nothing better than a stake, and loses all stability and respect. The characters of those who exercise it become increasingly debased, until in the end the Palace of Command gets a tenant who decides not to let himself be driven out: the tyrant.

When that time comes, he can, with hardly an addition to Power's attributes on paper, found the most hideous despotism. Each of its successive conquerors before him has, for his own ends, created some new office, and if the state, already monstrous in size, had not in those days crushed all life, the only reason was that it was continually changing hands. Let it once come to rest in the same hands, and its weight will be felt.

## 7. Of the Formation of Power

The strength of Power and its extent are two very different things. It may be confined within a very narrow range of attributes and, in its own domain, act energetically and receive complete allegiance. Or it may again have vast attributes but a constitution which renders it nerveless and so deprives it of public respect. In this case, however, it is in uncertain equilibrium: either it must work within narrower limits or it must strengthen its constitution. At the time of Pompey the government of Rome had become unfitted to govern a vast empire: everywhere was felt the need for a system of command which would be at once more concentrated and more stable. It was to be the Empire.

Just as the territorial conquests of Republican Rome called into being the Empire, so the extension of the attributes of the state in democracies made inevitable the coming of authoritarianism.

It could, no doubt, have been avoided if there had been a stable, vigorous, and unified executive to which the legislature acted merely as limitary principle. But in fact, as we have seen, the contrary happened: the legislature made itself the ruling sovereign. The only effect of the proclamation of the sovereignty of the people was to substitute for a king of flesh and blood that hypostasized queen, the general will, whose nature is always to be adolescent and incapable of personal rule; the occasional inconveniences which arise in a monarchy during the minority or mental incapacity of the sovereign being now permanently present, the aforesaid queen boldly entrusted her person to a succession of favourites, who abused their position the more freely the less she became an object of controversy. The only possible safeguard was in the sense and morals of that regency council, the sovereign assembly.

In this respect antiquity furnished an admirable model in the shape of an assembly, the Senate, which had known how to build and govern the Roman Empire: the slackness which made a personal authority necessary was not the fault of this assembly but rather of the disorders which ensued on the decline of its strength.

The Senate, however, even though in the great period of Roman history it did actually exercise sovereignty as if it were a modern parliament, was far from proceeding from the same principle. The legislative authority belonged, not to it, but to the people, acting on the impulsion of its chosen magistrates; the Senate was thus, not the parliament of the people, but the council which the executive magistrates had to attend, and these it kept in an ever tighter control. This illustrious chamber was composed only of men who had filled the highest executive offices, to which they had risen only by way of a succession of minor posts. The Senate, therefore, consisted exclusively of men who had grown grey in the public service; of these none was missing, and all were vested with a sacred character and made irremovable.

It has been today's folly to imagine that assemblies which have not enjoyed these advantages of careful selection, long experience, and great stability are capable of playing the same managerial role as the Senate. The importance of their composition being a good one has, no doubt, been recognized. But it has been hard to reconcile this desideratum with the principle that they must embody the general will.

Recourse has to be had to the idea that everyone cannot take part in the formation of the general will because everyone is not independent and enlightened and for that reason cannot be an active citizen. As Kant says:

> The right to vote is the only test of citizenship; but this right presupposes the independence of him who wishes to be not only a part of the Republic but also a member of it—a part, in other words, that acts as it sees fit in conjunction with the others. Action in this capacity compels a distinction between the active citizen and the passive. . . .[15]

Kant ranked among the passive citizens "all those who to preserve their lives, their nourishment, or their protection depend on someone else";

15. Kant, *Métaphysique des Mœurs,* First Part, xlvi. Trans. Barni (Paris: 1853) p. 170.

he would, in other words, have denied the vote to all the salaried employees of a factory. Among other thinkers, not independence, but leisure, becomes the test of civic rights. And in this may be felt the influence of Aristotle: what makes the citizen is having the time to think about public affairs—in fact, no time, no citizen. There appears in Sieyès and even in Rousseau a shamefaced nostalgia for the facilities for forming an enlightened opinion which in ancient days slavery conferred on the freeman.

> Among the Ancients, the slavery of a large number of individuals had [said Sieyès] a refining effect on the classes of freemen. The result was that every freeman could be an active citizen. In our days, fortunately, society has a broader base, our principles are more humane and the law offers protection to all alike. But for the very reason that the inhabitants of every floor of the social structure are citizens, there are men among us whom their state of intelligence and feeling alienates from society's interests much more than could ever have been the case with the humblest citizens of the free States of antiquity.[16]

Rousseau comes near to saying that the abolition of slavery makes a republic on the ancient model impossible:

> What is this? That liberty requires slavery to maintain it? It may be so. Extremes meet. Whatever is unnatural has its disadvantages, and that is truer of civil society than of anything else.
>
> Circumstances unfortunately arise in which a man can keep his liberty only at the cost of another's, in which the citizen can enjoy perfect freedom only on the condition of the slave being very much a slave. Such was the position of Sparta. You, ye modern peoples, have no slaves but you are slaves yourselves; the slaves' liberty is paid for by yours. Do not claim credit for this state of things to me; I see in it a proof, not of humanity, but of pusillanimity.[17]

He marks in several passages his distrust of a crowd incapable of sound judgment.

Our authors were, then, in agreement in refusing to admit all the members of society to the task of forming the general will.

16. Cf. Paul Bastid, *Sieyès et sa pensée* (Paris: 1939) p. 391.
17. *Du Contrat social,* Book III, chap. xv.

But [asks Sismondi] how are we to distinguish those who have a will from those who have not? Everyone has a right to happiness, everyone has a right to perfect himself. By what signs can we recognize those whose imperfections are a menace to the happiness and progress of the rest? Lines of division have had to be drawn but they are almost capricious. . . . The belief has been entertained that those whose poverty condemned them to unceasing manual labour, who had no time left for reading, reflection or conversation with their neighbours on more serious subjects, had no will of their own. It has been sought to exclude them—even though it was well recognized that there were exceptions to the rule.

This philosophy, of a regime based on intelligence tests, was formulated at the representative Council of Geneva, and Geneva furnishes the most perfect example of such a regime in operation.[18] It gave good practical results,[19] but could not, in spite of them, maintain itself. There is no country in which it has maintained itself.

Entrusting the function of voting to a part only of the people—which was what it came to—could not be made consistent with the totalitarian aspect assumed by Power. Power tolerates no resistance from society, allows no sectional interest's right to oppose the general interest as incarnated by itself. That being so, to have no share in the formation of Power is to be completely defenceless. Nor is it compatible with justice to exclude any class of society from voting. It is, no doubt, undesirable that the *Lumpenproletariat,* as Marx called it, should affect foreign policy by its votes. But the political structure has been built in such a way that there is no means of depriving the voters of the power to bedevil diplomacy without robbing them at the same time of the power to defend and ameliorate their condition.

18. Cf. the remarkable study by William E. Rappard: *L'avènement de la démocratie moderne à Genève, 1814–1847* (Geneva: 1936). In it may be seen, in the microcosm of Geneva, the general movement of the period.

19. "The aristocratic regime of the Genevan Restoration did not die from the revolt of the victims of its abuses. . . . Though some of its leaders gave the impression of being limited, tyrannical and of an irritating arrogance, this regime was always honest and humane. And it was for a long time remarkable for the disinterestedness of those who served it and for the intelligence and talent of many of them. An even-handed justice was administered to all. The public finances were managed with an economy which was the more remarkable in that the regime was neither insensitive to misery nor indifferent to enterprise of public utility. Indeed, it is possible that Geneva has never known so little material suffering and so much intellectual distinction as on the morrow of the aristocratic restoration." W. Rappard, pp. 424–25.

It is a melancholy but indubitable fact that in a democracy each social category can get what is due to it both in justice and in humanity only in so far as its voting power makes possible its extortion. No working-class vote, no laws protecting the worker. No women's vote, no laws protecting women.

And so, since the various sectional interests have no other means of expression or weapons of defence on which to rely, sovereignty has to be shared with social categories which are incapable of passing a sound judgment on matters of general interest.

Democracy being a battle for Power, those who are not represented necessarily go under. Children, for instance, having no vote, get little attention, and what concerns their well-being tends to be neglected. For this to be remedied under the present system they would have to receive in their cradles the ballot papers which are the sole means of self-defence.[20]

This is the preposterous result of the confounding of interests and opinions. If interests were guaranteed and given their own means of expression and action, Power could then be formed by a clash of opinions only and could be thrown open to enlightened opinions only. In the absence of this basic distinction, Power is the plaything of interests which, disguised as opinions and served by passion, do battle for a majority, to be the arbiter of problems on which it is ignorant.

## 8. Of Parties

The phenomenon which denotes a democracy is the activity of voting: but its nature is not self-explanatory. Do men in voting exercise a right or do they perform a duty? Are they choosing a policy or representatives who will work out a policy for them? What jurists have said on this point is of less importance than the general feeling. It is certain that the average citizen looks on voting as a right. It is no less certain that in early days he conceived himself to be choosing a man but that, as time went on, he came to see himself as choosing a policy. The cause of this change is the rise of political parties; its consequence is that the regime of parliamentary sovereignty has been gradually transformed into a plebiscitary regime.

20. [In the application of this statement of England it may be observed that family allowances were introduced nearly forty years after old age pensions. Even then, so Lord Beveridge has said, the balance of his plan was, for political reasons, disturbed for the benefit of the old, to the disadvantage of the children.]

So long as the people, gathered together by constituencies to nominate its national representatives, has regard to the personal merit of each and not to his political label, the assembly consists of an elite of independent personalities. Groups are formed in it by those who think alike, but these can only live in a perpetual flux of disintegration and reconstitution; the reason is that men who were in agreement on one piece of legislation, touching, for instance, questions of defence, may be in disagreement on fiscal matters. The result is a living assembly in which opinions are always free and do battle with one another for the country's good and the education of the public.

But when, as happens in democracies, the representative assembly becomes the repository of Power, the appetite for command impels the members to group themselves in permanent factions, thereby sacrificing something of their own personalities to the effective cohesion of the group in its quest for victory.

The forthcoming elections are then no longer regarded as held with the object of bringing to the assembly an accession of fresh talent but rather of strengthening or weakening the various groups to which all belong. Anxious to strengthen itself, the group makes its presence felt in the electoral body, from which it asks that it choose a man who stands in the name of the group in preference to a man with distinguished personal qualifications. "In voting for a man as such, you are abandoning your sovereignty to him," is the way in which it is put to the electors— and it is true.

> Vote rather for an opinion: that is to say in practice for a man of whose merits, like himself, you are necessarily ignorant, but who is the standard bearer of an opinion. In this way you will be exercising your sovereignty, and will be impressing on the government the way in which it is to go.

Through the prestige of its leaders and the popularity of its principles the group brings victory to its candidates, whom it has chosen less for their personal worth than for the pledge of their obedience to itself; moreover, they will be the more faithful to their party from their inability to make their way without it.

The first result of this is a degradation of the assembly, which no longer draws its recruits from the best men. A man must now be ready to rely on the support of the controller of his group's votes and to let his name be boosted for election by his whip. He must be ready to become a mere numerical, and not a qualitative, addition to the assembly.

Another result is the debasement of the elector's position. He is now regarded only for the weight which he can throw into one or the other of the scales. By hook or by crook the vote of which he disposes must be got from him. When the Reform Act of 1832 had widened the franchise, the chief preoccupation of the two English parties was to get put on the register the electors whose support each believed itself to have won, and to fetch them in carriages on polling day, for fear that otherwise they would omit to record their vote. The spectacle was not so much that of people proudly exercising their rights as citizens, as of two factions touting in every way open to them for the votes which could confer Power.

So far the debasement of the electors and the degradation of the assembly are only accidental. They are to become by progressive stages systematized. Syndicates of interests and ambitions will soon take shape which, regarding the assembly as a mere adjunct of Power and the people as a mere cistern for the assembly, will devote themselves to winning votes for the installation of tame deputies who will bring back to their masters the prize for which they have ventured everything, the command of society.

### 9. Of the Political Machine

The political machine is perhaps the most important discovery of the nineteenth century; the credit for it must, it seems, be given to an American, Martin Van Buren.

Like every other machine, it has the advantage of effecting a great economy of effort by dint of being immensely complicated.

During his campaign, the candidate must try to convince the electoral body that his opinions are the soundest and his character the worthiest. The machine saves him most of this work by bringing him supporters who cleave to his views without his having had to set them out and who cheer his name without ever having heard it before. When the period of the elections opens, the elector has to weigh the pros and cons of the programmes and personal merits of the respective candidates. This worry is saved him by the machine, which hands him out a ready-made list of those whom he must support.

All that is needed to produce these desirable results is organization. In this respect the city of New York has long since shown the way. In each quarter of the town each party has an office staffed by permanent and salaried agents, who, in a descending hierarchy down to the leader of a block of flats, maintain contact with each single person who may one day be called on to vote. It is all a question of linking people to the party in such a way that their support may be counted on. Is hammering at their eardrums with political ideas the best way of doing this? Are men as susceptible as all that to intellectual arguments? Do not the emotions hold greater sway over them? Do they not attach themselves to those who, in times of difficulty, have helped them with kind words and material succour and have found them work? If they have opened for them gambling and drinking clubs where they meet the same companions every evening, do they not develop an *esprit de corps* which makes them feel proud of the party emblem looking down on their festivities? When the moment has come, will they refuse to give what costs them so little, the insertion in the ballot box of a voting paper bearing beneath the usual emblem a list of names?

They were rare spirits, the Rousseaus and the Jeffersons. The manipulators of the machine make fewer pretensions; but they know the real man, who needs warmth, comradeship, the team spirit, and can make noble sacrifices for his side. The machine whose foundations are laid in an empirical psychology can make the pretensions of political philosophy look meaningless and ridiculous.

Stupid slogans, which come trippingly to the tongue and are a pleasure to repeat,[21] songs which exalt the "comrades" and ridicule the "enemy," these are the stuff of politics. Mix with it a little doctrine, but only a very little, and reduce it to the simplest propositions.

A good regimental officer may explain to his men what they are fighting for, but in the day of battle that will not avail him if he has not first kept them in good humour, convinced them that he is at all times there to help them, and inspired in them trust and affection.

The squalid side of Tammany Hall has been thrown into relief many times; but it has not been sufficiently brought out, so it seems to me, that this machine of the Democratic party has been of service, materially

21. [Cf. George Savile, Marquess of Halifax, *The Character of a Trimmer:* "Amongst all the engines of dissension, there hath been none more powerful in all times than the fixing names upon one another of contumely and reproach; and the reason is plain in respect of the people, who, though generally they are incapable of making a syllogism or forming an argument, yet they can pronounce a word; and that serveth their turn to throw it with their dull malice at the head of those they do not like."]

and morally, not on the plane of charity, but on that of comradeship. For the machine's officers, both the commissioned and the non-commissioned, there are solid rewards in store. Long and useful service earns them at length posts, graded according to their importance, in the administration; in these they are allowed a few peculations so long as they do not cause too great a scandal. Their installation in these posts is all the easier because, in accordance with ancient custom, many of them are elective, and, for the rest, it is the usual thing to dismiss office holders who were put in by the beaten party. For "to the victors belong the spoils." Such was the nature of the Tammany Hall machine; though today it lies broken, it can still take pride in having set in motion a completely new scheme of politics.

The prescient of every country have transplanted this experiment; they too have made organized love to the electors.

The bosses of the machine were at first looked on by the great party leaders as useful but lowly auxiliaries. In much the same way there was a time when navigating officers looked down on engineers. But the men of the machine lost little time in making their importance felt. All the work of an election had been made cut and dried beforehand by them: why then should they let candidates who had not received their blessing profit by their labour? Soon they secured for themselves the selection of the candidates, and, naturally, chose men in their own likeness: they did not choose Catos. From this has followed a prodigious drop in the level of parliaments and in the level of government.

### 10. From the Citizen to the Campaigner: The Competition for Power Takes Military Form

The history of the machine in the United States and in England, where it was introduced by Joseph Chamberlain, has been admirably recorded by Ostrogorski, a Russian.[22] His book has been translated into several languages, and each country has taken it to heart. The lesson has been learned everywhere that, since votes give Power, the supreme art of politics is getting voters to the polls. And that is the concern of organization and propaganda.

So far as organization is concerned, the task has been one of perfecting

22. M. Ostrogorski, *La Démocratie et l'organization des partis politiques* (2 vols. Paris: 1903).

the achievement of Tammany Hall; there has been no element of innovation, and even the National Socialist party created nothing which was
not to be found in embryo in the ancient doings at New York.

But so far as propaganda is concerned, what an advance is here! The
fathers of democracy held the view that an election campaign was a season
of popular education by means of the full exposition of contrary policies;
they attached special importance to the publication of parliamentary
debates which would, by being reported, enable the citizen to follow the
activities of government and so fit him more and more to pass judgment.
If the participation in sovereignty of an ill-informed man was not without
its drawbacks, these would in large measure be compensated for by the
gradual mitigation of the prevailing ignorance through the medium of
discussion, to which even the meanest intelligences could not help paying
heed. The fact that the larger spirits would have to solicit the votes of
the smaller would mean that the latter, their intelligences once formed in
such a school, would at long last be fitted for the leading part which had
been assigned to them without exception. Of all the arguments in favour
of democracy this was the noblest.

The men of our day, however, being circumspect people, have realized
that the cultivation of the electors' intelligence is at least as likely to open
a window on the arguments of their opponents as on their own; therefore
it is labour lost.

The faculty of reason may lie relatively unused in the majority of a
people, but there is not a man anywhere who is incapable of emotion.
And it is to the emotions, therefore, that appeal must be made. Rouse in
your behalf trust, hope, and affection; rouse against your rival indignation,
anger, and hatred—and success is yours. It is truly complete when a
public meeting can be induced to cheer a speech which it cannot
understand, and to greet the other side's reply with stampings of the feet.
Its path of duty is marked out for it by the proceedings of the national
assembly itself. The result is that good citizenship, so far from being
awakened among those who are as yet without it, gets extinguished in
those who already have it.

To stifle the curiosity which may be aroused by an outstanding orator
on the other side, to kill the desire for the knowledge which comes from
an understanding of the arguments on both sides, to destroy the natural
amiability which predisposes a man favourably to his neighbour, the
chord of party loyalty is struck. To read the enemy's newspaper becomes
a treason, no less than to attend his meetings except for the purpose of

drowning his voice and afterwards confuting him with the help of a manual for hecklers. For the political battle is a war in the true sense. Baudelaire, even in his day, marvelled at the military jargon employed in it: "The advance guard of democracy, in the forefront of the battle for the republic, and others." The poet was right. The electors had been transformed into soldiers engaged in a campaign, the reason being that their leaders were out to take possession of Power.

## 11. Towards the Plebiscitary Regime

The further the organization of parties is pushed and the greater the part that is played in winning elections by "the flag" and "the machine," so much the more complete is the subjection of the member of congress or parliament to that machine, which is the real holder of his seat. Parliament is then no longer a sovereign assembly in which an elite of independent citizens compare freely formed opinions and so arrive at reasonable decisions. It is now only a clearing-house in which the various parties measure their respective parcels of votes against each other's.

The more powerful the machine becomes and the tighter the bonds of party discipline are drawn, the less does debate matter: it no longer changes votes. The bangings of desks take the place of arguments. Parliamentary debates are no longer a school for citizens but a circus for boobies.

In the beginning it was the machine that made away with men of intelligence and character. Soon they are making away with themselves. The tone and behaviour of the assembly are in a continuous decline. At length it loses all consideration.[23]

As the parties take on a greater consistency and discipline, so does all effective authority leave the assembly. If one of them disposes of sufficient votes to dominate it, then the assembly becomes merely the office in

23. Just after the conclusion of the First World War Lord Bryce wrote at the end of a survey of the great modern democracies: "Persons of age and experience say everywhere and in terms much the same, that there is less brilliant speaking than in the days of their youth, that the tone of manners has declined, that the best citizens are less disposed to enter the chamber, that its proceedings are less fully reported and excite less interest, that a seat in it confers less social status, and that, for one reason or another, respect for it has waned." James Bryce, *Modern Democracies,* Vol. II, p. 367.

(Bryce admits that *laudatio temporis acti* has probably played a part in this—but only a part.)

which that party's decisions are registered. Under these conditions the only possible government is that which the party wills; it is the party's government.

The relations between cabinet and parliament then become reversed, a phenomenon of which Dicey, writing in 1889, was already aware. After recalling that in England the executive was in principle independent of Parliament, that ministers were named and retired by the king alone, he went on to note that in practice "the cabinet is a parliamentary executive, for it is effectively chosen, though very indirectly, by the House of Commons, which can at any time dismiss it; further, its members are chosen invariably from among the members of both houses." But, as Dicey saw, the cabinet was starting to extricate itself by progressive stages from its dependence on Parliament. The consultations with the electorate having now the character of battles waged between the various machines, the victorious machine can install its leader in power; and he need then hardly concern himself with the assembly, in which a stable majority will be guaranteed him by the whip.

> It is at any rate conceivable [said Dicey] that the time may come when, though all the forms of the English Constitution remain unchanged, an English prime minister will be as truly elected to office by a popular vote as is an American president.[24]

In 1904 Sidney Low remarked the same phenomenon:

> An English prime minister, with his majority secure in Parliament, can do what the German emperor and the American president, and all the chairmen of committees in the United States Congress, cannot do; for he can alter the laws, he can impose taxation, and repeal it, and he can direct all the forces of the state. The one condition is that he must keep his majority.[25]

Now, keeping his majority is easy enough when the party machine controls the elections, when the member who falls out with his machine is certain to lose his seat, and when he is, morally and socially, of such a kind that the loss of his seat means his relapse into insignificance.[26]

24. A. V. Dicey, *Introduction to the Study of the Law of the Constitution*, p. 483.
25. Sidney Low, *The Governance of England*.
26. The dictatorship of the machine is slowed down in a country whose people, being long accustomed to aristocratic government, continue to choose their representatives from among persons of distinction: this is the case with England. Hence it is that this country, though it was the first to make the acquaintance of parliamentary sovereignty and the first

The more the machine controls the way in which votes are cast, the more the individual member sinks to the condition of a mere arithmetical symbol and the more the leader of the party tends to exercise an absolute and undivided *imperium*. We have seen the fruits of this system in Germany, where in 1933 the National Socialist party manœuvered in Parliament as at a military word of command, thereby assuring the absolute rule of their leader. Had the Communists, who were organized after the same fashion, had the same weight of numbers in the French Parliament in 1936, the same result would have followed. And so the action of parties has caused sovereignty to pass from parliament to the victorious machine, and elections are now no more than a plebiscite by which a whole people puts itself in the power of a small gang.

## 12. The Competition of "Mechanized" Parties Ends in the Dictatorship of One Party

Let one of these machines put more method into its organization and more cunning into its propaganda, let it boil down its doctrine still further into propositions which are at once simpler and falser, let it surpass its adversaries in insult, treachery, and brutality, let it once seize the coveted prey and, having seized it, never let it go—and there you have totalitarianism.

All those in outer darkness then break out in angry laments. Yet have they not contributed to this result?

A man or a gang now disposes of vast munitions which had been long accumulating in Power's arsenal. Yet who heaped them all up there if not those others who, when they were in office themselves, were always for an extension of the state?

There is now no makeweight in society with the strength to stay Power's advance. And who, if you please, destroyed them, those powerful groups of men on which the monarchs of former days dared not lay a hand?

A single party leaves the marks of the master's talons on every inch of the nation's flesh. Who at first was it that aimed at crushing all personality beneath the deadening weight of party? And who looked for the triumph of his own party?

---

to have experience of party government, has not been the first to feel its logical consequence, the dictatorship of party.

This tyranny is accepted by the citizens, who come to hate it only when it is too late. Yes, but who was it that disinclined them to judging for themselves and made them take the loyalty of the campaigner in exchange for the independence of the citizen?

There is no more liberty, for liberty is a property only of men who are free. And who bothered himself about forming men who were free?

### 13. The Degradation of the Regime Is Linked to the Degradation of the Idea of Law

All discussions of democracy, all arguments whether for it or against it, are stricken with intellectual futility, because the thing in issue is indefinite. As many writers, so many definitions—a confusion which is a function of contradictory notions being covered by the same word. In essence these notions fall into two groups, the one, that of law and liberty, the other, that of absolute sovereignty of the people.

It is overlooked that, in the life of a democracy as it is in fact lived, these two principles conflict; and astonishment is felt when, supposing ourselves to be the witnesses of successive advances of democracy—as measured by the triumphs of popular sovereignty—we see in the end the emergence of a despotism, of a regime from which law and liberty have taken flight.

This is the process on which we have tried to throw light. Let us recapitulate.

In the beginning, thought laid down liberty as the end. It was sought to ensure to the individual the maximum of independence that was compatible with life in society, to protect him from every arbitrary will, and to guarantee his rights effectively.

With this end in view, proclamation was made of the sovereignty of the laws. The laws were, in accordance with Rousseau's formula, placed above the man. And nothing else other than the laws was to be above him. He would have no need to go in fear either of an individual who was more powerful than himself or of a group which was formidable by weight of numbers, for between their force and himself stood an inexorable justice which would decide in accordance with the laws established. Equally he would have no further cause to fear the rulers, whose expansionist tendencies would be held in check by the laws, to serve which would be their only function. And in this way there opened before the citizen such a vista of freedom and inviolability as no other system could procure him. The will of the human being was enfranchised from all other masters save the law, which was conceived as a binding force at once sovereign and salutary.

This system could only last so long as the law inspired a religious veneration. While it was sacred and immutable, it could hold sway over a society which was based on law and liberty: whether the rulers held office on a permanent tenure or were elected at intervals made no real difference if, in any case, they themselves were subject to something which did not change.

But is it possible for law not to change at all? Certainly it is not. What was possible, and what to preserve its sacred character was necessary, was that a change in it should be either the imperceptible labour of time, the slow work of custom, helped by the invisible and silent toil of scholars laying precedent on precedent, or else a solemn act, looked on by all as dangerous and impious, justifiable only when it seemed amply probable that the substance of what was effected conformed with the dictates of objective reason. There had, to put it shortly, to be a belief in the necessary character of the laws; they had to be looked on as inscribed in the nature of things, and not merely as a product of the human will.

What in fact happened was that the laws came to be looked on as mere regulations which were always open to criticism and revision. And the task of their unending amendment was entrusted now to a parliamentary body and now to the people itself: it became in either case a function of opinion. The reason for this was not a prior admission that the laws could be what anyone wished them: their necessary character was still accepted, but it was thought that the "necessary" law would be given to the people by revelation, at a time when, as was supposed, passion and interest would be dumb. This is a conception which merits a careful consideration in its own right,[27] but must not detain us here. Our concern is not with the result predicted but with the result obtained. And that result was that the supreme rules of social life became matter for political disputation.

From then on, the particular wills, which it had been sought to keep in subjection by proclaiming the sovereignty of the laws, were free to act, for they were now competent to make or unmake these same laws. Whereas formerly only the choice of the rulers was committed to the strife of parties, there was now not a single rule of social life which did

27. Cf. my essay on "The Political Thought of Rousseau," appearing as introduction to my edition of *Du Contrat social* (Geneva: Constant Bourquin, 1947).

not depend for its continuance on the issue of an election. The life of democracies has been marked by a growth in the precariousness of laws. Kings, chambers of peers, senates, anything that might have checked the immediate translation into law of whatever opinion was in vogue, have everywhere been swept aside or rendered powerless. The law is no longer like some higher necessity presiding over the life of the country: it has become the expression of the passions of the moment.

Changes in the laws react on every social relation and affect every individual life. They affect them the more as men grow bolder as regards the laws, as they extend their scope and are at greater liberty, as they think, to make them. The citizen has now no longer a fixed and protected right, for justice has become the servant of changing laws. He is no longer safeguarded against rulers, when their aggressions are backed by laws which they have made to suit themselves. The hurts which a new law may inflict or the advantages which it may confer are now on such a scale that any change in the law tends to induce in the citizen a mood of total fear or total hope. As the only way to subdue the legislative authority, which is now one with the executive, is by means of a well-organized faction, factions are for ever gaining in cohesion and violence. The more of possibility and the more of menace that Power holds, so much the fiercer grows the strife of factions, and so much the more precarious the tenure on which Power is held.

The reality of Power is now no longer held by the titulars of office; it is scattered among factions, only the leaders of which draw profit from the loyalty felt by a percentage of the population to the heads of the state and to the magistrates—a loyalty which, in a republic worthy of the name, should be the possession in common of the entire people.

These factions are states within the state;[28] sometimes they hold each

28. The word is used in its literal sense. The phenomenon of party has undergone a rapid evolution, more or less advanced according to the countries and parties looked at. By the time the evolution has run its course, the position of a party in the body of the nation is that of a similar but narrower body. The party has its slang and its own folkways, its own particular heroes, and its own universities in which its own conception of the world is taught (propaganda schools); it has its central government, its budget, and its armed forces (militia, shock troops, etc.). It has its flag, its party hymns, its prophets, and its martyrs to the cause. In short, it boasts a "patriotism" which is fiercer because narrower than a patriotism; the two things merge only so far as the nation becomes the chattel or instrument of the party.

In many respects a party is like a warrior tribe led out to the conquest and exploitation of the nation; it resembles the Norman bands who long ago took over England. We find other in check to the enfeeblement of the public authority, at others they succeed each other in office, changes which take on the character of earthquakes.

But, whether their equilibrium produces anarchy or their alternate victories a contrariety of extreme courses, in either case the resulting uncertainty becomes so great and the prerequisite conditions of social life are laid in such ruin, that in the end the peoples, tired of the impotence of an *imperium* which is ever more hotly disputed, or of the ruinous oscillations of an *imperium* which bears ever more hardly, aspire to stabilize this crushing burden of Power which changes hands at random, and find in the end disgraceful consolation in the peace of despotism.

---

again, in short, the primitive phenomenon of a society being conquered by a smaller society, already studied in chapter vi. Party conquest reproduces all the main features of barbarian conquest.

# BOOK VI

⌒

# Limited Power

# or Unlimited

# Power?

A Prince that will say he can do no good, except
he may do everything, teacheth the people to say they
are slaves, if they must not do whatever
they have a mind to.—HALIFAX, *Maxims of State*.

# XV.

## *Limited Power*

POWER HAS TWO ASPECTS, of which sometimes the one and sometimes the other is the more present to men's minds, according to the character and the situation of the onlooker, and, above all, to the circumstances of the time.

It is a social necessity. By reason of the order which it imposes and the harmony which it creates, it enables men to attain a better life.[1] These services rendered by it have made so great an impression on the majority of writers, and the idea of a governmental vacuum (Hobbes,[2] Ihering[3]) has filled them with so much horror, that in their conception no foundation could ever be dug too deep for the rights of Power. And this held good whether its rights were derived from God or from society, of which it was the supreme expression (Kant) or the predestined guide (Hegel).

---

1. André Berthelot remarks in an article entitled "État" in the *Grande Encyclopédie*: "In Central Africa, Baker was much struck by the contrast between the Ounyoro, who are subjected to a bloody despotism which kills or tortures on the slightest provocation, and the neighbouring territories, in which the tribes have no chiefs. The former have a flourishing agriculture, industry and even architecture, and a well-clothed and well-fed people; the latter are so many naked bands of savages, who live exposed to the torments of hunger."

2. See the quotations from Hobbes in chap. ii.

3. Cf. Ihering: "Anarchy, that is to say the absence of state force, is not a state at all, and anyone who puts an end to it by any means whatsoever, whether he be a usurper from within or a conqueror from without, renders a service to society. He is both a saviour and a benefactor, for of all states the most insupportable is that in which there is no state." Quoted by M. Prélot, *Dictionnaire de sociologie*, article entitled "Autorité."

These theories we attacked *in limine*, and we demonstrated that Power's undeniable blessings could be explained on a quite different hypothesis, and one which had the advantage of not obscuring its other aspect.

It is also a social menace. It is not a thing of reason but a living complex, animated by a dynamism which impels it to take over the forces developed already in the human congeries under its sway, that it may use them to its own purposes.

The basic condition of all political science is to see Power, as it were, stereoscopically, from both angles.

The very possibility of such a science is, in truth, open to doubt. For there is no branch of study in which the intelligence gets so easily led astray from the path of neutrality by prejudice and interest, none in which the strict meanings of words suffer a like corruption from use in popular controversies and from the call to action which they sound: instance the words "democracy" or "socialism," which are charged with so many different hopes as to have lost all precise meaning.

To the observer who is inside the test tube and not above it, it happens inevitably that he exaggerates the importance of the reaction which is all about him, and views as an advance what is merely an oscillation. And so it happens that the solutions found in times past to the problems which agitated the finest spirits of their age are in the sequel forgotten or regarded as otiose: yet their value remains.

The doctrine of limitation of Power is the most striking example of this.

### *1. Limited Power*

This doctrine has had a strange destiny. In the course of a single century it has burned brightly, concentrated on itself the attention of every thinker of eminence, grown in attraction by reason of the frightful spectacle presented by the outbreak of an unbridled absolutism, been the fixed guiding star of all political navigation; it has then, in the very hour of its triumph, paled its fires to the point at which what was in 1840 a truism seems today a paradox. To understand how it came into being, we must return to the ancient society of that Middle Age from which we are descended.

What we find there is a complex of authorities which all limit one another. That of the king, the state's in other words, is only one of them. And he, like all the others, lives in what may be called an atmosphere of right. By this I mean that certain ideas are so much the heritage of all that not even the most outstanding of these authorities is in a position to modify them: it must submit to them. So said John of Salisbury in the twelfth century: "The difference between the prince and the tyrant is that the prince obeys the law and governs his people in accordance with right." This formula receives its full force only if it is remembered that what is here referred to is a law and a right which issue from a source higher than Power.

We are acquainted with the process by which the state has grown at the expense of all other authorities. Not only has it subdued them to its overlordship, but in addition, thanks to the dismemberment of the Church, the temporal monarch has claimed to be in direct communion with the divine suzerain, and has in this way justified his assumption of a measure of legislative power, a goal towards which he had long been moving. Though the measure of it seems to us a small thing, it seemed to contemporaries a daring innovation.

In this way Power, which had till then been on a footing with the other authorities and the prisoner of right, tended to absorb within itself the various social authorities and even right itself. The notables, that is to say, could not maintain their position but by its pleasure, and ideas of the just depended for their continuance on its decree.

Our understanding of the old society is so imperfect that we tend to regard the seventeenth and eighteenth centuries as still a time of feudalism and clericalism; whereas to contemporaries, when they compared them with times past, it seemed that the state was well in the saddle. An unparalleled concentration of functions in the hands of Power was already tending to make participation in its exercise more sought after than ever before; its favours were becoming more lucrative, its mistakes more fraudulent, and its vengeance more formidable.

Government is not at its most stable when its powers are at their most extended. Then, rather, is the time when it disturbs most interests, and the weight which it lays on them stimulates them to discharge, if they can, the burden onto other interests. This they cannot do so long as the strength of the government is in proportion to the extent of its claims. Their time for action comes when government is weak.

Such a combination of circumstances leads inevitably to troublous times. The criticisms directed against the actual rulers, the attacks launched against the doctrines of which they make use, and the denunciation of the interests which they serve or protect, take on a tone, at any rate among some sections of the population, of hatred and warlike violence. By legal means, if such there are, if not by violence, they are ejected from their places by other men, basing themselves on other doctrines and allied to other interests, who harry, punish, and execute their predecessors, together with their auxiliaries, partisans, and colleagues. But before long these new arrivals, who are the more rabid from coming to Power with fresh appetites and all the strength given by victorious passions, evoke in another section of the community a no less fanatical rage.

The time of proscriptions opens. The wiser heads then bethink them that what renders this succession of rulers, their doctrines and their interests, so altogether hateful is the possibility which they enjoy of an exclusive dominion.

When, for a whole half-century in England, poison, confiscation, burning, and capital punishment had been successively meted out to heterodox opinions and opposition parties, Locke, from his Dutch retreat, considered that security, liberty, and peace could be the lot of the citizen, only if Power were deprived of the right to prescribe all, to direct all, and to impose all.

It is the eighteenth century's title to fame that it tried to find means of effecting this limitation. Its jurists, to start with, furbished anew the principles of natural right. These, in the Middle Ages, had been founded on the direct command of the divine will, but this foundation had been laid in ruins by the break-up of Christian unity, the great diversity of sects, and the advance of free-thinking. A substitute, though, truth to tell, a less robust one, was found in reason. The thing of importance was to uphold a legislation of universal extent, such as no human will could bend to suit its fancy or its interests.

Next, Montesquieu demonstrated the need for makeweights. *"All history shows that every man who has authority is led to abuse it; he does not stop until he comes up against limitations.* It is a hard saying, but limitations need to be set even to virtue herself." Shades of Calvin, Savonarola, and Saint-Just! But what is the way to get these limitations respected? "Things must be so arranged that *one authority checks another.*"[4]

## 2. Of Internal Checks

The checking of one authority by another is a difficult conception for countries in which the various public authorities are dependent parts of one centralized machine, all set in motion by one authoritative will.

---

4. *L'Esprit des lois*, Book XI, chap. iv.

Such is the structure of the European states today. In them the governmental machine was the work of the absolute monarchy, and its task is still the execution of orders which emanate from one supreme organ. Thus, the democracies which we know are in reality monocracies.

But the republics of antiquity, Rome especially, were quite other. There the different magistracies were independent, and there was no concentration of the *imperium* except when, under pressure of events, a temporary dictator was appointed. Each office, moreover, had its own authority or *potestas*. The result was that the various authorities were liable to cross one another's paths and act as a check on one another. This process of check offered by one authority to another was an essential part of Roman constitutional law. One magistrate could stop another either by prohibiting a step intended or by annulling a step taken. Thus, the consul could check the praetor and the tribune the consul. And the contribution to Roman political history made by the tribune's power of check has been the most important of any.

To men familiar from childhood with Roman history and knowing it infinitely better than that of their own country,[5] the idea of one authority checking another seemed natural enough. The difficulty consisted in finding an equivalent suitable for introduction into modern constitutions. It was perhaps neither practical nor prudent to introduce internal tensions into a Power which had been a unity for centuries. But Western society did, as history showed, offer the possibility of limiting Power by means not of an internal but of an external check. Power could, without falling over itself, come up against makeweights.

### 3. Of Makeweights

What is a makeweight? Clearly it must be a social authority, an established sectional interest; such were in Montesquieu's day the higher ranks of the English aristocracy, which he so much admired, and the Parliamentary class in France, to which he himself belonged. In our own time the syndicates of workmen and employers answer to the description. So do in all times the various conglomerations of interests and loyalties which arise spontaneously in society and which Power seeks instinctively to dissolve.

---

5. The reason why Israel, Athens, and Rome served for illustration rather than more modern instances was that there were good studies of the distant past, but none of the recent. The researches of Montesquieu into feudal institutions excited astonishment and derision. After him they multiplied rapidly.

At different times it is, as is natural, different sectional interests which display sufficient character and energy to "form a body" and play the role of makeweights. It would be as absurd to entrust a political role to a social class which was devoid of any energy of its own as to refuse it to one which had and asserted such an energy. Interests, moreover, make themselves sufficiently prominent by their own dynamism. What Montesquieu means is that their defence of themselves, however egoistical it may be in principle, goes to form a social equilibrium, marked by the existence of makeweights which are capable of checking Power.

Bodies of this kind were found by Montesquieu in every part of the society of his own time. There were the nobility, whose influence had declined with the decline of their social importance. There were the clergy, also in decline, but still kept independent by their large estates and by the extent to which they acted as a ladder for the rise in the social scale of men of intellect. Over against these bodies in decline was one in the ascendant, that of the Parliament men with official freeholds, who would often turn back the royal authority. There were the surviving assemblies of the States in the provinces, who guarded jealously the privileges earned by loyalty and were sustained by a vigorous parochialism. There were besides the corporations, also in a decline, confronted now by the rising power of the commercial or industrial companies which tended to dominate the chambers of commerce and make of them their instrument.[6]

The tradition of the monarchy inclined it to the suppression of these centres of social life, not so much those which were, like the nobility, dying by inches as the more vigorous ones. The spirit of authority and centralization, which was to triumph with the Revolution, was already at work.

Montesquieu took advantage of a pause in this process to denounce it as harmful: "Monarchy is lost," he said, "when the king, concentrating all power in himself alone, summons the state to his capital, the capital to his court and the court to his own person."[7] For him the social equilibrium is assured by incessant warfare between the various authorities. And this becomes readily intelligible when it is remembered that it was at this time that the doctrine of the balance of power and European equilibrium first saw the light in diplomacy.

6. Witness the campaign of the Normandy Chamber of Commerce in 1787 and 1788 against the Anglo-French Commercial Treaty.
7. *L'Esprit des lois*, Book VIII, chap. vi.

The Continent of those days swarmed with petty states, whose lives depended on the rivalries of the larger; everywhere one power checked another and so enabled these tiny sovereignties to live in the interstices between the great. And by analogy Montesquieu seems to have sought the preservation of individual liberty in social equilibrium.

Further, just as the *jus gentium*, which could not by itself have saved these small sovereignties, came to invest them with sanctity and respectability, so the judicial authority furnished additional guarantees to individual liberty.

The sale of offices guaranteed the complete independence of the judicial authority in its dealings with the state. The king must stop removing cases to his privy council. Thus there was to be a justice which would be the more objective, in that, laws being still few and far between, decisions must be mainly based on natural law, on contract, and on custom. Such a justice would, moreover, be constantly tempered by interpretations which were in accord with the movement of ideas: the English jury system was to be introduced, and with it the intervention of what modern sociologists would call "the contemporary social conscience." The final requirement was that this justice should be put within the reach of all.

## 4. The Makeweights Crushed and Law Subordinated

Such in outline was the system of Power which was conceived by the choicer spirits of the eighteenth century. They had no need to concern themselves with the problem of the formation of Power: the eighteenth-century solution of that was heredity. Nor with the problem of the formation of right. There had come down to them a transcendental right: philosophy did no more than rub the corners off it. No: for them the great problem was that of the limitation of Power, and they focused attention on formulas for doing it. At that moment a sudden earthquake occurred—political, but intellectual as well. Its harbingers had been Rousseau and Mably.

The sovereignty of the people was asserted against the sovereignty of the king, and triumphed. The old Power, whose virtues and vices were, like its nature, known to all, was suddenly replaced by a new Power.

Among such of the men of the Convention as did not merely ignore him, Montesquieu was treated with a superior and disdainful amusement. He had met with it before from his correspondent, Helvétius. Let us not waste our time, said they, on framing an elaborate machine to check the anti-social activities of Power. There is but one effective remedy—to overturn it. What made the old Power bad was the law of its being: "We are only too well aware," said Grégoire, "that there has never been a dynasty which was not a race of devouring monsters living on the people's blood."[8] The Power which we are now building is one which will be, by the law of its being, good. Thus we make of government a thing commensurate with the interests of society.

The problem of the limitation of Power, so it was supposed, only arose from the defective solution found in earlier times for the problem of the formation of Power.[9] If the source of government is undefiled, then liberty is the offspring, not, as formerly, of its weakness, but of its strength; it is no longer Power's growth that will be anti-social, but any obstacle which it is sought to oppose to its growth.

Thus it happened that the enemies of Power[10] became the fanatical agents of its growth and realized in a few months the absolutism which had for centuries eluded the grasp of the monarchy.

> The French monarchy [said Odilon Barrot] had spent whole centuries in dissolving all the various forces in society which resisted its will—yet it had still left in being some few scattered remnants of the institutions of the Middle Ages. What next? The Constituent Assembly made a clean sweep of all these last remaining obstacles: independence of the clergy, tradition of the nobility, municipal bodies of towns, syndicates of guilds, States provincial, local Parliaments, hereditary offices, all disappeared in a day, not to make way for more liberal institutions, but to enrich with their effects, and to augment still further, the central authority.[11]

So complete was the work of destruction of the makeweights which the wild men of the Revolution effected, that for many generations to come the French nation, with no other object before its eyes than the state, would come to place in it all hope and all fear, would seek

8. Sitting of September 21, 1792.

9. "In a monarchy," asserted Billaud-Varennes, "the nation is tyrannized over in proportion to the vigour with which the prince's ordinances are carried out." *Rapport sur le mode de gouvernement provisoire et révolutionnaire*, made in the name of the Committee of Public Safety.

10. Among them Saint-Just, who said: "A people has only one enemy who is dangerous—its government." *Rapport au nom du Comité de Salut Public* of the 19th vendémiaire, year II.

11. Odilon Barrot, *De la centralisation et ses effets* (Paris: 1861).

unceasingly to change its ministers, and would lose in the end the instinct of association and the tendency to form societies within society, which had in other days been the precious bulwarks of liberty.

There is good reason for the growth which we have seen in "this universal and passionate desire for public offices," of which Tocqueville said that it was giving to politics the proportions of an industry, but "an unproductive industry, which disturbs the country without fertilizing it."[12] The growth is the natural result of the fact that in modern society the subject's condition has become, under onerous and arbitrary administration, a hazardous one; whereas the career of administrator has become a safe one. A man needs to be in the machine if he is to avoid being helplessly in its grip.

Nor was that the end. There was, overarching Power, natural law, which is, as was said by Cicero,[13] valid for all nations and all times; we cannot be freed from its obligations by senate or people.

The men of the Revolution pulled down this sovereign law from heaven and handed it like a bauble to Power.

It had needed the hardihood of a Hobbes to assert that the state is the source of law, that "when a republic is formed, there are laws and nothing antecedent to them,"[14] that "every law, written or unwritten, derives its force and authority from the will of the republic, that is to say from the will of its representative, be he monarch or assembly," that it is by these laws alone that man "distinguishes good and evil; in other words, what is contrary to and what is not contrary to the statutes of the realm."[15]

The Revolution took these principles to its bosom. Law is a creation of the general will, of parliament,[16] in fact, which has become in a trice the only competent authority not only for manifesting but for forming this will.[17] The effective sovereign is parliament,[18] on which unlimited

---

12. *Démocratie en Amérique*, III, 406.

13. *De Republica*, III, xxii.

14. *Leviathan*, p. 138 of the first edition of 1659.

15. *Ibid.*, p. 139.

16. [With the coming of the Revolution, "parliament" now takes on its modern meaning.]

17. The system of Sieyès, which passed into French constitutional law, denied the nation's ability to form a general will except in an assembly. And as the assembly of the nation is impossible in practice, the National Assembly was by a fiction deemed to be the assembly of the entire nation.

18. "The French representative system," wrote Carré de Malberg, the jurist, "deviated in 1789–1791 from the principle of national sovereignty: by confounding the general will with the legislative will of Parliament, it made Parliament the peer of the sovereign, or

authority has been conferred not only to make of government a hurtful business but to crush with the whole force of the law the individual liberties which had just been proclaimed.

Doubtless the men of the Constituent Assembly had originally had a restrictive intention: they realized that there was nothing a government could do except in virtue of a law, and that no law could be made except in virtue of an assent by the people. But the logical end of their system could only be to make possible any act of government whatsoever, provided that it was authorized by a law,[19] and to make possible any law whatsoever, provided that Parliament voted it.

This absorption of law within the state, combined with the destruction of the various social formations, laid the twin foundations of what has in our time been called "the monolithic state." There is no authority outside the Power which the state exercises, no law outside the law which the state has formulated.

### 5. Unlimited Power Is Equally Dangerous Whatever Its Source and Wherever It Rests

This whole scheme of political philosophy reposed on a fallacy which Montesquieu had exposed in advance: "As in democracies the people appears to do very nearly what it wills to do, liberty has been supposed to reside in governments of this species: *the Power of the people has been confused with the liberty of the people*."[20] The Power of the people was but a fiction[21] in a regime which was for practical purposes a parliamentary sovereignty.[22] But the fiction justified the blotting out of liberty on a scale never known before in Europe.

---

rather made it the effective sovereign." R. Carré de Malberg, *La Loi, expression de la volonté générale* (Paris: 1931) p. 72.

19. We have already seen how the prohibition laid on the courts to interfere with any act of the administration gave arbitrary rule a much freer rein than it had under the *ancien régime*.

20. *L'Esprit des lois*, Book XI, chap. ii.

21. "The French Revolution solemnly affirmed the principle of national sovereignty, but it applied it not at all; for, as has already been said, this famous principle is nothing but a decoy, a fiction and a governmental device, which has no more real validity than the principle of divine right." Léon Duguit: *L'État, le droit objectif et la loi positive* (Paris: 1901) p. 251.

22. "The French Revolution gave the death-blow to divine right and legitimacy. But no more do sovereignty of the people, and the general will which governs and makes law through representatives, find any acceptance among thoughtful people. The state is command

These, it has been said, were but the birth-pangs of a new principle. Where is the novelty? It had already been condemned by Cicero.[23] Its consequences had already been illustrated by sufficient examples, drawn both from ancient and from modern history, to enable a commentator[24] on *L'Esprit des lois* to write almost at the time of the publication of the *Contrat social:*

> Whenever the governing body within a state is enabled by the possession of a majority to command what seems good to it, it becomes a despotic government just as surely as one in which one man alone commands in obedience to no other law than his own will and pleasure.

Even after more than twenty years, Benjamin Constant could still not talk of the despotism of the Convention without a spasm of horror and anger:

> When no limits are set to the representative authority, the representatives of the people are not the defenders of liberty but the candidates for tyranny. Moreover, once tyranny comes to be, it may well be the more hideous for the tyrants being more numerous. . . .
> An assembly which can neither be suppressed nor restrained is, of all possible authorities, the blindest in its movements and the most incalculable in its results, even for the members who compose it. It plunges into excesses which, on a first view, seem inconceivable. An ill-considered bustle about everything; an endless multiplicity of laws; the desire to gratify the passions of the popular party by self-abandonment to their pressure or even by

---

and everyone cannot command. The truth is that the general will is a fiction." Gumplovicz, *Die Sociologische Staatsidee* (1902) p. 3.

23. "There is no government to which I should more quickly deny the title of commonwealth than one in which everything is subject to the power of the multitude. For as we have decided that there was no commonwealth at Syracuse or at Agrigentum or at Athens when those cities were ruled by tyrants, or here at Rome when the decemvirs were in power, I cannot see how the name of commonwealth would be any more applicable to the despotism of the multitude. For in the first place a people exists only when the individuals who form it are held together by a partnership in justice, according to your excellent definition, Scipio. But such a gathering as you have mentioned is just as surely a tyrant as if it were a single person, and an even more cruel tyrant, because there can be nothing more horrible than that monster which falsely assumes the name and appearance of a people." Cicero, *De Republica*, III, xxxiii.

24. Élie Luzac, a member of a family of Protestant refugees in Holland, who published in 1764, at Antwerp, an annotated edition of *L'Esprit des lois.*

encouraging them to press; the rancorous hatred inspired in it by the resistance which it meets or the disapproval which it senses; the flouting of national sentiment and the stubborn clinging to error; often enough the *esprit de corps* which gives strength but for usurpation only; the alternation of rashness and timidity, violence and feebleness, favouritism to one and distrust of all; the motivation by purely physical sensations, such as enthusiasm or panic; the absence of all moral responsibility, and the certitude of safety in numbers from either the reproach of cowardice or the dangers attending on rashness; such are the vices of assemblies when they are not confined within bounds which they cannot overstep.[25]

Another writer of the period concludes as follows:

Too long have we asserted that opinion was queen of the world—opinion, changing, passionate and capricious opinion, is a tyrant whom we should distrust not less than other tyrants.[26]

More, indeed, for there is no tyrant who dares go to such extremes as those who give themselves the airs of popular sovereignty.

When the general will is all-powerful, its representatives are the more to be feared for giving themselves out as nothing more than the docile instruments of this alleged will, and for possessing the means of compulsion or persuasion by which to canalize it into whatever channel suits them. What no tyrant, acting in his own name, would dare to do, these men legitimate by the limitless extent of the power of society. For the increase of taxation made necessary by their requirements they go to the freeholder of this power, to the people, whose omnipotence serves no other purpose than to excuse the encroachments of their representatives. Laws the most unjust, institutions the most oppressive, are rendered obligatory for being the expression of the general will. . . . The all-powerful people is as dangerous as a tyrant and more so; or rather it is certain that tyranny will usurp the right which is the people's. It need do no more than proclaim the omnipotence of its people in the act of threatening it, than speak in its name in the act of silencing it.[27]

Such were the lessons taught by a generation which had learned wisdom by suffering. For a whole quarter of a century they had witnessed

25. *Cours de politique constitutionnelle* (ed. of 1836) pp. 16–17.
26. Sismondi, *Études sur les constitutions des peuples libres* (ed. of 1836) p. 204.
27. B. Constant, *op. cit.* (ed. Laboulaye, of 1872) pp. 279–80.

a succession of mutually incompatible regimes, whose only point of resemblance was in the obedience which all alike exacted, and in the assurances of zeal, devotion, and enthusiasm which had to be showered on them. The characters of men had been degraded before their very eyes by fear, which sought to avert the tyrant's blows, by malice, which strove to point them at others, and by greed, which rushed in wherever they had been struck. Proscriptions had been the lot of the proud, honours that of the renegades, safety that of no man.

Daunou, in the year 1819, raised this protest against the revenges which terror wreaked on terror:

> The restoration of the liberties of the individual is for a revolution a vain objective; at no point in its course does it return them. Ambition, greed, hatred, vengeance, the violent or hurtful passions of every kind, lay hold on revolutionary movements; and if, during the long night of disorder in which the victors and the vanquished take turns in being lost and crushed, voices are raised reclaiming order and safety, their advice is held for treacherous or untimely; the perils of the time, which could in fact be cured only by the application of the safeguards of ordinary laws, are made the excuse and banal watchword for welcoming every fresh act of injustice and disorder. For the space of thirty years arbitrary acts of every kind have been multiplied, unavailingly, to the point at which not a single citizen remains who has not, once or more times, suffered from them: unavailing it has been, for the power to commit more goes on being demanded at intervals in the sacred name of public security.[28]

This is an instance of experience echoing a meditation of Montesquieu's:

> Great vengeances, and the great changes which flow from them, cannot be undertaken without placing great power in the hands of a few citizens. ... There is need for government to return at the earliest possible moment to its ordinary channel, in which the laws are all-protective and show their teeth at no man.[29]

### 6. Thought Swings Back to Limited Power Lessons Drawn from England

The thinkers of the Restoration had received their political education in the school of twenty-five years of despotism and proscription. The

28. Daunou, *Essai sur les garanties individuelles* (Paris: 1819) pp. 23–24.
29. *L'Esprit des lois*, Book XII, chap. xviii.

similarity in the situations confronting each sent Benjamin Constant back
to the truths which Locke had perceived.

> The establishment of sovereignty of the people in an unlimited form is to
> create and play at dice with a measure of Power which is too great in itself
> and is an evil in whatever hands it is placed.[30]

The principle of the limitation of Power is rediscovered.

> Entrust it [unlimited Power] to one man, or to several men, or to all men,
> as you please; whichever it is, the results will be equally unfortunate for you.
> You will then wax hot against the actual holders of this Power, and will,
> according to circumstances, accuse in turn monarchy, aristocracy, democracy,
> mixed governments and the representative system. You will be wrong; it is
> the measure of force that is the culprit, not its holders. Your indignation
> needs to be directed against the sword and not against the arm. There are
> weapons which are too heavy for the hand of man.[31]

The entire work of this great liberal writer is a repetition of this one
idea. The problem was to apply it.

How did omnipotence rise to the top? By destroying in the name of
*the mass*, which it claimed to represent, though its existence was only a
fiction, the various *groups*, whose life was a reality. By making a handmaid
of the law to which in former times the public authority had itself been
subject.

The logical way to remedy this would have been to let free associations
develop, whether they were founded on locality or function, and to restore
to a position of complete independence the processes of forming and
administering the law. But the custodians of Power were disinclined to
lose the immense resources placed at their disposal by the Revolution and
the Empire. In 1814 the France of the departments seemed to the Duc
d'Angoulême a much easier country to govern than the France of the old
provinces, "which was a veritable hedgehog of liberties."[32] The opposition,
in a parliamentary regime in which it might one day come to power, was
no longer concerned with cutting down the substance of an authority

---

30. B. Constant, *op. cit.*, p. 8.
31. *Ibid.*, p. 8.
32. Maurras, *Action française*, May 15, 1930.

which it might one day hope to inherit. The social impulsion to form groups and the spirit of independence among the lawyers had been left enfeebled by a long enslavement: the thought was rather to get from Power what could be had than to dispense with it. This was to be noted later by Odilon Barrot:

> The wider you set the bounds of Power, the more people will there be to aspire to it. Life goes where there is life, and when a nation's entire stock of vitality is concentrated in its government, it is only natural that every man should seek a place in it.[33]

The circumstances of the time and the tendency to "catch the nearest way" brought the entire principle of limitation of Power down to a formal system of separation of powers. Had not Montesquieu praised this aspect of the English Constitution in a famous chapter of *L'Esprit des Lois?* As it was a big, fat book, the reading of a single chapter was held to qualify for the office of interpreter. And so this doctrine, at once simple and formal, took root in the political science which was spread by the French all over the Continent, that there must be an executive, a lower chamber, and an upper chamber—and then all would be well.

It is true enough that English analogies had an immense influence on the men of that time. They saw in Elizabeth, James I, and Charles I the prototypes of the French absolute monarchy; in the English Revolution the prototype of the French; in Cromwell a cross between Robespierre and Bonaparte; in Charles II, Louis XVIII, and James II, they saw Charles X; and they believed that the men of the July monarchy had given France a William III, and with him the stability which England had displayed since 1689.

Therefore, it was natural for them to look across the Channel for a model for French institutions. But they needed also to look behind the established powers of government to the social foundations which gave them a solid strength.

The English Parliament had then been in existence for nearly six centuries. In truth, however, it was born along with the monarchy itself, being the child of the *colloquium* in which the king, to furnish himself with the sinews of action, assembled the effective custodians of the various social forces and had to bargain with them. As the small fry of the esquires

33. Odilon Barrot, *op. cit.*

and the commonalty in the various counties grew in capacity to give him "aids," he made place for them in his counsels. The "King in Parliament" was supreme because the social forces supported him; and Parliament had no need of special rights, being itself the congress of independent authorities of whom Power must make request.

The social importance of the peers had not diminished with time. Their special position of territorial magnates still assured them a power of the purse even after they had lost their military power. When wool was the leading industry, they were its principal purveyors; when the growth of population in the eighteenth century raised the price of commodities, they reaped the most advantage from the rise. They were to do so again in the nineteenth century from the rise in land values and from the extraction of coal, for in English law the owner of the land is owner also of what is below the land. Tied as they were to the land, they were tied also to the men who lived on the land, and in the strength of their roots in the soil lay the secret of their political durability.

The system of pocket boroughs, vicious as it was, assured the automatic representation in Parliament of all that was eminent in society, for wealth took the form of estates; with estates went rotten boroughs, and rotten boroughs carried seats in Parliament.

Thus the two chambers were in fact the organ of the actual social forces. From this they drew their strength, which they did not borrow from any form of constitution: from this again came their caution.

They did not so much balance Power as hem it round. Though they could have crushed it and taken its place, they refrained by reason only of a good sense of which de Lolme has come upon the secret: they saw that a Power as circumscribed as this, and as remarked by all, was much less dangerous than would be its successor if it perished, for its successor would enjoy all the advantage of surprise and all the prestige of novelty. Yet the social forces, each time that they so wished, could dictate Power's course, as had been seen in 1749 when they drove Walpole into war.

Thus, the "separation of powers," as seen in England, was in reality the consequence of a process of recoil of the royal *imperium* before the social forces. The institution of Parliament was the constitutional expression of forces which were in league against Power, acted as its overseers and controllers, and doled out to it its sinews of action, by which means they kept it always in check and decided its course with ever greater frequency. Such was the position in the time of Montesquieu, and such it was still in that of Benjamin Constant. The profound transformation which has since taken place is another story.

### 7. The Formal Separation of Powers

The mere recital of the circumstances which gave birth to the duality of powers in England reveals how arbitrary was the introduction of the system in France. In the history of France the central Power and the social authorities had never had a meeting-place; the centralized *imperium* had lived in victorious isolation. Duality in France had not been the creation of events: it was an artificial duality introduced by the makers of constitutions. The *imperium* was cut into three slices, the king's, the lower chamber's, and the upper chamber's.

But habits are stubborn things. Each slice of the serpent tended to reproduce the complete serpent: the king regarded himself as the heir of a king who was absolute, and the assembly regarded itself as the heir of an assembly which was absolute. Both of them tended naturally not to remain within the limits of the part written for them by a constitution, but to make themselves masters of the *imperium* conceived always as a whole. In the same way the Augustuses and the Caesars, between whom Diocletian had made so ingenious a division of the Empire, never regarded their respective territories except as bases from which to make themselves masters of the undivided Empire.

In the event, as we know in France, the monarchy made the running by successive encroachments, and the appeals of Parliament to the people led in the end to the Revolution of 1848. The hopes to which the July monarchy had given birth can be measured in the accents of woebegone astonishment with which men like Augustin Thierry greeted its sudden fall. It had been supposed to be going to last for centuries! And there it was, dead after eighteen years! Popular sovereignty had triumphed, and the problem of the formation of Power was no more.

The sequel was the reappearance of the fundamental mistake of the first revolution, the illusion that any Power which is founded on a good principle must be infinitely beneficent. Listen to Lamartine: "A strong, centralized Power such as is this, is, it is true, dangerous where the government and the people are not one, but it ceases to be so when the government is merely the nation in action, that and no more."[34]

34. *La France parlementaire*, Vol. II, p. 109.

All the same the National Assembly, in honouring the shades of Rousseau by acclaiming the sovereignty of the general will, burnt a candle to Montesquieu as well by organizing the separation of powers.

Then ensued the *pons asinorum* of constitution-makers. Never was seen such light-mindedness! One power, they said, would check another—and no doubt it would if each distinct institution was the organ of a force pre-existent in society. But if both are emanations of the same force, never.

To oppose, as the Second Republic did, an assembly elected by the people to a president elected by the people was not the organization of a true equilibrium of social elements, but merely the introduction of dispute between men invested by the same authority. In the matter of equality of rights, the president was bound to win the day over a body of men with disparate wills. Taught by experience, the makers of the constitution of 1875 no longer provided for the election of the president by the people. But in that case the Chamber, which drew its power directly from the sovereign people, was bound to win the day over the president and annul his powers.

There was in all this a fulfilment of the prediction uttered by Sismondi:

> Whenever it is recognized that all power issues from the people, then those who hold it most directly from the people and those with the largest number of electors are bound for that reason to think their power the most legitimate.[35]

The different destinies of the third element, the upper house, under different constitutions, illustrate the conditioning of an institution's political existence by the social background.

It is noteworthy that the Senate in France has resisted stoutly the onslaughts of the lower house, the reason being that it was the true reflection of a distinct social force, the small country oligarchies. It is still more noteworthy that, of the two American chambers, the one which has had the greater success in creating a balance with the President is not the one which has, like him, been elected by universal suffrage: had the latter stood alone the President would have mastered it, as Louis Napoleon mastered the National Assembly. It is the Senate which has for many years counterbalanced the presidential authority; the reason being that, composed as it is of two members from each state, without regard to

35. Sismondi, *op. cit.*, p. 305.

statistics of population, it is representative of separate local entities, of established groupings and the oligarchies which run them: of anything, in short, except the people.

Volumes have been written on the usefulness of a second chamber in moderating the transports of the first. But, as Mill wrote,

> its efficacy in this respect wholly depends on the social support which it can command outside the House. An assembly which does not rest on the basis of some great power in the country is ineffectual against one which does.[36]

For this reason the House of Lords, which in the thirteenth century had been able to hold Power in check, and at times even to keep it in tutelage, could hold back the movement of the people only so long as the lords were still social forces[37] and were for ever admitting fresh social forces by a wise course of policy.

The House of Lords has, in fact, recoiled further and further before the Commons: indeed it saved what is left to it of its power of check only by resigning itself—in 1911—to being no more than a hindrance. Today it is little more than a school of academic debate.

Constitutions may contrive admirable organs, but these get life and force only so far as they are filled with a life and force derived from a social power which it is not within the capacity of the constitution-makers to create. It is, therefore, a mere conjuring trick to parcel out into distinct organs a Power which derives from one solitary source, the majority of the people. So long as the pieces remain apart, there is, admittedly, conflict, but it is the deleterious conflict of the ambitions of men and bodies of men, not the health-giving conflict of different social interests. When this point is reached, there goes with the enfeeblement and the discrediting of authority a vast increase in the responsibilities of the state. But in the end, when nothing keeps the pieces apart but constitutional devices and the *amour propre* of the different species of representatives, they come together again in the winning organ whose absolutism is now unlimited.

Power cannot, therefore, be limited by the mere dismemberment of the *imperium* into constituent parts each with its distinct organ. For

---

36. J. S. Mill, *Representative Government*, p. 233.

37. As already noted, the landed aristocracy became the natural beneficiary of the rising demand for coal.

limitation of this kind to succeed, there must be in existence sectional interests in a sufficiently advanced state, conscious of their identity, and armed with strength to stop the encroachments of Power on their own spheres, together with a system of law which is independent enough to arbitrate their clashes and escape from being the instrument of the central command.

The nature of this social equilibrium raises vast questions. Can it be fitted up and kept alive by legislators of vision? Or must it not rather be a situation of a kind which is met with at certain stages in the course of historical evolution, when an ascending scale of the social balance is symmetrically in line with a descending—a position which any continuation of the movement inevitably disturbs? This may happen when the scale of political power rises in the midst of social powers which were at first unbounded. Or again when social powers renew their strength against a political power in its decline.

We will not now handle this problem in which are implicit the freedom and effectiveness of the human will, and, it may truly be said, the limitations of the human being. Let us be content to note that the second hypothesis would, if true, explain those brilliant appearances and long eclipses of individual liberty which strike the historian as a recurrent phenomenon.

The explanation of this liberty would in that case be the momentary inability of any one of the powers at strain to impose itself absolutely, an inability which cannot last, because each of these various bodies lives its own life, some sinking into decay and others taking on fresh strength. And the precariousness of liberty would then be seen to be a social fatality, for liberty cannot continue to be, either when the family, the commune, the squire, or the employer enjoy an absolute autonomy, or equally when the state has total sovereignty.

Here too would lie the explanation of the remarkable decline in the status of the individual in the nineteenth and twentieth centuries. First came oppression by the state, following the destruction of the makeweights by the French Revolution. Followed the rise, thanks to the enfeeblement of Power by its own internal divisions, of new social forces, which were at first capitalist and later trade unionist. Soon a certain tendency to oppression showed itself in some of these new forces, wherever they achieved a measure of autonomy. Then Power started to gather strength again, and the social forces were attacked by the state, an attack which, at the start, had as its aim to protect the human being, but, pushed to its conclusion, was logically bound to enslave him.

Again, it must be noted that Power which is founded on the sovereignty of the people is in better shape than any other to fight and conquer. If sovereignty resides in a king or an aristocracy, so that it belongs to but one man or a few, it cannot markedly extend its scope without clashing with the interests of the majority; and if only these interests are provided with an organ of their own, however restricted its power—such as the tribunate in the early days of Rome—the vast forces which in this way find expression will expand the organ by degrees, just as an army which is vastly superior in numbers will necessarily spread out once it has secured a bridgehead. But with an organ of resistance possessed by a minority against the power of the multitude, the opposite must happen; it is sure to wither away by progressive stages, just as a bridgehead narrows when it is held by an army which is much inferior in numbers.[38]

We see, then, that the opposition evoked by Power will be strong enough to limit it only in the case of a Power which is of a minority character. But a majority Power can proceed to absolutism itself; such an absolutism reveals, by its mere existence, the lie in such a Power's soul—though it styles itself "people," it has never ceased to be Power.

38. "I cannot think that, where democracy is the ruling power in society, the second house would have any real ability to resist even the aberrations of the first." J. S. Mill, *op. cit.*, p. 235.

# XVI.

## *Power and Law*

THE ABSENCE IN SOCIETY of any concrete authorities capable of restraining Power does not matter if Power itself makes humble submission before the abstract force of the natural law. The idea of the limitation of Power by such a law puts no trust in material makeweights, which are in their nature egoist and may as often hinder Power's beneficent action as check its malignant use; rather it calls into being a spiritual process to take the place of a mechanical. It takes the form of a general distaste for the rulers aroused in the entire nation, and of a prick felt in their own consciences; it may end up in the setting in motion against them of a judicial machine by which, their great place notwithstanding, they are brought to book.

Beyond all question, the supremacy of law should be the great and central theme of all political science. But, make no mistake about it, the necessary condition of this supremacy is the existence of a law older than the state, to which it is mentor. For if law is anything which Power elaborates, how can it ever be to it a hindrance, a guide, or a judge?

The same passions and the same ideas as those which laid in ruin the social authorities deprived law of its autonomy.

This process we are now about to follow into its furthest consequences, in full knowledge that the widespread feeling of the supremacy of law which haunts men's souls makes easier of achievement the restoration of its independence.

## 1. Is Law a Mere Body of Rules Issued by Authority?

The man in the street, in unconscious repetition of the medieval theologians, requires of those who rule society that they be just.

But what is justice? It is defined in the Institutes of Justinian as "the permanent and unshakable will to give to each his due right." Nothing could be clearer than that: each of us has his rights, which are called subjective rights, and these live and meet in an objective law—the elaboration of a moral code which is over all and which Power must both respect and make respected.

We agree with Duguit when he says: "The end of public authority is to realize law." And when Power is exercised in accordance with this law, it becomes legitimate, whatever its origin.[1]

But what, you will say, is this law? Let us see what the jurists say. The answer given by most of them is that the law is the epitome or consequence of the rules of conduct given out by the competent authority. "So that," one of them adds, "what is in conformity with the laws is good, and what disregards them is bad."[2] "The art of distinguishing the just from the unjust," defines another, "is one with the art of knowing and applying the laws."[3]

We are now going round in a vicious circle! Political authority should be just; it needs, that is to say, to act in conformity with the law. But the

---

1. "Political Power being an artefact, men have well understood, from the first day on which they entertained the notion of natural law, that the orders of this Power were only legitimate if they were in conformity with this law and that the use of material constraint by political Power was only legitimate if its purpose was to ensure the enforcement of this law.... No man has a natural right to command others: be he emperor, or king, or parliament, or popular majority, none may impose their will as such; their acts can have no authority over the governed, unless they are conformable with law. Seen from this aspect, the much discussed question of what is the end of the state, or, more accurately, of political Power, is resolved in the following way: the end of political Power is to realize natural law; it is compelled by this law to do all it can to ensure its reign. The state is founded on force; but this force is only legitimate when it is exercised in conformity with the law.... In different centuries there have been different formulas, but the foundation has always been the same. In the tenth century, under the Church's influence, this idea, that God had raised up princes that they might cause this law and justice to reign, had deeply imbued men's minds. M. Luchaire has clearly shown that the power of the Capetian monarchy reposed essentially on this belief, that God had instituted kings that they might render justice to men and above all ensure peace, and that that is their first and most essential duty." Léon Duguit, *Traité de Droit constitutionnel*, Vol. I (Paris: 1921) pp. 518–19.

2. Marcadé.

3. Demolombe. Quotations taken from H. Léby-Ullmann, *Éléments d'introduction à l'étude des sciences juridiques*, I, "La définition du Droit" (Paris: 1917).

law, we are told, is nothing more than the epitome of the rules given out by political authority itself. Therefore the authority which makes laws is, by definition, always just.

Here is sophistry and to spare! Evidently, however, it takes some avoiding, since even a Kant arrived at this all-embracing justification of Power. As he writes in his *Metaphysic of Ethics*:

> The people is never entitled to resist the supreme legislator of the state; for a rule of law is only made possible by the submission of all to the legislative will. Any right of rebellion, or even of sedition, is, therefore, totally inadmissible. . . .
>
> The people's duty to put up with abuse of the supreme power, even when it finds it insupportable, is based on the consideration that resistance to the sovereign body of laws should never be regarded as other than illegal, and as involving, even, the overthrow of the entire legal constitution. For the people to have a right to resistance, there would first need to be a public law permitting it to resist; in other words, the sovereign body of laws would need to contain a provision making it no longer sovereign.[4]

The logic is impeccable. Laws are the only source of the law. Therefore, whatever is in a law is law, and there can be no remedy against the laws. Accept it, and to seek in law a bulwark against Power becomes pure illusion.

The law is, as the jurists put it, "positive."

> The very essence of the Rule of Law [writes a contemporary authority] is that it be instantly enforceable by weapons. Law, therefore, necessarily supposes a public authority capable of compelling individuals to obey the orders given out by itself. For the same reason it is clear that law can be conceived of only in terms of positive law.[5]

## 2. Of Unlimited Legislative Authority

Must we, then, in the face of such authorities as these, renounce as illusion the idea of a law capable of checking Power, and see in law merely a creature of the state and one which is powerless against its creator? Yet

4. *Metaphysic of Ethics* (Fr. tr. Barni. Paris: 1853) first part. xlvi.
5. Carré de Malberg, *Contribution à la théorie générale de l'état* (Paris: 1920) p. 57, note 6.

has not history shown us[6] a law whose credentials are of a different standing, being founded on the divine law and custom? And even today does not the general sentiment attest the fact that anything that is in a law is not necessarily law? Let us rather inquire, therefore, how this aberration, to the existence of which we have just called so much evidence, came to be, and what produced the subjection of law.

We are now at a point at which several streams of error, starting from very different sources, meet—the mistake of Hobbes, the illusions of Rousseau and Kant, and above all the transgressions against common sense of the hedonist or utilitarian school, as represented by such men as Helvétius,[7] Bentham, and Destutt de Tracy, whose understandings were as moderate as their influence was great.

Hobbes, we know, saw in Power the only begetter and maintainer of order among men. In times before it or without it there was nothing but the brutal clash of appetites. Again, "when a republic is established, there are laws and nothing antecedent to them." Further,

> for each subject the civil law is the body of rules which the state, orally, in writing or in any other way that sufficiently indicates its pleasure, has communicated to him in order that he may employ them to discern good and evil, evil being what is against the rules.[8]

This definition bears a close resemblance to that of some modern jurists! Given these principles, where does it all end?

> The sovereign of a republic, be he a man or an assembly, is not subject to the civil laws. For he, having the power to make and unmake the laws, can, when he pleases, escape from subjection to them by abrogating those which impede him and making new ones.[9]

Hobbes, at any rate, both saw and wished the consequences of the principle which he was laying down. His imagination took pleasure in a

6. Cf. chap. xi.

7. [Helvétius (1715–1771), French philosopher of the utilitarian school and one of the Encyclopaedists; he held that all man's faculties may be reduced to physical sensation, that self-interest is his only motive, and that ideas of justice and injustice, not being absolute, change according to custom. His chief work, *De l'Esprit*, was published in 1758 and raised such a storm that he published three separate retractions.]

8. Hobbes, *Leviathan*, second part, chap. xxvi, p. 137 of the first edition of 1651.

9. *Ibid.*, pp. 137–38.

total Power, and he painted its horrific features with a logician's fanaticism: lord of all property, censor of all opinion, above reproach in all its actions, since it alone was judge of the social good and all morality came back to the social good.

The case of Rousseau and Kant is quite other. They carefully refrained from entrusting this unlimited legislative authority to either a monarch or an assembly. No! Such an authority could belong to none other than the entire people and, on that condition, seemed to them innocuous. For, argues Kant, "when a man decides on something in regard to another, it is always possible that he may do that other some injustice; but injustice is impossible in what he decides for himself (for *volenti non fit injuria*)." [10]

From this line of reasoning, which would be in strict logic supportable if everyone subject to the laws had without exception given an effective assent to each of them, is deduced, with the help of numerous fictions, the essential justice of the legislative authority.

Fiction number one: that a people as a whole, speaking *ex cathedra*, can do no injustice to any man in its decisions.

Fiction number two: that a people as a whole formulates a considered determination at all; have we not lately observed the American people, which had voted as a whole the Prohibition law, giving the lie to its vote at any hour of the day or night?

Fiction number three—and a most important one: that the people is consulted on each law; that happens only in Switzerland, and even there only on certain laws.

The unlimited legislative authority with which Kant and Rousseau endowed the whole of society was bound inevitably, as Benjamin Constant said, "to pass from the whole to the majority, and from the majority into the hands of a few men, often into the hand of one. . . ." [11]

However, what were potentially the evil effects of this idea were held in check by the conception of society which was entertained by Rousseau, Kant, and the men of their time. The one reality seen in the entire social complex by these men of enlarged understanding was the human being, and they proclaimed the dignity and rights which were his in his capacity of man, in language of an admirable elevation. What they did not sufficiently see was that these rights of his might come into conflict with

10. *Op. cit.*
11. B. Constant, "De la Souveraineté du peuple," in the *Cours de politique constitutionnelle* (ed. Laboulaye. Paris: 1872) Vol. II, p. 9.

unlimited legislative authority. But it is certain that in that event they would have fought for them and not against them. Rousseau's point of view in the matter was made clear for all to see by the defence of the *liberum veto*[12] which he undertook. And in the nineteenth century it is on the whole true to say that the separation, though inevitably provisional, of the executive and the legislature, and above all the individualist ideas which were everywhere in vogue, acted as a safeguard against the possible consequences of an extreme application of the idea of legislative omnipotence. The truth is that the various declarations of rights played the part of a natural law set above the laws.

### 3. The Mistake of the Hedonist and the Utilitarian

The hedonist and utilitarian mistake is grosser.

It is the end product of the rationalist crisis. Nothing, said Helvétius, is good or bad in itself: "The different peoples of all ages and countries have at no time applied the name of virtuous to any actions except those which either were, or were at any rate believed to be, useful to the public."

But they were, of course, often wrong on what was useful. Help was brought to them by the new science of utility and Bentham's doctrine of "the greatest good of the greatest number."

The first thing to do is to banish entirely the "archaic prejudice" of an objective morality which is compulsive in itself.

> It is a very old and very ridiculous mistake [said Destutt de Tracy] to suppose that the principles of morality are as it were immanent in our heads and are the same for everyone, and then to posit for them some kind of celestial origin . . . let us recognize that morality is a science which, as with the other sciences, we make up as we go along, that it is only the knowledge of what consequences our inclinations and feelings will have for our happiness . . . of all the sciences it is always the last to achieve perfection, always the least advanced, always the one on which there must be the widest

12. [The *liberum veto*, which was introduced into the constitution of Poland in the seventeenth century, gave each single deputy the right of vetoing any measure introduced into the Diet, even if the rest of the house approved it. It need hardly be said that, when at the time of the first Partition the partitioning powers presented the Poles with a new constitution, they retained a feature so well adapted to keep a country infirm of purpose.]

differences of opinion. So we shall find, if we look closely, that our moral principles are so far from being uniform that there are in this respect as many modes of seeing and feeling as there are men, that it is this diversity which accounts for diversity of character and that, without our being aware of it, each of us has a system of morals which is proper to himself, or rather a confused mass of inconsequent ideas, which does not deserve the name of system but for all that takes the place of one.[13]

The reader will perhaps shrug his shoulders and consider that Tracy[14] may be dismissed as a second-rate thinker who cannot have had much direct influence. Possibly, but he describes to perfection the dispersal of beliefs and feelings which followed on the rationalist earthquake. Good and evil, justice and injustice, have now become a matter of opinion.

Persisted in, these opinions will find expression in laws, and these laws will be the foundation of law, by deciding what shall be just and what unjust. Tracy is aware that there is here the possibility of great confusion. Therefore he wishes to entrust to "the legislator, who is primed on every aspect of morality by methodical and strictly deductive reasoning," the duty of issuing practical moral precepts, the reasons for which it is impossible to explain in detail. How are men to be got to obey them? "The most powerful of all moral instruments, in comparison with which the rest are almost a nullity, are repressive laws and their entire and perfect execution."[15]

The modern problem is here posed for us. When law has ceased to be a thing in its essential parts untouchable, a thing sustained by the beliefs held in common by the whole of society, when it has become, even in respect of fundamental morals, a thing modifiable at the pleasure of the legislator, one of two consequences must follow: either a monstrous spawning of laws at the bidding of every interest which agitates and of every opinion which stirs, or else their planned economy by a master who knows his mind and will drive society to accept whatever rules of conduct he thinks it necessary to prescribe.

This dilemma is the inescapable consequence of two connected facts: the throwing of all first principles into the melting-pot of a scepticism

13. Destutt de Tracy, *Éléments d'idéologie,* Vol. IV, pp. 456–59.

14. [Destutt de Tracy (1754–1836), French materialist philosopher, whose tenet it was that to think is to feel. His chief work, *Éléments d'idéologie,* was published in 1817–1818.]

15. *Ibid.,* p. 454.

which is as unrestrained as it is unmethodical, and unlimited legislative authority.

### 4. Law Above Power

Loud and clear we proclaim it—the mounting flood of modern laws does not create law. What do they mirror, these laws, but the pressure of interests, the fancifulness of opinions, the violence of passions? When they are the work of a Power which has become, with its every growth, more enervated by the strife of factions, their confusion makes them ludicrous. When they issue from a Power which is in the grip of one brutal hand, their planned iniquity makes them hateful. The only respect which they either get or deserve is that which force procures them. Being founded on a conception of society which is both false and deadly, they are anti-social.

It is untrue that the supremacy of law can be procured by Power working alone. By far the most of the work is done by beliefs and folkways, of which there must be no incessant calling in question; their relative stability is an essential condition of the welfare of society. The necessary cohesion of society cannot be procured by Power alone. There must exist, rooted in a common faith, a deep community of feeling, passing into an acknowledged ethic and maintaining an inviolable law.

Power can achieve nothing of all this. Once this community of feeling is in dissolution, and law is delivered over to the good pleasure of the legislature, then no doubt Power not only can but must extend. It must intervene, widely and continuously, to restore, if it can, the threatened cohesion.

Thus is explained the rise of Power at the time when the Catholic faith was shaken. Thus, too, is explained its further advance coincident with the effective abandonment of the individualist notion of subjective rights affirmed in 1789. While this belief in inherent subjective rights was a less effective bulwark than the Christian faith from which it was left over, yet it was very precious as against the abuses of man-made law.

In France it was the Catholic jurists who first recalled to mind that there exists an absolute law, to give expression to which is the only function of laws.[16] It was a truth which, though it had seemed self-evident

16. "A law, considered as an instrument of social discipline, has no more validity than force, when it is itself only the expression of force; the truth is that law itself has its laws which govern it, and is, if it goes beyond them, of no more worth than the dangers which

to Montesquieu,[17] raised, in our own day, a veritable outcry—so strong was the conviction that there was no institution so fundamental and no principle so primary as not to be infinitely variable at the pleasure of whatever wish or opinion happened to be predominant for the time being.

It was to the accompaniment of an orchestra of protesting noises that Duguit enunciated the true doctrine of law, and its political function:

> Whatever idea of the state is formed . . . it needs energetically and pertinaciously restating that the activity of the state in all its manifestations is limited by a law which is superior to itself, that there are things which it cannot do and things which it should do, and that this limitation does not apply merely to this or that organ of it but to the state itself. . . . It is essential never to weary both in understanding and in asserting that there is a rule of law which is superior to the public authority, a law which comes to limit it and lay on it obligations.[18]

## 5. A Period of Ambulatory Law

The conception is one which, no sooner formulated, forces itself on the mind. It alone can give meaning to what are otherwise mere games with words: the talk heard nowadays of installing the reign of law between nations signifies nothing at all if every people claims to possess an unlimited right of deciding what it will do.

But, however true may be the idea of a rule of law laid on Power, its implementation is in our time a matter of great difficulty. For, even if the principle of laws being conformable to a law is admitted as an obligation, what is there to prevent a Power which presents a law and a group which mobilizes opinion to get it passed, from claiming that the law in question is an expression, manifestation, and realization of law? And, on my calling

---

it is its purpose to avert. . . . They (these laws which are over the laws) make up the natural law, giving to this expression the highest meaning of which thought can conceive: it is the ideal which marks out and illumines the road which legislation must follow. . . . A law is not law; it is but law's accidental manifestation, its temporary or local expression or, as it were, its instrument." Ch. Beudant, *Le Droit individuel et l'État*, pp. 12–13.

17. "Before there were any laws made, there were intimations of justice. . . . To say that justice and injustice are only what is commanded or forbidden by positive laws is tantamount to saying that, until a circle had been traced, the radii were not all equal." *L'Esprit des lois*, Book I, chap. i.

18. Duguit, *Traité de droit constitutionnel*, Vol. III, p. 547.

it iniquitous, I shall merely be told that my conception of law is false or, a still more crushing retort, out of date.

Law, like morality, which is its stay, is, we are told, ambulatory;[19] both are in continuous movement and neither, therefore, has any fixed mark.

The genius of our time finds quite instinctively this repartee to the principle of the supremacy of law. Having found it, it comes to terms with the principle fast enough, even to the point of invoking it! The attack on those same individual rights which in 1789 had had their sacredness proclaimed, the privileged position accorded to certain groups or the discrimination exercised against certain others, the character of uncertainty stamped on every interest, and the unconditional surrender of them all to Power, all were explained, justified, and extolled as reflecting an ever more advanced and elevated conception of law.

And what answer can be made? In what does the substance of law, as opposed to ambulatory law, consist? It has now lost the two stays which formerly kept it on its base: as to its essential parts, faith in a divine law, as to the rest, respect for ancestral observances. The second root could not, it is true, hope to survive in a time of rapid change. But how about the first?

The man of today, owning neither superior nor ancestors nor beliefs nor folkways, stands completely defenceless before the glittering prospect which is now held out to him, of a better state of things to be achieved, of a larger social welfare to be realized, by means of legislation, which, though it offend an outmoded law, is inspired thereto by today's better law!

It is, then, quite useless to look for the defence of an unsettled law from a hesitant public opinion. The feeling of law is still alive, but it is now called out effectively only by violence in its most naked forms—it does not respond, and is quite without means of responding, to the challenge of daily and surreptitious aggression.

## 6. Remedies Against Laws

Is there, then, any way of assuring effectively the supremacy of law unless it be by first formulating expressly its fundamental rules, and then

19. [The word "ambulatory," which is here chosen to translate *mouvant*, is found in *Religio Medici* in just this context.]

establishing a concrete authority, which will have the task of bringing laws to the test of law, and rejecting those which offend it?

That was the system which Marshall, the American jurist, was able to get accepted in the United States in 1803. Against a law which violates the rights guaranteed him by the Constitution, the citizen can have recourse to the judicial machine, in the final resort to the Supreme Court; this can invalidate as respects the suitor the provisions of the law in question, which, being now inapplicable, is thereafter a dead letter.

In this institution the Americans have found the bulwark of their liberty and the dam to Power's encroachments. It has checked the passions to the play of which the democratic form of constitution abandoned the legislative machine—it has prevented them from using this machine to the detriment of this or that class of citizens.

The proposal was made to bring this institution over to France and to make of the Declaration of Rights of 1789 the fundamental and inviolable law. The tribunals and, in the last resort, a supreme tribunal would then adjudicate between the impatient legislator and the wronged citizens.

The project would certainly have tied up with the real intentions of the men of the Constituent Assembly. They are now made fun of for having inscribed "immortal principles" at the head of the legislative structure which the rulers of today were to build. Here, as often happens, it is the sceptic that was the fool, and the enthusiast who was the wise man. Once the decision was taken to entrust to men the vast responsibility of making the law, they needed for their guidance a fixed framework to direct and limit their activities. The Declaration was the more or less legitimate descendant of the divine law. But a much less effective one!

Is it now possible to make the Declaration effective by bringing over an American institution? Let it be remembered that this institution grew and flourished only from being the natural offspring of the Common Law which the immigrants had brought with them from England, a law which has not, or has not for a long time had, its equivalent on the Continent.

If the judge in America can now rebuff the legislator who invades the domain of private liberty, the reason is that the judge in England had been able before him to rebuff the agent of Power who encroached on this sphere.

A judicial bit was in the mouth of the executive, and it was, therefore, logical, at a time when the legislature was taking a big step forward, to put a bit in its mouth, too. For what did it profit the citizen to be protected by a judge against an agent of Power come without legal warrant, if, as nowadays happens, the agent could return the next day, and be acting this time in the name of the law? This is the danger which is parried by the Supreme Court. And, as we see, the innovation of 1803 was in line with earlier conceptions of the judge's role and of judicial authority which are, unfortunately, foreign to France, at least to the France born of the Revolution.

## 7. When the Judge Checks the Agent of Power

The eighteenth century conceived for English liberties an admiration which has echoed down to our own time, but it was quite wrong in ascribing the principle of them to the parliamentary regime. It was really embedded in the judicial regime.

When the agent of Power comes to lay hands on a man in his private domain, whether to force him to do or to prevent him from doing, he is backed by a complete apparatus of constraint to which a solitary individual can make no resistance. He is, if left to his own resources, a slave of Power. He only ceases to be so if a makeweight can hold back the arm of government. That was the primary function of the tribunes of Ancient Rome, from whose establishment the *plebs* dated the beginning of its emancipation. It is a task which both in England and, derivatively, in the United States, devolves on the judge.

In every civilized country the judicial function consists in punishing the criminal and righting the civil wrong done by one man to the rights of another. It implies, logically, ability to take the preventive steps needed to terminate the tortious act.

Now, in what are called the Anglo-Saxon countries the right of justice to take these steps is not limited to the actions of one private individual in regard to another, but extends also to the actions of an agent of Power in regard to a man in a street.

A secretary of state [said Dicey] is governed by the ordinary law of the realm both in his official conduct and in his private life. If, in an access of anger, the Secretary of State for Home Affairs assaulted the Leader of the Opposition or had him arrested because he considered the liberty of his political opponent dangerous for the state, this minister would in either case expose himself to proceedings and to all the other penalties laid down by the law for the case of acts of violence. Although the arrest of an influential politician, whose speeches might excite disorder, is a strictly administrative act, that would not excuse either the minister or the policemen who had obeyed his orders.[20]

This example throws into relief the essential difference between British and Continental society, and makes clear what is the real foundation of English liberty. It is not where search has been made for it, in political institutions, which have been copied to no purpose, but rather in the conception of law.

Political thought in France places Power above the ordinary law. In that way it divides the members of the community into two clearly defined classes. All who are on the state's side of the line may proceed against all who are on the people's without becoming accountable to the ordinary tribunals.

> In England, on the other hand, the idea of legal equality, or of the universal subjection of all classes to one law administered by the ordinary courts, has been pushed to its utmost limit. With us every official, from the prime minister down to a constable or a collector of taxes, is under the same responsibility for every act done without legal justification as any other citizen. The reports abound with cases in which officials have been brought before the courts, and made, in their personal capacity, liable to punishment, or to the payment of damages, for acts done in their official character but in excess of their lawful authority. A colonial governor, a secretary of state, a military officer, and all subordinates, though carrying out the commands of their official superiors, are as responsible for any act which the law does not authorize as is any private and unofficial person.[21]

The effectiveness of these guarantees derives not so much from the sanctions which they carry as from the state of mind which they induce. The subaltern, being punishable for the orders which he executes, reflects before he executes, and the primary conceptions of the Common Law serve him as a measuring-rod. Whatever lies outside it is suspect to him. As for his superior, the threat of legal proceedings reminds him unceasingly that he is as much a citizen as everyone else; these results do not follow when, as in France, the legal remedy, offered as an act of grace to the

20. A. V. Dicey, *Law of the Constitution* (London). [*Publisher's note:* Liberty Fund republished the eighth edition (1915) in 1982.]
21. *Ibid.*, p. 189.

private person against authority which has abused its power, does not strike the actual men who have done the wrong.

## 8. Of the Authority of the Judge

The French Revolution was, as we saw, bent on destroying this precious guarantee of liberty against the acts of Power, which is conferred by the judge's intervention. None of the succeeding regimes has suffered it to reappear.

Today we can hardly realize its worth: for in our times the idea of the sufficiency of a law to arm the agent of Power seems natural enough. And if in the United States the judge can annul the law itself, he cannot do so in England.

That the power of check possessed over the executive (but giving way before the will of the legislature) could be of immense effect will be recognized by those who remember that for a long time the legislative power was feeble in the extreme or even non-existent, and that law signified a fixed code of rights which all were agreed on keeping fixed: *Nolumus leges Angliae mutari.*

Nevertheless, this code of rights developed, though imperceptibly, by means of decisions given in particular cases, decisions which, under the need to decide on more and more diverse sets of facts, were brought together and created a body of precedent.

It was a difficult science and made to look forbidding both by the fictions to which recourse had to be had and by the Norman patois with which it was studded, with the result that the law was to some extent the preserve of those who handled these sacred mysteries.

In this way there came into being a law which drew its inspiration not at all from the specific needs of Power but responded only to those of the body of society. The arcana of the law gave birth to what are called in England the principles of the Constitution,[22] being nothing more than "a generalization of the rights which the courts secure to individuals."[23]

Forming, as it does, a world apart, exercised in the grave discharge of its solemn and to some extent mysterious function, the English bench of

---

22. "In England the so-called principles of the Constitution are inductions or generalizations based upon particular decisions pronounced by the courts as to the rights of given individuals." *Op. cit.,* p. 193.

23. *Ibid.,* p. 196.

judges has accumulated in the course of centuries a prestige and a moral authority which explain the respect in which Parliament holds what has been rightly styled judicial legislation. Parliament, though "it can do anything," has observed great circumspection in regard to the law thus formulated: "upon the degree of authority and independence to be conceded to the Bench depended the colour and working of our institutions."[24]

And the same reasons explain how the same prestige, of which the American courts are the heirs, has caused those courts to have entrusted to them the right of pronouncing on the laws themselves. But in recent times the rising flood of laws has not, in England, spared the fabric of the ancient law. And in the United States Power has rebelled against the hindrance opposed to it by the Supreme Court, which has been accused of not moving with the times.

Having joined issue with Power on a terrain which suited Power well and itself badly, the Court found itself against public feeling and, after a Pyrrhic victory, had to turn down its wick: there has been talk of its twilight.

The fact is that public feeling today, which apprehends things in terms of a delusive simplicity, declines utterly to permit the opinion of a few men to act as a brake, all on its own, on what the opinion of society as a whole demands. That, it is thought, is a sin against the principle of popular sovereignty.

The reason why in France laws have been completely removed not only from the control of the courts but even from interpretation by them is, as Gény truly said, "the feeling, vague and instinctive but deeply rooted in Frenchmen, that in emasculating, even by judgments given in concrete cases and which have small validity outside the facts of those cases, the certain authority of statutory dispositions, our magistrates would in the end reach the position of restraining the supreme power of the legislator, and that in that way the judicial authority would become, merely in the process of strictly carrying out its duties, superior to the legislative, the latter being the authority in which your modern man wishes to keep sovereignty exclusively vested."[25]

The legislative authority, now regarded as the expression of the will of

---

24. *Ibid.,* p. 224.

25. François Gény, *Science et technique en droit privé positif* (4 vols., 1914–1924) Vol. IV, p. 93.

all, or, more accurately, of the whole, exercises a total sovereignty. Who dares to hinder it?

So long as the question is posed in terms of the opinion of a few as against the opinion of all, the answer does not admit of doubt. But this misses the point, for it is not a matter of *opinions* on one side or the other. On one side is a passing emotion, which a government or a party can fan into flame with the greatest ease, thanks to the improved and still improving methods of agitation which are available to them. And on the other are the verities of justice, with which there is no shuffling. No doubt the slightest false step on their part gravely discredits the guardians of these verities.[26] But they do not on that account lose their obligatory character.

## 9. Does the Movement of Ideas Affect the Fundamentals of Law?

The verities to be defended, however, must be eternal verities. The mistake of the United States Supreme Court was to defend against political opportunism principles which themselves partook of political opportunism.

The founders of the American Constitution were independent proprietors and they legislated for independent proprietors. At the time of the conflict which brought about the eclipse of the Supreme Court, Power had the backing of a mass of proletarians who were suffering from the consequences of a monstrously distorted conception of the rights of property. It is because it took its stand on the terrain of perishable verities that the Court has seen its authority temporarily in abeyance.

Similar in kind is the mistake of those who say that the natural or fundamental law should follow the movement of ideas. This high-sounding title masks in truth only the flux of interests. The various classes and social groupings are in continuous change as regards both their composition and their relative strengths. And the phrase really means that law must adapt itself to these changes.

But there is in law an immutable element, and we human beings are not, as I see it, alas, equal to the task of evolving a bubbling stream of ever new verities. Ideas are, more truly, like infrequent oases in the barren

---

26. As, for instance, the ill-advised opposition of the Court in the United States to some timely social insurance legislation.

wastes of human thought; once discovered, they are for ever precious, even though they are left to be silted up by the sands of stupidity and ignorance. Where is this stream of yours, that it should cause me to change direction? A mirage. There must be a return to Aristotle, St. Thomas, Montesquieu. In them is substance, and nothing of them is divorced from reality.

## 10. The Way in Which Law Becomes Jungle

The capital blunder of our time is, probably, this: that everything has come to be regarded as eternally abiding our question. No society, as Comte said, can continue at all in which certain fundamental notions are not accorded a unanimous respect, as being beyond the pale of discussion. And, said he,

> there can be no true liberty without a rational submission to the unique dominion, properly authenticated, of the fundamental laws of nature, in which is shelter from all arbitrary rule of men.[27] The metaphysic of politics has tried in vain to give its realm an odour of sanctity by investing with the honourable name of *laws* any sort of decisions, confused and irrational as they often are, taken by sovereign assemblies, whatever may be their composition; decisions which are conceived of, by a basic fiction which is unable to change their nature, as a faithful expression of the popular will.[28]

Can we fail to see that a delirium of legislation, such as has grown up with the last two or three generations, creates, by accustoming minds to look on fundamental rules and notions as infinitely modifiable, the most favourable conditions for the despot?

Ambulatory law is the sport and instrument of the passions. The despot whom a political wave carries to Power can twist into the most fantastic shapes what had already lost all certainty of form. Immutable verities being things of the past, he can now impose his own—intellectual monstrosities resembling those creatures of nightmare with the head taken from one animal and the limbs from another. By setting up a kind of

27. This is an almost word-for-word reproduction (was Comte aware of it?) of Locke's thought.
28. Comte, *Philosophie positive*, Vol. IV, p. 157.

vicious "alimentary circle" he is enabled to feed the people on ideas which they return to him in the guise of general will. This general will is the breeding-ground of laws which are ever more divorced not only from the divine but also from the human intelligence.

Law has lost its soul and become jungle.[29]

29. In the *Encyclical Mit Brennender Sorge*, of March 14, 1937, may be read: "He who takes the race, or the people, or the state, or the form of government, the bearers of the Power of the state or any other fundamental element of human society—which in the temporal order of things have an essential and honourable place—out of the system of their earthly valuation, and make them the ultimate norm of all, even of religious, values, and deifies them with an idolatrous worship, perverts and falsifies the order of things created and commanded by God. Such a one is far from true belief in God and a conception of life corresponding to true belief. . . .

"It is part of the trend of today to sever more and more not only morality, but also the foundation of law and jurisprudence, from true belief in God and from His revealed commandments. Here we have in mind particularly the so-called natural law, that is written by the finger of the Creator Himself in the tables of the hearts of men and which can be read on these tables by sound reason not darkened by sin and passion. Every positive law, from whatever lawgiver it may come, can be examined as to its moral implications, and consequently as to its moral authority to bind in conscience, in the light of the commandments of the natural law. The laws of man that are in direct contradiction to the natural law bear an initial defect, that no violent means, no outward display of power, can remedy. By this standard must we judge the principle: 'What is of utility to the people is right.' A right meaning may be given to this sentence if it is understood as expressing that what is morally illicit can never serve the true interests of the people. But even ancient paganism recognized that the sentence, to be perfectly accurate, should read: 'Never is anything useful, if it is not at the same time morally good. And not because it is useful is it morally good, but, because it is morally good, it is also useful.' (Cicero, *De Officiis*, III, 30.)

"Cut loose from this rule of morality, that principle would mean, in international life, a perpetual state of war between the different nations. In political life within the state, since it confuses considerations of utility with those of right, it disregards the basic fact that man as a person possesses God-given rights, which must be preserved from all attacks aimed at denying, suppressing, or neglecting them. To pay no heed to this truth is to overlook the fact that the true public good is finally determined by the nature of man with its harmonious coordination of personal rights and social obligations, as well as by the purpose of the community which in turn is conditioned by the same human nature. The community is willed by the Creator as the means to the full development of the individual and social attainments which the individual by a give-and-take process has to employ to his own good and that of others. Also those higher and more comprehensive values, that cannot be realized by the individual, but only by the community, in the final analysis are intended by the Creator for the sake of the individual for his natural and supernatural development and perfection."

# XVII.

## *Liberty's Aristocratic Roots*

WHERE IS LIBERTY?

For two centuries now this European society of ours has been seeking it; what it has found has been the widest, the most cumbersome, and the most burdensome state authority ever yet experienced by our civilization.

That being so, when we ask where liberty is, "they" refer us to the ballots in our hands; over the vast machine which keeps us in subjection we have this one right: we, the ten- or twenty- or thirty-millionth of the sovereign, lost in the vast crowd of our fellows, can on occasion take a hand in setting the machine in motion. And that, "they" tell us, *is* our liberty. We lose it whenever an individual will takes sole possession of the machine: that is autocracy. We regain it when the right of giving the machine a periodical mass-impulsion is restored to us: that is democracy.

This is all either misdealing or cheating. Liberty is something quite different. Its essence lies in our will not being subject to other human wills: in our will ruling alone over our actions, only being checked when it injures the basic, indispensable requirements of life in society.

Liberty is not our more or less illusory participation in the absolute sovereignty of the social whole over the parts; it is, rather, the direct, immediate, and concrete sovereignty of man over himself, the thing which allows and compels him to unfold his personality, gives him mastery over and responsibility for his destiny, and makes him accountable for his acts both to his neighbour, dowered with an equal right claiming his respect—this is where justice comes in—and to God, whose purposes he either fulfils or flouts.

It is not as an element in the happiness of the individual that the loftiest spirits have vaunted liberty, but rather because it consecrates the dignity of his personality and thus saves the human being from playing the merely instrumental role to which the wills of authority tend ever to reduce him.

Why is it that these lofty intentions have been completely lost sight of? That participation in government (absurdly called "political liberty" when it is in reality one of the *means* given to the individual of safeguarding his liberty against the unending onslaught of the sovereignty) has come to seem to him more precious than liberty itself? That this participation of his in Power has sufficed to induce him to raise up and encourage state encroachments, which have, thanks to the approval of the mob, been carried to much further lengths than absolute monarchy could ever have carried them?[1]

The phenomenon looks paradoxical but only until it is analysed.[2] It is easily accounted for when once a sufficiently clear idea has been formed of the thousand-year-old duel fought between sovereignty and liberty, between Power and the freeman.

## 1. Of Liberty

Liberty is not a recent invention; on the contrary, the idea of it forms part of our oldest intellectual heritage.

When we employ the terminology of liberty we rediscover naturally formulas which had been elaborated in a social past far distant, long before the appearance of absolute monarchy, which is, properly speaking, the first in time of the modern regimes and first set in motion the destruction of subjective rights to Power's advantage. For instance, when

1. [Cf. "And one sad servitude alike denotes The slave that labours and the slave that votes."—Peter Pindar.]

2. It was foreseen, notably by Benjamin Constant: "The abstract recognition of the sovereignty of the people makes no addition to the sum of individual liberty; and, if this sovereignty is given an extension, which it ought not to have, liberty may be lost in spite of *or even because of this principle*." B. Constant, "De la Souveraineté du peuple," in *Cours de politique constitutionnelle* (ed. Laboulaye. Paris: 1872) Vol. I, p. 8.

we say that no man may be imprisoned or dispossessed unless in virtue of the law of the land and the judgment of his peers, we are getting back to the language of the Magna Charta.[3] Or if we seek with Chatham to affirm the inviolability of the private dwelling-house, we are unconsciously bringing back to life the imprecation contained in the ancient law of Norway: "If the king violates a free man's dwelling, all will seek out the king to kill him." And again, when we claim the right to act as we will, subject to liability for the consequences of what we do (which is, for instance, the state of British law in regard to freedom of the press), we breathe the air of the very earliest Roman law.

We form an idea of liberty "instinctively," or so we think; but it is in reality a throwback of the collective memory to the day of the freeman. Unlike man in a state of nature, the freeman is not a philosopher's dream, but actually existed in those societies which Power had not invaded. It is from him that we derive our notion of individual rights. All we have forgotten is how they were hedged around and defended. We have become so inured to Power that we have now come to regard our liberties as held in grant from it. But viewed historically, the right to liberty was not an act of generosity on the part of Power: its birth was of another kind. And the chief clash with our modern ideas lies in this: that in the past this right was not of general extent, based on the hypothesis that there was in each man a dignity which Power had on principle to respect. It was the personal right of certain men, the fruit of a dignity to which they had enforced respect. Liberty was an achievement, which won the name of subjective right by self-assertion.

It is against this historical background that liberty must be viewed if we are to see its problem aright.

## 2. The Distant Origins of Liberty

Liberty is found among the most ancient groupings of the Indo-European peoples known to us.

It is a subjective right which belongs to those, and to those only, who

---

3. "Nullus liber homo capiatur vel imprisoneretur, dissessietur de libro tenemento suo nisi per legale judicium parium suorum vel per legem terrae."

At the same period in France, Matthew Paris wrote (1226): "Quod nullus de regno Francorum debuit ab aliquo jure sui spoliari, nisi per judicium parium suorum."

are capable of defending it: to the members, that is to say, of certain virile families which have, with a view to forming a society, entered into a sort of federation. Whoever belongs to one of these families is free, because he has "brothers" to defend him or avenge him. These can, if he has suffered injury or death, beleaguer in arms the dwelling-place of the murderer; they can also, when he is the accused, range themselves at his side.

In this powerful family solidarity all the most ancient forms of procedure find their explanation. As, for example, the manner of serving a writ, the record of which is preserved for us in the laws of Alfred:[4] acceptance of service was obtained by a mimic assault on the defendant's house—a clear indication of the fact that a suit was at first a recourse to arbitration held with a view to obviating a physical combat. It also explains why the suit took the form of a piling up of oath against oath, with that suitor winning the day who could bring up the larger reserves of "sworn men" to put their hands under his and swear in his behalf:[5] it was an obvious trial of strength, in which the more numerous and united family was bound to carry the day.

It was these powerful families, jealous of their independence but assiduous in matters of common import, that gave their tone to libertarian institutions. Unwilling at first to accept a leader at all except when circumstances made one necessary,[6] they ended in submission to a regular government, but always refused to admit that anything other than their express consent tied them to it. All the authority, strength, and resources at Power's command were those which were lent to it by assemblies of freemen. Life in cities disintegrated the clans progressively into families in the strict sense, but the chief still embodied the fierce spirit of independence which marked the beginnings of society. Witness the most

4. Cf. Glasson, *Histoire du droit et des institutions de l'Angleterre* (Paris: 1882) Vol. I, p. 240.

5. *Ibid.*, p. 251.

6. Cf. Mommsen: "The members of the community [in earliest times at Rome] came together to repel, by uniting their strength, the foreign oppressor, and they also helped each other in the event of fire; for purposes of this defence and this assistance they provided themselves with a leader."

Except in the aforementioned case of necessity, there was no sovereignty *intra muros*, and "the leader of the *domus* could at first count only on himself and his household and was his own court of law." Mommsen, *Le Droit pénal romain* (Fr. tr. by Duquesne. Paris: 1907) Vol. I.

ancient Roman law, which was built on the principle of the autonomy of the individual will.[7]

### 3. The System of Liberty

To us it is hardly credible that a society can remain alive in which each man is the judge and master of his own actions, and our first reaction is that the most hideous disorder must reign wherever there is no Power to dictate to men their behaviour. Patrician Rome is evidence to the contrary. It offers us the spectacle of a continuing gravity and seemliness which suffered no decline until after a lapse of centuries; and disorder set in at the very time that rules started to multiply.

Why is it that the autonomy of individual wills did not produce what seem to us its natural results? The answer lies in three words: responsibility, ritual, folkways.

The Roman was, it is true, free to do anything. But let him have answered imprudently the question "*Spondesne?*" and he was bound; that he misunderstood, that he was deceived or even coerced, helped him nothing: there was no coercing a man; *etiamsi coactus, attamen voluit.*[8] He was free, but, through carelessness, imprudence, or stupidity, he promised to pay a certain sum, and cannot: behold him now the slave of his creditor.

A world in which the consequences of mistakes were liable to be so heavy both required and formed virile natures. Men meditated long their actions, and, as though to induce reflection, their every action wore a ceremonial aspect. All might be done, the sale of a son or the substitution

---

7. Ancient law was based on the principle of the subjective will. According to this principle the individual is himself the foundation and the source of the law he owns; he is his own legislator. His decisions have, within the sphere of his authority, the same character that those of the people have in theirs. In either case there are *leges*: in the first *leges privatae*, in the other *leges publicae*; but in respect to the foundations of law there is complete identity between them. In all that concerns his house and his private interests, the head of the family possesses the same legislative and judicial authority as the people have in what concerns the generality of the citizens. *The idea which lies at the root of ancient private law is that of autonomy.*

"The *lex publica* limits the domain of private legislation only where the interest of all makes it imperatively necessary. These restrictions are of small importance, compared with those of the law of later times: centuries were needed to destroy the old conception and to dissipate the fear, which was its offspring, of restricting private liberty." Ihering, *L'Esprit du droit romain*, Fr. ed., Vol. II, p. 147.

8. *Ibid.*, pp. 296–97.

[*Spondesne?* (Do you promise?)

*Etiamsi coactus, attamen voluit.* (Even though compelled, yet he decided.)]

for him in the inheritance of a stranger in blood, but the necessary ritual had to observed. At the height of Republican Rome this ritual was strict in the extreme; and brought it home to men that their decisions and acts were grave and solemn things. It gave to their steps a measured and majestic gait.[9] Unquestionably nothing did more to give to the Senate its air of an assemblage of kings.

Finally we come to the essential factor in the ordering of society, to the folkways.

The early imprinting on the mind by a feared and venerated father of the cult of the ancestors,[10] a severe and uniform education,[11] the formation in common of adolescent training centres,[12] the early spectacle of behaviour

9. "The era of liberty in its fullest bloom saw also the reign of the sternest rigour in regard to form. Form lost its severity at the same time that liberty began insensibly to go under, and, when liberty crashed completely and for ever beneath the unflagging pressures of the regime of the Caesars, the forms and formulas of ancient law were buried beneath its ruins. It is a fact to rivet our attentions, thus to see form disappear just at the time that the sovereign's good pleasure seated itself on the throne, openly and undisguisedly proclaiming itself the supreme principle of public law. But more than this, the epoch of the Byzantine Emperors, the funeral oration which they pronounced over the death of form, their unconcealed dislike of and contempt for it, will bring home to us the connection which lies between liberty and form. Sworn enemy of the arbitrary, form is the twin sister of liberty. In effect, form is the bridle which checks the excesses of those whom liberty hurries into licence: it steers liberty, it controls and protects it. Fixed forms are the school of discipline and order and, therefore, of liberty; they are a bulwark against attack from without; they may break, but never bend. The people that places a real value on liberty knows instinctively the value of form; it realizes that it is no external yoke, but the palladium of its liberty." Ihering, *op. cit.*, Vol. III, pp. 157–58.

10. Instances observable today testify to the discipline exercised on a society by the cult of the ancestors: "Among the Fangs, the permanence and uniformity of the people's soul are assured by a patriarchal feeling which is the strongest in the whole of tropical Africa. Every man of this people, interesting on so many accounts, lives in the shadow of the ancestors; they impose on each of its tribes certain oral traditions which have been handed down for generations; they communicate to them a veneration and respect for illustrious actions, and a kind of discipline which is at the same time individual and social.

"The cult of the ancestors gives to each of this people's social groups a cohesion which, owing to the absence of any political organization, it would otherwise be without. Their high birth-rate, their steady conquest of their neighbours, their irresistible expansionism and their uncouth originality, would all show, if demonstration was not superfluous, the tremendous power of a common faith upon associations of human beings." Dr. A. Cureau, *Les Sociétés primitives de l'Afrique équatoriale* (Paris: 1912) pp. 337–38.

11. In an aristocratic society, education is the essential factor in the preservation of folkways. The English are not far wrong in stressing "the playing fields of Eton."

12. As, for instance, the Greek institution of the ephebi: "When they are eighteen years of age, the republic collars the young and gives them schoolmasters, with a view to training

commanding respect,[13] this and all else conditioned freemen to certain modes of behaviour. Should they fall short, whether through whim or weakness, there fell on them the force of public censure, which checked their careers and might even go so far as to deprive them of their status of freemen.

The reason why Plutarch makes such elevating reading is that his characters, from the best to the worst, play their parts one and all without commonness or meanness. It is not surprising that they have furnished tragedy with almost all its heroes, for, even while they were alive, they were in some sense already on the stage, trained to play certain characters and fixed in their parts by the exacting expectations of the spectators.

The climate of opinion when Republican Rome stood at its summit was that of a small, privileged society, free from all menial work and sordid preoccupation and nurtured on tales of heroic exploit; a betrayal of this standard, and its doors closed for ever against the offender. Let us remark in passing that it was because the political thinkers of the eighteenth century conceived of opinion after these classical models that they sought to entrust it with so large a part. They failed to notice that the object of their admiration was neither general nor natural, that it was the opinion of a class and a product of meticulous training.

## 4. Liberty as a System Based on Class

The system of liberty rested entirely in those days on the assumption that men would use their liberty *in a certain way*.

---

them to be generals or archons or counsellors; it subjects them all to a political novitiate. The college is not only a school of philosophy and rhetoric, a gymnasium or a religious association; it is more than anything else a place of instruction for citizenship; the types met there are as numerous as the duties of an Athenian are complex and varied. The Athenian is a soldier, he speaks and votes in the public assemblies, he makes and unmakes the laws; he must celebrate his country's cults strictly and exactly, for that is a duty laid on him by both politics and religion; having the status of freeman, he must possess the qualities which distinguish freemen from slaves; he must be read in the poets, whose works are a part of the sacred heritage bequeathed by the past, a storehouse of ancient traditions, and hymns of praise to the gods and to the mighty exploits of the ancestors; he must practise the arts which are the life and soul of Athenian culture, gymnastics and above all music, that he may realize the ideal man of Aristotle, when he delineated the citizen of a free city, descended like Helen from the immortals and born through the favour of the gods to breathe the loftiest air of thought and feeling. Such should the Athenian be, and such will be the ephebe." Albert Dumont, *Essai sur l'Éphébie attique* (Paris: 1876) Vol. I, p. 7.

13. It was with a view to impressing the minds of the young that the Roman senators brought their children to attend the sittings. Naturally the required effect would not have been produced if these had not differed widely from our parliamentary debates.

This assumption implied no estimate of the nature of man as such. Speculations of that kind made their appearance only when Greek civilization was in decline, and came to Rome as an importation from abroad.

Reliance was placed on the observable fact that men—men, that is to say, of a certain class—in virtue of acquired characteristics which could be maintained in vigour, behaved for all practical purposes in this particular way. With them, and for them, the system of liberty was workable.

It was a system based on class. There lies the gulf which separates the city of antiquity from the state of today, ancient thought from modern.

The word "freeman" does not sound to our ear as it did to those of the men of old. The emphasis is, for us, entirely on the "man." In it is the substance, and the adjective is a mere redundancy which only develops an idea already contained in the noun; whereas for the Romans the emphasis was on the "free," so much so that they telescoped the noun and the adjective into a single noun: *ingenuus*.[14]

The freeman is a man of a particular kind, and has, if we are to accept Aristotle, a particular sort of nature. It is to this nature that the privileges of liberty are linked. The moment a man belies it, they are lost to him— as, for instance, to the Roman who let himself be taken prisoner in war, or became a notorious evildoer, or, for the sake of security, placed himself in another man's power.

Freemen are, taken as a body, capable both of ruling others and of agreeing among themselves, and rest their pride simultaneously in the majesty of their own persons and in that of the city. Men of their breed, whether Spartiates or Romans, will never submit to slavery whether from within or from without. They put up a superb resistance to the aggressions of Power seeking expansion, while bringing to the discipline and defence of society a proud and assiduous succour.

They are the soul of the Republic, or rather they are the entire Republic. But what about the rest?

It is passing strange that our philosophers of the Revolutionary period should have formed their conception of a free society by reference to societies where everyone was not free—where, in fact, the vast majority were not free. It is no less strange that they never stopped to ask whether perhaps the characters which they so much admired were not made possible by the existence of a class which was not free. Rousseau, in

14. In the early Middle Ages the word signifying liberty was placed in front of the other: *Liber Homo*.

whose philosophy were many things, was fully conscious of this difficulty: "Must we say that liberty is possible only on a basis of slavery? Perhaps we must."[15]

## 5. The Free, the Unfree, the Half-Free

The system of liberty in the ancient world rested on a social differentiation which the modern spirit finds profoundly shocking. At Athens there were from fifteen to twenty thousand free citizens, as against four hundred thousand slaves. And the slavery was, even in the eyes of the philosophers, the condition of the freedom; a section of humanity had to be tools. "The usefulness of slaves diverges little from that of animals," said Aristotle; "bodily service for the necessities of life is forthcoming from both."[16] It is thanks to them alone that freemen had the leisure to raise themselves to the true condition of man, as it was defined by Cicero: "The name of man is generally bestowed but is in fact earned only by those who cultivate knowledge."[17]

But, even so, the position at Athens in the time of Aristotle and at Rome in the time of Cicero, in which a large class of freemen rested on a bed of slaves, marked a stage in a long trail of generalization of liberty.

It is far from the case that in the epoch in which liberty glittered most brilliantly all who were not slaves were free. Full liberty belonged only to some, but there were many who enjoyed what was called by Mommsen half-liberty.

Full civil and political rights were at first the portion only of the eupatrids or the patricians, members at one and the same time both of the founding families or clans and of the warrior bands in whose assemblage the strength of society consisted; the phratries and curias kept alive the memory of these bands.[18] The plebeians who lay outside these categories, or entered them only in the capacity of dependants, were not citizens and freemen in the true sense.

15. *Du Contrat social*, Book III, chap. xv.

16. Aristotle, *Politics*, Book I, chap. ii, para. 14.

17. Cicero, *De Republica*.

18. On the true nature of the curias, cf. especially Vasilii Sinaiski, *La Cité quiritaire* (Riga: 1923) and *La Cité populaire considérée au point de vue de la Cité quiritaire* (Riga: 1924).

"The curia," says Sinaiski, "was truly an association of courageous men who bore arms. It was a group of warriors, bound together by common sentiments." *La Cité quiritaire*, p. 17. A *quiris*, or freeman, is a member of one of these groups.

Naturally the mass of plebeians brought social pressure to bear on the privileged aristocracy, and this pressure had the effect of diffusing the system of liberty, though it also altered its characteristics.

To us, who are not satisfied with a liberty that is undiffused, this pressure, and its diverse forms and consequences—which are not, as we shall see, what was intended—are full of valuable lessons.

### 6. Incorporation and Differential Assimilation

Out of an extremely complex process (one on which historians have been too silent) it is only possible here to disengage the three main forms of emancipation, to which we shall give the names of "incorporation," "differential assimilation," and "counter-organization."

It is certain that in the earliest days of Roman history whole families were taken into the patriciate. The authorities tell us of several occasions on which this happened, as, for instance, at the annexation of Alba, when the great Alban clans were taken in on a footing of equality. Enlargements of the patriciate effected after this manner did no harm to the system, any more than did the frequent admissions of individuals by way of adoption. The effect was merely that people who had the habit of liberty received an accretion of like-minded people, or, in the case of individual admissions, of people who were considered to display in the highest degree the characteristics proper to a state of liberty. The admissions of individuals went on almost uninterruptedly and greatly reinvigorated the patriciate. The admission of whole families, on the other hand, soon came to an end.

The result was that, instead of virile plebeian families coming in to enlarge and fortify the patriciate, they remained part of the *plebs*, gave it its leaders, and conducted a long-drawn-out political warfare, in the course of which the right of plebeians to hold the various public offices was progressively recognized. Then these plebeian families, in the pride of offices held and administered, joined up with the patriciate to form a new governing class: the *nobilitas*, which presided over the destinies of Rome in the most glorious hours of her history.

In the course of its struggles with the patriciate the condition of the *plebs* changed, for it won for itself civil and political rights.[19] These were

19. "The *plebs* acquired citizenship bit by bit. First came the *jus familiae* and the *jus patrimonii*, then the right to bear arms, next the right to sit in justice, the right to vote and the right to marry, next the right to become magistrates and priests; these were the phases

not, properly speaking, the patrician rights, and this is why the expression "differential assimilation" has been used. For instance, the form of patrician marriage, the *confarreatio*, was bound up with rites which were purely patrician; other forms of marriage had, therefore, to be found. Again, the manner of making a will by means of a solemn declaration of testamentary intentions made before the *comitia curiata* was unsuited to the plebeian; so there was invented the disposition by way of a fictitious sale of the estate. All these forms of plebeian usage were, moreover, of greater practical convenience than the ancient forms, which were in the end to be abandoned even by the patricians themselves.

The spirit of the law underwent a change. So long as Roman society was powerfully organized in private groupings, each of them presided over by a man of strong will, whose will had been disciplined by beliefs and folkways, all the law that was necessary was to keep some sort of watch on the various crossroads at which collisions were possible.

But behaviour became less calculable when it was a case of a crowd of men whose wills had received less conditioning. Weaker characters, of men who had not previously enjoyed complete autonomy as regards law, could not be made subject to the cruel consequences of mistakes, which would be more frequent. It became necessary to temper and humanize the law. Public authority, in the form of the praetor, was brought in to protect individuals. Regulations multiplied under it.

Nor was that all. Primitive law could do without means of coercion. Judgment was an arbitral award accepted in advance. Maine noted the entire absence of sanctions in the earliest systems of law. Now, when it was in operation over a wider area, justice acted in a sovereign rather than in a mediatory capacity. She needed the wherewithal to execute her will.

Liberty, now cut to the habits of more people, lost something of its primitive stiffness and haughtiness. Yet it still reigned, though the phenomenon that was to destroy it was already forming.

### 7. The Advance of Caesarism

The acquisition of civil and political rights was a very big thing for the plebeian. It was a big enough one even for the strong characters and bold

of this evolution, which did not for the most part occur in virtue of a single act in a particular year." Mommsen, *Manuel des antiquités romaines* (Fr. ed. Paris: 1887) Vol. VI, first part, p. 74.

spirits who had made their own way and founded powerful families, thereby putting into the shade many enfeebled patricians and gathering about them in their turn a numerous retinue of dependants.

In law there was, it is true, no longer a *plebs*, but there was still one in fact. In the mistress of the world that was now Rome, inequality of conditions took a form far different from that taken in the days when even the proudest patricians were no more than swollen peasants. Prodigious fortunes were now amassed, to which the inviolability of individual rights gave the same protection as formerly it gave to the peasant's field.

The men of the people came thereby to set less store by their legal status of freemen than by their participation in the public authority. By means of the first, whether through their own fault or that of circumstances, they could not make progress adequate to their situation. The second was to be their instrument, and they were to make such use of it as would destroy liberty itself, their own along with that of the mighty who kept them down. The tribunate and the plebiscite would, between them, produce this result.

In the time when the plebeian had no rights, he had obtained, by means of the celebrated secession of the plebeians to the Aventine, the institution of inviolable tribunes, armed with complete powers for protecting him and with the right to halt for his behoof any activity of the government. This tribunician power had about it an arbitrary character which was necessary at first to make up for the plebeian's lack of rights: it should, logically, have disappeared as soon as equality of rights had been realized. Far from that, however, it continued in existence, backed by the Senate, which made clever use of it to check the designs of magistrates who were too independent, and to concentrate finally in its own hands all public authority.[20]

20. "The transformation by which the tribunician power, intended at first as a weapon against the hereditary nobility, was at a later date, when it had passed into the hands of the new 'magisterial' nobility, used by the Senate against the magistrates, and later still served the ends of the budding monarchy against the Senate, is matter for history rather than for public law. This strange institution, the fruit less of practical needs than of political tendencies, without positive function and intended only for negation, could according to circumstances serve the ends of every party in turn, and it did in fact serve for and against all of them in succession. It was one of the justified ironies of the spirit that rules the world that the tribunician power, in its deepest root a revolutionary power, should in the end have legitimated monarchy." *Ibid.*, Vol. III, p. 355.

The Senate permitted the tribunes to unite the *plebs* as a separate community within the city, and to arrange for it to pass by vote resolutions of its own, *plebi scita*, resolutions which acquired in the end the status of laws in the true sense.[21]

These laws were very different both in intent and content from those which had in former days been presented by the magistrates, the Senate consenting; the latter had been limited to the formulation of general principles. The tribunician plebiscites, products for the most part of the needs or passions of the passing hour, came often into conflict with the most fundamental principles of the law.

In this way there was introduced into Roman society the essentially erroneous notion that it is the business of legislative authority to prescribe or forbid anything whatever. Anyone who put forward a proposition of a nature seemingly advantageous for the immediate future was blindly applauded, even though his proposition subverted the entire permanent edifice of order. It was the tribunate which habituated the people to the idea of a saviour redressing at a stroke the social balance. Marius and Caesar were to be its heirs, and the emperors would find it an easy task to establish themselves on the ruins of the Republic and liberty.

And who were the men who would try to stay this process? Freemen of the old school. Brutus's dagger, so dear to the Jacobin heart, was wielded by an aristocratic hand.

## 8. The Conditions of Liberty

The death of the Roman Republic may be ascribed with equal truth either to the fault of the masses or to the failure of the great.

The system of civil and political liberty could be made to work so long as it was not extended beyond men whose folkways accorded with it.[22]

---

21. For these resolutions to acquire the force of laws, the consent of the Senate to them was at first necessary. But in the end its consent ceased to be necessary. Whatever the *plebs* voted was then law.

22. Rousseau stressed this in a passage which his more conventional expositors tend to pass over in silence. Addressing himself to the Poles, he wrote this: "I am conscious of the difficulties in the way of the plan to free your peoples. What I fear is not only misconception of their interests, amour propre and prejudice on the part of the masters. This obstacle surmounted, there are still to fear the vices and poltrooneries of the serfs. Liberty is a succulent food but takes a good digestion; only healthy stomachs can stand it.

"I am moved to laughter by those debased peoples who, lured into rebellion by strong drink, talk grandly of liberty without having the least idea of it, and, with their hearts full

But it ceased to be workable when once it had come to include strata of men for whom liberty was as nothing beside political authority, who expected nothing from the one and hoped everything of the other.

So far the responsibility for error is that of the masses. But that of the great is just as heavy. They had changed from the austere patricians of old into greedy capitalists, enriched by the pillage of whole provinces, by the illegal occupation of conquered territories, and by the squalid practice of usury. There were those who, like a certain Caecilius Clodius, had come to possess 3,600 pairs of oxen and 257,000 head of cattle. As absences on military service ruined the small proprietors, the capitalists acquired their land, and—an eloquent symbol, this!—ruined the once fertile soil by periodical changes of pasture for their vast herds of cattle, to such an extent that it was to be out of cultivation for nearly two thousand years.[23]

It thus appears how right Tiberius Gracchus was in seeking to limit the large and multiply the small estates, thus tightening the dangerously relaxed bonds of the social order.

In so doing he hit on a fundamental truth—on what may truly be called the secret of liberty. A libertarian regime—one, that is to say, *in which subjective rights are inviolable*—cannot be maintained if the majority of those members of society who take a part in politics are not concerned to keep them intact. How can they be made concerned? By all the citizens having interests—not, it is true, of the same extent, but at least of the same kind and not differing too widely in degree—interests which all are glad to see protected by the same rights.

In the heyday of the Republic the more fortunate citizens had been able without occasioning discontent to predominate at the elections, just as in war they were in the forefront of the battle. The reason was that their interests, though large, were not different in kind from the smaller ones of their neighbours.

---

to the brim with all the servile vices, imagine that to be free it is only necessary to be mutinous.

"High and sacred liberty! If these wretched people could know you, if they could realize the price that must be paid to win you and keep you, if they were conscious that laws are sterner taskmasters than tyrants, their feeble souls, enslaved by the passions which must be kept down, would fear you a hundred times more than slavery; they would flee you in terror as a burden too great to be borne."

23. Cf. Alb. Grenier, "La Transhumance des troupeaux en Italie," in *Mélanges d'archéologie et d'histoire* (1905) p. 30.

But this natural harmony could endure only so long as the material conditions of life stretched in an uninterrupted chain from highest to lowest, a chain in which the various links were not too far apart. It was utterly destroyed when there came to be at one end of the social ladder a disinherited mass, and at the other an insolent plutocracy. The subjective rights, regarded as legitimate when all that they included was the modest holding of a *quiris*, came to inspire hatred when immense fortunes, however acquired, however large, and however used, sheltered beneath them. Thereafter the social pressures were directed against just those individual rights which should have been dear to each single member of the body politic, but had in fact come to be regarded by most of them as a mere blind, as the jealously guarded abuse of a small minority. From that time the majority laboured for the destruction of those rights. And liberty foundered with them.

## 9. The Two Possible Directions of People's Parties

It would be an error, disastrous alike to intelligent historiography and to the formation of political science, to confound in one and the same bland admiration everyone who has "espoused the popular cause," without distinguishing the two ways of serving it and the two roads along which, in pursuit of this end, society can be brought.

The situation to be coped with is the same, whichever way is taken: it is the vast gulf set between the legal status and the economic status of the ordinary man.

Whereas at Rome, in the first period of growth, economic independence and personal autonomy in matters of everyday life had gone on broadening down at the same pace as the right to political liberty, or even at a faster pace, a second phase arrived in which this independence and this autonomy started contracting, while the right to liberty continued to be extended to those members of society who were as yet without it (instance the admission to citizenship by Marius of the *capite censi*).

In this way a position was reached in which a large crowd of individuals, weak and wretched in isolation, had at their collective disposal a great influence on public affairs. Naturally financial advances were made to this influence by the plutocratic factions. But in the end, as was certain to happen, it was caught by the popular leaders.

When that point had been reached, there were two courses open to the popular leaders. The first was that of Tiberius Gracchus. To him it seemed that the spirit of citizenship, the will to safeguard and defend common interests and sentiments, gets at once lost sight of both at the top and at the bottom when the capitalists have too much to defend and the proletarians not enough. Therefore he sought to re-establish as between citizens a real similitude, together with the solidarity which flows from it: to put an end to the existence side by side of a plutocracy and a proletariat, and to arrange matters so that each single citizen could enjoy effectively an independence and an autonomy such as would bind all together in defence of the system of liberty.

The second course, to which Gaius Gracchus allowed himself to be committed by the failure of his brother, was quite different. To him the monstrous individual strength of the grandees and the utter individual weakness of the ordinary man were accomplished facts on which there was no going back, and he set himself the task of installing a public authority as manager of the people's affairs on their behalf.

The contrast between the policies of the two brothers at once leaps to the eye; the aim of the elder was to restore every citizen to the status of owner, whereas the younger got a law passed which allotted to each citizen his ration of corn at a low price, soon to be given gratis.[24] This measure went in the diametrically opposite direction to the policy of Tiberius Gracchus. Tiberius had sought to multiply the numbers of independent proprietors; Gaius brought into Rome the last of them, lured there by free rations.[25]

The result was that, instead of the physical independence of society's members becoming generalized, the bulk of them became the dependants of the public authority.

---

24. Law of P. Clodius, 58 B.C.

25. [The reference here is to the *lex frumentaria* of 123 B.C. by which Gaius Gracchus fixed the price of corn at six and one-third *asses* to the *modius*. The view that this measure had the effect suggested in the text, though it has often been taken, is not accepted by the writer in the *Cambridge Ancient History* (vol. IX, chapters II and V), who maintains that, even though the law was repealed some four years later by reason of its cost, the price of six and one-third *asses* was probably not much below that at which the state might, with judicious buying, have hoped to sell without serious loss to itself. It is now, not surprisingly, impossible to determine with any sort of certainty what, on any hypothesis, was the economic price of corn at Rome in 123 B.C. The view taken in the text can, it is thought, claim this much at least of justification: even on the most favourable view of the *lex frumentaria* as such—even if there was no offence in it to the most "classical" of economists— it set a course which led, first to the proposal of Saturninus in 103 B.C. to fix the price of the *modius* at only five-ninths of an *as* (though neither the figure nor the date can be

To carry out its new duties, that authority had necessarily to build up a separate administrative corps. It was, in time, to turn into the Empire, which lost no time in creating permanent officials and praetorian guards.

In truth there is no republic except where Power does not take the form of a concrete entity with its own members, where the citizens may almost without distinction be called on to manage temporarily common interests commonly conceived, and where none has a motive to increase the burdens which all support.

On the other hand, Power comes into being (a state in the modern sense) as soon as the gulf between individual interests has become so deep that the weakness of the mass requires the permanent protection of an all-powerful care, which cannot but behave as master.

### 10. The Problem Is Still with Us

Shall I be reproached for having buried my head too deeply in ancient history? But I have buried it in very recent history, too.

I find a remarkable counterpart to the story of the two Gracchi in that of the two Roosevelts.

Theodore Roosevelt, considering that the physical independence of the majority of citizens was the essential condition of their attachment to libertarian institutions, applied himself to fighting a plutocracy which was transforming citizens into salaried dependants. He came to grief on the same blind egoism of the men of great place as caused the downfall of Tiberius Gracchus.

Franklin Roosevelt accepted the accomplished fact, took up the defence of the unemployed and the economically weak, and constructed, by means of their votes and to their immediate advantage, such a structure of Power as recalled in striking fashion the work of the first Roman emperors. The individual right—the shield of each, which had become the bulwark of a few—had to bow down before the social right. And the free citizen passed a milestone on his way to becoming a protected subject.

The phenomenon, when once its essence has been grasped, throws a flood of light on the political history of Europe. We may pass over the evolution of the Italian republics, which, in their progress from the

---

regarded as certain), and then to the free distribution by Clodius in 58 B.C. It can, in short, be fairly said that it was Gracchus who "fished the murex up."]

patriciate to the tyranny, exactly reproduce the course of events at Rome; for it is not by these, but rather by the monarchies, that the modern states have been created, receiving from them indelible characters.

An important class of freeman can be dimly discerned in the darkness of the Merovingians.[26] But troubled times cast them into a *de facto* dependence—to become *de jure*—on a powerful squirearchy. The kingdoms of the early Middle Ages may be conceived of as a species of vast and loosely knit republics in which citizenship was the perquisite of only a few notables.

But, as we have seen, the chances of preserving libertarian institutions are bound up with the proportion of the politically effective members of the society in question who desire benefit from them. We ought not, therefore, to feel surprise at the wide measure of support accorded to kings in their attempts to substitute their own authority for liberties which benefited only the few and were an oppression to the many.

Those historians who are impelled by an inner need to take sides are much embarrassed by this struggle between monarchy and aristocracy. How should they pay tribute to the authoritarian labours of kings, which rescued men from feudal servitude? Albert de Broglie had described this tendency:

> We have had already, and even from the highest quarters, theories of French history which were very consistent, very well pieced together, and in which the whole construction stood its ground to perfection. According to these system-builders, the two principles which have always taken charge of the development of France are also the fulfilment of all its prayers—Equality and Authority. The greatest measure of equality possible protected by the largest amount of authority imaginable, there is the ideal government for France. That is what the crown and the Third Estate were seeking in common all through our long convulsions. To suppress both the superior ranks which dominated the bourgeoisie, and at the same time the intermediate authorities which inconvenienced the throne, to reach by that road complete equality and unlimited power, that is the final and providential tendency of French history.
>
> A *royal democracy,* as it has been called, in other words a master but no

26. [The Merovingians were the first dynasty of Frankish kings in Gaul. It was founded by Merovech in A.D. 448; his grandson, Clovis, established its fortunes. The Carolingians succeeded in A.D. 752.]

superiors, equal subjects but no citizens, no privileges but no rights, such is
the constitution which suits us.[27]

Will historians, in their passion for libertarian and anti-absolutist
institutions, admire the resistance of aristocracy to the formation of
absolutism? Sismondi, for instance, states that in the Middle Ages "all the
real advances made in independence of character, in the safeguarding of
rights, and in the limitations forced by discussion on the caprices and
vices of absolute Power, were due to the hereditary aristocracy."[28]

Only the English political scene does not impale the historian on this
dilemma, and that by reason of certain historical peculiarities which have
been well set forth by de Lolme. There, in effect, the authority of the
crown was from the first sufficiently great and security sufficiently assured
to save the large class of freemen from shrivelling into a narrow caste.

Instead of the ambitions which had been thwarted and the activities
which had been exploited by the oppressive measure of liberty enjoyed
by the notables finding, as in France, a rallying-point beneath the royal
banner, the political strength of what may already be termed "the English
middle class" was mustered in the wake of the squires (regarded as large-
scale freemen) under the banner of liberty. The phenomenon is one of
decisive importance: for it has had the effect of forming, for and
throughout whole centuries, an English political outlook very different
from that prevailing on the continent of Europe.

## 11. Of the Historical Formation
## of National Characteristics

J. S. Mill, in a famous passage, threw into contrast the different political
tempers of the peoples of France and England:

> There are two states of the inclinations, intrinsically very different, but
> which have something in common, by virtue of which they often combine
> in the direction they give to the efforts of individuals and nations; one is the
> desire to exercise power over others; the other is disinclination to have power
> exercised over themselves. The difference between different portions of

27. Article in the *Revue des Deux Mondes*, January 15, 1854, cited by Proudhon in *De la
Justice dans la Révolution et dans l'Église*. [In stressing this tendency, de Broglie was animated
by the wish to fight the Bonapartism for which it had paved the way.]

28. Sismondi, *Études sur les constitutions des peuples libres* (Paris: 1836) pp. 315–16.

mankind in the relative strength of these two dispositions is one of the most important elements in their history.[29]

Barely troubling himself to camouflage the cap, Mill then fits it on the French, who sacrifice their liberty, he explains, to the most exiguous and illusory participation in Power.

There are nations in whom the passion for governing others is so much stronger than the desire of personal independence, that for the mere shadow of the one they are found ready to sacrifice the whole of the other. Each one of their number is willing, like the private soldier in an army, to abdicate his personal freedom of action into the hands of his general, provided the army is triumphant and victorious, and he is able to flatter himself that he is one of a conquering host, though the notion that he has himself any share in the domination exercised over the conquered is an illusion.

A government strictly limited in its powers and attributions, required to hold its hands from overmeddling, and to let most things go on without its assuming the part of guardian or director, is not to the taste of such a people; in their eyes the possessors of authority can hardly take too much upon themselves, provided the authority itself is open to general competition. An average individual among them prefers the chance, however distant or improbable, of wielding some share of power over his fellow-citizens, above the certainty, to himself and others, of having no unnecessary power exercised over them.

These are the elements of a people of place-hunters; in whom the course of politics is mainly determined by place-hunting; where equality alone is cared for, but not Liberty; where the contests of political parties are but struggles to decide whether the power of meddling in everything shall belong to one class or another, perhaps merely to one kind of public men or another; where the idea entertained of democracy is merely that of opening offices to the competition of all instead of a few; where, the more popular the institutions, the more innumerable are the places created, and the more monstrous the over-government exercised by all over each, and by the executive over all.[30]

The English people, on the other hand, according to Mill, "are very jealous of any attempt to exercise power over them, not sanctioned by long usage and by their own opinion of right, but they in general care very little for the exercise of power over others"; the English have little

---

29. J. S. Mill, *Representative Government* (London: 1861) p. 82.
30. *Ibid.*, pp. 82–83.

sympathy with the passion for government, but "no people are so fond of resisting authority when it oversteps certain prescribed limits."[31]

To the extent to which these two pictures seem to us to be true, how are we to explain such a contrast? By the characteristics acquired in the course of two quite different historical evolutions.

In their capacity as leaders of the middle classes, the English aristocrats, ever since Magna Charta, associated them in their own resistance to the encroachments of Power. From that ensued a general attachment to safeguards for the individual and to affirmation of a law which was independent of Power and, at need, opposable to it.

In France, on the other hand, it was around the monarchy that the middle classes rallied in their struggle against privileges. The victories of state legislation over custom were popular victories.

So it came about that the two countries entered on the democratic era with very diverse dispositions.

In one of them, the system of liberty, from being a right of persons of aristocratic origin, was to be progressively extended to all. Liberty would become a generalized privilege. For this reason it is misleading to speak of the democratization of England. It would be truer to say that the rights of the aristocracy have been extended to the *plebs*. The British citizen is as untouchable as a medieval noble.[32]

In France, on the other hand, the system of authority, the absolutist machine constructed by the Bourbon monarchy, was to fall into the hands of the people, taken in mass.

In England, democracy would take the form of the extension to all of an individual liberty which was provided with centuries-old safeguards; in France, that of the attribution to all of a sovereignty which was armed with a centuries-old omnipotence and saw in individuals nothing but subjects.

### 12. Why Democracy Extends Power's Rights and Weakens the Individual's Safeguards

When the people appears in the political arena in the leading part, it enters on what has been for centuries the battle-ground of monarchy and aristocracy. The former has forged the offensive weapons of authority, the latter has strengthened the defensive positions of liberty.

31. *Ibid.*, p. 84.

32. Even in our time, however, it has been perceived that, if all are entitled to the enjoyment of aristocratic liberty, all are not equally well-fitted to uphold the conditions

According as the people has, during its long minority, rested its hope in the monarchy or in the aristocracy and collaborated in the extension or in the limitation of Power, according as its admiration has traditionally gone out to kings who hang barons or to barons who turn back kings, it will have formed potent habits of mind and inveterate sentiments which will lead it on to continue either the absolutist work of the monarchy or the libertarian work of the aristocracy.

Thus, the English Revolution of 1689 invoked the name of Magna Charta, whereas in the French of 1789 praises of Richelieu rang loud; he was canonized as "man of the mountain and Jacobin."

But even in countries where popular authority is orientated by potent memories towards the safeguarding of individual rights, it will inevitably tack about to Power's side, and its breath will come, sooner or later, to puff the sails of sovereignty.

This tacking about takes place at the bidding of the same causes as we have already seen at work at Rome. So long as the people, consisting of freemen participating in the work of government, comprises none without some individual interests to defend, so that all feel an attachment to subjective rights, liberty seems to them precious and Power dangerous. But so soon as this "people with voting power" comprises a majority of persons who have, or think they have, nothing to defend, but are offended by great material inequalities, then it starts to set no value on anything but the power which its sovereignty gives it of overthrowing a defective social structure: it delivers itself over to the messianic promises of Power.

Louis Napoleon, Bismarck, and Disraeli perfectly understood this— great authoritarians all of them, who realized that, by enlarging the franchise at a time when property was becoming a closer preserve, they were, by calling in the people, paving the way for the distension of Power. It was the politics of Caesarism.

What folly it is to remit the judgment of events to posterity when contemporaries often see so much more clearly! Those of Napoleon III saw very well that he was not acting illogically in instituting universal

---

which are necessary to it. D. H. Lawrence has given forceful expression to the deep-seated but unavowed convictions which not so long ago were still held:

"Now Somers [a character in the book] was English by blood and education, and though he had no antecedents whatsoever, yet he felt himself to be one of the *responsible* members of Society, as contrasted with the innumerable *irresponsible* members. In old, cultured, ethical England this distinction is radical between the responsible members of Society and the irresponsible." D. H. Lawrence, *Kangaroo*.

suffrage while at the same time favouring the concentration of wealth and the accentuation of social inequality.[33]

Only three things matter to Caesarism. First, that those who are oldest in liberty within the society should lose their moral credit and become incapable of imparting to those who enter on the heritage of this liberty a pride of personal status embarrassing to Power. Tocqueville has remarked on the part played in this respect in France by the complete extirpation of the ancient nobility.[34] The second factor necessary to Caesarism is that a new class of capitalists should arise, without moral authority and possessed of an extreme of wealth which sets them apart from their fellow-citizens. Lastly, there is the third element, which is the union of political strength with social weakness in a large dependent class.

Though they heap treasure on treasure and think themselves thereby more powerful, the "aristocrats" of the capitalistic creation, by awakening the resentment of society, disqualify themselves for ever from being its leaders against the inroads of Power. Whereas the infirmities of the multitude find a natural haven in the omnipotent state.

In this way is removed the only obstacle that Caesarism has to fear—a movement of libertarian resistance, emanating from a people with subjective rights to defend and under the natural leadership of eminent men whom their credit qualifies and whom the insolence of wealth does not disqualify.

33. In 1869 it was already possible to write as follows: "Banks, credit societies, steamship lines, railways, big factories, large-scale metallurgical industry, gas, all undertakings, in short, of any importance, are concentrated in the hands of 183 persons.

"These 183 persons dispose as they please of the accumulations of capital which they control, amounting to more than twenty milliards of issued shares and bonds, the best part, in other words, of the public wealth; and above all they dispose of all the great industrial machines on which the rest of productive industry, for all its alleged freedom, has to depend."

As we see, the phenomenon is older than is usually supposed. The author from whom we quote considers that its development has proceeded at a greatly increased pace since the revolution of 1848. Cf. G. Duchêne, *L'Empire industriel. Histoire critique des concessions financières et industrielles du Second Empire* (Paris: 1869).

34. "The uprooting of the nobility deprived the nation of a necessary portion of its substance and inflicted a wound on liberty which will never heal. A class which has for centuries marched in the front rank acquires, during its long and uncontested primacy, dignity, pride of heart, natural confidence in its strength and a habit of being looked up to which makes it the most stubborn element in the body of society. Not only are its own dispositions virile; its example increases the virility of other classes. Its extirpation has enervated even its enemies. Nothing can replace it completely; it can never be reborn; it may recover its patents and bonds, but not the soul of its fathers." Tocqueville, *L'Ancien Régime et la Révolution*, p. 165.

# XVIII.

# Liberty or Security

THE HISTORY OF WESTERN SOCIETY was interpreted in the nineteenth century as an uninterrupted progress of the peoples towards liberty. Two periods were discerned.

In the first, men, who had till then been closely bound in chains of dependence on and exploitation by particular masters, were seen being progressively extricated by means of the struggle in progress between these masters and political authority.

In the second, being now more or less freed from their masters, they were in the enjoyment of a measure of civil liberty, but under the rule of a state which lived far above the heads of every social authority. All that still remained to do was to transform this supreme master of society into its servant. That was the task of democracy which, once realized, brought in its train political liberty; by this was meant the giving of obedience not, as previously, to masters, but to stewards whom the rules had, for the furtherance of the common good, themselves appointed.

This process of liberation in the material sphere was accompanied by a similar process in the spiritual. Instead of being subjected, as in the past, to the categorical imperatives of creed and conduct, men rid themselves of these superstitions and took to sitting in their own judgment seat as to what they should believe and in what manner they should act.

Such were the convictions of the nineteenth century, which were, it is true, slow to penetrate certain spirits.

But today it is a very different evolutionary process which the contempo-

375

rary observer finds to record. Power, which had been refashioned for the service of society, is in reality its master. It is the less contested for claiming itself to be society's offspring. It is the more irresistible for meeting with no authority outside itself with the strength to limit it. The dethronement of the old faith, to which the state itself was subject, left an aching void in the room of beliefs and principles, a void which enabled Power to enunciate and impose its own. The appeal to the state against the exploiters of human labour ended in the substitution of it for them. The result is our present tendency towards the concentration in the same hand of a unified political command and a unified economic command, towards, in other words, an absolute *imperium* such as was never imagined by our forefathers, to find the like of which we must turn to other civilizations, such as the Ancient Egyptians.

At the summit of our society are regents who, that action may be harmonized, have an eye to the harmonization of thought. At the base is a mob which is, taken all in all, obedient, credulous, and laborious, which dutifully receives from the sovereign its orders, its faith, and its daily bread, and which lives more or less in a state of servitude to a master who is immeasurably distant and impersonal.

The proposition that this state of public servitude is the inevitable culminating point of the historical sequence formed by the successive stages of a civilization, can be supported with many more proofs than are available to demonstrate the interpretation of a progress towards liberty. But it would be exceeding our knowledge to assume that the sequence has a culminating point. As to that we know nothing, and we are acquainted with too few civilizations in the successive stages of their development to justify us in making their histories the norm of our own.

We do no more than record that every society which has evolved in the direction of a state of individual liberty turns aside from that liberty suddenly and abruptly just when it seems on the point of attaining it. And what interests us are the reasons for this phenomenon.

## 1. The Price of Liberty

It is a mysterious excellence of language that it expresses more truths than are clearly conceived of by the speaker. We say, for instance: "Liberty is the most precious of all goods," without noticing everything that this formula implies in the way of social assumptions.

A good thing which is of great price is not one of the primary necessities. Water costs nothing at all, and bread very little. What costs much is something like a Rembrandt, which, though its price is above rubies, is wanted by very few people, and by none who have not, as it happens, a sufficiency of bread and water.

Precious things, therefore, are really desired by but few human beings and not even by them until their primary needs have been amply provided. It is from this point of view that liberty needs to be looked at. A fable will, perhaps, render her more intelligible to us.

A man is wandering in the jungle, relying for his food on the uncertainties of the chase, in constant danger from wild beasts of all kinds. A caravan comes by him; he runs to it and is glad to find rest in the security of numbers and an abundance of provisions. He becomes the most docile of all the chief's servants, and arrives under his aegis at the city. At first he enjoys the wonders of the city, but, getting quickly acclimatized to his security, it comes over him that he is now a slave, and he seeks his freedom. In the end he becomes free. But just at that moment the city is overwhelmed by nomad tribes who pillage, burn, and massacre. Our man flees into the countryside and takes refuge in a fortress in which a baron shelters beasts and men: he pledges to this protector all his productive energies, the consideration being the life which has been saved to him.

But a strong Power brings back order to life, and our man is soon heard complaining of the baronial fatigues; these he transforms into a tribute of money which he contrives to make progressively smaller until in the end he sets up as an independent proprietor. Or again he sets off for the town, where he seeks to hire out the labour of his hands as it pleases him, or to find an opening in some industry which fits his capacity. Then there is a sudden economic crisis. The farmer and the industrialist can no longer sell at the anticipated price. The worker is thrown on to the street. Once more our man looks for some master with whom he is safe for a regular pittance, either by having a stated quantity of what he produces taken at an assured price or by having guaranteed him stable employment and a stable wage.

In this way we see how, in the case of the hero of our allegory, the will to be free is in time of danger extinguished and revives again when once the need of security has received satisfaction.

Liberty is in fact only a secondary need; the primary need is security.

The idea of security merits, therefore, some examination: examination at once reveals its complex nature. For which reason its opposite, insecurity, is more manageable. This we will define as the carking anxiety of being threatened with a disastrous occurrence. Insecurity, as is at once apparent, is a function of three variables. To start with, what is a disastrous occurrence? For one man a mere loss of money answers the description, whereas another will not so regard death itself. It follows that, as greatness of soul is more or less present, the number of disastrous occurrences is more or less extensive. Take the case of an individual for whom any one of a given number of occurrences is disastrous. The chances of one or another of these occurrences happening are greater or smaller according to the age in which he lives and his own condition. The chances of violent death are different in the nineteenth century from what they were in the time of the barbarian invasions. But men do not submit these risks to the process of mathematical calculation. A sanguine man underestimates them, a nervous man exaggerates them.

The feeling of insecurity may, then, be represented as a function which carries different intensities for each member of any given community at any given time, according to the number of things feared by each, the mathematical probability of one or another of them happening, and the propensity of each to exaggerate or underestimate this probability. The greater this feeling of insecurity and the stronger the individual man's desire for protection, the higher also is the price which he will pay for this protection.

The feeling of security is, as we said above, the opposite of this feeling which is, in principle, of measurable intensity. In that case security too is of measurable intensity, and the more strongly it is felt the stronger also will be the will to liberty.

## 2. Ruunt in Servitutem

The conclusion is that there never was a time in any society whatsoever when some individuals did not feel themselves to be insufficiently protected, and others did not feel themselves to be insufficiently free. The former I will call "securitarians" and the latter "libertarians."

This line of reasoning, as is at once apparent, forces on us a correction of our earlier hypotheses concerning the relations between Powers and the social authorities. The social key positions may in time lapse into the hands of securitarians, who will not rest until they have exchanged the independence which might have been theirs for a guarantee from the state. We shall consider the consequences of this phenomenon later.

It is also apparent that, taking one country with another and assuming that the risks are equal, the spirit of liberty will be more prevalent where the spirit of men is prouder, or even where their temperaments are merely cast in a more sanguine mould.

If, then, character is debased by an effeminate education, or if life takes new forms which generate anxiety without the real risks being increased, the proportion of securitarians will go up.

If, again, the real likelihood of terrible occurrences is suddenly intensified, almost the whole of a society may go securitarian.

It is for this reason that the freemen of the eighth to the tenth centuries rated their liberty cheaply. Seeking a strong right arm to protect them against the fury of the Saracen or the Norman or the Magyar, they made haste to raise up with their own hands the citadel which was to be for centuries their descendants' prison. Bold and few were to be those who would, later, venture themselves outside their lord's domain, those whose adventurous peddling was to found the fortunes and the dynasties of the merchant patriciate. It was to require the increasing warmth of the king's peace to melt off from the iceberg of feudal servitude its most capable and energetic elements; these became the bourgeoisie of the towns while the rest lingered on in feudal bonds.

The history of the intelligentsia shows how surely infeudation follows in the wake of insecurity.

The murder of Archimedes at the siege of Syracuse symbolizes the intellectual's fate in ages of violence. Let an ancient society be invaded by barbarians or let passion arouse in it the barbarism that slumbers there, and the first victims are sure to be the intellectuals.

What is the intellectual to do next? At the time of the downfall of the Roman Empire he took precipitate refuge in the Church. That for him was the safe life and it was also, thanks to the munificence of the new masters, to be a life of rapidly growing opulence. For more than five hundred years every intellectual was in religious orders. Not, we may be sure, that every intellectual was a believer, but because an intellectual and social discipline was the price paid for security.

As physical security came to seem better assured, some few ventured to step outside this tutelary watch and ward. But the great majority of the intellectuals remained within the family of the Church, from which they drew a pittance, small but certain. For instance, even as late as the eighteenth century, men like Condillac and Sieyès were abbés.

### 3. Of the Architecture of Society

He who has grasped the conception of the libertarian and securitarian sentiments being measurable quantities of opposites can envisage any society whatsoever, at any given moment of its existence, as a multitude of specks, each corresponding to an individual, which can be arranged in tiers by reference to their libertarian content. The most securitarian among them will, as I see it, be quite at the bottom and the most libertarian right at the top; and the rest will be spread out according to the ratio between their aspirations to liberty and their need for security. We may conceive this image as bearing the general appearance of a pyramid or a spindle. Whichever we take, there will in either case be an arrangement of horizontal tiers, acting as lines of demarcation, in each of which is found a particular group of individuals, categorized by reference to temperament. These categories we may call alpha, beta, gamma, and so on, starting from the top.

But still using the simile of specks to represent the members of society, we can also distribute these specks by reference to another principle, namely their position in society. Social position is something which does not admit of logical definition but which we know by feeling it. Leaving aside for the moment, as being unnecessary to our purpose, any attempt to give precision to the idea of social position, we will, trusting to impression alone, present yet another image, that of the arrangement of society in tiers by reference to stations in life. Here too are lines of demarcation, separating off what are commonly called "classes." Let us call them A, B, C, and so on.

If we now bring these two images together, what is the conclusion which their confrontation suggests to us? Will there be a correlation of classes and categories, so that A corresponds to alpha, B to beta, and so on?

There certainly will not be an absolute correlation. All the A's will not, through pride of rank, be seen disdaining every form of protection. Nor will all the Z's find their impotence so alarming as to have no other concern but that of getting themselves assistance. In each class and for each society there will be a certain degree of correlation.[1]

One thing is certain: that the correlation will be at its maximum either in a society which is in process of formation or in one which has just undergone a complete overthrow. It is in such times as those that audacity takes wing. By accepting all risks and seizing all initiatives, the bold become the rulers. Whereas, on the contrary, the timid run to cover and support; so that the degree of their subjection will give the almost exact measure of their fears.

There are in a society of this kind great inequalities; but there is in it, notwithstanding, a social equilibrium for the reason that liberties enjoyed are in proportion to risks taken.

This equilibrium, however, is soon, inevitably, disturbed. The nature of men is such that they organize into subjective rights the positions which they have won for themselves; they monopolize them and pass them on to their descendants. No doubt it is true that the force of example, education, and perhaps heredity, of which we have still so much to learn, tend to preserve in each class the characteristics proper to each. But the process is an incomplete one: men of libertarian temperament make their appearance in the depths, and the men on the top show more and more marked securitarian trends. The result is that the arrangement in tiers by reference to stations in life ceases to correspond with that by reference to temperament: the degree of correlation is lowered and the social equilibrium is destroyed. If society was so fluid a thing that some went up and others down without impediment, the equilibrium could be maintained. But in fact, as has been said above, a powerful instinct for acquisition and conservation is at work, which tends to stabilize the status quo and render the barriers impassable.

The various turns which events may take are all easily imagined. Sometimes it happens that, as at Sparta, the upper classes long succeed in continuing to produce virile types of men, by means of a severe training and a rigorous exclusiveness. Sometimes it happens that, without disturbance to the existing arrangements of tiers, they throw open their ranks to fresh infusions of energy; that happened at a certain period of

1. The degree of correlation may be defined as the proportion of individuals in Class A who are also in category alpha, the proportion in Class B who are also in category beta, etc.

Roman history, and at a certain period of English history, but the most striking instance of it is seen in the Middle Ages, up to about the time of St. Louis. Then the baron who led to the wars the most valiant of his men-at-arms would often knight the serf who had displayed outstanding courage, and the origin of the true feudal nobility was no other than that. At a later date, with the development of economic activities, wealth became the road to nobility. Let a man buy a noble fief and himself fulfil its military obligations, and he had only to show that he had "lived a noble's life" for three generations to place beyond dispute his status as noble.

Power may also be the upward path to social distinction. But of all the means of replenishing the upper strata this is the least adapted to reviving their libertarian virtues.

### 4. Power and Social Promotion

In the image in which we represented the architecture of society, the body of officialdom found no place. There was reason for this. For in a nascent society, or in one which is making an entirely fresh start, there is not and cannot be a political authority as distinct from the social authority. In them political authority can be the product only of the willing assent of men who have risen spontaneously to positions of command. A Power which looked elsewhere for support would be nerveless, and it receives their support only at the price of gaining their assent to its decisions.

But this coalescence of political Power with the social authorities does not endure for ever. The reasons for its disappearance are various, but chief among them is the coming of a "head chief" whose policy it is to reduce his peers to a subordinate position—in other words, a king. As we have seen, his next step is to court an alliance with the inferior classes; but what is emphasized here is that it is to the more vigorous elements of those classes that he goes for support, to those whose station in life is out of relation to their energies. The more difficult the process of transition from one class to another is made, the greater is the commotion among these elements to find an outlet; the king provides them with the outlet which they need by enrolling them in his service, and the body of the state draws fresh life from their young strength. This is the first phenomenon to mark: the encroachment of political Power on the aristocratic authorities. A second, already described by us, accompanies it: with a view to breaking down the resistance of the aristocracy, Power strives to loosen the hold of the notables on their dependants. This results in a change of status for the dependants. To be at the mercy of a single master is a wretched condition. But when there are two masters, squire and state, battling for their allegiance, the intervention of Power creates for them a sort of liberty. Not, it is true, the liberty which comes from a man's own assertion of his own rights, but a poorer quality of liberty, liberty by another's intervention, than which the securitarian temper can know no other.

The third phenomenon to mark is the progressive invasion of the high social strata by elements from below; they ascend by the official ladder and then, grown rich in the service, break away from it.

It is far from being the case that these new aristocrats show all the characteristics of the old, or even of those who have climbed the rungs of society's ladder by their own unaided efforts. It is one thing to rise at the riser's own risks, another to owe promotion to a master's favour. A pirate like Drake, enriched by his voyages, the importance of which his ennoblement, if nothing else, attests, owes everything to himself and makes a very different sort of aristocrat from a public administrator grown great in public offices often by qualities of flexibility rather than of energy.

No absolute rule can be laid down, and there have been public functionaries who have displayed the most virile qualities. But often also, as was seen in the late Roman Empire, the functionary is only a freedman who has never shaken off the characteristics of a slave. Recruited from these freedmen, the ruling class of the late Empire became tame and spiritless.

Towards the end of the *ancien régime* the French aristocracy, too, felt the effect of the ways in which most of its members had obtained their elevation, as may be seen in the astonishing picture of Pontchartrain given us by Saint-Simon.[2]

## 5. *The Middle Class and Liberty*

The tone of an aristocracy gets transformed by the process of internal decay, along with its restocking by elements with little in them of the libertarian spirit: securitarian elements come to predominate in it.

2. [Pontchartrain, Jérome, Comte de, 1674–1747. Secretary of State, 1699–1715. His administration of his office was deplorable and Saint-Simon's memoirs are studded with unflattering references to him. He obtained his elevation through the influence of his father, who was Chancellor.]

It is the most pitiable spectacle to be found in social history. Instead of maintaining their position by their own energy and prestige, as men who are always ready to take the initiatives, responsibilities, and risks which are too formidable for the other members of society, the privileged, whose role it is to protect others, aim at being protected. Who alone is placed high enough to protect them? The state. They ask it to defend for them the positions which they are no longer capable of defending for themselves and are therefore unfit to occupy.

When the French nobility, recruited as it then was by the purchase of public offices, was no longer capable of excellence in war, then was the time that it got reserved to it by law the officers' berths. When to the merchants who, like Sindbad, embarked in a voyage their entire capital there had succeeded a prudent generation of traders, the latter sought to have the king's navy secure to their travellers exclusive rights to some distant coast—from which their ancestors would have kept all intruders away themselves by their own artillery.

How can men whose authority rests on Power's guarantee oppose to it the proud independence which honourably distinguished the ancient aristocracy? Lacking now all strength of their own, they no longer uphold Power; no longer upholding Power, they have become incapable of limiting it. The notions of aristocracy and liberty have parted company.

The heirs of their libertarian aspirations are the middle class. We will define the middle class, if we must, as composed of those who have enough social strength to stand in no need of any special protection and to desire the largest measure of liberty, but have on the other hand not enough strength to make their liberties oppressive to others.

A class of this kind can only develop when general security has reached a certain level. For in a time of general insecurity the elements of society must combine into sufficiently large aggregates for safety, and the result is squirearchy. It is only at a later date, when the public Power is sufficiently in the saddle, that less force is needed to maintain an independent existence; when that has happened the hour of the middle class has sounded. It then becomes, as Aristotle stressed, the most important element in the body of society. If it is a case of disciplining an aristocracy which is making disorderly use of its strength, it is the natural ally of Power. Whenever the state tries to stifle liberty, it is the natural ally of the aristocracy.

Its specific interests make it the champion of a republic in which the order necessary for the maintenance of security is made compatible with the tolerance necessary for the practice of liberty. It is, as a class, so attuned to a regime of moderation that, wherever it flourishes, such a regime comes into being, and, whenever it disappears, such a regime sinks without trace. It is a well-known historical fact that when at Rome this class of the population had been decimated and proletarianized by a succession of wars, the Republic broke down.

It is a no less safe generalization that its shipwreck is the proximate cause of modern despotisms. Tyrannies made their appearance in step with the inflation which destroyed the independence and security of middle-class liberalism.

## 6. One Level of Liberty or Several Levels

We can take things a step further. The position of this class is, as we have said, sufficiently secure for it to have no other wish than liberty.

Suppose that Power has come into its hands. It then has a choice of one of two courses. Either it retains this liberty for itself without generalizing it, while contriving for the lower strata all the security which they need, and permitting and even facilitating migration from the securitarian zone to the libertarian. Or else it extends this liberty to everyone. In the eighteenth and nineteenth centuries it followed, as we have seen, the second of these two policies.

But there was a fatal corollary. By sharing with all the degree of liberty which was suited to itself, it withdrew from the classes below it the means of protection which it did not need itself. In this the logical connexion is clear enough, but misconception on the subject seems to be so widespread that we must pause a moment to clear it up.

An example will assist. One of the most important aspects of liberty is liberty to contract. It is consistent with the dignity of a freeman that he should be able to engage and bind himself by his own voluntary act. That was the view of the Romans, who used the same word, *leges,* to denote laws which were binding on everyone and contracts which were binding on parties. The same idea turns up again in the French civil code: contract is the law of the parties. It has been a fixed tenet of jurists, arguing irrefutably from these premises, that the worker was bound by his contract of service, and that a strike was a unilateral breach of this contract, which gave the employer the right to sue for damages. In our own time even the illustrious Duguit has refurbished in peremptory style this line of reasoning. But the consequences of this logic proved unacceptable, as working out too hardly for the employee—just as it also worked out too hardly to place on him the economic burden of every injury caused him at his work which did not result from the fault of his employer: and yet that is the way in which things should have gone since what was in question were the relations between two freemen, each of whom should take the consequences of his own clumsiness or mischance.

A whole code of social legislation has stepped in to protect the worker and confer on him privileges. Nor were the superior classes, who had to support the burden of it, in good case to be heard in protest against it. For in this way there was established, bit by bit, the securitarian body of law, which will always be necessary for most men. But at the same time the obverse side of this securitarian policy seems to have been imperfectly discerned: in effect, it imports a discrimination between men all of whom enjoy the nominal status of "free," and denies to the multitude the risks, the responsibilities, and, as a natural consequence, the preferments of liberty.

## 7. A Securitarian Aristocracy

This retreat from the obligations of liberty was the less remarked because at the other end of the social ladder the same phenomenon was happening, though here it was without the excuse of necessity.

If it is the function of an aristocracy which disposes of large resources and enjoys a large measure of liberty to prevent abuses and disorder by means of a strict self-discipline, then no aristocracy ever failed in its duty more completely than that which was raised in the soil of the employing class. If an aristocracy is false to its duty when it takes to shuffling out of responsibilities and risks, and making its sole aim the security of its possessions and position, then no other aristocracy ever made greater haste to leave its post than the capitalist.

How has it in fact functioned? Whereas in the early decades of the nineteenth century there were to be found a large number of proprietors each of whom bore the risks involved in his particular undertaking, by the end of the century there was a much smaller class which, with the aid of the limited liability company and the money market, controlled gigantic enterprises and regulated all economic activities. An aristocracy indeed! But without the honour that belongs to aristocracy and directs its actions in well-ordered channels; one which was careful to divorce from the command, which it exercised, the responsibility, which it rejected, and the risks, which it palmed off on to the shareholders.

It can scarcely be denied that this small capitalist aristocracy has dealt more generously with its employees than did the large proprietary class which preceded it. For all that, it is not surprising that it has aroused more anger and hatred. For men put up with any masters who show themselves brave and self-disciplined. The Roman legionaries did not grumble when the consul, who had given them throughout one example of endurance after the other, took the lion's share of the spoils for himself. But when intrigues at home enabled clever men to appropriate the greater part of the *ager romanus,* that was taken badly.

Similarly, the bourgeois who was seen by all to be devoting all his time and his entire fortune to a business which bore his name and to which his honour was pledged, won men's respect. But under the reign of anonymity the case was different.

Every method of shaking off risks came alike to the new aristocracy. And more and more, following the usual securitarian procedure, it came to monopolize the positions which it had won and to shore them up with the authority of the state. The breaking of the storm is the signal for big business to panic. In the name of the general interest it supplicates Power to support and save it.

## 8. Disappearance of the Libertarian Element

At the time of the twenty-year crisis between the two wars, the proletarians were in a fair way to assure themselves of a miserable sort of security, the outward expression of which was unemployment benefit. The aristocrats had found in the backing of the state another and more gilded kind. Between them lay a middle class, which had been already, according to the country to which it belonged, half or wholly proletarianized by inflation. It too had been struck by the great wave of insecurity. The upheaval was on a scale that gave the lie to the wisdom of a thousand years.

It had been held an assured truth that a man of character and capacity never lacked work. And yet highly qualified engineers, like the lowest grades of unskilled labour, were given to understand that their services were not wanted. The disgrace of unemployment quickly gave birth to the idea that to obtain work was a matter of luck or nepotism.

Another adage which generations had consecrated was that to produce more was to improve the producer's standard of life. The vine-grower, the fisherman, and many others besides were now to be taught the lesson that increases in production may reduce profit and reductions in production may increase it.

Lastly, it had been taken as proved that abstemiousness in the present would assure to a man a better future for himself and his family. A fresh wave of devaluations now completed the lesson of the war and made a mockery of individual forethought; contrary to all right and reason, the debtor waxed fat on the loans granted him, loans which impoverished the creditor.

A whole science of living, which, simple though it was, had till then sufficed, went by the board. It was as though a crowd of fishermen, each in control of his own boat, had had all their plans upset by the sudden unaccountable behaviour of the tides, the wind, and the fish. What was to happen next? This is what happened. Note was taken of the existence of certain sheltered occupations. The official was seen to be in a comfortable niche and to be safe for his pension. The great public utility undertakings, in their monopolistic positions, were seen to be maintaining and even improving on their normal profits. It was, then, to these sheltered sectors that the crowd inevitably gravitated in its bewilderment. And as there was not room in them for everybody, the natural desire of all men was to include their own sectors of activity among the sheltered.

### 9. *The* Pactum Subjectionis

The essential psychological characteristic of our age is the predominance of fear over self-confidence. The worker is afraid of unemployment and of having nothing saved for old age. His demand is for what is nowadays called "social security."

But the banker is just as timorous; fearing for his investments, he places the capital monies at his disposal in government issues, and is content to credit effortlessly the difference between the interest earned by these securities and the interest which he pays out to his depositors. Everyone of every class tries to rest his individual existence on the bosom of the state and tends to regard the state as the universal provider. And President Franklin Roosevelt came out as the perfect psychologist when he laid down as "the new rights of men" the right of the worker to be regularly employed at a regular salary, the right of the producer to sell stable quantities of goods at a stable price, and so on. Such are, in substance, the securitarian aspirations of our time.

The new rights of man are given out as coming to complete those already proclaimed in the eighteenth century. But the least reflection is sufficient to show that in fact they contradict and abrogate them. The old ones, in decreeing liberty, made each man the sole master of his own actions; the state could not guarantee their consequences, which had to be borne by the individual alone. Whereas, on the other hand, if the state is to guarantee to a man what the consequences of his actions shall be, it must take control of his activities. In the first case, a man is thought of as an adult, he is freed from tutelage and left to face the risks of life himself. Whereas, in the second, the purpose is to keep him out of the way of risks; he is treated as an incapable and put in leading-strings. The conclusion is, then, that the promises of today in fact close the cycle which was opened by the declarations of earlier days. The liberty then given is taken back in exchange for a security which is desired by all.

The mind of man needs, like his heart, objects of affection; they land him in the same evasions. All that he wants to see in any given phenomenon are those aspects of it which flatter and exalt him, not those which offend and mortify him. He dissociates what life has made inseparables, praises the cause and condemns the consequence, applauds the end and repudiates the means, affirms an idea and denies its corollary. Thus the Rights of Man fill us with exaltation; but the bourgeois ferocity of society in the days of Louis Philippe, its indifference to the unemployed man and its cruelty to the bankrupt offend our sensibilities. So we refuse to see in all this merely two closely linked aspects of the same spirit.

The spirit was that of a class which, seeking a full outlet to its energies, sought to throw down all barriers to its activity, like the giant seen on the frontispiece of a well-known pamphlet[3] with this epigraph: "Take his chains off him and let him go." Its aim was the removal of all obstacles from the social arena, without pausing to consider that these had been necessary as hand-rails and useful as supports. It decreed that a man should be the sole ruler of his conduct and the sole author of his fate. But, once this course had been set, the rule of life could only be that which Carlyle formulated in anger:[4] "Every man for himself and let the devil take the hindmost."

3. Dupont de Nemours, *Réponse aux observations de la Chambre de commerce de Normandie.*
4. Cf. the immortal pages of *Past and Present* (1843).

The plenitude of liberty carried with it the plenitude of risks. There could henceforward be as little succour for the weak as there could be restriction on the strong. It was the survival of the fittest, an idea which, as is known, was not suggested to Darwin by the spectacle of nature, but was, on the contrary, taken by him from the philosophers of individualism.

The full harshness of a regime of this kind was bound to fall on those who were "bad starters," namely the proletariat. A society in which there was the same degree of liberty and the same absence of protection for every one of its members created for those who were worse placed an insecurity which was insupportable. These were the first to protest against a right to liberty which was common to all and to demand protective measures.

But even those who were deemed strong, they too took fright in their turn. The whole of society without exception reached the point of demanding security. Security has to be paid for. It is for that reason that we are today the participants in what the old writers called a *pactum subjectionis,* by which men surrender to the state their individual rights in consideration for the social rights received back from it.

## 10. Social Security and State Omnipotence

What concrete proof is there, we may be asked, that those who seek social security find an authoritarian state?

The facts are clear to see.

In two countries with opposite political traditions, two men, than whom two more different cannot be imagined, were simultaneously carried to Power by the same securitarian aspiration of a people maddened by the post-war crisis. We must keep in mind the complete contrast between the two nations and the two rulers, but it is even so most noticeable that the role of saviour assumed by Power justified both in the United States and in Germany a prodigious step forward by the state, the symptoms of which were the same multiplication of officials, the same triumph of the central authority over the regional authorities, the same subordination of business to politics.

It is true that the process went further in Germany than in America. But then they started from very different positions. In the case of Germany a federal state was converted into a unitary state; but the unitary principle was already implicit in the Prussian predominance in the Reich. Whereas only the tiny District of Columbia was governed directly from Washington. The strength and vitality of the states' governments were so great that the subordination of those governments in the space of a few years verges on the miraculous.[5]

America was a country which was a stranger to compulsory military service, in which the tradition was to elect officials to office, and in which Power was subject to judicial control. Is it not astounding that Power was able in a few years to reduce this control nearly to the vanishing-point, to build up a vast bureaucracy, and to invest this bureaucracy with such wide powers that a number of federal agencies have been established simultaneously to formulate rules, to apply them, and to punish breaches of them—to act, in other words, as legislator, executive, and judge?

Finally, nothing has strengthened Power's grip so much as its continuance, however unconstitutional, in the same hands. Thus, two states, as dissimilar as they well could be, both swept forward simultaneously towards omnipotence, borne on the wave of the same securitarian aspirations.

We have already seen how greatly aspirations of that kind serve to distend the state. Let us now examine how they do it.

The state is expected to be a shelter from the blast; the result is seen in an eagerness to accept its growth on the part of all the candidates for security; it comes to be looked on as a sort of living umbrella, and its proliferation is received not only with complacency but with enthusiasm. For instance, the criticisms with which every increase in the bureaucratic machine would have been received in other times are quickly stifled when it is a case of putting into force schemes of social insurance.

The state, when once it is made the giver of protection and security, has but to urge the necessities of its protectorate and overlordship to justify its encroachments. Bismarck realized long ago that this was the road which led to enlarged authority.[6]

---

5. The revenue required by the federal government was twenty-four times as much in 1938 as it had been at the start of the century.

6. "In seeming tender to the welfare of individuals, state socialism works above all for the state. The great political realist who officially patronized and enthroned socialism in Germany knew what he was about. He saw that the state, by accustoming the citizen to turn to it to beg of it a law, a statutory order or an ordinance of police, binds him to itself in bonds of dependence and subjection. He saw clearly that the state as state strengthens its hold by what look like concessions. Its political forms may change with time, but the

The sense of insecurity, which, in growing more general, generalizes also the eagerness to undergo authority, acts on Power as a stimulus and excitation.

Power draws its energy from the social atoms which furnish it forth. In a time of security, men of energy and enterprise tend to find in society the means of raising themselves, and not to enter the service of the state machine. But a time of social confusion deflects them towards Power. Anyone analysing the new entries into new regimes, whether at Washington or Berlin, would find them composed of elements which would not, for the most part, have been attracted to government in normal times.

In a time of insecurity such as ours, we find, then, these two factors which seat a social protectorate in power—in society a marked predisposition to be governed, and in government a personnel of unusual drive.

## 11. The Social Protectorate; Its Justification and Purpose

Every people is today being swept along on the same current, though not all at the same rate, towards the social protectorate. The interests which uncertainty has frightened, the reason which disorder has offended, the feelings which misery has revolted, the imagination which the vision of future possibilities has inflamed, all these call with one voice for a manager and lawgiver. The pressure of needs, desires, passions, and dreams helps him, once found, to overthrow every constitutional obstacle, legal or moral, that stands in his path: obstacles which were already in dissolution, thanks to the decay of absolute values, the hatred felt for acquired rights, and the fierce and vengeful spirit of parties. To do all, Power must be lord of all. The peoples reckon that it will continue to be the docile recipient of their impulses while at the same time it secures for them concrete results which can only be obtained by the continuous pursuit of systematic policies. The experts expect it to plan all social mechanisms by reference to objective reason, when it is nothing better than a bubbling cauldron of subjective wills. Everything beckons on the agents of Power to vaster ambitions. The noblest of these ambitions are not on that account the least dangerous: their aim is to be the architects of public happiness and historical progress.

---

sum total of authority and constraint, which the old forms bequeath to the new, continue to grow." Henry Michel, *L'Idée de l'état* (Paris: 1898) p. 579.

From the time that religion lost its empire over the spirit of man, the avowed end of human existence has been happiness. The American Declaration of Independence included in the catalogue of the rights of men "the pursuit of happiness." In the view of the Founding Fathers it was the business of each man to secure his own happiness. But could not the vast resources of the state help in securing it for him? Should they not be used for this purpose? As long ago as 1891, Joseph Chamberlain expressed the view that the state was entitled to pass any law or perform any action which might increase the sum of human happiness.[7]

The scientists having reduced the human being to one animal among many, another notion came to birth: that of the perfectibility of the species. Was it not Power's business to impel the human animal along the path of his perfection?

Human behaviour was made the object of studies which stressed its irrationality. The eighteenth century had trusted to instinct to guide man in accordance with his best interests once he had been freed from restraints and superstitions. Instinct is today regarded, not as an infallible natural guide, but as a collective memory which is rich in nothing but slowly realized accretions. So imperfect a guide does it make that there are savage peoples who have been known to let themselves starve to death in the near vicinity of herbs and roots which they had never been taught to regard as edible.

Examined in the light of science, human behavior looks to be susceptible of many improvements which would increase individual happiness and advance the progress of the species. It is far from being the case, to take some of the commonest examples, that the family dietary is well balanced and intelligent care taken of the body. How infinitely fair and healthy men could be, would they but cease to be the slaves of habit and the playthings of chance! And what a welter of a world is this in which children who were conceived in inadvertence grow like wild grasses, in which towns spread as greedy speculators direct, like blind animals sprawling in their own excrement!

I pity the man who has never experienced the noble temptation to play the gardener to this disorder, to build Cities of the Sun, which shall be peopled by a nobler race. But there is in these visions a danger. Men whose stock of knowledge is small find them intoxicating and may be readily convinced by them that the happiness of a continent requires

7. House of Commons, March 23, 1891.

the complete suppression of fermented liquors, or, worse still, the extermination of an entire race whose blood is deemed impure.

Only a man who has himself gone in search of truth knows how deceptive is the blaze of evidence with which a proposition may suddenly dazzle his eyes; the light soon fails, and then the hunt is on again. The entire field of knowledge would have to be covered to measure how few discoveries are sufficiently well grounded to justify a man in basing on them any actions which affected the whole of human society; or to appreciate as well the difficulty of reconciling the often discrepant indications furnished by independent branches of learning.

In the absence of this intellectual realization of the limits of knowledge, the worldly wisdom of ancient aristocracies may often shield us from the various enthusiasms which, in their desire to be constructive, come near to being incendiary.

Everywhere, however, it happens that the handling of public affairs gets entrusted to a class which stands in physical need of certitudes and takes dubious truths to its bosom with the same fanaticism as did in other times the Hussites and the Anabaptists.

## 12. Theocracies and Wars of Religion

Faith has been pitchforked out of the political scene, but to no purpose. Religious aspiration is natural to man, so much so that he even invests interests and opinions with the haloes of idolatrous cults: he commits his gold rings to any Aaron who makes for him a god. For that reason Power, on passing into the hands of a victorious sect, takes on the character of a theocracy, a character without which it could not hope to win the degree of obedience necessary to the accomplishment of its tasks as protector of all.

These tasks, in fact, make higher demands on discipline than would ever be met by the rational assent of the citizens, who have been known, even after giving their express approval to a particular measure, to obstruct its application with virtual unanimity.[8] Therefore, there must be means of constraint. The growth of the police, in numbers, importance, and dignity, is a universal phenomenon at the present time. But this direct constraint must be used sparingly. The secret of success is to reach the mind, and propaganda is the indispensable adjunct of the police. But this

---

8. Prohibition in the United States was a striking example of this.

propaganda, too, has its requirements, which are certain master words, thrilling in all who hear them chords that are stretched on one and the same faith.

Thus, all stands firm in the structure of the new state. There are no limits to the Minotaur's beneficent protection; there can be none, therefore, to his authority. To be always sure of himself, he must be convinced; and, to be obeyed, he must convince: so he unites in his own person the spiritual and temporal powers, joining together what Western civilization had always until then kept separate. In that separation lay its unique achievement, and perhaps the secret of its tremendous success.

It is astounding how little conscious we are of the pace at which we are moving towards a regime of this kind. With it as the goal, political struggles take on a new sharpness and cruelty. Men feel in their bones that there is now no longer room for what used to be called "private life."

Such is the Minotaur's success in moulding the lives of individuals that escape from him is impossible; there is, therefore, no salvation but in seizing him. The words "I will live in a certain way" are now pointless; what must be said is, "To live in a certain way myself, I must seize the controls of the great machine and employ them in such manner as suits me."

It is a time of proscriptions and civil wars. It is also a time of wars between nations, for these Titans are allergic to each other. And what wars they are! For what is now at the disposal of rulers is not a mere segment of the national resources, but the entire spiritual and material resources of whole communities, to which they have become the poor-box, the housing authority, and the god.

# XIX.

## *Order or Social Protectorate*

WE ARE THE WITNESSES of a fundamental transformation of society, of a crowning expansion of Power. The revolutions and *coups d'état* which are a feature of our epoch are but insignificant episodes heralding the coming of the social protectorate.

A beneficent authority will watch over every man from the cradle to the grave, repairing the disasters which befall him, even when they are of his own making, controlling his personal development and orientating him towards the most appropriate use of his faculties. By a necessary corollary, this authority will be the disposer of society's entire resources, with a view to getting from them the highest possible return and in that way multiplying the benefits which it confers.

Power takes over, as it were, the whole business of public and private happiness, and it is an indispensable clause of the contract that all possessions, all productive energies, and all liberties should be handed over to it, as being the labour and the raw materials without which it cannot accomplish so gigantic a task. The business is one of setting up an immense patriarchy, or, if anyone prefers the word, a matriarchy, since we are now told that collective authority should be animated by maternal instincts.

It is, no doubt, true that not every mind has a clear conception of the goal to which the pressure behind the idea of a social protectorate is driving. But it is obvious enough to the thoughtful. There are those who denounce it in panic, but with no clear perception of the force and complexity of the causes at work. There are those who welcome it, but with no care for all the ensuing consequences. In truth the atmosphere of the whole debate is less that of two doctors calmly discussing a course of treatment than that of two swimmers swept away by a current, against which one struggles while the other deliberately abandons himself to it: it is an atmosphere not of reason but of emotion.

Our analysis of the growth of Power has put us in the way of understanding the great phenomenon of modern times. We will now set down the reasons for which it is opposed, recall the immediate factors which fight for it, underline its dangers, and, finally and above all, plumb the profound causes which in present conditions make it inevitable, that we may ask ourselves whether their nature partakes of absolute or of contingent necessity.

## 1. The Liberal Negation

The Liberal school of thought denies flatly that it is any business of the state to undertake the tasks to which it is now bidden and on which it enters with enthusiasm; for they lie, it says, outside the normal sphere of its competence.

The very terms used remind us that we are at this point entering a fresh field, that we are leaving behind us the examination of Power as a phenomenon, for the ethical study of the state. This change of terminology is not only permissible but obligatory, for we are now done with inquiries as to what is, and are facing up to various opinions as to what ought to be. But the new departure needed to have attention called to it: for nothing is worse than to jumble up the normative and the positive.

What we are told, then, is that the state is leaving the normal sphere of its competence. Let us see what the Liberal has to say on this, basing ourselves on the arguments of a man of clear intelligence, Émile Faguet.[1]

The state, you tell us, has a normal sphere of competence. Agreed, but how do you define it? "To assure internal order and external security."[2] What has determined it? The nature of society, which is formed for the defence of all against aggression from without and of each man against assault by his neighbour! But at this point I pull you up. Who compels

1. Cf. notably É. Faguet, *Le Libéralisme* (Paris: 1903). A fine book, containing many excellent truths.
2. *Ibid.*, p. 102 and in several other passages.

me to subscribe to your conception of society? Were I a small peasant proprietor, living autarchically with my family, for me, no doubt, society would be merely an institution of repression, assuring me my security by means of the soldier and the policeman. But were I, on the other hand, a worker, producing what is useless to myself and receiving my requirements through the complex mechanism of the labour of a crowd of others, for me society would tend rather to wear the aspect of a workers' association. I should be led to regard it as being in essence a cooperative institution, by means of which I receive, in exchange for a given quantity of work, a given quantity of goods and services. And if this exchange is irregular or seems to me inequitable, why should I not invoke the intervention of Power to regularize the cooperation, just as you yourself, my Liberal proprietor, invoke it to suppress any attack on your property?

Then what becomes of your "normal sphere"? It is now nothing but *your* conception of what the public authority ought to be: it is in my view a narrow, out-of-date conception, which does not respond to my needs. I oppose to it *my* conception, and I will bring mine out on top. But I go further; I want to accept your definition of the "normal sphere." You said "external security." Very well; it is apparent that neighbouring states are controlling and disposing of the entire resources of their nations with a view to producing the maximum military strength. That being so, the duty of defence, which you include among the normal duties of the state, forces our Power to control and dispose of everything.

You also referred to "internal order." But what sort of order is this, in which I cannot find employment for my stock of labour, I am not sure of procuring for my children what the young of savages receive from nature, and the slightest financial shock may render useless a lifetime of forethought? So even your own formula refutes you!

It gives me no pleasure to crush in argument the Liberal standpoint. Its mistake is to have taken up positions which are as untenable in discussion as they are irrelevant to the needs and passions of men.

The image in which it makes Power does not respond to the reality of any time or country. Power has never regarded as forbidden territory the domains of social and economic interests. When the French Civil Code prescribed the division of property on death, it was prescribing what was, both in intention and in effect, a social and economic measure. And the law of 1867 on limited companies has also had momentous consequences of the kind.

The Liberal negation is, therefore, in the forms in which it is clothed, quite utopian.

## 2. The "Legalitarian" Criticism

That is not in the least to say that no other critical standpoint is possible. To establish it, let us borrow from theology certain elementary notions. When the intelligence, unsupported by either study or revelation, applies itself to its essential objective, the knowledge of God, it forms by a natural process two antithetical conceptions. One is that of a miraculous Providence, which is reached and set in motion by prayers for particular objects and then intervenes to disturb for the benefit of its invoker the natural course of things. And the other is that of a supreme Wisdom, which has subjected everything to laws of a majestic regularity and then leaves them to operate unchecked.[3]

Theology has, as is known, admirably reconciled the two conceptions in the account of the Divine Nature which it has drawn up. It is enough for our present purpose to have borrowed from it the antithesis in its crudest form that we may apply it to the government of human affairs.

This government may take one of two forms, the legalitarian or the providential. It may buttress with sanctions fixed and relatively unchangeable laws, and see to their exact execution, while treating with respect whatever consequences they have; or else it may take occasional interventions and bring to each situation as it arises its own remedy, with the result that there are no longer fixed laws but rather an uninterrupted series of "miracles" or arbitrary acts.

Political philosophy in every age has thrown into contrast the two conceptions, which twenty-five centuries ago were called by the Chinese "government by the laws" and "government by men" respectively.

The first, clearly, is an ideal which does not admit of more than a partial attainment. We will examine it summarily, and endeavour, in doing so, to introduce for the sake of clarity a little order into the many and various notions evoked by the word "law."

The material world is governed by laws, to which we, as physical beings, are necessarily subject: if, for instance, I am hoisted into the air

---

3. "Fixit in aeternum causas, qua cuncta coercet Se quoque lege tenens." Lucan, Pharsalia, II, 9–10. ("He established the chain of causes for all eternity and bound himself as well by universal law.")

and support is withdrawn from me, I *must* fall, in just the same way as an apple falls. Our submission to these laws is absolute, and let me not be told that science frees us from them, when in fact all the successful discoveries are in essence only an intelligent and profitable submission to these very laws.

When we talk of the natural laws of society, we come at once to something quite different: a population of nomadic shepherds, for instance, whose pastures are ruined by drought, *must* emigrate. But in this case the necessity is not, as in the former, a mechanical one: the population may refrain from emigrating—and die in consequence.

Lastly, we come to laws our submission to which is neither mechanical nor vital, to the moral law which it lies in our power to violate, and to the civil law which it lies in our power to transgress. The moral law prescribes what is good absolutely, the civil law what is useful to society. The positive legislation of a society buttresses with sanctions these prescriptions of the good and the useful, while paying attention to the necessary subordination of the useful to the good.

We see, then, that government by the laws is, in essence, that in which those rules are sanctioned which are of useful effect to men dedicated to the good; they are set in a framework which is determined, generally, by the physical laws of nature and, especially, by the natural laws of society.

When Power confines itself to enforcing respect for those laws, the individual moves over ground on which there are both barriers erected and roads marked, but on which, on condition that he respects those barriers and follows those roads, he is free, in the sense that no human will can, by a sudden and arbitrary intervention, disturb his plans and constrain his will. He is recognized as being the master of his fate and responsible for it. He has a consecrated dignity.

Human infirmity, no doubt, will always stand between us and the complete realization of such a system as this. Our power of discerning the good is not flawless and, still more, our ability to anticipate the useful is unequal to taking into account all possible circumstances. Our laws, in consequence, can never be of an absolutely unalterable and immutable character; unceasing vigilance is needed to provide for particular cases, and wisdom must from time to time take a hand in revising the rules. Yet it is certain that this vigilance carried to excess and these interventions multiplied unduly will diminish the liberty and dignity of the individual. The conclusion is, then, that government by the laws, undiluted, is in its perfection unrealizable, but remains ever the model and the touchstone, the myth and the inspiration. The cause of social order and human dignity is best served when this ideal is made the goal.

We may say of each successive society which has crossed the stage of civilization that it has, at one moment in its career, drawn near to this perfection—but only to sheer off again before long and to move headlong towards arbitrariness in government and servility in the hearts of the subjects.

Of the various reasons for this it will be sufficient to enumerate a few. First is the fact that the interplay of positive laws deemed the most adequate still leaves only too much for scores of individual miseries and misfortunes. This feature of human laws need not occasion much surprise to the public man when its presence in the divine law is freely admitted by the theologian. But it would be asking too much of the victims to expect so serene a spirit in them; they desire—nay, they demand—a providential intervention to mend the consequences of their misfortunes. This "variable" of present discontents is liable to take on sudden accretions at certain periods, either because, owing to a change in the actual circumstances of life, the civil law ceases to supply the needs of society in a satisfactory manner; or because, through a change in the psychological outlook of individuals, what was previously regarded as satisfactory is no longer so regarded; or for reasons which are still more serious: that men deny the need to subordinate the useful to the good and, taking the view that the useful is the good, in that way break the connecting chain which keeps in coherence the various kinds of laws; or again because, flown with a false conceit of human capabilities, they think themselves endowed with power to abrogate the natural laws of society by means of positive laws.

It may happen that all these reasons will be found working together, and it is in fact the lesson of history that they are usually found in conjunction.

Between them they furnish dormant ambition with a wonderful opportunity for putting life into Power, and for restoring to it those aggressive and arbitrary characteristics of which its nature partakes.

It goes without saying that, thanks to the ingrained habit of legality, the interventions on which Power now embarks take on at first the form of laws. But these are but counterfeit laws, concerned only to provide for the situations of the moment, owning the imperious sway of current passions and requirements. Under the cloak of objective legislation, every subjective desire enjoys a saturnalia, as is shown both by the rapidity and the inconsistency with which these so-called laws multiply. Principle and certitude are things of the past; the desires of the moment become "your only lawgiver," no respecters these of the notions of moral good and natural necessity, which they confound with that of utility in its most transitory shape. Utility itself has come to mean, not the permanent utility of society as a whole, but the passing utility of a sectional group which accommodates virtue and knowledge to its interests and passions.

Whatever pretensions are made that this is the way to be of service to man, the fact remains that he thereby loses all liberty and all dignity. For he can now no longer plan his course by reference to any given certainties, and the knowledge that any activity of his own will avail him much less than to stand well with Power disposes him towards ambition of a servile kind—to be of those who are in touch with the author of all miracles, to be a beneficiary of arbitrariness.

Would anyone dare to deny that this is the general tendency of our time? And is not its danger patent? Very strong inclinations are at work on its behalf. Where the idea comes from that men hold despotism in detestation, I do not know. My own view is that they delight in it.

We need look no further than at the fortunes which they embark in games of chance, *paris mutuels,* and lotteries, to measure the extent of the glamour which the hope of a casual increment holds for them, as well as of the sacrifices which they are ready to make to give themselves a chance of gaining it. Now arbitrary Power is a lottery of a kind: and there are prizes in it for the fortunate.

Or look at the novels, plays, films, and news items which have a popular success: it will be found that here, too, there is a very wide demand for events, shows, and characters which are out of the common run. Arbitrary Power answers to this need.

In this way human nature makes straight the way for the coming of arbitrary Power, the summons to which is given, as it was sure to be, by the tasks committed to the social protectorate.


### 3. The Modern Problem and Its Absurd Solution

We will now try to expound in a series of simple propositions the problem in our own time.

Firstly, the social evil to which a remedy is sought in the institution of the protectorate is no imaginary evil. In the vast industrial complex there is, in a very real sense, a failure in the adjustment and correlation of the relations between the parties which cries out for correction. And there is also a widespread discontent, due to the conviction that the complex does not distribute to each his fair social share.

Secondly, anyone supposing that adequate remedies can be found within the framework of the legalitarian system, by means of one of those applications of positive exactments to new situations which are from time to time necessary in such a system, will find that it is impossible in practice to make an application of that kind effective. For the new laws required would need to be the fruit of enlightened study and meditation. Whereas in fact legislative activity, as it is called, is nothing better than the hurried botching of short-sighted interests and blind passions.

So that, thirdly, these outpourings of so-called laws are in reality merely so many acts of government, busy in its daily task of coping with the day's situations. Power in any case, whether it keeps or spurns the thin disguise of legality, proceeds in fact by way of arbitrary decisions.

Fourthly, the arbitrary Power, swept on by the passions of the mob and swayed by the ardours of the holders of office, lacking rule and bit and limit, constitutes, for all its tinsel dresses, a despotism such as the West has never known before. It is none the less dangerous for being unstable—all despotisms have been unstable. As none is outside its power, it makes for servility; as every conquest is open to it, it breeds ambition.

And, lastly, the demand for order, with which we began, ends in letting loose disorder on a gigantic scale.

At this point we should be justified in bringing our investigation to a close, for we have done what we set out to do. We aimed at explaining the successive stages of Power's growth and its monstrous efflorescence that is now before our eyes. The inquiry is finished, the dossier is complete, the reasons have been made good and the consequences foreshadowed.

Yet we cannot bring ourselves to leave the subject without pillorying the error which is guiding our epoch to the absurd solution of making general disorder the remedy for particular disorders.[4]

It should be clearly understood, however, that this supplement to our investigation is no more than a rapid and superficial glimpse of another vast field of study which we hope one day to explore.

---

4. For, no matter what particular order it may procure, I cannot but see in despotism the disorder of disorders.

Let us, in this spirit, go back to the various phenomena of social and moral disharmony which in our own time favour the rise of absolute Power.

### 4. The Miracle of Confidence

The entire existence of man in society rests on confidence. The stranger whom we meet constitutes no menace either to our persons or to our property. We see in him, on the contrary, one of those countless anonymous fellow-workers who guarantee to us the daily satisfaction of needs which have in the course of centuries gradually multiplied. Nor do we rely only on his negative virtues, as when we leave valuable objects in the care of whoever happens to be our neighbour; our well-being depends on his active cooperation as well, as when we trust ourselves to the diligence of a host of intermediaries to get a message through to its destination and to get for us at every hour of the day our necessaries of life.

Our security turns on the admirable regularity with which a whole host of services is rendered to us by a countless number of members of the same society who do not know us and whom we do not know. We, too, play our part, but its efficaciousness and value are due to all the parts being concerted.

The mind slips all too easily into the passive acceptance of this harmonious working; once meditated on, it becomes both astonishing and admirable, and is sufficient proof that "Each for all and all for each" is not the motto of an improbable Utopia but the formula of society in being.

It is, evidently, a false and superficial view of the matter to regard the great mass of the "administered," the users and the consumers, as being served by certain independent "organs," such as the police, the railways, and commerce generally, for these so-called organs are in truth only the services guaranteed to each other by the members of the mass. The true picture of the social order is rather that of the miraculous conjunction of millions of separate trajectories. The various services are regularly rendered by the appropriate agents, and the users regularly served, the condition being the amazing adherence of each social atom to its own trajectory and its wonderful loyalty to its own appropriate line of conduct in its double capacity of agent and user.

Think of the ensuing disaster if a railway signalman leaves for only an hour his normal course of conduct! Nor is his case in any way exceptional, though it is certainly one to strike the imagination. Each single irregularity causes a shock, and the machine can only function at all so long as the peccant behaviours do not exceed in number the lowest margin which it can rectify in its stride. Irregularity on a widespread scale would bring our species to an end, for there is no individual who can provide for his own needs. So aware are we of this that, even when faced with disturbance on the most colossal scale, we immediately and instinctively start to tie up again the threads which bombardment or insurrection have broken.

But how, you ask, has the division of labour come about, how have men fallen into their several divisions, and how is the necessary internal adjustment brought about?

One possible answer—the first that occurs to men in general—is that it is the work of a single will. There is a wide variety of myths, the systematic study of which has still, unfortunately, to be undertaken, explaining the functional division of men into different categories with each of which there goes along a certain type of behaviour. This form of social organization, say the myths, has been decreed by one particular lawgiver, demiurge, hero, or even fabulous animal, as the case may be, so that slavish adherence to the traditional behaviour is the fruit of veneration and fear. In one myth[5] the ordering of all things, natural and social, is represented as a combined and simultaneous operation. In another, on the other hand, it is recognized that objects which are incapable of the act of willing are not regulated in the same way as are human beings. Human beings are allowed by this myth to have had their own particular teacher, who ceases in time to arouse any superstitious veneration: at that stage the myth degenerates into something worse than the mythical—false history. Since, it is said, the organization of society is the work of a man, it is open to other men, if they please, to rebuild it on other foundations. Thus to the superstitious horror of change succeeds naturally a belief in the possibility of any change whatsoever. The fixation-ist error has given birth to its contrary, the utopian error. The reason is that ideas are still bound by the same conception of the social order being subject to a will.

5. I use here deliberately the vague formulas "In one . . . in another" without any suggestion of a logical and connecting link. In this way I emphasize that I have not set myself the ludicrous design of compressing into a single page the whole study of myths and doctrines concerning the order of society. I touch on the subject only to the extent to which my theme makes it necessary to do so.

By the time that the legalitarian conception makes its appearance the development of human intelligence has proceeded a certain distance: its starting-point is the affirmation that, on the analogy of the laws of nature, human society also has its natural laws. With these the social order is secured and preserved; they mend it without ceasing and in doing so complicate it no less continuously. Whatever the other merits of this thesis, it is in its concrete applications vitiated partly by the hasty assimilation of the "forces" which move men to the "forces" of nature, and partly by an inability, for which there is some excuse, to distinguish between the laws which govern objects without souls and those which control beings who have received liberty and will. The upshot of it is a tendency to quietism.

Epitomized, these two points of view, the voluntarist and the quietist, issue in the ordinary conceptions of socialism and liberalism respectively, which do not merit discussion. No positive study has yet been made of the means by which the harmony of society is maintained and mended, nor can there be any question of making one here. All that can be done will be to give certain indications, which will be developed elsewhere and, where necessary, revised.

## 5. Concepts of Right Conduct

Let us begin in a small way by considering any given man in society, fulfilling any given function and pursuing any given line of behaviour. He suggests naturally to the mind the image of a mobile object describing a given curve. What is the force which binds him to this curve and causes him to follow this trajectory?

Egoism, answers the school of Hobbes and Helvétius; concern for his own self-interest! From that starting-point every social institution has been explained as an emanation of the natural and necessary complex of egoistical interests. Intellectually, nothing could be finer than some of the workings-out of this theory,[6] and it would be ridiculous to impugn the intentions of its authors. What attracted them to this hypothesis was the desire, coming naturally to savants, to find in the moral order one simple principle corresponding to energy in the physical order.

However reluctant we might be to accept their assumption, we should

6. See in particular Ihering's coherent structure of reasoning in *L'Évolution du droit* (Fr. ed. Meulenaere. Paris: 1901).

be in their debt if they had really succeeded in building a coherent structure. But they have not done so, and the only way which they have found of making egoisms the instrument of the common good is by endowing them with calculations which show a more human degree of enlightenment. But men take short views where their interests are concerned, and this fact leads our philosophers to secure by constraint the order which the reason is too feeble to establish. Starting from the all-sufficient efficaciousness of egoism, they reach the necessity of repression, to which in the end they ascribe a most exaggerated role.

This twofold misconception, of basing social order either on enlightened self-interest or on repressive constraint, is due to defective observation.

Neither the most far-sighted calculation nor fear of punishment determines to any marked extent the conduct of man in the concrete, either in what he does or in what he refrains from doing. His actions are governed by feelings and beliefs[7] which dictate to him his behaviour and inspire his impulses. Not a man of us asks himself, when the time comes for us each day to go out into the fields, or the factory, or the office, "Shall I go or not?" Just as none asks himself, seeing a child in danger, "Shall I save it or not?" Or, seeing a neighbour fingering a well-filled wallet, "Shall I take it from him or not?"

Man is an animal made for life in society. The intelligent awareness of our interests and the fear of punishment are but complementary forces, which are useful for checking the occasional aberration. But such occasions are infrequent. In general we behave as good neighbours and scrupulous cooperators, for that to us is second nature, a nature which has moreover grown in the soil of a sociability and benevolence which should not be underestimated.

And now how does this nature work? He would be a bold man who claimed to have the explanation of it; yet it seems clear to me that it works by way of concepts. Common speech often provides the key to the workings of psychology, and when we say, "I do not see myself doing something or other," we are revealing that we are controlled by concepts of right conduct.

In childhood a host of educational influences play their part in forming these concepts. Not only parents and teachers and priests and masters,

---

7. Let us note that our particular interest, when it consciously motivates us, can only be regarded as one more belief, since quite clearly we are never in possession of all the relevant factors so as to be able to disentangle our real interest.

but some fellow-pupil whom we admire, some colleague who attracts us, some dead man whose example stirs us. What may be called "social heredity" operates here with a power incomparably greater than that of physical heredity: the family into which we are born, the country to which we belong, the career on which we enter, all these have for us an immense power of suggestion.

All that is around us whispers to us our duty: we have but to copy and repeat. The conduct always seen around us and the actions always held up for our admiration provide our spirit with models which we follow without thinking. Even on their death-beds, some of the greatest men have repeated formulas and gestures which they have taken from history or poetry.

These potent concepts are the guides to our behaviour; it is they which make it calculable to our fellows and compatible with their behaviours. It is they which maintain the social harmony.

## 6. On the Regulation of Society

From this it follows that, whenever the current concepts of right conduct are disturbed, the social harmony is in danger. Disturbance may happen even in a fossilized society, in which the same tasks and the same employments have been shared in the same proportions for generations. And it happens almost inevitably in a rapidly developing society, in which new functions and new ways of life are continually coming into being.

Take the first case. Each new arrival in such a society, in whatever situation and social employment, arrives as a successor already formed by example and teaching. He has served his apprenticeship, whether as a medieval mason or as a Roman emperor, at the side of the man he is to replace. His duty is a simple one, though all the same he may prove unequal to it; that is the phenomenon of the decay of folkways, a theme to which the ancient authorities devoted a most intelligent attention.

The debasement of religious beliefs may set it in motion, accompanied by a rationalist outbreak which fastens on all the determinants of behaviour, gives every proof of its inability to replace them, and ushers in the reign of intellectual anarchy. But the trouble may also be caused by the corruption of the ruling classes, a corruption which leads to the rupture of the true social contract: that, namely, by which each man behaves in character with his functional type on condition that everyone else with whom he has relations acts in character with his. In those conditions irregularity of conduct spreads from top to bottom, and in many cases the intellectual upheaval is little more than the consequence of the moral, for it is part of the average man's make-up to feel religious doubts on account of doubts concerning his bishop rather than to feel doubts concerning his bishop on account of religious doubts. And so, even in a fossilized society, harmony is destroyed.

Far more difficult is the task of maintaining it, or rather of unceasingly restoring it, in a developing society, in which there is a continuous addition of new activities to old, bringing new behaviours in their train and making necessary the adaptation of such of the old as they do not directly modify.

Once the complexity of the problem is grasped, the functional disorders which in fact occur in a developing society seem less matter for surprise than the high degree of adjustment secured it by a hidden automatism, the admiration felt by the men of the nineteenth century for self-regulating mechanisms is understandable;[8] but these disorders explain how it is that in the end an accumulation of troubles comes to exceed the tolerable limit, especially if the mechanisms are in continuous process of losing their virtue.

These mechanisms are much misconceived, for the study of them has hardly begun. How so? you say; have not the economists analysed meticulously the delicate interplay of forces? True enough, but there lies the mistake, in thinking that the whole problem in its entirety falls within the province of the economists. Economists can explain to us the way in which a growing supply of automobiles lessens progressively the demand for horses and carriages until these completely disappear, in which automobile factories absorb the men engaged in coachmaking and saddlery and draw in more besides, in which stables are transformed into garages. But when the process of quantitative adaptation has been brought to its inevitable perfection, there remains outstanding the whole of the infinitely more important question of qualitative adaptation. Between a master saddler living above his workshop in the Temple[9] quarter, and his son lost in the nameless and cosmopolitan crowd of Citroën workers and living in a suburb, there has been a prodigious transformation of folkways,

8. An admiration of which Spencer is the most characteristic interpreter.

9. [A quarter in the centre of old Paris in which the Templars lived. The name has survived.]

beliefs, and sentiments, a transformation which cannot but leave its mark on the whole tone of society and in the end even affect the interplay of supply and demand.

What makes it possible for political economy to be a science at all is that it looks on social life, and all the activities, relationships, and satisfactions of human beings, as the regular flow of one and the same energy: sometimes—as in the case of labour—active, sometimes—as in the case of wealth—potential, but homogeneous and always measurable in units of value. But the very feature which makes a science of it makes it incapable of explaining the whole of social reality, or even of taking account of all the phenomena which occur within its proper sphere. It reveals the reasons for which local savings are diverted from accounts kept locally by local bankers, as in former days they were, and are attracted into vast central reservoirs from which they are distributed nationally and even internationally; but it is no part of its business to stress the fact that the manipulators of savings are now not the same set of men, and that the old and the new types are quite different, in nothing more unlike than in their respective concepts of right conduct. It justifies the money market as a useful piece of regulative machinery, but is not concerned to know what temperaments it attracts and what characters it develops. It is a valuable science, but one grafted on to a false psychology, which regards the race of men as a physical mass pin-pointed in place and acted upon only by the mechanical force of self-interest.

Hence it is that the point of view of the economist is the worst of all for discerning social disharmonies: these must react on quantitative adaptations before they receive his attention. That is what in the end happened. Disturbance in the sphere of economic functions appeared as a sort of tertiary ague compelling attention to a social disease which had been long in progress.

## 7. New Functions Necessitate New Constraining Concepts

This disease takes the form of a social fissiparousness, of a defective medley of inharmonious behaviours.

These are occasioned by the disturbance, which goes along with the evolution of society, of the concepts of right conduct, and there is delay in finding substitutes which are at once sufficiently clear-cut and sufficiently binding to guide mankind when they find themselves in novel situations. Men become the natural prey of interests which, even when restrained by the fear of penal sanctions, show themselves impotent to procure harmonious behaviours.

The phenomenon of being thrown out of his element and out of gear is substantially the same whether it is a case of a peasant being flung into a factory or of a small employee becoming a big speculator. It is not merely, as has sometimes been said, the too rapid change of condition which constitutes the essential danger, but rather that, on reaching their new condition, the men who have either got on or been uprooted are without concepts of right conduct to prompt them in their new parts. They retain, no doubt, certain moral ideas, which they learnt in childhood. But casuistry, which means the application of general precepts to particular situations, is a difficult art and only for the few. And so long as there is no code of practical rules suited to any given condition, general principles by themselves are impotent.[10] The task of elaborating this code of rules is not the business of the legislative authority, which cannot go into details of that kind; it is no director of consciences.

It belongs to the creators of the new conditions, to the innovating elites, guided to the extent needed by the spiritual authorities, to create the code of behaviour and the concepts of right conduct which are needed to harmonize the new function with the order of society. These innovating elites[11] must consider, while innovating, the personnel whom they attract, and make ready for their reception frameworks of morals as well as the raw materials of their work.

Each function, in a word, has its law of chivalry and its duty of leadership. In the social movement of today, the innovators have neither elaborated these laws nor been conscious of these duties.

### 8. Social Authorities Without Ethical Codes

Let us look at some actual cases.

The man who thought of the bearer share of low nominal value made possible the association of small and medium savings with large-scale

10. Taken in this sense, the formula of Durkheim is correct: "Morality is not the product of two or three very general principles which act as a guiding thread to life and which we have but to elaborate as circumstances make it necessary; rather it is the product of a very large number of specific precepts." Durkheim, *De la Division du travail*, p. 16.

11. In this context the word "elites" connotes, as is clear, force of personality and creative energy, not moral worth.

economic enterprises. The role of the financiers who mobilized the people's savings was a very beneficent one on two conditions: first, that the enterprises on whose behalf they raised the capital were advantageous to the community, and secondly that they had a care for the security of the savers. It would be unfair to deny that many financiers have been conscious of this double responsibility; but no such binding financial ethic has ever been constructed as to keep every financier without exception in the narrow path. On the contrary, an ever growing irresponsibility has marked this particular category of society. The annals of capitalism show instances of numerous issues which have had no other aim than that of robbing the investors, by, for example, selling them a limited liability concern at a price well above its true value (watering the stock), provoking an exaggerated fall in the price of the shares, and then buying them in at a low price. Even apart from the numerous instances of devices which are openly fraudulent, there are many others in which the promoters are quite indifferent as to both the security of the capital and the purposes to which it is put, their sole concern being their own brokerage and commission.

They justify their indifference by two notions, both of them false. The first is that the extent of the flow of capital towards a particular enterprise is determined by its profitability, which in turn measures its social utility and the need for its extension, conclusions which are quite erroneous, being based on an ill-founded confidence in economic automatism. The second is that the promoter of an issue contracts on equal terms with the investor: this is one of the absurd consequences of the egalitarian fiction which is the presiding genius of modern law.

Now let us pass on to the industrialist who, fortified by a vast provision of capital, opens a large factory. In his capacity as a supplier of goods and employment he is a social benefactor, but only, of course, on the two conditions that the goods supplied are useful and that he is conscious of his responsibility for the fate of the army of workers which he musters.

The first of these two preoccupations is, unfortunately, removed from him by the utterly false dogma that demand is the measure of utility, whatever the way in which this demand is stimulated, and even if it is the fruit of an impudent publicity.

As for the second, it gets dispensed with by the fiction of equality. The industrialist is not now the lord, protector, and guardian of those who are to work in his service, but only a man who contracts on equal terms with equals. Hence came the nineteenth century's folly of supposing that the obligations of contract were the long and short of the obligations of the employer to his men. Anyone studying the case law and legislation relating to industrial accidents will think himself in a madhouse as he contemplates the legal fictions to which recourse has had to be had to justify the responsibility of the employer, a responsibility which should, on the contrary, have flowed naturally from the positive recognition of the duties inherent in an economic overlordship carrying with it all the obligations of protection and help.

Next we come to the proprietor of the popular newspaper. Such a man is not a mere seller of paper in obedience to a popular demand; he is, rather, a propagator of opinions, an awakener of emotions, a builder or destroyer of concepts of right conduct. Yet, from the day that the first "ha'penny paper" was launched until now, the big circulations have never built up an ethic. The spread of education, which was designed to counteract the consequences of universal suffrage by providing the citizens with the minimum of knowledge necessary to enable them to form sensible opinions, has in fact furnished the purveyors of cheap emotion with an inexhaustible reservoir of consumers.

To superficial minds the only point of consequence lies in the direct influence exercised by the press on the course of politics, but that is not the essential feature of the phenomenon. It is, rather, the propagation of concepts of right conduct which are anti-social[12] and the habit of emotional processes of thought which it engenders.[13]

The shock administered to "good manners" by the press, not unassisted by the film, is almost incalculable. And the journalist world, though much more honest in the narrower sense than is often thought, is quite unconscious of its responsibility in the wider.

One more example: that of the publicity agent, the worker in persuasion, who hires his services to all comers whether he gives the public a taste for patent medicines which are either actively harmful or completely useless, or teaches them habits which may do them harm, or propagates

12. The sensational newspaper gives a vast publicity to peccant behaviours and exceptional fortunes. It breeds the illusion that society is made up of Landrus, Staviskys, and Garbos. The exception seems to become the rule, and faithful adherence to social forms of behaviour is correspondingly discouraged.

13. This is probably its most important aspect; it cannot, however, receive proper treatment in such a cursory review as this.

destructive political principles, a form of advertisement which is called, for short, propaganda.[14]

## 9. Consequences of a False Conception of Society

To sum up this cursory *tour d'horizon,* it is clear enough that the financier, the industrialist, the journalist, and the publicity agent, even when they are perfectly decent people, are all guilty of social misbehaviour, for the simple reason that they have no professional code which is sufficiently precise and binding to canalize their activities towards social ends.

The unedifying character of such codes and concepts of right conduct as they have is due in part to the rapidity of society's evolution. But a further and much more important reason is the lack of spiritual and social authorities.

The task of the spiritual authorities should be to keep close on the tail of the evolution of society, and to formulate specific obligations, flowing naturally from the moral truths of universal extent, for each situation as it arises. It is a pure waste of time to preach in a church frequented by stock-jobbers the rules formulated for a patriarchal peasantry. After listening respectfully, the stock-jobbers will go away without having received the smallest guidance for life.

But the assurance needed to play so active a role is lacking to spiritual authorities whose title deeds are in dispute and who in consequence fall back defensively on the mere performance of ceremonial.

The task of those who are for practical purposes rulers, leaders, employers, squires, and guides of the people, should be to take good care where they are going and whither they are leading. But in fact, the words "ruler" and "leader" are not applied to them; they are denied this style and title. The false dogma of equality, so flattering to the weak, results in practice in a chartered libertinism for the strong.

At no time in history has social elevation carried with it fewer obligations, or actual inequality proved more oppressive, than since the

14. [Miss C. V. Wedgwood, in a notable essay entitled "The Historian and the World" (republished in *Velvet Studies;* London: 1947), has written on the need for "concepts of right conduct" in historians: "Misinterpretation of past ages is more or less inevitable, and, although a respect for truth is an essential quality for the good historian, his understanding will always be limited by individual peculiarities. That is why it is important, if his style is persuasive and his learning impressive, that he should also be a good man. The dead can look after themselves; the living cannot . . . it is all too easy, armed with this romantic, this most appealing of weapons, to play unfairly on the wishful thoughts of the ingenuous."]

incorporation in positive law of an equality in principle, bringing in its train the negation of all the duties that belong to station. What we now see are the developing consequences of hasty thinking, which has refused to see in the mechanism of society anything except the individual men and women who make it, and a central mainspring, the state. Everything else it has disregarded, and the role of the spiritual and social authorities has been denied.

There were intellectual reasons for this mistake: into a new sort of studies was carried the presumption of an adolescent science, grown drunk on Newton, which could see in the whole universe nothing but the simple play of elemental forces.

And there were political reasons too. The state and the individual were just emerging triumphant from their long struggle waged in common against the social authorities, which were hateful to the one as rivals and to the other as tyrants.

How would they share the spoils between themselves? Either the individual would reap all the benefit of a twofold enfranchisement—the individualist solution—or else the state would be heir to the functions hitherto filled by the now banished authorities—the *étatiste* solution. The nineteenth century essayed at first the first of these solutions: Power, which had no master, mastered itself, trusting to the interplay of individual interests to bring about the best of all orders, a spontaneous order. We have seen how, thanks to this forbearance, new social authorities sprang into the saddle,[15] unrecognized as such and finding in the foolish denial of their existence the opportunity for doing infinite mischief. And we have witnessed, too, the appearance of the most fantastic candidates to spiritual authority: the most moth-eaten heresies have reappeared in the guise of new ideas, and around them have sprung up those militant and aggressive churches, the parties of today.

The result has been that in the end the insolence of interests and the confusion of beliefs have made necessary the restoration of some sort of order. The only available disciplinary authority being Power, it has had to have conferred on it an unlimited restraining capacity.

### 10. From Chaos to Totalitarianism

Leaders of groups, such as the feudal baron or the captain of industry, have always existed in every society known to history and will continue

---

15. Authorities which are called "the money power," and also the influence of the press.

to be in every conceivable society. This fact carries with it a twofold responsibility for the leaders, as to the harmonizing of the group with the whole and as to the well-being of the group. Both these responsibilities are natural ones: they continue just the same even if positive law neglects them or refuses to give them countenance. Similarly, there are in each social authority, whether ancient or modern, those who set the pace and lay down standards of behaviour: the elders, whose responsibility it is—it, too, a natural one—to set an example.

There are many different species of "notables," and there are Elders for each of the many roles played in the drama of society. No social order could either maintain or restore itself if the controllers of groups and masters of colleges ceased to carry out their essential purpose, to which the spiritual authority must continually recall them.

It is an idle metaphysic that denies their existence and treats them as ordinary citizens: it results, not in suppressing their authority and influence, but only in freeing them from the honourable disciplines which make them the servants of the common good. On interest becoming their only principle of action, the very men whose duty it is to secure order spread disorder. The troubling of the concepts of right conduct spreads from top to bottom, and individuals, whatever their stations and functions, lose the precise and detailed picture of their duties on which their effectiveness as fellow-workers depends.

When that happens, cohesion can be restored to society only by Power's formulating in the greatest detail the rules of behaviour which are appropriate to each separate function. And since habits and folkways, those powerful internal regulators of the concepts of right conduct, have ceased to bring about a spontaneous conformity, conformity must be secured by repression.

But repression cannot be made effective at every turn and everywhere; that would need as many policemen as there are citizens. Therefore it is sought to supply the defect of external compulsion by a form of constraint which is really the most efficacious of all, that which the forum of a man's own conscience exercises over his actions. Concepts of right conduct are put into him from without, for which purpose use must be made of the squalid weapons of mass suggestion and propaganda. The upshot is squalid concepts, undifferentiated by reference to function, as those which spring from moral influences and observed examples are differentiated.

The social cohesion created in this way is of a far rougher and more primitive kind than the one which has been allowed to perish. The divergences which troubled society are diminished, but at the price of the differences which gave it its civilization.

This is the totalitarian solution, an evil called into being by the individualist evil, for the contrary of an error is not truth but only another error.

## 11. The Fruits of Individualist Rationalism

From not having known how to preserve, and from not knowing how to restore, the delicate and living harmony of a highly civilized society, we are returning to the form of cohesion which is that of the primitive tribe. Out of common frenzies are forged powerful sentiments, comporting with their totems and taboos, for failure to feel which the penalty is to be treated as a *hostis* or foreign enemy.

What would the individualists and freethinkers of the eighteenth and nineteenth centuries say could they but see what idols a man must now worship, to what jackboots he must now pay homage, if he is to escape being hunted and stoned? Would not the superstition which they fought seem to them the very acme of enlightenment, compared with the superstitions which have taken its place? And how mild is the despotism which they threw off by the side of those which are now crushing us!

So careful of the individual life, so delighting in refinement of manners, so critical of the criminal law's severity, so scandalized by legal injustice, think of the horror with which they would compare the society which made them with the society which they have made! For, however strong an attraction individualist ideas may have for us, it must be admitted that it is impossible to condemn totalitarian regimes without also condemning the destructive metaphysic which made their happening a certainty.

This metaphysic refused to see in society anything but the state and the individual. It disregarded the role of the spiritual authorities and of all those intermediate social forces which enframe, protect, and control the life of man, thereby obviating and preventing the intervention of Power. It did not foresee that the overthrow of all these barriers and bulwarks would unleash a disorderly rout of egoistical interests and blind passions leading to the fatal and inauspicious coming of tyranny.

Tocqueville, Comte, Taine, and many another redoubled their warnings in vain. Were all the prophecies poured out by so many of the finer spirits to be set down in sequence, a whole book would be the result.

Useless Cassandras! And why so useless? Perhaps societies are governed in their onward march by laws of which we are ignorant. Do we know whether it is their destiny to avoid the mortal errors which beset them? Or whether they are not led into them by the same dynamism which carried them to their prime? Whether their seasons of blossom and fruitfulness are not achieved at the cost of a destruction of the forms in which their strength was stored?[16] After the firework display, the darkness of a formless mass, destined to despotism or anarchy.

16. [Cf. Halifax, *A Character of King Charles II:* "Formality is sufficiently revenged upon the world for being so unreasonably laughed at; it is destroyed, it is true, but it hath the spiteful satisfaction of seeing everything destroyed with it."]

# Epilogue

## Written by the Translator

ENCOURAGED THERETO BY THE AUTHOR, I am minded to write a few sentences of my own on a work which has occupied so much of my time.

This book ranges over the great open spaces of place and time, but its kernel can be bounded in a nutshell: it is a study of the expansionism of Power at the hands of men of great place, called throughout *les dirigeants*.

At the root of Power is force, and its ultimate appeal is to the egoistical side of men. From the resulting deterioration in themselves and their policies the *dirigeants* can be saved, if completely, only through the undeviating acknowledgment of an absolute code, which neither they nor their supporters made or can alter, but which can instantly deprive of all validity, other than that given by force, their own laws and ordinances. *Lex iniqua non habet rationem legis:* the words beat like drum-taps, but their sound is often low through the grinding of political axes. The people can, for all a Durkheim's advocacy, do wrong; and, when a majority holds power over a minority, justice may as easily as with a despot turn to being the interest of the stronger—unless they (or he) keep a vigilant and instructed conscience which impels to the unquestioning recognition of the obligatory character of the objective moral code. "They made it known," wrote Acton of the Stoics, "that there is a will superior to the collective will of man and a law that overrules those of Solon and Lycurgus. That which we must obey, that to which we are bound to reduce all civil authorities and to sacrifice every earthly interest is that immutable law which is perfect and eternal as God Himself."

Ideas such as these were once the commonplaces of Western Europe—the nations of which now resemble nothing so much as Athens and Thebes and Sparta bickering in the shadow of Macedonia, with Trieste or Salonika cast for the part of Olynthus. But we in our time have changed all that. Disliking the minority rule of one person (or even of three), we have increasingly organized ourselves in the light of our mass recipes for what a statesman (heaven help us!) has called "the science of happiness." "We have," said an eloquent and progressive French orator of some forty years ago in a much applauded peroration, "pulled down the stars from heaven." He would be thwarted no longer.

Recent events confirm the teaching of earlier ones as to the capacity for sin of *dirigeants*,[1] whose oratory is still expended on the soundness of "the people's heart" (the general will) and in exalting, for purposes more their own than his, the moral and intellectual competence of the ordinary man. (They "praise my Lord Such-a-one's horse when they mean to steal it.") Therefore, it is now said of him, whatever he (vicariously) decrees or decides, under whatever pressure of emotion or interest, is as good law as God's, if he has but decreed or decided it by a sufficient majority. To this claim it must be replied, as the book makes reply, that Power, even when based on popular sovereignty at its broadest, is still not God; that the natural law need never justify itself to any man, to any assembly, or to any tribunal; that neither the largest of majorities nor the most powerful of despots can ever meet it on its own ground; that, in short, Antigone was right and Creon wrong, notwithstanding Hegel's attempt to confuse that particular issue. The angels fell from spiritual pride, and the people would be well advised to stop their ears against the exaltation of their merits by seekers after Power; else their ultimate disaster will be the greater.

From the Power-bred instinct of *dirigeants* to persuade their subjects that they are the only providers of the best of a wide variety of worlds, the tendency to confound categories by conferring on words the meanings best suited to the users' purposes has taken vigorous wing. Upon corruption of will has been piled obfuscation of intellect. One of the first casualties in times of discord is, as Thucydides noted, the meanings of words, and to the Thucydidean list of inexactitudes it is time to add the

1. [Cf. Swift, in a letter to Bolingbroke of April 5, 1729: ". . . for I will venture all I am worth that there is not one human creature in power, who will not be modest enough to confess that he proceeds wholly upon a principle of corruption."]

current equation of liberty with security and the possession of a vote, of justice with equality as, too often, envy has conceived it to material ends, of idealism with the not always disinterested exaggeration of man's moral capacity, and of "democratic" with whatever the user of the word happens to approve. Humpty Dumpty has succeeded to the chair of more precise thinkers.

The remedy for which the author calls is simple to state, but none the easier on that account to compass, being in fact the return to the acknowledgment of a code which is not relative to some contemporary set of interests and pressures, but lives and moves

> Beyond time's troubled fountains
> On the great Atlantic mountains.

This process is, whatever else, certainly different in kind from the standard preoccupations of displacing this ruler by that, raising to Power that state or class or party in preference to this, and substituting one piece of political or economic machinery for another, all to the sound of self-appreciative chatter.

*Debemur morti,* and now an almost simultaneous doom (in less lethal times Clemenceau could at least predict the survival of a few Negroes in the Congo) is, if we may believe half we hear, quite possibly round the next corner: the planetary epitaph, if the djinn gets really out, should be in these terms only:

> We have erred and strayed from thy ways like lost sheep.
> *Hic jacemus.*

THE END

# *Index*

**423**

Parliament, English 44, 230
absolutism and, 279
authority of, 46
development of, 265–270, 327–328
imperium and, 278–279
legislative authority and, 277–279
monarchical power and, 208, 211*n*,
212
peers in, 328
pocket boroughs and, 328
political machines and, 304
popular sovereignty and, 278
respect for judicial legislation, 348
separation of powers and, 328
two chambers of, 328
Parliament, Long, 249
Parliamentary sovereignty. *See* Sovereignty
Parties, political, 126*n*, 135, 297–299
competition of, 305, 306
Democratic, 300–301
influence of on elections, 303–305
as states within states, 308*n*
totalitarianism developed from, 305
Pascal, Blaise, 232*n*
Paternal authority. *See* Authority, paternal
Patriarchy
vs. avuncular social structure, 89
government as, 95–96
war and birth of, 92–93
Patrician, patriciate, 101, 361, 362
Paul V (Pope), 36
Peace time and resources for war, 152–153
People, the, 94, 101
*See also* Bourgeoisie, the; Common
people, the
general elections and, 289
power of, confused with liberty of, 322
rule of law and, 336
sovereignty of, 282, 286–291, 333,
353*n*
tyranny of, 324
Philanthropy, 186
Philip II, 119, 141
Philip III ("The Bold"), 6*n*
Philip IV ("The Fair"), 183*n*, 204, 248
Philip of Valois, 7
Philosophers
perfect society models and, 146–147
tyranny, relationship between, 145–149
Pirenne, Jacques, 188
Plato, 146–147, 172–173, 232–233

Plebians, 360, 361
*Plebiscita*, 272*n*, 364
Plebiscitary regime, 297
Plebiscite, 15
influence of political parties on elections
and, 305
*Plebs*, 93–95, 101, 345, 361, 363
*See also* Common people, the; People,
the
Pliny, 234
Plutocracy, warrior aristocracy and, 93–95
Pocket boroughs, 328
Poland, 339*n*
Police, growth of, 394
Poligamy, 94
Political authority. *See* Authority, political
Political economy, 410
Political machines. *See* Machines, political
Political organization. *See* Organization,
political
Political parties. *See* Parties, political
Political rivalry. *See* Rivalry, political
Political science. *See* Science, political
Politics
dynamism of, and the state, 191–192
metaphysics of, 350
military jargon and, 303
*Politics* (Aristotle), 19
"Polity," 280
Pollard, A.F., 230
Pontchartrain, Jerome, Comte de, 383*n*
Pope, 35
Popular will. *See* Will, general
Pot, Philippe, 206
*Potestas*, 317
Power
*See also* Authority; Authority, legislative;
Government(s); Monarchy;
Sovereignty; State
abatement of, 63–64
absolute, 11, 12
advance of, 156–158, 171–172
Ancien Régime and, 244–245
in the ancient world. *See* Greece,
ancient; Rome, ancient
anonymity of, 13
arbitrary, 144, 402, 403
aristocracy and, 97–98, 99, 102–103,
173–174, 176, 180–183, 193, 193-
213, 382–383
army, the, and, 198–199, 208–209

The text of this book was set in Galliard, a sixteenth-century old-style
face made available to contemporary printers in 1978 by the
Mergenthaler Linotype Company. This adaption was drawn by the
English type designer Matthew Carter.

Printed on paper that is acid-free and meets the requirements
of the American National Standard for Permanence of Paper
for Printed Library Materials, Z39.48-1992. ∞

Editorial services and index by Harkavy Press,
New York, New York

Design by Madelaine Cooke, Athens, Georgia

Composition by Monotype Composition Company, Inc.,
Baltimore, Maryland

Printed and bound by Sheridan Books, Inc.,
Chelsea, Michigan